North by South

North by South

THE TWO LIVES OF
RICHARD JAMES ARNOLD

Charles Hoffmann and
Tess Hoffmann

The University of Georgia Press
Athens and London

© 1988 by the University of Georgia Press
Athens, Georgia 30602
All rights reserved

Designed by Sandra Strother Hudson
Set in Linotron 202 10 on 13 Janson by the Composing Room
of Michigan
Printed and bound by Thomson-Shore
The paper in this book meets the guidelines for
permanence and durability of the Committee on
Production Guidelines for Book Longevity of the
Council on Library Resources.

Printed in the United States of America

92 91 90 89 88   5 4 3 2 1

Library of Congress Cataloging in Publication Data

Hoffmann, Charles.
  North by South.

  Bibliography: p.
  Includes index.
    1. Arnold, Richard James, 1796–1873—Diaries.
  2. Slaveholders—Georgia—Bryan County—Diaries.
  3. Businessmen—Rhode Island—Diaries.   4. Bryan County
  (Ga.)—Biography.   5. Plantation life—Georgia—Bryan
  County—History—19th century.   I. Hoffmann, Tess.
  II. Title
  F292.B85A753   1987   975.8'73203'0924   87-13278
  ISBN 0-8203-0976-1 (alk. paper)

British Library Cataloging in Publication Data Available.

FOR ARTHUR ARNOLD ROGERS,

WITH GRATITUDE AND AFFECTION

Contents

Illustrations

Other illustrations are gathered in a separate section.

THE ARNOLD FAMILY CHART

Welcome Arnold[1]
1745–1798
m. February 1773
Patience Greene
1754–1809

Mary[2]
1774–1851
m. May 1801
Tristam Burges
1770–1853

Samuel Greene
1778–1826
m. September 1813
Frances Rogers
1786–1865

RICHARD JAMES[3]
1796–1873
m. May 1823
Louisa Gindrat
1804–1871

Eliza Harriet
1796–1873
m. May 1817
Zachariah Allen
1795–1882

1. Welcome and Patience had fourteen children,
   of whom four survived.

2. Mary and Tristam Burges had seven children,
   of whom one survived.

3. Richard and Louisa had nine children,
   of whom seven survived.

4. Louisa was Samuel, Jr.'s first cousin.

Cornelia
m.
Timothy Ruggles Green

Samuel Greene, Jr.
m.
Louisa Gindrat[4]

Mary

Candace

Anna

Eliza Harriet
1825–1906
m. June 1846
William Brenton Greene

Louisa Gindrat[4]
1828–1905
m. November 1848
Samuel Greene Arnold, Jr.

Richard James, Jr.
1834–1899
m. October 1860
Mary Clarke

Thomas Clay
1836–1875
m. December 1870
Elizabeth Screven

William Eliot
1838–1883
m. August 1871
Helen Foreman

Mary Cornelia
1841–1928
m. June 1861
William Talbot

Susan Allen
1843–?
m. September 1872
Dr. John M. Johnston

Preface

Fifteen miles southwest of Savannah and three miles due east of Interstate Highway 95 lies the plantation land on the Ogeechee River in Bryan County, Georgia, once owned by Richard James Arnold (1796–1873) of Providence, northern businessman and Rhode Island citizen as well as southern planter and slave owner. Today nothing remains of White Hall, Arnold's home during the winter season. The broad front avenue that once led to the manse, a sight which in 1853 charmed the northern journalist Frederick Law Olmsted, is now a tangle of dead live oaks and undergrowth where snakes abound. Even the cemetery in which Louisa (Gindrat) Arnold's parents are buried is overgrown and the tombstones desecrated. When Richard Arnold died in 1873 he left behind a thriving business enterprise, the largest rice plantation in Georgia and the second largest in the old rice kingdom that stretched along the coastal tidewater region from the Carolinas to Georgia. Two years later, with the death of his son Thomas (1836–1875), the plantation was sold at auction.

What has survived are business records, family letters, and other documents. They all provide an insight into the dual life of the younger son of a prominent Rhode Island family, who decided in 1824 to use the remainder of his inheritance ($30,000) to buy a second plantation and to double the number of slaves he had acquired when he married Louisa Gindrat the previous year. From that point he spent half the year in Georgia managing the plantations and their slaves and the other half managing his varied business interests in Rhode Island, a man with two lives who ultimately signified in microcosm a divided nation moving toward civil war.

In this book we examine Richard Arnold's life in the context of the social, economic, and political milieu of antebellum Rhode Island and Georgia, and we analyze the tensions that developed between the two worlds. The details of his divided life as revealed in his personal papers and business records reflect the growing dichotomy in antebellum America between the North and South brought about by the issue of slavery. Paradoxically, these documents reveal the easy accommodation of most upper-class white northerners to the institution of slavery as part business and property and part paternalistic society. Arnold moved easily between the two worlds, for he was the personification of the wealthy, successful, paternalistic entrepreneur. The social and cultural disguises that the two lives required, however, became more difficult to maintain as political events divided North from South.

Ultimately, secession with its threat of disunion rather than moral outrage turned the powerful northern social and economic class against the South. Arnold's decision to oppose secession in Georgia gained him continued acceptance within this class in Rhode Island, even though it physically divided his family and cost him some friends in the South. It did not, however, cost him a single slave until the Emancipation Proclamation freed them legally, and it did not cost him a single acre of land until he was ready to return to the South after the war and reconstruct his life there.

Richard Arnold was not unique as a Yankee who acquired land and slaves in the South. Indeed, long before him, his mother's cousin, General Nathanael Greene, at whose Georgia plantation Eli Whitney invented the cotton gin in 1793, was a plantation slave owner after the Revolutionary War. There were many who came after him, including Thomas Green Clemson of Pennsylvania, founder of Clemson University, who like Arnold married a southern woman, the daughter of John C. Calhoun, and became a plantation slaveholder in South Carolina. Similarly, Richard Peters, also a Pennsylvania Yankee, purchased a plantation and slaves in Georgia and introduced agricultural reforms, making the plantation into a model farm with diversified crops and livestock breeding. Like Arnold, Peters opposed Georgia's secession from the Union, but unlike Arnold he remained in Georgia during the Civil War, a loyal citizen of the Confederacy. The 1860 census reveals that nearly 360,000 former Yankees lived in the Old South, engaging in various occupations from agriculture to teaching school. There was even a colony of 120 New York families who settled in Virginia and purchased 24,000 acres of worn-out plantation land, farming it scientifically and hiring free labor, both white and black, to work it. By and large, these Yankee immigrants remained in the Old South, becoming citizens of their adopted states.

What was unusual was that Arnold, following the pattern established by other planters in the area of spending the malaria season in the North, maintained two complete establishments and lived two different, if not entirely separate, lives as a southern planter and a northern businessman. As a paternalistic slave owner he ran a model plantation, achieving a reputation as a good and kind master so that Olmsted, reporting back to the *New York Times* in 1853, praised "Mr. X" as a "father" caring for his "children." As befitted a member of the white, Anglo-Saxon, Protestant middle class that dominated

Rhode Island politics and social life throughout most of the nineteenth century, Arnold immersed himself in the details of his shipping, mining, manufacturing, and real estate interests and in the political, social, and cultural life of his native Providence. He saw no conflict between owning slaves in the South and being appointed a member of a blue-ribbon committee to investigate the facts of a Providence race riot in 1831. From his New England background developed the religious, social, and economic attitudes that enabled him to become a slave owner in Georgia, a role he actively sought rather than passively accepted as part of his wife's dowry.

The one life never denied the other: events outside his control forced him to choose between his Georgia plantations and his Rhode Island citizenship during the war. It was symptomatic of the deep division within the United States that two of the Arnold sons remained in Georgia as slave-owning Confederates while the rest of the family lived in the North. Arnold insisted to all who would listen to him in the North that he had opposed secession at the risk of losing all his friends in the South. Louisa Arnold, however, was a secessionist and remained so throughout the war. Although she loyally accompanied her husband and children to Rhode Island after the outbreak of hostilities, her sympathies were with the South and her two Confederate sons. The Arnold daughters Louisa (Mrs. Samuel Greene Arnold) and Mary Cornelia (Mrs. William Talbot) sided with their Unionist husbands, but the rest of the children apparently agreed with their mother. No member of the family was an outright abolitionist.

Richard Arnold survived the war, and although nearly seventy, he decided to rebuild the plantations, using northern capital to expand rice production and pay his ex-slaves their wages. Since his son Thomas had managed the plantations during the war, he could carry on after him. The death of father and son within two years of each other ended fifty years of enterprise.

Arnold's plantation journal for 1847–1849, which forms the structural focus of this study, covers only two of those fifty years. Thus by itself the journal is only a fragment, beginning with an unreadable first entry dated January 9, 1847, and stopping short on April 21, 1849. Even within the journal's time span there are two major gaps, one of six and a half months and the other of seven and a half months, which thus divide the journal into three sections. The time gaps are accounted for by the fact that Arnold kept the journal only while actually in residence at the plantation.

Although interesting as a partial record of an antebellum plantation in Georgia, the journal must be placed within a context that gives it meaning beyond the daily details recorded in the entries. Therefore, we decided not to limit ourselves to an edition of the journal with an introduction providing the background. There have been several such editions beginning with Ulrich Phillips and James Glunt's pioneer work, *Florida Plantation Records* (1927), the partial records of the Florida cotton plantations El Destino and Chemonie, which belonged to George Noble Jones and his wife, Mary Nuttall Jones. The limitation imposed by this approach is that it focuses mainly on the workings of a plantation and largely ignores the social milieu to which the Joneses belonged as they summered in Newport, Rhode Island, or in Europe and wintered in Savannah, Georgia, living a cosmopolitan life off the labor of their slaves. Aristocratic planters, the Joneses and the Arnolds not only belonged to the same social and economic class, sharing the same racial attitudes inherent in the fact that they owned slaves, but they were also close friends, related by marriage, visiting back and forth and living as neighbors in Newport in the late 1850s.

A later study, *Planter Management and Capitalism in Ante-bellum Georgia* (1954), by Albert Virgil House, which includes an analysis of a rice plantation belonging to Hugh Fraser Grant based on his edited journal and other business records, is more relevant to our interests. House places Grant's rice plantation in an economic and agricultural context directly related to Arnold's enterprise, for Grant's plantation was located in the same general tidewater area farther down the Georgia rice coast. House's discussion of the capitalistic economics of rice plantations provides an insight into one facet of Arnold's approach to his plantations as a business operation. Although House does provide a biographical summary of the Grant family, his study is largely limited to the economic and horticultural aspects of plantation management and rice culture.

A more recent edition of a rice plantation journal together with related documents, James W. Clifton's *Life and Labor on Argyle Island* (1978), is also relevant to our study in that the Argyle Island plantations, Gowrie and East Hermitage, were rice plantations run in tandem as one plantation by Charles Manigault and his son Louis, just as Arnold organized White Hall and Cherry Hill, his two main plantations. The Manigault documents are arranged chronologically so that they tell their own story, but since they deal largely with "life and labor" on the plantation, the narrative *behind* the documents is lost, and no attempt is made to identify persons and events internally. For example, January 1847, the date of the beginning of our segment of Arnold's plantation journal, finds Charles Manigault in Paris. Manigault, like Jones, was an absentee planter. Both shared a love of France, and although the Manigaults were Charleston-based and the Joneses were Savannah-based, they had many friends in common, including the Middletons and the Izards of Charleston and Newport, the Manigaults being related to both families. The Manigaults, father and son, maintained strong business ties in Savannah, using the firm of Robert Habersham and Son as their factor, as did Grant and Arnold. It was an interrelated world these southern planters inhabited, and the fact that a New Englander, by reason of marriage, broke into this circle of southern friends and relatives intrigued us about Arnold as a slave-owning citizen of a free state.

The organization of this study was suggested by the natural division of time in Arnold's plantation journal between winter and summer as the Arnolds resided at White Hall from November or December until April or May, when they annually migrated North to escape the danger of malaria, returning to Georgia after the first frost. Thus we decided to alternate chapters, using the appropriate time segment of the plantation journal as an interchapter, to suggest the alternating pattern of Arnold's dual life. Since the journal is the record of a working plantation containing detailed information of each work day, it naturally follows that most of the references in the text are to be found in the plantation chapters, but the chronology of the book is by no means limited to the two years covered by the journal itself. This study spans the entire career of Richard Arnold as a cotton and rice planter from the 1820s to the 1870s, for the journal is the touchstone by which themes and topics are explored and analyzed. For example, references to visitors at White Hall, such as Mary Nuttall Jones, are the occasion for an exploration of the Arnolds' social life. Illness among whites and blacks described in the journal suggests another topic for analysis. Arnold's dismissal of the tutor for his sons leads to a discussion of education among whites of the upper middle class and its lack among blacks in general and slaves in particular. Allusions to slave marriages in the journal suggested another topic for discussion. The journal, therefore, is not merely a record of plantation operation and organization; it is a social document revealing the moral and religious attitudes of its author as well as his economic interests. Even the absence of entries for Sunday is a clue to the close tie that existed among southern planters between religious beliefs and an economic system based on slavery. Sunday was the day set aside to worship the God who sanctioned slavery as a master-servant relationship, a day to be spent by both whites and blacks in contemplating who was master and who was servant.

Further details about Arnold's dual life came from family letters, journals, business records, and other plantation documents, such as slave lists, instructions to overseers, and contract agreements with overseers. Very few of the letters sent by overseers to Arnold survive, but a series of letters spanning twenty years from his "engineer," the favored slave Amos Morel, son of the Arnolds' "mammy," proved invaluable as source material. The travel journal kept by Eliza Harriet Allen, Arnold's twin sister, of her visit to White Hall in the spring of 1837 revealed family and New England attitudes toward slavery. Paternalism was the key to the social acceptability of Arnold as slave owner by his northern friends and family, and religious doctrines and property rights were the moral and economic justification. The portrait that emerges from the documents is that of a kind and good master, an image he himself fostered. This benevolence only reinforces the essential evil of the institution, for such a man of good intentions in turn based his justification for owning human beings on his good intentions and therefore was incapable of perceiving the evil he perpetuated.

Although available documents dealing with Arnold's plantations and life in Georgia are scattered, with serious breaks in the continuity of some of the records, nonetheless a clear picture emerges of a wealthy New Englander who, having married a young southern woman educated in the North, decided to invest his own not inconsiderable inheritance on expanding his wife's dowry, devoting the rest of his life to the business of running a plantation, accumulating through the years 11,000 acres of land and more than 200 slaves. The New England work ethic was strong and Arnold was not content to live a leisurely life like George Noble Jones or Charles Manigault. While in Rhode Island six months of the year, he not only kept in touch with his overseer, as did Jones and Manigault, but he developed his northern business interests, which often provided capital to expand the plantation enterprise and to tide him over during a poor crop year.

Rhode Island was never in the forefront of the abolitionist movement like its neighboring state Massachusetts. The merchants of Rhode Island had found the slave trade and the distilling of rum too profitable to be ardent abolitionists, and their heirs who invested that money in cotton textile mills were not eager to disturb the status quo in the southern states. Slavery itself was not abolished in Rhode Island until 1842, although it had ceased to be an economic factor in the state by the end of the eighteenth century. Despite the fact that his uncle was prominent in the anti–slave-trade movement and his father as a state legislator had voted for abolishment, Richard Arnold as a slave owner was eminently acceptable among his Rhode Island peers. If they thought at all about his owning slaves, beyond his owning a rice plantation on which they worked, it was within the framework of Christian paternalism and the master-servant relationship. Furthermore, Newport, where the Arnolds spent the hot summer weeks long before they built a home there, had been a summer haven for southern slaveholders since colonial times. Arnold was as much a part of the white power structure in the city of Providence as was his brother-in-law, Zachariah Allen, textile manufacturer and heir to a fortune based in part on the slave trade.

In the 1830s and early 1840s, racial turmoil in Providence and political upheaval in the state found Arnold, not surprisingly, on the side of property rights and law and order and against mob rule. In 1842 he was assistant adjutant general in charge of supplies for the state militia during the Dorr War, in which the maverick politician Thomas Wilson Dorr, his nephew by marriage, had set up a rival People's state government, thus precipitating a constitutional crisis. Arnold, Georgia slave owner, was much more acceptable in the white power structure of Providence and Rhode Island than Dorr, abolitionist and populist, who sought to enfranchise the growing number of immigrants who had come to work in the textile mills of Rhode Island.

By the 1850s Newport was a cosmopolitan summer resort where Philadelphians, New Yorkers, and Bostonians were building cottages and villas to distinguish themselves from the transient visitors who took rooms by the week in the hotels and boardinghouses and the day trippers from Providence and Fall River who descended on the public beaches during the hot summer days. By then, the long-standing, South Carolinian slave-owning families—the Middletons, Izards, Pinckneys—were joined by the Joneses and others to form a nucleus of residents who held slaves in the South and, indeed, brought their body servants with them from the plantations. Politically, Newport had long been prosouthern and antiabolitionist, if not outright proslavery, and therefore the southern enclave found the political as well as the social atmosphere congenial. The Arnolds were attracted to this haven for southern planters at first as transient visitors and by the late 1850s as permanent residents.

Still, the slave owners did not have Newport all to themselves—Emerson, Longfellow, and Whittier were summer visitors; Samuel Gridley and Julia Ward Howe lived on the outskirts at Portsmouth; and such local black leaders as Isaac Rice and George Downing were ardent abolitionists. But by and large, being a summer resort, Newport was more casual than confrontational, more conversational than controversial. Cosmopolitan residents such as Henry James, Sr., although opposed to slavery, were not active in the abolitionist movement. And if Andrew Robeson, Sr., was an active abolitionist and supporter of William Lloyd Garrison, his son Andrew, Jr., became Arnold's nephew by marriage and George Noble Jones's neighbor by choice.

The interrelated web of relatives and friendships—Julia Ward Howe and Richard Arnold were distant cousins, Samuel Howe and Richard Arnold were members of the Newport Reading Room—kept the tensions beneath the surface even during the war.

The outbreak of the war caught the Arnolds unprepared, still at the plantation, separated from their two married daughters and recently married eldest son in the North. To complicate matters further, their daughter Mary Cornelia was engaged to marry William Talbot that summer in Newport. Talbot rushed down to Georgia to bring his fiancée back to Rhode Island, since the Arnold family was divided on whether to remain at White Hall that summer and wait out the war, which neither side expected to last long. In the end, all but two sons, Thomas and William Eliot, went back to Rhode Island in May 1861. Before he left, Richard Arnold sold the plantations to Thomas to prevent expropriation by the Confederates. Both Thomas and William Eliot considered themselves Georgians first and joined the Confederate army, although Thomas remained primarily at White Hall to manage the business and protect the property, including the slaves, from becoming "contraband" of war.

As the casualties mounted for both North and South—many of the Arnolds' personal friends in Providence and Newport lost sons in the war—the Arnolds worried about their sons in Georgia, since communication with them was almost impossible. As Sherman's army approached the Ogeechee area late in 1864, the anxiety within the Arnold family mounted for the lives of their sons and the safety of their property. But whatever divisions existed within the family about the war, they all closed ranks when William Eliot was taken prisoner of war on December 13, 1864, while defending Fort McAllister on the edge of the plantation. Richard and Louisa Arnold rushed down to Savannah, which had been captured by Sherman shortly after the fall of Fort McAllister. By then, William Eliot had been transferred to a northern prisoner-of-war camp, but eventually, after family political pressure was exerted in Washington, he was paroled to the care of his brother-in-law by order of President Lincoln.

The Arnolds were survivors, and the Arnold family was reunited in Newport during the summer of 1865. The two lives of Richard James Arnold, North and South, came together as the family spent the summer in Newport planning the reconstruction of White Hall. Also there with them was Amos Morel, former slave, now a free man, but loyal to his master. With his skills as a mechanic and blacksmith he could have survived on his own, but his one thought in the confusion and turmoil after the war was to be reunited with his "poor" master. Earning enough money for his passage from Savannah, Amos Morel joined the Arnolds in Newport. His skills as an "engineer" were needed back at White Hall to help rebuild the rice mill destroyed in the war, and thus he became part of Arnold's plan for reconstructing the past. But for the moment there was little for him to do except, as befitted a former servant, to be hired as the Arnolds' waiter, the job he had spurned thirty years earlier in order to become a blacksmith on the plantation. Before he left Newport to return to White Hall with Thomas and William Eliot, Amos Morel sat at his own request for a photograph, the sitting and copies paid for by Richard Arnold. Arnold's paternalism survived emancipation and the war itself; he gathered around him many of his former slaves as servants and field hands to run the postbellum plantation, paying them wages instead of rations.

Our research began at the Rhode Island Historical Society Library with Eliza Harriet Allen's journal of her 1837 visit to White Hall plantation. The summers of 1980 and 1983 were spent at the University of North Carolina (Chapel Hill) reading in the Southern Historical Collection and participating in two summer seminars sponsored by the National Endowment for the Humanities, one conducted by Dr. Louis D. Rubin, Jr., on southern literature, and the other led by Dr. John S. Reed, on southern culture. The direction of the projected study was helped immeasurably by the comments and suggestions of the seminar directors and fellow participants and especially by Dr. Carolyn A. Wallace, director of the Southern Historical Collection, who had originally catalogued the Arnold family papers and who introduced us in 1983 to Mrs. Edward Caldwell of Chapel Hill, Richard J. Arnold's great-granddaughter. Mrs. Caldwell's permission to edit Arnold's plantation journal provided the final impetus toward the shape and focus of this book.

A fortuitous meeting with Arthur Arnold Rogers of Deerfield, Massachusetts, at the Rhode Island Historical Society Library in August 1985, just as the book was taking final shape, made available to us the Arnold-Rogers collection; the collection is owned by the descendants of Samuel and Louisa Arnold, who as the Lazy Lawn Realty Trust have been gathering together the scattered letters, photographs, and documents that collectively fill out the story of that branch of the descendants of Welcome Arnold, Richard's father. Permission to use the Arnold-Rogers collection has allowed us to complete the story of Richard Arnold's two lives.

In addition, we wish to acknowledge the following librarians and their institutions for the courteous and unfailing help they gave us during the years in which the book was in progress and for permission to quote from their holdings: Brown University Archives (Martha Mitchell); John Hay Library (Dr. Mark N. Brown); Newport Historical Society (Mrs. Peter Bolhouse); Rhode Island College (Ms. Linda Green); Rhode Island Historical Society (Harold Kemble); Southern Historical Collection (Dr. Richard Shrader). Our colleagues, Dr. C. Annette Ducey (Rhode Island College) and Dr. Nancy A. J. Potter (University of Rhode Island) gave encouragement at crucial times. A grant from the Rhode Island College Faculty Research Fund helped defray some of our research expenses. An understanding dean (Dr. David L. Greene) and chair (Dr. Robert E. Hogan) provided released time from teaching. And a sympathetic brother (Michael C. Carlos) unstintingly and generously supported two research expeditions to Savannah and Bryan County, Georgia.

Providence and Newport
1986

CHAPTER ONE

Prologue

On January 29, 1853, a Saturday, Frederick Law Olmsted, the future creator of that man-made paradise New York City's Central Park, arrived at a different kind of "paradise," the rice plantation on the Ogeechee River near Savannah, Georgia, owned by a New Englander identified only as Mr. X in *A Journey in the Seaboard Slave States* (1856). Olmsted waited in the parlor while the house servant Tom announced him. Although Olmsted introduced himself to the master of White Hall as the author of *Walks and Talks of an American Farmer in England* (1852), he also brought with him a letter of introduction from Mr. McCurdy of the New York firm of commission merchants, McCurdy, Aldrich and Spencer, to balance the scales. He stayed only until the following Tuesday, February 1, but the mistress wrote to her daughter that same day, "I was quite ready for him to go." It was not that Olmsted had incurred the displeasure of his hostess—"we found him quite pleasant"—but that she was unexpectedly busy with her family. Her two younger sons were supposed to be in Rhode Island. Instead, they were at the plantation together with their tutor and his wife, a last-minute change of plans. With a slave wedding planned at the manse for Saturday night, February 5, there was enough to keep her occupied without having to entertain a northern visitor or worry whether he was receiving a proper introduction to plantation life.[1]

Olmsted's impression upon awakening on the morning after his arrival and looking out the window of his bedroom was that he had come to a veritable Garden of Eden: "A grove which surrounded the house was all in dark verdue: there were green oranges on trees nearer the window; the buds were swelling on a jessamine-vine, and a number of camelia-japonicas were in full bloom. . . . Sparrows were chirping, doves cooing, and a mocking-bird whistling loudly."[2] He also described in considerable detail the social and economic organization of this plantation in his letters and subsequent book.

His conclusion, based on one working day, was that Mr. X's plantation was an ideal place where the institution of slavery could be observed at its best as a system of labor, and that Mr. X himself was a paradigm of the paternalistic slave master whose plantation was "a model of what he [Olmsted] believed slavery should be in America—a benevolent, patriarchal and civilizing institution."[3]

Olmsted's journeys in the slave states of the South and his views on slavery based on his first-hand observations are well-documented, but the untold story is that of Mr. X, who was Richard James Arnold (1796–1873) of Providence, Rhode Island. Arnold divided the year between White Hall, his plantation in Bryan County, Georgia, and Rhode Island, traveling back and forth according to the seasons. How the younger son of a birthright Quaker and successful Yankee merchant, Welcome Arnold (1745–1798), came to be a southern planter and slave owner as well as a northern businessman and citizen, maintaining a dual existence throughout the antebellum period, is in itself fascinating.[4] But the social, economic, and political implications of this division between the two segments of his life are of more lasting significance. The paradoxes and contradictions that existed between Olmsted's paradisial view from his window of a Sunday morning and the realities of Arnold's slave plantation were symptomatic of the national duality.

Thirty years earlier, in December 1823, Richard Arnold had arrived at White Hall plantation for the first time to see for himself the approximately 1,300 acres of rice and cotton land and sixty-eight slaves he had acquired through marriage six months earlier to Louisa Caroline Gindrat (1804–1871). It was primarily as a young Yankee businessman that he evaluated the present and future prospects of the plantation. The economic reality was that he could neither sell nor run it profitably: the 1823 crop, although admittedly a poorer harvest than usual, did not exceed ninety barrels of rice, six bags of good cotton, and four bags of stained cotton, hardly enough to cover the plantation expenses and current wages due George Waters, the administrator of her parents' estate. Part of the land, called Mulberry Hill, was heavily mortgaged and was to be sold at auction the following month; the remaining cultivable land was not enough for the large work force of slaves he owned. Either he would have to buy more land or sell some of the slaves: on the one hand, he was "very much opposed to laying out money in this section of the country," as he wrote to his brother, Samuel, but on the other hand "negros bring now nothing—owing to the distressed state of the country, they are selling very often & in large gangs to satisfy sheriffs executions at public auction."[5] From the beginning he viewed the slaves as a type of property with a fluctuating cash value.

Arnold's decision to buy more land rather than sell one-fourth of his slaves was basically economic; it made more business sense to buy additional land at a low price than to sell part of his capital assets in the form of slaves at a time when slaves were worth less on the market. He would ensure a more productive plantation, efficiently using his labor force, and he could always sell the plantation land and slaves when times were better. Consequently, he followed the advice of neighboring planters to buy more land, and at the end of January 1824, he "purchased a Tract of Prime land opposite White Hall," consisting of 600 acres, for $3,500.[6] This purchase did not permanently commit him to the life of a southern planter and he had the option of being an absentee owner, putting the plantation in the hands of an overseer to manage while he remained in the North. Instead, late in 1824 he decided to invest the remainder of his inheritance—a $30,000 cash settlement from his brother—in additional plantation land and slaves, which committed him irrevocably to slavery. He purchased Cherry Hill plantation, paying $9,500 for the land and buildings and nearly twice that for the sixty-three slaves who worked and lived there. The purchase of this second plantation fulfilled his plan to operate the two plantations in tandem, making efficient use of his work force from one to the other and diversifying his crops, for Cherry Hill had the best rice land and White Hall the best cotton land. Although he made many other purchases of land in later years, it was this first major expansion of his holdings in land and slaves that committed him to being a southern planter. It also committed him by his own act and decision rather than by inheritance to a dual existence as a northern citizen and a southern slave owner.

Richard Arnold's decision to invest his inheritance in the plantations came as a shock to his twin sister, Eliza Harriet Allen (1796–1873). What had shocked Eliza Harriet (called Harriet by the family) was not that her brother was a slave owner and that he had purchased slaves with the remainder of his inheritance but that he had decided to invest his money in an enterprise that would require his residence in Georgia at least six months of the year. She could not bear the thought that she would be separated from him for such a long period; furthermore, he had agreed to the cash settlement with brother Samuel without consulting her or her husband, Zachariah Allen (1795–1882), who as a trustee of Arnold's northern holdings had worked hard to gain a favorable settlement of the Welcome Arnold estate for the twins. But since the decision had already been made, she wished him well in his enterprise and reconciled herself to being separated from him half the year.[7]

Louisa Arnold presumably never doubted the desirability of keeping White Hall plantation, for as far as she was concerned it was home. She had been born on the plantation and had spent her early childhood there; her parents were buried in the small family cemetery within walking distance of the manse. Returning to White Hall as Richard Arnold's wife was a homecoming, the plantation being her marriage dowry as it had been her mother's in 1803 when she married Abraham Gindrat.[8] Many of the slaves (numbering fifty-seven in 1803) were still alive in 1823, and their children had been born on the plantation. Olmsted, writing of Louisa, perpetuated the mythology of the special relationship between slave-owning whites and their slaves in order to explain the Arnolds' paternalism, based as it was on "the ties of long family association, common traditions, common memories, and, if ever, common interests, between the slaves and their rulers."[9] The mythology persisted long after the institution itself had been abolished.

It was to Louisa's friends and relatives that Richard Arnold looked for advice, for they lived in Georgia and knew the situation, being planters themselves. It was only to be expected that Arnold would turn to Thomas Savage Clay (1801–1849), who had grown up with Louisa, and to Clay's uncle, William Savage, "the principle [sic] planter in the country."[10] They had advised him to buy more land rather than sell the slaves, and Thomas Clay suggested that he buy Cherry Hill, since through his mother (née Mary Ann Savage) he planned to buy and manage Richmond-on-Ogeechee plantation adjacent to Cherry Hill. The Clays, the McAllisters (Thomas Clay later married Matilda McAllister), who owned Strathy Hall on the other side of White Hall, and the Savages were a small, tight circle of friends and relatives. Like-minded in their attitudes toward plantation life in the South but with strong links through family and friends to the North, they divided their time between Georgia in the winter and the North during the summer malaria months. Thomas Clay's father, the Honorable Joseph Clay, Jr. (1754–1811), could well have served as Richard Arnold's role model, for Clay (graduate of Princeton in 1784 and with an honorary master's degree from Brown University in 1806) led a dual life in reverse as a native Georgian and slaveholding plantation owner in Bryan County, Georgia, and pastor of the First Baptist Church in Boston, Massachusetts.[11] Louisa Caroline Gindrat had grown up in this society, so she and her husband were welcomed as family rather than as strangers. Something of Eliza Harriet Allen's jealousy of this closed circle is apparent in her letter to Richard upon learning he had invested the rest of his inheritance in Georgia: "I shall lose my brother & one whom I have always considered as a part of myself—& for this I suppose I am in part indebted to Mr. Clay, for which I owe him no thanks."[12]

Richard's ending up as a southern rice planter might never have happened, for until March 1820 he was engaged to Abby Mason, daughter of a Providence physician, businessman, and United States congressman (1815–1819). Consequently, young Richard Arnold seemed destined for a business career in Rhode Island, perhaps in the family shipping business with his brother, Samuel, perhaps in textile manufacturing with his brother-in-law Zachariah Allen, perhaps in one of the enterprises of his future in-laws. The death of her father in the summer of 1819, however, coupled with the fact that Richard Arnold was still in Europe on his grand tour, led to behavior on Abby's part that, according to Richard's older sister, Mary Burges, "has been far from correct," and what was worse her coquetry had got her "talked about" all over Providence.[13] Eliza Harriet could only speculate that either Abby had heard the rumor that Richard had "lost property," which was untrue, or that Abby had "found somebody she liked better in Boston," which would explain her behavior. In any event, Abby returned Richard's engagement ring with the explanation that "a change in her feelings toward him renders an union altogether impractible [sic]."[14] The returned ring was the traditional, symbolic gesture of breaking an engagement, but Abby also signified the end of the relationship by sending back at the same time Richard's miniature portrait which had been delivered to her in October 1819, presumably as a sentimental gift so that she would have his likeness while he was absent in Europe.

Three years later Richard married Louisa Gindrat. Her plantation and slaves in Georgia were presumably incidental to his proposal, since he had no need of her estate, encumbered and tangled as it was, on which to build his fortune. His father, long since dead, could not advise him, but presumably he would have disapproved of the dowry, if not the marriage itself. Welcome Arnold had been directly involved in the movement to abolish slavery and the slave trade in Rhode Island. In 1779, when he was a deputy of the General Assembly of Rhode Island and member of an ad hoc committee of three, Welcome Arnold prepared a bill to prevent slaves in Rhode Island from being purchased and carried out of the state against their own consent in violation of the manumission act of 1774. This was no abstract issue, for the assembly on the same day also directed the sheriff to detain certain slaves who had been purchased from being carried South against their consent. More important, as a member of the upper house of the general assembly in 1784, he was instrumental in the successful passage of the bill for the gradual emancipation of children born to slaves in Rhode Island.

Certainly, it is difficult to imagine that Richard's uncle, Thomas, still alive at the time, approved of his nephew's becoming a slave owner. Thomas Arnold (1751–1826), together with his brother-in-law Moses Brown (1738–

1836) and other fellow Quakers, agitated against the flourishing slave trade in Rhode Island. In 1787 they succeeded in having a law passed that prohibited anyone in the state from participating in the slave trade. The law, however, was unevenly and loosely enforced, and the slave trade continued to flourish illegally in Rhode Island until 1807, when federal law abolished it. To monitor the state law, the Quakers organized the Providence Society for the Abolition of the Slave Trade in 1789 with Thomas Arnold as secretary and Moses Brown as treasurer. Moses Brown's brother John violated the law and was unsuccessfully prosecuted in 1796 by the society.

To understand how Richard Arnold, coming from a New England anti-slavery family with a Quaker background, could end up as a slave owner in Georgia, one must understand the duality of New England and, in particular, Rhode Island attitudes toward slavery in the eighteenth and early nineteenth centuries. In 1755, when Louisa Gindrat's great-grandfather was first acquiring White Hall plantation, there were 4,697 slaves in Rhode Island, twice as many as existed in Bryan County, Georgia, in 1823. A gradual emancipation act was passed in Rhode Island in 1784 (all children born of slave mothers after March 1, 1784, were to be considered freeborn citizens although bound to their former owners as servants until age twenty-one), but slavery itself was not abolished in Rhode Island until 1842. In 1820 there were still 47 slaves in Newport and 4 in Providence, according to the federal census.

The duality of northern attitudes toward slavery is exemplified in the career of General Nathanael Greene (1742–1786), a Revolutionary War hero from Rhode Island, who accepted the gift of Myrtle Grove plantation near Savannah from the citizens of Georgia for his services during the war as commander of the Army of the South. Since General Greene had broken with his Quaker principles to fight in the war, his acceptance of slave ownership after the war created no religious dilemma for him. Having married Catherine Littlefield in 1774, he settled down after the war to a pattern of wintering on the Georgia plantation and summering at Newport, Rhode Island.[15] His sudden death in 1786 left his widow with five children, but she continued to run the plantation with the help of an overseer, dividing her time between the North and the South according to the season. Indeed, it was by her invitation in the summer of 1793 while still in the North that the New England schoolteacher Eli Whitney stopped at her plantation in Georgia. His invention of the cotton gin at Myrtle Grove is part of American legend, but it was also part of American or at least southern agricultural economics that the invention of the cotton gin locked the slave into the Cotton Kingdom as surely as the cotton gin freed the southern planter from limitations on cotton production.

Although Welcome Arnold owned shares in many ships during and after the Revolutionary War, as well as owning his own ships, there is no evidence to suggest that he ever took part in the slave trade as did many of the shipping merchants of his generation in Rhode Island, including some of the most prominent and wealthiest families in the state—the Browns, the D'Wolfs, and the Allens. The merchants of Welcome Arnold's generation made their money wherever they could, whether it was privateering during the war or the illegal slave trade after the war, and even Welcome Arnold profited from privateering and from the sugar and molasses that was imported into Rhode Island as part of the triangular slave trade of molasses, rum, and slaves. In 1796, the year of Richard Arnold's birth, twenty-one slave ships sailed out of Rhode Island ports, carrying 274,068 gallons of rum to purchase 2,165 slaves.[16] It was an average year; over the years Rhode Island slave traders controlled from 60 to as much as 90 percent of the American trade in African slaves, and the trade actually increased after it became illegal. Many of those ships sailed out of Providence harbor within sight of the Arnold home.

The sons of these wealthy, successful merchants invested their inheritances in the growing textile manufacturing industry of the early nineteenth century, but they did not look too closely at the source of their inheritances. Richard Arnold's brother-in-law Zachariah Allen inherited nearly $100,000 from his father and invested it in the building of a textile mill and its satellite village in 1822. He did not question that at least a small part of his inheritance came from his father's ownership of two slave ships, the brigs *Nancy* and *Susannah*, which made several illegal voyages out of Rhode Island during 1793–1795.[17] From Richard Arnold's early letters and business records it is apparent that he saw himself as a pragmatic Yankee entrepreneur, the mirror image of his brother-in-law, who invested in Rhode Island's expanding textile industry. From that perspective Arnold's decision to buy more land rather than sell some of his slaves at White Hall plantation was the converse of Allen's decision to shut down some of the machines in his mill and dismiss half of the work force when he calculated he was losing fifty cents on every yard of broadcloth he produced. The mercantile justification in either case was profitability, the one expanding his business to make it more profitable and the other contracting.

Zachariah Allen and Richard Arnold had much in common as young men of wealth who had money to invest in business enterprises that would be their life's work and career. Both graduated from Brown University, Phi Beta

Juſt imported in the Ship Charlotte, John Rogers,
Maſter, and to be Sold by
CALEB GREENE,
AND
WELCOME ARNOLD,
At their Store near the Great Bridge, in Providence,
being the ſame lately occupied by LOVETT and
GREENE,
A new and compleat ASSORTMENT of
English and India
G   O   O   D   S,
Suitable for the Seaſon, which they will ſell on the
loweſt Terms, for Caſh.
   They have likewiſe for Sale, LIME, warranted
good, by the large Quantity, or ſingle Hogſhead.
Any Perſon applying may be ſupplied on the ſhorteſt
Notice, the Lime Burners in Smithfield and North-
Providence, by reaſon of their living at a Diſtance
from the Market, having appointed the ſaid Arnold
their Factor, to diſpoſe of all the Lime they make.

*Newspaper advertisement of Caleb Greene and Welcome Arnold
for English and India goods,* Providence Gazette, *May 1,
1773. (Courtesy of the Rhode Island Historical Society.)*

Kappa, Zachariah in 1813 and Richard in 1814. Both had many possibilities
open to them as the younger sons of a prominent family, law and politics
being definite opportunities. They both studied law after graduation from
Brown, and Allen was admitted to the bar in 1815, but neither of them
actually practiced law. Allen served on the town council of Providence for
several years, but Arnold's life as a planter in Georgia precluded a political
career in Rhode Island. Still, both were active in civic affairs, including the
founding of the Rhode Island Historical Society and the Providence Athenaeum. Both became trustees of Brown University for life, and both served
on a blue-ribbon committee to ascertain the facts of the 1831 Providence race
riot.

   As young gentlemen of property and social standing they completed the
grand tour of Europe, but as sons of self-made Yankee merchants they never
cultivated a feeling for leisure. Even their European jaunts had a practical

purpose, Allen's to investigate the state of the art in textile-mill machinery, Arnold's to act as European agent for the shipping firm founded by his father and continued by his brother, Samuel. Both Allen and Arnold inherited small farms, but considered themselves gentlemen farmers and continued to live in the city.[18] One of the anomalies of Arnold's dual life was that while residing in Georgia he left his North Providence farm in charge of Prince Bent, a former slave who had earned his freedom by joining the Rhode Island Black Regiment during the Revolutionary War, and while residing in Providence he paid a white overseer as required by Georgia law to manage the plantation.

In the end, Zachariah Allen and Richard Arnold chose careers at each end of the Cotton Kingdom (although Allen began in wool manufacturing, he eventually turned exclusively to cotton manufacturing, and although Arnold eventually concentrated on rice culture, he continued to grow cotton for export to the North and to England). The lord of the loom and the lord of the lash were joined more by their concepts of business than they were by a product. Whatever their cultural ambitions, they were ultimately pragmatic men who pursued the American dream of material success.

Both Allen and Arnold imposed their own sense of order and time upon the river landscape where their enterprises were located. Place for the mill owner like Zachariah Allen was measured in water power, and the water rights, or mill privilege as it was called, made the river land valuable. He paid twice as much per acre for the land he would flood when he built his dam as for the land on which he would build the houses for his workers. The site on the Woonasquatucket River north of Providence was valued for the fourteen-foot fall of water that could be translated into horse power to run the mill machinery. Richard Arnold valued his plantation site on the Ogeechee River southwest of Savannah for its accessibility to the Savannah market, the river functioning as a highway to bring in supplies and ship out the cotton and rice. But even more important was the fact that the Ogeechee was a tidal river, essential to the tide-flow method of rice culture by which the flow and ebb of the tides were used to flood and drain the rice fields. A system of dikes, ditches, and floodgates, more elaborate than any used by textile manufacturers for their mills, controlled the water.

Woonasquatucket is an Indian place name meaning "at the head of the tidal river," for the Woonasquatucket joins the tidal Providence River at the farthest reach of the tide. The Narragansett Indians once hunted and fished in the wilderness of the river's watershed. Similarly, Ogeechee is an Indian place name meaning "clear water." The Yamassee Indians, allies of the

Creeks, hunted and fished in the area. By the time Zachariah Allen and Richard Arnold arrived on the scene, the Indians had long ago disappeared from both areas. Tribal memory of the river died, since place to the Indians was a living stream encompassing the whole of tribal history at that location. This sense of place as a function of time in a continuum of tribal past and present grew out of the fact that American Indian tribes considered their land to be communal property belonging to the tribe and not private property to be bought and sold separately by individuals.[19]

A different perception of time and place had taken over by the time Allen established his community on the banks of the Woonasquatucket River. Time and place were money, and Allendale was a white man's place name imposed on the natural landscape, even though the river itself retained its Indian name. Allen literally counted the cost per yard of manufactured cloth and spent the rest of his life experimenting with the speeding up of his machinery in order to increase his margin of profit.[20] He automated where possible and increased the number of machines a single operator handled as well as their speed. In a system of labor where the laborer's time was the property of the employer, idle machines meant lost money. The cost in human terms was never calculated, and Allen's employment of children as young as seven and his imposition of a dawn-to-dusk workday for operatives were common practices among textile manufacturers in New England throughout the antebellum period. Allen's image of himself was that of an engineer perfecting his machinery and of a father caring for his family of workers.

Arnold brought with him to the plantation this northern sense of time. He had been born and raised a stone's throw from the port of Providence with its busy wharves filled with sailing ships from all over the world, including slave traders and the Yankee clippers engaged in the China trade. Some of these ships, the masts visible from his bedroom at Sabin Tavern, were owned first by his father and then by his brother, Samuel, older by eighteen years, who ran the shipping company.[21] Second-generation money went into the textile manufacturing companies, as, for example, Zachariah Allen's, and even brother Samuel owned shares in various cotton mills, such as the Lyman Manufacturing Company and the Georgiaville mill which Allen purchased and rebuilt in the 1850s. Providence was a busy commercial port in the 1820s, as was Savannah, where ships carried the cotton and rice to the northern states or to England and brought back supplies on the return voyage. The plantations, however, were backwaters, slow moving like the river itself, to say nothing of the stagnant swamps which harbored the miasma of summer.

Arnold had been at White Hall no more than three weeks when he ex-

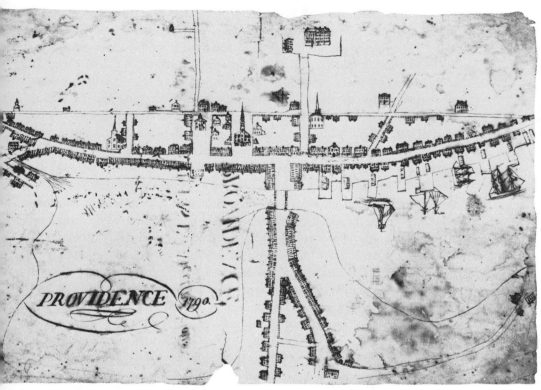

Map of Providence, 1790, by John Fitch. The town spreads on both sides of the Providence River, which is spanned by the Great Bridge. Welcome Arnold's store, wharves, and the Sabin Tavern face the river to the right of the bridge. (Courtesy of the Rhode Island Historical Society.)

pressed his impatience with the pace of doing things in the South: "I am at the Plantation where every thing goes in negro fashion, which is tediously slow," he wrote to his brother.[22] It is apparent from his early letters and business records that he had hoped to apply a greater sense of time and efficiency to his two plantations, each with its own work force and separate slave community, the work gangs interchangeable according to need. Nevertheless, he soon had to adjust his northern sense of time and speed to the natural rhythms of plantation work based on the task system. The rate of work for each task—such as hoeing, plowing, sowing—was established by a "task slave," usually a slave driver, who sought the middle ground between the slave's desire to do the least amount of work in the greatest amount of time and the master's desire to get the most work possible out of his slaves each day. Since the usual rate for most tasks was well established by long-standing custom, there was little room for change. Unlike the textile mills, it was a labor system geared to the slowest worker rather than the fastest. The natural rhythms of nature from planting to harvest determined the overall work routines. Unlike the small farm back in Rhode Island there was no slack season at the plantation because of its large size and the long growing season. After the harvest came the equally important work of preparing the rice and cotton for market, organizing repairs to the ditches and floodgates in the rice fields, and clearing new land before the next planting season. There was always something to do on the plantation, but the key to success was to make sure that it was done efficiently and productively. In common with the other planters of the area, Arnold sought an efficient balance of work force and cultivated land.

Speed was not the quickest way to profitability on the plantation. Because he depended on traditional methods of farming in a labor-intensive business, Arnold concentrated on using his organizational skills in assigning tasks and his business acumen in acquiring more land. As is evident in the plantation journal for the years 1847–1849, as well as in his account books and other journals, he had a passion for detail. This attention to minutiae, combined with a willingness to invest capital in new land and equipment, such as rice and sugar mills, made him a successful planter. His financial success, however, depended upon diverse business enterprises in both North and South. He never relied solely on the plantation for his livelihood.

As he prepared to make his rounds of the plantation on Monday, January 11, 1847, Richard Arnold was the third largest planter in Bryan County, surpassed only by his two friends and neighbors, Thomas Savage Clay and George Washington McAllister. He was a southern slave owner, the master of two hundred slaves, with all it entailed socially and culturally. But he was also the citizen of a northern free state, where he owned property and made investments and where he lived during the malaria season. His two lives coexisted more or less smoothly without interruption for nearly forty years, until 1861, when events outside his control forced him to choose between them. By then his identity was as divided as the nation itself, for he was as much southern planter as he was northern businessman.

In 1847, however, the Arnolds appeared to enjoy the best of both possible worlds, wintering in Georgia and summering in Rhode Island, respected in both communities. By this time, Arnold's image of himself as a southern planter concerned with the efficient economics of the plantation system had enlarged to include Christian paternalism—he was a kind, good master who had by chance of marriage "inherited" his slaves and who was deeply concerned for their social and moral welfare. From that point of view all aspects of the system, including slavery itself, were part of God's design to Christianize and civilize the slaves. Thus Olmsted, accepting Arnold's self-image, could describe him in 1853 as a "religious man" without calculating the moral cost of his owning slaves.

CHAPTER TWO

Bryan County, Georgia

On Monday, January 11, 1847, Richard Arnold, as was his custom while in residence at White Hall, rode to Cherry Hill, the larger of his two crop-producing plantations and a distance of about four miles from the White Hall mansion house. Arnold used the shorter track through the woods to the rear of White Hall rather than the broad front avenue which led to the main road. The mansion itself "was a structure of wood, with double roof, dormers and belvedere gallery; the principal apartments on the second floor, with the doors and windows opening upon broad piazzas."[1] To the rear of the house but separated from it were the kitchen, the house servants' quarters, the store house, barns, and the stables. Not far from the house, but hidden from the manse by a grove of cedars, were the cabins occupied by the White Hall field hands.

Since his overseer, Charles W. Ferguson, who lived at Cherry Hill, was still ill with pleurisy, Arnold checked thoroughly on the work being done there besides making his usual rounds to inspect the physical plant for any special attention. Normally, Ferguson would supervise the slaves so that Arnold could make any necessary adjustments to the work orders for the next day or week, but Ferguson had been bedridden for the past five days.

The slave families at White Hall and Cherry Hill lived in duplexes. "Each cabin was a framed building, the walls boarded and whitewashed on the outside, lathed and plastered within, the roof shingled; forty-two feet long, twenty-one by twenty-one; each tenement divided into three rooms—one the common household apartment, twenty-one by ten; each of the others [bedrooms], ten by ten. . . . Each tenement is occupied, on an average, by five persons."[2] Between each cabin and the next was an enclosed area for fowl and pigs, and in the rear were gardens, a half acre for each family. The cabins fronted on a wide "street," two hundred feet wide, more of a common, where many of the fowl roamed freely despite the coops in the back. The swine were allowed to root in the woods to the rear.[3] The housing accommodations Arnold provided his slaves did not quite meet the "ideal" suggested by some planters in various farm journals such as *De Bow's Review* in that "the ideal slave home was thought to be a well-constructed single family dwelling."[4] Each unit, however, was somewhat larger than the sixteen-by-eighteen-foot log cabin proposed by others as the ideal and was of a higher standard than the typical slave quarters which "were crowded and unhealthy and cabins were poorly constructed, in a state of disrepair, too small and dirty."[5]

Arnold encouraged his slaves to be as self-sufficient as possible by growing vegetables in gardens tended after the field work was finished, which, because of the task system, could be as early as three or four o'clock in the afternoon.[6] He also encouraged his slaves to keep fowl by buying their surplus eggs for family or plantation use, giving them credit at the store for whatever they sold him, including any game they had caught or shot and hogs they had raised.[7] Such luxury items as coffee, tobacco, and spices (but not liquor) could then be purchased. On April 12, 1837, his twin sister Eliza Harriet Allen, visiting the South for the first time, seemed puzzled at receiving from the slaves at a neighboring plantation a gift of thirteen eggs, "which I was told not to refuse."[8] While it is obvious she was much more delighted to have tasted the first strawberries of the season the same day she received the gift of such a common thing as a baker's dozen of eggs, the eggs were more precious to the slaves than the taste of early strawberries: they were a gift of money. "Eggs," Olmsted explained, "constitute a circulating medium on the plantation. Their par value is considered to be twelve for a dime, at which they may always be exchanged for cash, or left on deposit, without interest, at his [Arnold's] kitchen."[9] It was not egg money, however, but gifts (one is tempted to say "tips") that enabled Tom Morel ("my Head Waiter," as Arnold called him in his account books) to "loan" eighty dollars on December 6, 1854, to his master to keep for him while it earned interest![10]

The practice of giving monetary credit to the slaves in exchange for the fruits of their labor on their own time after the completion of their assigned tasks was not unique to Arnold's plantations; it was also customary on other plantations in the low-country region of South Carolina and Georgia during the antebellum period. The purchase by the master of produce, hogs, and game from his slaves led to a de facto ownership of property by the more enterprising plantation slaves despite the fact that legally the slave was himself property and could own nothing. It was with amazement that on Sunday morning, January 30, 1853, Olmsted watched Arnold's head house servant, Tom Morel, mount his own horse and tip the boy who held the horse for him; and that he received a salute that same morning from the watchman, Amos Morel, mounted on one of his three horses. Olmsted reminded his readers, however, that such evidence of paternalistic generosity on the part of Richard Arnold, the master, and enterprise on the part of the Morel brothers, was still within the slave system.[11] Arnold, despite his original misgivings concerning the task system's inefficiency, had by the 1840s accepted it as an institutionalized method of plantation labor that worked, as is evident from his plantation journal. To compensate for the low productivity of the task system, he sought to increase efficiency on his plantations by introducing more modern machinery such as the steam engine, which Amos Morel serviced, and to increase productivity through the building of the sugarhouse at Cherry Hill plantation.

Cherry Hill was the main working plantation of the Arnold estate. In addition to the slave quarters, the plantation was the site of the nursery (a combined baby nursery and day-care center) and the overseer's house, the rice mill, the elevator building which housed the shafting and gearing, a brick outbuilding which held the steam engine, the grist mill, and the corn house, as well as stables and barns. The new sugarhouse would soon be built there, the first shipment of bricks having been unloaded at the wharf from the *Cotton Plant* on Friday, January 8. The cottonhouse, however, was located at White Hall because it was the cotton-producing plantation.

All this was a far cry from the disappointing 1823 cotton and rice crop when Arnold first took over White Hall. By 1836, for example, the plantations were producing nearly 10,000 bushels of rice worth over $8,000, and nearly an equal amount of cotton in value, although Arnold had to hold off selling some of the cotton because of the low market price during the Panic of 1837.[12] He was storing more bushels of rice just for use on the plantations than the approximately 300 bushels he was able to sell on the market that first year. After the purchase of Cherry Hill plantation and its slaves, Arnold gradually expanded his holdings, waiting for the right opportunity to buy, since prime rice-producing land was scarce and expensive, and his neighbor Thomas Clay held most of the river land between White Hall and Cherry Hill. Sans Souci plantation, which Arnold purchased in 1835, was mostly pine land, and in order to get the rice fields at nearby Sedgefield in 1848, he had also to purchase two tracts of pine land totaling 1,200 acres from Edward Pynchon.

Although Arnold was the third largest planter in the county, after McAllister and Clay, his was a relatively small operation compared with the huge holdings of South Carolina rice planters like Nathaniel Heyward, who owned seventeen plantations and 2,000 slaves and produced 6,700,000 pounds of rice in 1849. It was not until after the war that Arnold rivaled these grandees of the antebellum rice-planter class. Then he became the largest rice producer in Georgia, and in the whole coastal plain area of tidal rivers, essential to rice production by the tide-flow method, he was second only to Heyward.[13] But by then everything had changed, and Arnold was able to expand because he provided northern capital to buy land cheap and pay wages to his former slaves.

Rice culture as practiced during the antebellum period was a labor-intensive business, more so than it need have been, but there was little incentive for the planter to introduce labor-saving methods when a ready supply of enforced labor was available to him at practically no cost as long as he had already "invested" his capital in slaves. Cultivation was so primitive—by hand and hoe—that animal-drawn plows were not introduced on the Heyward plantations until about 1860.[14] Arnold was already using plows drawn by mules or oxen in 1847, but only in the older, established fields; the new ground being cleared in January was cultivated and planted, as well as cleared, by hand. And even in the older fields, bedding cotton land—plowing into broad ridges preliminary to seeding—was sometimes done by hand, especially if the plows were being used elsewhere.

Olmsted reported that although the slaves on Arnold's plantations were humanely treated, "with as much discretion and judicious consideration of economy" as anywhere else in the slave states, he had observed many instances of "waste and misapplication of labor" directly related to the system of slave labor: "gates left open and bars left down, for instance, against standing orders; rails removed from fences by the negroes, as was conjectured, to kindle their fires with; mules lamed, and implements broken, by careless usage; a flat-boat, carelessly secured, going adrift on the river; men ordered to cart rails for a new fence, depositing them so that a double expense of labor would be required to lay them," and so on.[15] The slave, especially the ordinary field hand, had no incentive to work hard or be careful or learn new methods of farming. He was doubly enslaved—first as his master's property and second as one who was trapped by a system of labor economics that offered no hope of freedom. The master, in turn, even one as paternalistic as Richard Arnold, had little incentive to change established routines and traditional methods of work, let alone change the system itself. Incompetence, carelessness, indolence, and ignorance were largely absorbed into the system

By this Policy of Insurance, the Equitable Fire and Marine Insurance Company,

In consideration of —— Seventy five 62/100 —— Dollars.
to them paid by the assured hereinafter named, the receipt whereof is hereby acknowledged, DO INSURE

Richard J. Arnold

ACAINST LOSS OR DAMACE BY FIRE TO THE AMOUNT OF

Fifty five hundred dollars

On his Rice mill and other buildings and machinery, situate on his Plantation at Cherry Hill, Bryan County Georgia to apply as follows, viz.

$ 3200.	On Rice mill main building, used as a Rice mill
$ 350.	On Threshing machine contained in the above
$ 1200.	On Elevator building, shafting Gearing & elevators in the same
$ 400.	On Sugar House.
$ 100.	On Brick engine House.
$ 600.	On Steam engine and Boilers.
$ 200.	On Grist mill in elevator building.
$ 100.	On Corn House.
$ 150.	On Stable.
5,500	

With liberty for other insurance without notice until required.
$5500.   1 3/8 % $75. 62/100

And the said Company do hereby promise and agree to make good unto the said assured, his executors, administrators and assigns, all such immediate loss or damage, not exceeding in amount the sum insured, as shall happen by fire to the property, as above specified, from the Thirteenth day of September one thousand eight hundred and Sixty [at 12 o'clock at noon,] unto the Thirteenth day of September one thousand eight hundred and Sixty one [at 12 o'clock at noon,] the said loss or damage to be estimated according to the true and actual value of the property at the time the same shall happen; and to be paid within sixty days after notice and proof thereof, made by the assured, in conformity to the conditions annexed to this Policy. Provided always, and it is hereby declared, That this Company shall not be liable to make good any loss by theft or any loss or damage by fire which may happen or take place by means of any invasion, insurrection, riot or civil commotion, or of any military or usurped power. And provided further, that in case the owner of any other person or parties interested shall have already any other insurance against loss by fire on the property hereby insured, not notified to this Company, and mentioned in or endorsed upon this Policy, then this insurance shall be void and of no effect. And if the said assured, or his assigns or any other persons or parties interested, shall hereafter make any other insurance on the same property, and shall not with all reasonable diligence, give notice thereof to this Company, and have the same endorsed on the instrument, or otherwise acknowledged by them, in writing, this Policy shall cease and be of no further effect. And if any subsequent insurance should be made upon the property hereby insured, which, with the sum or sums already insured, should in the opinion of the said Equitable Fire and Marine Insurance Company, amount to an over-insurance, said Company reserve to themselves the right of cancelling this Policy, by paying to the insured the unexpired premium pro rata. And in case of any other insurance upon the property hereby insured, whether prior or subsequent to the date of this Policy, the assured shall not, in case of loss or damage, be entitled to demand or recover of this Company, any greater portion of the loss or damage sustained, than the amount hereby insured shall bear to the whole amount insured on the said property. And it is agreed and declared to be the true intent and meaning of the parties hereto, that in case the above mentioned premises shall, at any time after the making, and during the continuance of this Insurance, be appropriated, applied, or used, to or for the purpose of carrying on or exercising therein, any trade, business, or vocation denominated extra hazardous or specified in the memorandum of special rates, in the terms and conditions annexed to this Policy, or for the purpose of keeping or storing therein any of the articles, goods or merchandize, in the same terms and conditions denominated extra hazardous, or specified in the memorandum of special rates, unless herein otherwise specially provided for, or hereafter agreed to by this Company, in writing, and added to or endorsed upon this Policy, then and from thenceforth, so long as the same shall be so appropriated, applied, used or occupied, these presents shall cease and be of no force or effect. And it is moreover declared, that this insurance is not intended to apply to or cover any books of account, written securities, deeds, or other evidences of debt; and in all cases not herein otherwise specified, reference is to be had to and required to be used and resorted to in order to explain the rights and obligations of the parties hereto, in all cases not herein otherwise specified.

In Witness Whereof, The said EQUITABLE FIRE AND MARINE INSURANCE COMPANY OF PROVIDENCE, have caused these presents to be signed by their President, and attested by their Secretary, at their office in Providence, R. I. This Thirteenth day of September 1860

Thomas G. Turner President

[signature] Secretary

Equitable Fire and Marine Insurance Company policy insuring machinery at Cherry Hill plantation, September 13, 1860. (Courtesy of the Rhode Island Historical Society.)

and became institutionalized, demeaning both the worker and the employer. The slave used his ingenuity to get out of work as much as possible and assumed a mask of ignorance to escape blame and the whip. The master used the threat of the whip to keep control and get the work done, failure to perform a task satisfactorily being the most common reason for whipping.

It was, therefore, a matter of normal routine that because the slaves had "made out badly," clearing only one and a half acres of new ground, on January 11, 1847, Arnold shifted thirty-three of the Cherry Hill work force to clearing the next day. Similarly, on January 15, the women field hands were ordered to rework the tasks that had been done badly earlier in the week. That Amos Morel broke the axletree of his cart the next day was probably not due to carelessness and certainly not to ignorance or incompetence, for Amos, the blacksmith, was one of Arnold's most trusted, skilled, and competent slaves. The son of Mum Phebe, the Arnold children's mammy, Amos Morel was on his way to Savannah to sell the fish caught earlier in the Ogeechee when the axletree broke. The fact that he was sent twice the following week, and had permission to stay in Savannah over the weekend, is an indication of his favored position on the plantation. More typical of the kind of carelessness Olmsted observed was the incident on April 14 when the slave Battist and several other slaves, given the task of rounding up stray cattle, managed to drive off twenty head belonging to Arnold. If Arnold had not, by chance, seen it happen, he probably would have lost all twenty head. With the purchase of Pynchon's Sedgefield plantation and its herd, Arnold introduced branding as a means of identifying his cattle.

Although Arnold depended more and more on rice as his main cash crop, he minimized his risks by diversifying crops. He continued to produce fine sea island cotton at White Hall; the corn raised was used as a cash crop as well as a staple to supplement the slaves' diet. Sugarcane was raised in marketable quantities; and with the acquisition of new land, some of it suitable for grazing, he not only enlarged his herd of beef cattle but also maintained three hundred sheep. Even the river was fished and the surplus catch sold in the Savannah market. Every penny counted, and Arnold kept everyone busy. This diversification and the opening of new land, rather than the introduction of new methods of farming, enabled Arnold to use his work force more efficiently.

In order to increase profitability, Arnold concentrated more on mechanizing the final preparation of the crop for market, such as polishing the rice, which could not be done by hand, than on labor-saving machines for planting, which was done by hand. In the early 1840s with the expert help of his brother-in-law Zachariah Allen, Arnold purchased and shipped from Providence a steam engine to run the newly constructed rice mill at Cherry Hill. Previously, either he had to sell unmilled and unpolished rice, thus reducing considerably the price he obtained for it per pound, or else he had to pay another planter to mill and polish it. Similarly, unprocessed sugarcane fetched little on the market. The building of the sugar mill, begun in February 1847, was an attempt by Arnold to mechanize the processing of the sugarcane into sugar syrup so that he could go into large scale production. The venture, however, was unsuccessful because the sugar-mill equipment purchased from Lacklison of Savannah was defective. In the end Arnold sued Lacklison, but he continued to maintain a sugar mill at Cherry Hill throughout the rest of of the antebellum period; the sugar boilers and other equipment were sold by his son Thomas after the war.

Labor itself was a marketable commodity for the slave owner, and Arnold in common with other slaveholders hired out field hands and servants if they could be spared. He was not, however, in the business of buying and selling slaves, depending mainly on "a steady increase of his negro stock of five per cent per annum," according to Olmsted.[16] Arnold's "boasting" to Olmsted of this steady increase was in the context of proving to him that the Arnold slaves were healthy. As a northerner, Arnold was well aware of abolitionist agitation in New England and the impact of the recent publication of *Uncle Tom's Cabin* (1852). To put the best light on his own practice, Arnold had to balance the fact of a steady increase in "stock" with the countercharge that he was "breeding" slaves for sale. The 5 percent figure is generally borne out by the account books. After Arnold's initial purchase of the Cherry Hill slaves in 1824, he did not buy or sell slaves on any significant scale as a business practice, and no epidemic reduced his work force drastically.

Existing but incomplete account books suggest that Arnold was telling Olmsted the truth when he said that "he had sold but three slaves off his plantation in twenty years—and these either went willingly, or were banished for exceedingly and persistently bad conduct."[17] For example, on November 19, 1833—the day after he paid his slave Jim six dollars to cover the "expenses of bringing out the body of his brother March from Savannah"—Richard Arnold received from Thomas J. Parmalee of Augusta, Georgia, the sum of $750 for the sale of Stephen, sold "on a/c of his bad conduct, he being liable to lose his life should a prosecution be commenced against him at home." And on May 17, 1836, he received from Thomas Butler $1,300 for the sale of two slaves, Ned and Wally, so that they could be with their wives

and children on Butler's plantation in the western part of the state, sale subject to Butler's paying the $300 he still owed Arnold for the hire of these
slaves.[18]

The sales, totaling $2,050, along with the additional $750 Arnold had
earned from hiring Ned and Wally for four years, amply compensated his
humane motives. On the other side of the ledger, the cost of humaneness is
recorded in the purchase of various individual slaves or slave families. On
April 3, 1832, he paid $362 for the purchase of Celia. Perhaps to justify this
purchase, Arnold recorded the sale at length in his account book:

> To this sum pd by me this day at sheriff's sale for negro girl Celia that
> belonged to the Estate of the late A. Nethercliff & was sold under a judgment
> in favr of Doct. Bond & bid off by a Mr. Stoughton Hermans. But the Girl
> expressing a dislike to go to that gentleman & urging me very much to buy
> her, I consented to do so, as I owned her father, and I accordingly gave
> Hermans $4 to allow the titles to be made out to me—I paid in all, in order to
> T. B. Baker at the request of the sheriff $245.34   to Hermans $4—for title
> 1.25 & in order on E. Habersham payd to Wm Harn, sheriff or order on
> demand $110.66—
>
> Whole amt pd to be $361.25
> My expenses attending the sale   .75
> ─────────
> $362[19]

To keep a slave family together was a factor in all of Arnold's transactions
involving the buying of slaves. This motive was evident in his next purchase,
on January 22, 1834, of an entire slave family consisting of five individuals for
$1,900:

> To purchased 22nd inst of M. J. [Maria Jane] McIntosh, as per bill of sale, the
> following negroes that she inherited from her mother, which negroes are mar-
> ried or are to be married to my people & which purchase is made to prevent a
> separation of man & wife. They all belong to one family. Their names are
> Cinder, Flora, Tina, March & Dick, children of Cinder & Scipio, child of
> Flora. . . .[20]

Slave families had no status under the law in the slave states; parents could
be separated from their children and husbands from their wives by sale or
removal. Richard Arnold, however, consistently sought to maintain the in-
tegrity of his slave families. This paternalistic motivation involved him in
some complicated financial arrangements; when families are property, a monetary value is placed on their heads, and their worth as individuals may come

in conflict with their worth as property. On February 16, 1837, by request of the executors of the estate of the late Mrs. Ann Pray, Arnold set a price on each of her slaves, including a woman named Lissett whom Arnold judged as being worth "nothing."[21] On April 15, 1837, he concluded an agreement for the purchase of two slave families, consisting of nine individuals, from Mrs. Pray's estate, for $2,395.80. These slaves, Arnold explained in his account book, were "related to my people," including Sally, "wife of my man Abraham," and her two children. The other family, belonging to Lissett, he had not originally intended to purchase: "Lissetts family I positively refused to purchase at any price, and as she [Lissett] persisted so strongly I offered to give her fifty dollars if she would choose another Master. She would not do it & as she was Sallys sister & as she was so urgent to have me take them I reluctantly consented."[22] He did not want Lissett and had appraised her value as nothing because she was lame. Although useless in the fields, she would still have to be clothed and given the same food allowance as a full field hand. Since he himself had appraised and set the monetary value for the others in Lissett's family, he could not bargain about the price, and he did not want to break up the family. But if he could not bargain for their price, he could make certain before concluding the purchase that he was entitled to receive "a deduction of 10 per ct in conformity to Mrs. Pray's Will, she authorized that deduction in order to induce humane masters to take them."[23]

Perhaps the purchase of Mrs. Pray's slaves made Richard Arnold more cautious a year and a half later when the slaves of his neighbor, the late William Savage, were up for sale at auction upon the division of the estate. He wrote to Mary Nuttall (née Savage), who owned plantations in Florida, that "All the People I bot. [at the auction] I obtained at less than the appraisements.—And I bot. the 2d best family in the whole lot, being Isaacs." He acted as Mrs. Nuttall's agent in selling the slaves she had inherited from her uncle's estate: she preferred to sell them because "there are so many old ones." Her friends in Florida advised her to keep them, and she wrote to Arnold on December 20, 1838, requesting him to make arrangements to send them to her unless he had already finalized the sale. He had indeed negotiated to sell them, but the deal fell through, and on February 8, 1839, he wrote to her that "I have this moment delivered the Negroes to Mr. Clifford [to be transported to her plantation, El Destino, in Florida]—Forty eight in number. Old Ephraim has no connection among the People & was very anxious to remain and I consented to it.—He is of no value, & I believe he was so considered at the time of the appraisement."[24]

Nine slave children were born on the Arnold plantation in 1847, although

Richard Arnold's appraisal of Mrs. Pray's slaves, February 16, 1837. (Courtesy of the Rhode Island Historical Society.)

Quality's child, Washington, born on November 19, died ten days later. Several of the old people had died recently, including Old Dick in his seventy-seventh year and Old Sylvia in her hundredth year, both of whom died in late 1846. Old Dick had been the house servant of William Clark, Barbara Gindrat's first husband, and both he and Sylvia were among the twenty-two slaves made over to Barbara Clark and included in her marriage settlement in 1785. That left in 1847 only Gibb, Nanny (the cook), Adam, and Moses still alive from those original twenty-two; Kate, Moll, Sampson, Jinny, Morris, and George were still alive from the twenty-three other slaves drawn by Mrs. Clark in the division of Captain James McKay's estate upon his death in 1786.[25]

The new slave cabin Richard Arnold ordered built on January 14, 1847, may have been planned with other families in mind, but the timing was nonetheless fortuitous, for on that day Colonel Morris wrote concerning the sale of his slave Lissy:

> Your favour of 26th Dec. came round about to me and I have but recently received it. In answer to your purchasing Lizze   She became the whife of your Man without my knowledge and afterwards consented to what I could not help   I have been made to pay very high for leaving to my Friends to arrange for me, what I ought to have attended to myself, as in the instance of Jimmys Whife paying for her an[d] Infant $1150. I must therefore decline leaving it to Mr. Habersham or others to fix the value of Lizze   She is one of my formost women, and most fruitful, The value of such I am informed in Charleston is $600, which I will take for her   I am not desirous of selling only to gratify the desire of Man and Whife to be together.[26]

Colonel Morris was driving a hard bargain, and Richard Arnold knew it, but he had to take a white man's word on trust. Still, he tried to bargain with the colonel by making it a matter of honor:

> Your favr of the 14th Inst. is at hand, and I think there must be some mistake with regard to the value of such a woman as Lissy or any other woman that is a field hand in Charleston—If it is otherwise they [sell] much higher there than in Savh where she would not bring more than $500— & probably not more than $450.—For altho I do not doubt she is—, strictly prime as you state, yet you know she is undesired. I however have determined to unite them as man & wife & if on reflection & further inquiry, you do not consider the price mentioned by you as more than her real value, & will take less, I must pay the $600.—You will please send me a Bill of Sale after satisfying yourself as to the price together with an order for Lissy, and I will [pay] you the amount on receiving her.[27]

The colonel's bill of sale was for $600, the price that satisfied him from the beginning. Whether or not Richard Arnold really believed he was paying Colonel Morris "more than her real value," the potential value of his "property" doubled on July 26, 1847, when Lissy gave birth to Cora, thus increasing the number of his slaves from 202 to 203. It is unlikely that Colonel Morris knew Lissy was pregnant, for he would have demanded more money. It was not until February 20 that Arnold sent Cain to Colonel Morris's plantation to bring back his wife, Lissy. By then the overseer, Ferguson, was back on the job, having slowly recovered from pleurisy, going outside for the first time in three weeks on January 23.

This was only Ferguson's second year as overseer on the Arnold plantations, a position he was to hold for thirteen years, an unusually long tenure in a job which normally saw a turnover of personnel every two years. The ideal overseer would be a planter clone, for even the smallest detail overlooked, particularly in rice culture using the tide-flow method, could spell the difference between profit and loss. Were it not for the real danger of malaria, Arnold would have preferred to remain in Georgia most of the year, especially during the harvest season in late summer. At best, the overseer was a kind of superintendent who supervised the day-to-day operations of the business but who deferred to the decisions of the owner in important matters and did not take it upon himself to be a surrogate master, except in matters specifically authorized in the contract.

Richard Arnold held a low opinion of overseers in general, but as he told Olmsted, he found Ferguson to be "an uncommonly valuable one."[28] Even so, Arnold would rather not have had to employ an overseer and thus save the $1,000 a year he was paying Ferguson, but the law required "the superintendence or presence of a white man among every body of slaves." Ferguson was only the latest in a long line hired by Arnold since 1823. Arnold's troubles began even before this, since he claimed that John Miller, who had been overseer of White Hall, had wrongfully taken twenty-three of the White Hall slaves as his own. It took Arnold ten years of lawsuits to obtain a judgment against Miller in circuit court. It is no wonder, therefore, that Arnold was somewhat jaundiced about overseers, considering them necessary evils at best, and at worst, incompetent, stupid fellows.

From the beginning, Arnold sought to establish a firm hierarchy of authority and supervision because of his absence during the long summer season. Ben, one of the original White Hall slaves belonging to Louisa's mother, had run away the previous summer, but "he came back just before I came on [in December, 1823] & has been home & behaved very well all winter." Therefore, on May 15, 1824, explaining why he had delayed his return North, Arnold wrote to his brother, Samuel, "This is the season of the hardest work—and altho I have got thru the winter with very little trouble from them [the slaves] still they now are—trying my overseer—(to use the Georgia term) and unless he is firmly fixed in his command, before I leave, they may give him trouble."[29] Whether the slaves did not work hard enough in the master's absence or whether it was his incompetence, the overseer got very little productive work out of them. On his return to Georgia in November 1824, Arnold wrote to his brother, "His crop is all gathered & the value is not ⅕ of a crop.—And the stupid fellow has not repaired the dwelling House— and from his own a/c I cannot build a fire in it, or occupy two of the chambers, the windows having been broken in & now nailed up with rough boards."[30]

As a result, Arnold experimented with other arrangements, seeking to evolve the best system of management for his two plantations. For the year 1827, he entered into an unusual agreement by which his overseer, John James Snead, obviously inexperienced, was supervised by a neighbor's overseer.

> It is expressly understood that he [Snead] is to be under Mr. Martin the Overseer of Mr. Clay so far as respects the management of Cherry Hill when-ever said Arnold is not present. . . . Also the Said Snead is at all times when at a loss, or when any important work &c is to be done (in the absence of Said Arnold) such as flowing or leting off water, puting down trunks &c &c, to consult Said Martin & to follow implicitly his the Said Martins directions.[31]

Obviously, such an arrangement was bound to be unsatisfactory and at best served only as a temporary, stopgap measure. The following year, Arnold hired A. M. Sanford as overseer for White Hall only, Sanford being commit-ted to two other planters for that year. Since Sanford's work was apparently satisfactory and since Arnold wished to develop the two plantations together as one operation, Sanford was hired as overseer for both Cherry Hill and White Hall for the years 1829 through 1832.[32] This arrangement of one over-seer for both plantations with the work force interchangeable remained in effect throughout the antebellum period.

In common with other rice planters in the area, Arnold divided his field hands into work gangs ranging from twenty to thirty hands, each with a driver who functioned as a kind of foreman. There was nothing rigid about either the personnel or the size of the gangs, which depended on the task. In rice culture the task rather than the gang set the pace of work. Generally, however, Arnold retained the identity of the two separate slave communities, each with separate slave quarters. For example, in March 1847 Arnold calculated that his Cherry Hill work force consisted of the equivalent of sixty-eight and a half full hands and the White Hall force twenty-two and a half, each field hand being assigned tasks according to age and physical ability, ranging from one-fourth to full hand. Thus, the Cherry Hill work force consisted of ninety-two slaves and the White Hall work force, thirty-four, not counting the house servants, who normally did not do field work, and the children, who were not assigned regular field work until about twelve years of age but who were assigned such tasks as bird minding, fetching water, and other chores as needed. On the basis of his available work force Arnold calculated that for the 1847 growing season he should be able to plant 480 acres at Cherry Hill and 154 acres at White Hall in various crops—rice, cotton, sugarcane, and corn being the main cash crops. Arnold also assigned individual tasks to individual slaves, such as fishing and running errands, and the plowmen and the carpenters were special task forces within the work force because they were skilled.

The task system in effect on the Arnold plantation and elsewhere in the low-country rice-producing areas of South Carolina and Georgia in the 1840s and 1850s evolved during the colonial period, when rice culture with the use of slave labor began. By the mid-eighteenth century, when the importation of slaves was first permitted in Georgia, "the basic 'task' unit had been set at a quarter of an acre," and other tasks, such as the pounding of rice grain and the splitting of fence rails, had well-established quotas.[33] Therefore, when Arnold first arrived at the plantation in 1823 and wrote to his brother, complaining of the tedious slowness of "Negro time," he was actually commenting on "a prominent characteristic of the task system—a sharp division between the master's 'time' and the slave's 'time.'" His northern sense of time had to adjust to what was by then long-established practice in rice culture, paced according to what the slowest workers could be expected to complete within the allotted time. So institutionalized was the task system that a slave could "work intensively in his task and then have the balance of his time" as his own.[34] Like other planters of the area, Arnold made a virtue of necessity, impressing a northern visitor such as Olmsted with the humaneness of the amount of work required for any given task and with his paternalistic regard for encouraging his slaves to be more self-sufficient.[35]

The slave driver was responsible for seeing that the gang in his charge satisfactorily performed the assigned tasks, and he was also responsible for keeping discipline within the gang. Since satisfactory performance and discipline were almost synonymous from the point of view of the overseer and the planter (the pace of the task was set by the driver or someone under him), the driver was expected to punish by whipping those who consistently failed to do their share of the work. The driver was held accountable for the work being done properly and was also responsible for keeping discipline among his gang in the slave quarters, living with them and acting as a kind of resident policeman. It was this authority to discipline by whipping or flogging that often led to abuse. After the publication of *Uncle Tom's Cabin* in 1852, the public image of the slave driver, certainly among abolitionists in the North, was based on Sambo and Quimbo, who had been especially trained in brutality by their owner, Simon Legree.

Nonetheless, it was naive of Eliza Harriet Allen, Richard's twin sister, arriving in Savannah on April 1, 1837, to think that she would never see again what had so distressed her upon entering Savannah harbor, the sight of "a poor slave whipped by another."[36] In all likelihood Eliza Harriet would not find a slave whipping another slave on her brother's plantation because such a distressing sight would be kept from the master's sister, and at no time during her month and a half stay at White Hall did she actually go into the fields to see the slaves working. Her image of Richard was of a kind, benevolent, paternalistic slave master and Christian, and thus she could not believe that he would ever allow corporal punishment; also, she felt, the slaves loved him and Louisa, and therefore they would do nothing to warrant such punishment.

Although he did not witness any whippings on the Arnold plantations the few days he was there as a guest, Olmsted was not so naive and inexperienced an observer as to believe they did not take place, and Arnold was not so naive as to suggest that they did not. He indicated to Olmsted that his "children" like children everywhere would require punishment "sometimes, perhaps, not once for two or three weeks; then it will seem as if the devil had got into them all and there is a good deal of it."[37] The loving Victorian "father" required obedience of his children, and when they disobeyed they had to be punished, just as they were rewarded for good behavior. It would be a denial of the father's role if they were not disciplined for their transgressions, as much as it would be a denial of his love if they were not rewarded. Whippings were never administered by the master's own hand on Arnold's plantations (rewards, however, were usually handed out in person by the master or his wife).

The punishment of slaves on the Arnold plantations for "light" offenses, such as failure to work satisfactorily, "was administered with the whip, upon the back of the man or woman, without removing their clothes; the whip is a short stick, with a flatlash of leather."[38] The fact that the clothes were not removed may seem humane, for the women were not thus subjected to the indignity of exposure, but it also *hid* from sight whatever welts and bruises the lash raised. These whippings would not be reported in Arnold's plantation journal, since Ferguson and the drivers had discretion to punish ordinary offenses as long as no severity or cruelty was used. Ferguson in all probability verbally reported to Arnold any such whippings, but no written record survives. Nonetheless, on July 16, 1852, about six months before Olmsted's visit, Ferguson felt the necessity to write Arnold in Providence that he personally had "whiped some of them to make them work but had to give way" because they were actually sick and not feigning illness.[39] Ferguson may have feared the slaves would inform their master about the incident, and he was explaining his side of what had happened.

Solitary confinement rather than whipping was the punishment meted out for more serious offenses committed by Arnold's slaves: "The negroes were placed in solitary confinement in a small, dark house or jail kept for that purpose; and of this they had great dread. and much preferred being whipped."[40] It is understandable that a slave might possibly prefer the known physical pain of the lash to the psychological pains of solitary confinement in darkness for an indefinite period of time. It is even understandable in the context of the times why this form of punishment was used by slave masters, who adapted it for their purposes from current penal practice. Thomas Savage Clay, Arnold's nearest neighbor and friend, stated the rationale for this kind of punishment as early as 1833 in his monograph *Detail of a Plan for the Moral Improvement of Negroes on Plantations:*

> Corporal punishment, which was always degrading, should very rarely be inflicted in public, and *never* if the negro manifests penitence. This exhibition either hardens the spectators, or awakens sympathy for the guilty. The modes of correction I would recommend are, solitary confinement by night, separation from the other negroes by day, and the privation of such extra allowance as may be bestowed for the encouragement of industry and good conduct. The benefits of solitary confinement in reforming the depraved, and awakening a moral sense in the degraded, have been fully proved in our modern penitentiaries.[41]

The severest punishment, the ultimate threat, is to deny to the "child" access to the "father." Richard Arnold, whose own father had died when he was two years old and who had at first taken over the running of the plantation as a business proposition, had by reason of religion, personality, and paternalistic practice come to believe that he was paterfamilias to his "people" while he duly recorded their worth as property in his account books. After observing Arnold's treatment of his slaves, Frederick Law Olmsted, whose mother died when he was three years old and whose father shortly thereafter sent him to live at various "dames' schools" run by ministers' wives, wrote an apologia for the paternal role of the slave master:

> Here I see their master, dealing with them as a father might such children; guarding them sedulously against dangerous temptations, forbidding them to indulge in bad practices, rewarding the diligent and obedient, and chastising the perverse and indolent; anticipating and providing for their wants; encouraging them in the provident use of their little means of amusement, and comfort, and luxury; all the time furnishing them the necessary support of life; caring diligently for them in sickness; and only when they are of good age and strength, so long as he is their guardian, demanding of them a certain amount of their labor and assistance, to increase his own comforts, provide for his age.[42]

It was exactly the portrait Arnold would have wanted Olmsted to describe, not because he had deliberately misled him but because it precisely matched Arnold's self-image as a slave master, predestined by God to serve in that "station in life."

Paradise was not always idyllic, and on August 23, 1824, Arnold was billed for $5.68¾ by Isaac D'Lyon, sheriff of Chatham County, in which Savannah is located, for the apprehension and the jailing of his slave Sampson for 16 days at the cost of 16 cents per day. Whether it was unusual or not for a slave to run away from the Arnold plantation, the sheriff obviously considered such occurrences ordinary enough, for the bill presented was a printed form with the details inserted.[43] Sampson was one of the original White Hall slaves, aged forty-three in 1824; twenty-three years later, aged sixty-six, he was still listed as a full field hand capable of doing the same amount of work as in 1824, when he was in his prime.

On April 4, 1828, Arnold recorded in his account book the sum of $40.90 paid the previous day to George Miller, sheriff of Chatham County, Georgia, part of which was a reward for "apprehending my Boys," Sam and Wally. Wally was eventually sold, but Sam, twenty-two years old when he ran away, remained Arnold's slave throughout the antebellum period. Whatever Sam's difficulties that caused him to run away in 1828, he obviously settled down to accept his lot, because thirty years later he was listed by Arnold as a driver of one of the Cherry Hill work gangs, a position which Arnold would not have given him had he considered him unreliable.

One might speculate that Sam, a young man having just reached his maturity, was testing the limits of his master's paternalism. But what is one to make of Old Dick, one of the original slaves of White Hall plantation inherited by Barbara Clark Gindrat, who in March 1827 was apprehended by M. Richardson as a runaway slave? It was hardly youthful spirits, for Dick was fifty-seven. It could have been spirits, for Arnold had received ten gallons of whiskey earlier that same month as payment in kind from his neighbor, Thomas Clay. Whatever the cause, Dick had to be rescued from the Savannah jail, which, in addition to a bounty of $33.50 paid to Richardson, cost Arnold $5.35, the expense of sending the overseer, John James Snead, to Savannah in order to bring Dick home.[44] As late as 1841 (Old Dick died in 1846 at the age of seventy-six) Arnold's instructions to his overseer were filled with specific tasks for Old Dick—"Let Dick cut rushes and keep Old Sam supplied" making baskets, and "Dick can take care of the cattle hunt & mark all the calves & work in vegetable garden. . . . Dick must keep his quarter clear of grass."[45]

In the early fall of 1837, several months after Eliza Harriet Allen and the Arnolds had left for Rhode Island but still some weeks before the Arnolds' return to Georgia, Thomas Clay reported in a letter to Arnold that there had been several escapes from nearby plantations. Most runaways were caught immediately within a few miles of their plantation. This is what happened to two of them, one belonging to Patterson and the other, Simon, to William Savage, Mary Savage Nuttall's uncle. Simon, Clay informed Arnold, "has run away three times, & I presume will now be shipped [i.e., sold at auction]." The others, like many before them and many after them, hid in the swamps, eventually to be hunted like animals by posses of white men after the first frost. "It is intended," Clay wrote, "as soon as the accumulation of frost will render it safe [from malaria], to hunt for them by detachments until they are all caught or driven away." One of the hunted slaves was Dr. Rogers's man who "left home again & joined them." Their neighbor Colonel McAllister overtook one of the runaways belonging to George Washington Walthour, the largest slaveholder in nearby Liberty County, but when McAllister "demanded his gun, he replied he would give it up to no man. The Col. attempted to spring from his gig & seize him but came down on his lame leg & fell, on which the man escaped into the woods."[46]

It was not for the color of the soil that this rice-growing area of Georgia was known as "Black Ankle Country," and although the runaway slave might know the geography of the immediate area and how to survive off the land, the swamp land was as much a trap as it was a hiding place. Although the fugitive slave might hope to escape detection for a while, there was little chance he could escape to freedom in the North; indeed, most runaways had no thought of such freedom but rather were seeking to escape an immediate threatening or hopeless situation. As Gilbert Osofsky suggests in *Puttin' On Ole Massa:*

> In the deepest sense the entire South was a prison house, and all white men, solely because of their skin color, were prison keepers. By law and custom every white was permitted to stop any black along the road and ask him to present his pass or freedom papers or explain why he was away from the plantation. To collect the reward on a fugitive or perhaps claim the person of slave whose master could not be located must have been enticing bait for the poor whites who patrolled the Southern countryside. A good catch not only seemed a fulfillment of one's communal responsibility but also might mean instant wealth.[47]

Consequently, runaway slaves kept off the roads and hid in the swamps where the white man seldom went, especially in summer. The white enemy was visible and could be avoided, but, Osofsky continues, although most slaves and free blacks "were willing to assist fugitives . . . certain black Judases sabotaged the escape plans of many."[48]

In the summer of 1841 Arnold wrote to Thomas Butler King, United States representative from Georgia and at the time still in Washington, that Larkin, King's runaway slave, had been captured at White Hall plantation:

> It seems he has been lurking about there for some weeks & was seen by my Driver, but being so well armed he did not attempt to take him. He however heard him fire a gun, saw him kill a hog & then watched him until night, when he discovered where he slept. He then immediately informed the Overseer [J. Swanston] who took two other white men with him. & went with the Driver, secured him & sent him to Savannah Jail. When taken he had with him a Musket & Dirk. Knowing you are in Washington I thought it doubtful if you would hear of his being in Jail unless I informed you. I have written the Overseer to see Larkin & endeavor to find out where the others are to be found & use his best exertions to take them.[49]

In 1846, in his agreement with Ferguson, Arnold added "patrol duty"—that is, hunting for runaway slaves—to the other tasks of the overseer.[50]

It is not clear that Carpenter Peter, aged twenty-six, ran away from the plantation in the summer or fall of 1846, but the following winter his behavior was being observed. On January 9, 1847, Arnold recorded in his plantation journal: "C. [Carpenter] Peter on good behavior from this day."[51] Whatever his "crime"—mere failure to do his task would not have occasioned comment in the journal—reformation of character was required. Six years later, Carpenter Peter's behavior was good enough for the Arnolds to allow his wedding to take place at the manse, a practice usually reserved for favorite slaves. But in 1858 Carpenter Peter was again in serious trouble for stealing corn and molasses from the plantation. There is no doubt, however, that Arnold would have acted in both instances on the principle that there can be no moral improvement without punishment.

2

Antebellum Savannah was the commercial and financial center for the surrounding plantation country. The sale and shipment of rice and cotton and other commodities grown on the plantations were handled by commission merchants, called factors, who, like the Habershams, had their offices and warehouses along the wharves. The factors were a vital part of the plantation economy, for they not only arranged for selling and shipping the crops to northern or English ports, they also provided drayage, insurance, and temporary storage space. And if a large planter decided to withhold his rice or cotton from the market in the hope that prices would rise, his factor could provide longer-term storage facilities. In short, factors often acted as accountants and bankers debiting and crediting the planters' accounts according to the transaction, providing, for example, needed supplies for the plantation and even loaning money to the planters to tide them over from planting to harvest, particularly if the previous year's crop had been poor or if the market was depressed—all for a commission, of course.

By the 1830s, Savannah, although it had half the population, rivaled Charleston as a leading exporter of cotton, only New Orleans and Mobile being larger. With the building of the railroads during the 1840s and 1850s, Savannah's market expanded beyond the river by opening the upland cotton regions of western and northern Georgia directly to the port of Savannah. Savannah held the same relative position as the commercial and financial center for the rice and cotton planters of the coastal plains of Georgia as Providence held for the textile manufacturers of Rhode Island at the other end of the Cotton Kingdom. Richard Arnold, as befitted a man who had a foot at each end, owned stock in both the Bank of the State of Georgia and the Providence Bank.

It was not, however, as though the two worlds, North and South, were entirely separate and that once Arnold arrived at the plantation he doffed the

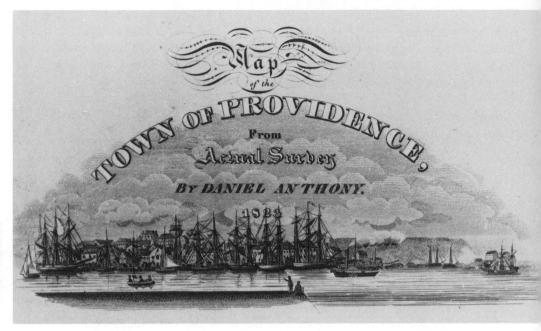

Cartouche from the 1823 map of Providence by Daniel Anthony showing Providence River waterfront. (Courtesy of the Rhode Island Historical Society.)

nineteenth-century equivalent of the gray flannel suit for the country tweeds and a southern drawl. Just as plantation matters and overseer reports followed him north during the summer season, so business accounts and trustee reports followed him south during the winter months. The Habershams and the Joneses had purchased or inherited wharfage on the Savannah River; the Arnolds and the Allens had purchased or inherited wharves on the Providence River. The coming of the railroad to serve the warehouses along the river was a boon to wharf owners like the Arnolds, but it also was a matter of concern to these shipping merchants whether the new railway might encroach upon their property and block the passage of ships or interfere with loading. Richard Arnold had noticed before he left for Georgia in December 1830 that the railway company's works had come very close to his wharf and had asked Zachariah Allen as his business agent to keep an eye on its progress. In late January 1831 Zachariah reported, "There is room enough left for the passage of vessels to your wharf, and from appearance, they have no intention of encroaching upon the gangway. Should they attempt it I will positively stop them and break up their proceedings at all events." The wharf, which he had inherited from his uncle Jonathan, proved profitable as the shipping business moved into the Age of Steam: "There is no one so convenient to the steamboats as yours for the storage of coal, as the boats will only require to be moved about their length to receive their complement of fuel," Allen reported to Arnold that spring. "I consider therefore that you have got a sort of monopoly of the chance of letting your wharf on very favorable terms" to the Sidney Coal Company.[52]

In Georgia, Arnold's factor, Robert Habersham and Son of Savannah, provided him with a variety of financial services throughout the year, but the factor's presence was especially valuable in the spring when Arnold left the plantation for the North. For example, on April 6, 1848, two weeks before the Arnolds were due in Savannah preparatory to sailing for Providence, the Habershams arranged for passage on the *Southerner*, leaving from Charleston; they paid $150 for staterooms 3 and 4, for which Arnold reimbursed them, entering the transaction under "Family Expenses" as was his custom in accounting for the cost of traveling back and forth between Georgia and Rhode Island. Since Arnold would not return until December 5, seven and a half months later, he needed to make various financial settlements before traveling north. Arnold took care of some bills personally, such as paying for the services of James, "a slave belonging to Estate of Jos. Jones" for masonry work "setting Kettles for Sugar House" the year before in April 1847. Payment of $25 for twelve and one-half days of work was made to Willis Ball, carpenter, a white man "sub-leasing" the labor of property owned by the Joseph Jones Estate. Similarly, but under "Family Expenses" rather than the plantation account, since this was the master's gift to his people, he listed various amounts credited for hogs and fowl, to Morris, Boston, Adam, Tom, and Harriet, and to Cain he paid sixty-two cents for a terrapin for the annual spring feast on April 15, 1848, the last Saturday before the Arnolds left for the North. The feast celebrated the final fruits of the year's harvest—1,500 bushels of rice loaded that day on board the *Cotton Plant* to be shipped to the Savannah market—as well as the new planting season—the finishing of fifty-two acres hoed at White Hall that same night.[53]

More typical of the kind of transaction carried out by the Habershams was the payment on April 21, 1848, of a bill for $153.47 for shoes and $362.40 for blankets and other items distributed to the slaves during the previous winter. In addition, on the same day, Arnold received $300.00 cash from Habersham and Son "on a/c."; of the money, $6.50 was "handed Mrs. Arnold in Savannah" and $4.50 was "handed my daughter Louisa in New York for her own use." Arnold was very much the Victorian father and husband, controlling the money and handing out presents whether to wife or daughter or servant. But he was generous also, and $135.00 of the expenses for the trip included china, carpets, and a sofa purchased at auction in New York, $14.50 for jackets for his sons, and $30 passage to Rhode Island for Catharine, the children's nurse, who was ill.[54]

Whether the amount was large ($992 to pay due promissory notes) or small (a $20 subscription to the Moravia Education Society in China), the Habershams provided an indispensable service that seemed to combine the services of banker, accountant, trustee, business adviser, and friend.[55] Even such a domestic service as mail delivery was provided by the Habershams; since there was no delivery to the plantation, mail was often sent to the Arnolds in care of the Habershams in Savannah. No wonder, therefore, that the Habersham family were welcomed guests at White Hall, and when Habersham himself dined at White Hall, as he did on February 5, 1848, undoubtedly he and his host mixed business and pleasure. The association covered nearly twenty-five years, although at the beginning Richard Arnold used Robert Habersham's services sparingly.

Arnold's trips to Savannah were usually a mixture of business and pleasure, especially if members of the family accompanied him. Savannah was the social center for the plantation country, and many planters maintained residences in Savannah during the winter social season. The Arnolds preferred to entertain at White Hall, staying while in Savannah with friends like George Noble and Mary Nuttall Jones, or residing at a hotel like the Pulaski House or a boardinghouse like Mrs. Maxwell's for short visits. Arnold's overnight visit to Savannah on March 21–22, 1848, however, was mainly for business; he paid bills and collected his dividend on the three shares he owned in the Planters Bank of Savannah. The $19 his daughter Louisa extracted from him upon his return was presumably painless compared with the $5 he paid a dentist earlier that day in Savannah.[56]

Richard Arnold was by no means the stereotype of the southern planter sitting on the piazza drinking mint juleps served by liveried house servants. He was deeply involved in the detailed planning and day-to-day operation of his business. Nonetheless, he and Louisa found time to entertain a steady stream of visitors to White Hall, some of whom stayed for extended periods. Daily visits from neighbors and friends, especially the Clays at Richmond-on-Ogeechee and the McAllisters at Strathy Hall, on either side of White Hall, were so common that they were not mentioned in his plantation journal. Admittedly, relations between Arnold and Thomas Clay had cooled during the winter of 1847–1848 because of a boundary dispute, probably in connection with Arnold's impending purchase of rice plantation land from Edward E. Pynchon, one of the boundaries of which ran alongside the old Clay canal.[57] But Louisa Arnold's friendship with the Clays went back to her childhood, long before she had met Richard Arnold. Not only had Louisa grown up with the Clay children, but Matilda McAllister had married Thomas Clay; the three families were in and out of each other's houses, and the Arnolds named their second son after his godfather, Thomas Clay. The rituals of southern hospitality, despite the long distances (as much as ten miles) between plantations, ensured that White Hall had many visitors from the outlying areas. For example, returning their hospitality of January 28, 1847, the Arnolds on February 9 entertained the Demeres, from whom they had purchased land many years earlier. The Demeres stayed overnight, and on the following day they were joined by the Pattersons, Dr. Charles William Rogers and family, Miss Woodford, and the Reverend Mr. Rogers of North Hampton, who, along with Miss Habersham and Mr. Buckley, was on an extended visit.

Such visits were the lifeblood of social intercourse among the planter families in antebellum Georgia. These were the friends and social peers of the Arnolds, a small circle of likeminded, upper-middle-class plantation owners who shared a pattern of social attitudes and who accepted the white southern way of life based on slavery. Many of these same people appear in Eliza Harriet Allen's journal of her stay at White Hall ten years earlier in the spring of 1837. The Starrs, for example, who dined as guests of the Demeres along with the Arnolds on January 28, 1847, were planters and distant neighbors; they greeted Eliza Harriet at the church on her first Sunday at the plantation and visited White Hall the next day, inviting her and the Arnolds to their home later in the week after they returned from a short stay in Savannah. Similarly, the following week Eliza Harriet and the Arnolds received a social call from the Rogerses (they were all absent, however, visiting the Clays), a courtesy which they repaid three days later by traveling to Otter Lee, the new home of Dr. Rogers, a distance of nine miles from White Hall. These were the same Rogerses who visited the Arnolds at White Hall on February 10, 1847. Dr. Rogers died in 1849, and his son the Reverend Charles William Rogers inherited his father's plantation. Although educated in the North (Yale and Princeton Theological Seminary) and married to a New Englander, Caroline Woodford of Hartford, Connecticut, once back in Georgia he refused to leave the South as a personal protest against the rising tide of abolitionism in the North.[58] While the Arnolds never went to that extreme, they presumably approved of his missionary work among the slaves as a Presbyterian minister and his general social and economic views: he too was a rich planter and owned more than 150 slaves.

On January 16, 1849, Richard and Louisa Arnold and their youngest daughter, Susan, began a week's visit to Savannah as guests of George Noble and Mary Nuttall Jones. Mrs. Jones was the former Mary Wallace Savage, whose aunt Mary Ann Savage Clay, then a widow, had assumed the care of the orphaned Louisa Caroline Gindrat in 1814 and raised her as a member of the Clay family. Although not directly related, Mary Nuttall Jones thought of the Arnolds as family and addressed them affectionately as uncle and aunt, and it was as family that they were welcomed at her home in Savannah and she at White Hall.

As usual, work continued at the plantation, and Arnold arranged that during his absence the carpenters, plowmen, and others would work in the rice fields at newly acquired Sedgefield. He also made arrangements to pay his overseer, Charles Ferguson, for the year ending December 31, 1848. While in Savannah he did not forget the "servants" belonging to the Joneses, buying $5.25 of calico cloth to be distributed as gifts and also presenting them with $1.75 in cash for their services in attending the Arnolds. He gave $12.00 to his wife for her use, having paid out of his own pocket for theater tickets to see the famous actor William McCready perform, probably in one of his Shakesperian roles. But since he had just received $2,325.49 from the sale of 137 casks of rice, he could afford to celebrate.[59]

Although both Richard Arnold and George Noble Jones were large slaveholding planters who spent the summer season in Rhode Island and eventually were neighbors in Newport, their life-styles were quite different. Both were from prominent colonial families in their respective states. Both had acquired plantations from their wives upon marriage, and both had discovered the finances of these plantations to be in a tangle, requiring lawsuits and investments of their own money. But there the similarity ended. Jones was Georgia-born, his great-great-grandfather, Noble Jones I, having been one of the original settlers of the colony and an aide to its founder, General James Oglethorpe. His family owned a large plantation in Jefferson County as well as extensive waterfront property in Savannah, where the Jones family were socially prominent. Jones, therefore, was no stranger to plantation life. His father died in 1819 when he was only eight, and eventually he took over management of the family plantation jointly owned by his mother and two aunts. Later, Jones inherited a third share of this large plantation, but by then he had already become a slave owner and planter in Florida through marriage.[60] Thus Jones, unlike Arnold, was experienced in plantation management when he married Mary Savage Nuttall, which may possibly explain in part his more casual approach; but more important, the two men were as different in temperament as their separate heritages could make them, the one southern and cosmopolitan, the other a New Englander and more parochial.

Jones was an absentee owner, leaving the day-to-day operation of his two Florida plantations to overseers (each had a separate overseer). Although like Arnold, Jones kept in regular correspondence with the overseers during his absence, which was most of the time, he interfered little with their treatment of the slaves except during a crisis. Because he was an absentee owner, there was no development of a paternalistic regime on the Jones plantations as there was on Arnold's.[61] Since George Noble and Mary Nuttall Jones belonged to prominent Georgian families centered in Savannah, they preferred to spend most of the winter social season in the city, where they owned a house and extensive commercial property. Arnold, on the other hand, although he was absent from the plantation five to six months of the year, was nonetheless considered a working planter who managed his own plantation while in residence in Georgia; even during the summer season he kept in close touch with his overseer by mail, besides leaving elaborate and detailed instructions before journeying north. The Joneses, on the other hand, were never tied down to their plantations, because El Destino and Chemonie were in Florida, a considerable distance from Savannah, the center of their social lives in the winter. They took along whatever servants they needed, as on March 27, 1847, when Mary Nuttall Jones arrived at White Hall with three of them.

El Destino, the home plantation of the Joneses when in residence in Florida, was a cotton plantation, and on March 29, 1847, the majority of the field hands were engaged in planting: of the forty-two hands working that day, twenty-eight were involved in plowing and planting. The Joneses were probably in residence for the first two weeks of January 1847, for the overseer's journal reported that the slave Venus, whose usual task was spinning, was assigned to the Jones house to do the cooking.[62] William Nuttall, being the personal servant of the Joneses, would probably have accompanied them from Savannah but would not appear in the overseer's journal. When in residence, the Joneses liked to entertain lavishly, and the wine cellar at El Destino was kept well stocked with French wines. A sportsman, George Noble Jones kept "fine fowling pieces and pedigreed dogs" on the plantation for the hunting season.[63] But whether the master was in residence or absent, the work on the plantation had to be done, the fields cleared in January and prepared for plowing, the wood cut, the rails split, the hogs minded, the plows repaired, the manure spread, the seed planted. The main difference between the Jones and the Arnold plantations was that the former was mainly a cotton plantation and the latter was a rice plantation. In either case, the actual work was done by the slaves.

The essential difference between Jones and Arnold was in their attitude toward the land. Both had roots in the land, but Jones saw the city—whether it was Savannah, Paris, or Newport—as the center of leisure and social life. Arnold, on the other hand, saw Providence as enterprise, the business center of his life in the North. His father, Welcome Arnold, had been born on a farm but had moved to the city to become a shipping merchant. Even the family farm in Smithfield was essentially a "business" rather than a traditional producer; it was a family enterprise of two farms that manufactured quicklime, which was transported in wagons to Providence to be shipped by boat to other ports in New England and as far as New York and Philadelphia. Welcome Arnold was a paradigm of the Yankee entrepreneur who left the farm to become a commission merchant, gradually acquiring his own fleet of ships.[64] His son Richard inherited shares in the family shipping company (his uncles and brother were still actively engaged in shipping when he acquired White Hall plantation). He also possessed his family's attitude toward the land as a source of enterprise in the linked chain of agricultural industry from product to shipping. Whereas Jones was content to live a life of leisure on the profits from his plantations and the rents from the Savannah River wharfage, Arnold was continually involved in his enterprises in the North, which included wharves on the Providence River, and in expanding and diversifying his plantation lands in the South. In the end, the difference explained in part why Jones fled to Savannah (and his family to Europe) when war broke out and why Arnold returned to Providence. Profit more than patriotism guided their flight.

By mid-March 1847 the fields of El Destino were ready to be planted in cotton. By late February, the first rice field at White Hall was ready—rice culture required staggered plantings so that the various jobs could be spaced at regular intervals. The weather was just right on February 26—rainy, too rainy for the Patersons and the Borlands to come for dinner but perfect for the field hands to trench and plant three and one-half acres of the old White Hall square. They planted the rest of the twenty acres the next day, and the "plough boys" followed behind to cover the seeds. Thus the first of the new rice crop, over sixty bushels of seed rice carefully saved from last year's harvest, was planted early enough to catch the March high tides for the sprout flow; to plant so early was risky, however, because the weather could turn cold and damage the crop after the seed had sprouted.

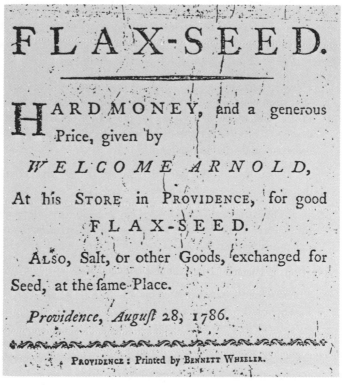

Advertising flyer for Welcome Arnold and Company, Providence,
August, 28, 1786. (Courtesy of the Arnold-Rogers Collection.)

In the spring of 1842 Arnold wrote out detailed directions for planting
rice, probably for his overseer, because in the early 1840s he had many different overseers working for him: "1—Sprout flow to remain from 2 to 5 days
according to the weather."[65] The purpose of the sprout flow—that is, flood-
ing the rice field for the first time—is to cause the rice seed to swell and
sprout; once the sprouts appear, in two to five days, the field is drained and
allowed to dry naturally for hoeing. The water from the tide-flow method is
not used to feed the plants but to *speed* up the growing season and to increase
production.

> 2[d]   Hoe for the first time about *one month* after planting—the land must be
> then *dug deep*. & the old Rice Roots well soiled over & weeds taken out with
> hands. . . . Do not flow the Point—flow unless fields are full of grass.—In
> these events—flow deep for three or four days & shallow afterwards until you
> see the grass killed—the Point flow is put on if at all before working.—If
> possible *avoid point flow*.

The point flow was used not only to kill the grass and weeds but also the wild or "volunteer" rice. The stretch flow (also called the "long flow") served the double purpose of hiving off any remaining grass and weeds and, when drawn down, of inducing growth in the rice plants.

> 3ᵈ   When the Rice is in *the 3ᵈ or 4ᵗʰ leaf* [of growth] at which time it ought to have been hoed a Second time & the large grass picked out, put on the water for the stretch flow. Keep it *three or four days over* the Rice deep then—draw it down to 5 or 6 Inches & so Keep it *from 15 to 20 days.*—If the point flow has been put on do not flow as long.

> 4ᵗʰ   About 8 days after the water is let off—Hoe the 3ᵈ time but hoe sooner if the land is dry *& pick grass carefully.*

> 5ᵗʰ   The Land must now be Kept dry & hoed fourth time if required   the Rice cleared of all grass the 3ᵈ hoeing   but if any is left be sure to take it out this time & pulverize the ground well with the hoe.—

Only then is the rice ready for the harvest flow:

> 6. When the Rice forms 2ⁿᵈ Joint—Some time about—latter end of June or 1st July put on the water & Keep it on until the Rice is in full Bulb—then draw it out & hand pick the field of the long grass—*Six* days after put in water & keep it in until—nearly for Harvest changing—*freshening the water every third or fourth day* always flowing deeper after the Rice has put forth its ears—of course—the flowing must depend on the Spring tides. . . .

> 7. Do not let your Rice be too ripe before you cut it.[66]

Nearly twenty years of experience in growing rice at Cherry Hill went into these directions. But all this experience would mean nothing if the migratory birds were not kept out of the rice fields, for they could strip the field in no time at all. Therefore, from March 3, 1847, some of the slaves, usually children or those slaves too old for other kinds of work, were sent out into the planted rice fields to drive the birds away. They were called "bird minders," and although their task may have been romantically named, there was nothing romantic about standing in the wet rice fields in all kinds of weather driving birds away from the sprouting seeds.

The first week of March was a busy one on the plantation. The Cherry Hill cornfield was bedded in preparation for planting, forty acres in all, ten of which were planted on Wednesday. Since Arnold was able on Sunday to sell to his factor five hundred bushels of corn at a dollar a bushel free of freight, all the corn he could spare, it was obvious that diversity paid off. Cotton and rice, however, were still the main cash crops, and the principal work on the plantation involved the preparation and planting of the fields for these two crops. For example, on Monday, March 1, the same day that thirteen hands were busy bedding the cornfield, Morris and several other hands were mending a break in the dam in number 18 square. A square was a self-contained, irrigated rice field of about twenty acres, and so the break in the dam did not affect any of the other fields. At the same time plowing was begun at White Hall preparatory to planting cotton. The work on the rice and cotton fields continued all week as did the planting of the corn, most of the field hands being thus occupied.

Even so, some hands were spared to unload the 12,000 bricks that arrived in the *Cotton Plant* on Wednesday, and the carpenters continued to work on the sugar mill along with two masons Arnold had hired to build the foundation. Charles and Bandy fertilized the potato field on Wednesday, having finished their harrowing, and Sambo and Jacob were put to work harrowing number 4 square that same day. Adam and George were kept busy carrying the fence rails to the Miller field and the pasture. All in all, it had been a good week for work despite the heavy rain on Thursday that kept the carpenters and masons from doing much work on the sugar mill. It had been a profitable week, for not only had Arnold been able to contract on Saturday for the corn, but on Friday the factors also took his total rice crop at a dollar per bushel, deliverable in Savannah. The only sour note during the week had been the fishing. There had been no catch from the previous Friday until Monday night, when twenty-six shad were caught, and on Friday only sixteen were caught. On that day he discharged Dean who had been working on the fish nets for the past fifty days. Since Dean was not one of Arnold's slaves, he had to pay his owner for labor as well as material.

While the field hands labored on the land, the house servants were also kept busy attending to the steady stream of visitors at White Hall—besides carrying out their usual assignments of cooking, cleaning, washing, polishing, sweeping, making up beds, and picking up after white folk, emptying their chamber pots, running errands for the family, and generally attending to their wants, whether it was starting the fire early in the morning to take the chill off the room or being on call late at night to attend to some request. These chores are not listed in the plantation journal, since that was intended only to be a record of field tasks, but Arnold also recorded in his journal the names of guests and the length of their stay. Thus on March 1, while the field hands were bedding the land for the planting of corn and cotton, Mr. Rogers, Mr. Buckley, and Miss Habersham all left White Hall, Miss Habersham having stayed for sixteen days, Mr. Rogers ten days, and Mr. Buckley the whole winter, the latter returning to White Hall on Wednesday. In addition, the Arnolds' daughter Harriet and their son-in-law, William Brenton Greene, were visiting, but Brenton had to return the next day to New York to his business career, managing a dry-goods store. The Greenes had been married on June 18, 1846, at the Arnold home in Providence. Greene had been born in Providence, a member of the same family that included Major General Nathanael Greene, a great-uncle, and Richard Arnold, a cousin. Harriet did not accompany her husband north, preferring to remain at White Hall, where she had been born on April 21, 1825. Undoubtedly, Mum Phebe had been in attendance at her birth, since she was the children's mammy until her death in 1841.

Despite the menial chores, the repetitive routines, the being on call twenty-four hours a day, and above all the necessary subservience to the moods of the master and mistress and the whims of the children and the guests, the household slaves, or house servants as the planters preferred to call them, were a more privileged class within the slave labor system than the field hands. Generally, they were better housed, clothed, and fed. On a large plantation like Arnold's with many household slaves, they had less work to do than house servants in middle-class homes in the North because they had only one kind of work assigned to them, there being a hierarchy of labor among the slaves. At the top was the legendary mammy, the symbol of all that was sentimental in the "moonlight-and-magnolias" legend of the Old South and, as Eugene D. Genovese observed in *Roll, Jordan, Roll*, the key to "understanding the tragedy of plantation paternalism, for the contradictions of that paternalism were represented in their most heightened form in 'Life in the Big House.' "[67]

Mum Phebe (alternatively spelled Phoebe) was the Arnold mammy, and in that role she accompanied the Arnolds to Rhode Island, leaving behind her two sons, Tom, born in 1812, and Amos, born in 1819.[68] Admittedly, by the time the Arnolds' first child, Eliza Harriet, was born in 1825, Tom was already listed as a house servant, being thirteen years old, but Amos would not yet have been assigned regular duties, being only six, young enough to miss his mother. The contradiction is inherent in the situation of a black mother's having to leave her own children to attend to the needs of a white mother and her children six months out of the year as the white family traveled north. The contradiction is inherent in the paternalism of presenting Tom and Amos three dollars each as a gift, duly marked in the account book under "Family Expenses," on May 25, 1837, shortly before the Arnolds and Eliza Harriet Allen left for Providence accompanied by Mum Phebe. Tom was already a young man of twenty-five with a family of his own and Amos a youth of eighteen, old enough to be hired out for his labor. By then they were used to their mother's going north every summer. Amos, for example, had earned as much for Arnold in one week as the three-dollar cash gift when Arnold hired him out to John Robinson of Savannah as a blacksmith and received from Robinson on December 19, 1837, the sum of $110 "for my Boy Amos Services as a Blacksmith from 9 May last to date."[69]

Eliza Harriet Allen does not mention in her diary the presence of Mum Phebe on board ship as they traveled together from Savannah to Providence, even though little Tommy Arnold, less than a year old, was very ill as they boarded the ship and his mother was seasick on the first leg of the journey to Charleston. Mum Phebe must have been constantly in and out of the Arnolds' suite, attending to both Tommy and his mother, but servants are invisible whatever their color. The only notice taken of Mum Phebe on the journey was the payment of one dollar for "clearance of Phebe" recorded in the account books.[70] Eliza Harriet Allen was sentimental about religion but not servants. Upon hearing of the death of Mum Phebe in 1841, she wrote to her brother, "Mum Phebe I think was a very good woman, & I doubt not the exchange is a happy one," presumably meaning the exchange of a worldly existence for the eternal rewards of heaven and not the bonds of slavery for the "freedom" of death. She was matter of fact about Mum Phebe's value as a servant: "She was not as efficient here [in Providence], but at the South she took much care from Louisea [sic]." Nonetheless, she paid tribute to the mythology of the mammy by adding "and a tie of so long standing cannot be broken without much pain."[71]

Whatever the rewards of green pastures, however, the pain of separation from her own family to serve the needs of a white family in a strange land where she knew no one and was kin to no one must have been great for Mum Phebe at the beginning. By 1837, having made the journey into exile more than a dozen times, she was probably used to it. Still, it was worrying to a slave mother that a new overseer had been hired. Tom, like most house servants, did not like the manual labor required of him—cutting enough grass each day for the horses and mules, polishing the carriage and harness, keeping the front yard hoed clean, and working in the garden. His mother might have worried even more had she known of Arnold's instructions to Swanston, the overseer, to supervise Tom's work, for "Tom is very apt to absent himself from his work & join Waters boy & Mr Savage's William in a hunt &c. this I wish put a stop to."[72] Was it, therefore, a happy exchange for a mother's anxiety on being absent from her family for nearly five months, that on October 14, 1837, the day they all left Providence to return to White Hall, Richard Arnold gave two dollars to Mum Phebe?[73]

3

As soon as they had completed their tasks satisfactorily, the field hands were free to return to their cabins to work on household chores or in their own gardens. The house servants, on the other hand, were under constant supervision by the master and his family. House servants may have been the elite of the slave community and dreaded banishment from the house to work in the fields. But field hands did not envy their close supervision or being on call day and night. On the Arnold estate the Cherry Hill slaves, separated in physical distance from the manse, existed as a separate community, freer to be themselves. They were all field hands except for the overseer's cook and two children, a boy and a girl, who ran errands for him, as specified in the contract. True, the overseer lived at Cherry Hill, but by tradition the drivers, not the overseer, policed the community unless there was a general outbreak of trouble or illness.

The field hands and their families looked forward to Saturday night, since Sunday was a day of rest on the plantation. The house servants carried on with their normal duties, especially if there were visitors at the manse. Liquor was forbidden on the Arnold plantations, and by the 1840s Arnold, by then a man of temperance, was alarmed at the problem created by the "grog shops" that had appeared on the fringes of the area plantations to sell liquor to the slaves. He specifically exhorted Ferguson in the overseer's contract "to do all in his power to prevent the negros from trading at the shop, & as far as in his power to prevent them introducing ardent spirits in either place & not set them the example of having it himself & to do all in his power to keep the people at home."[74] The plantation had not always been dry, for in the 1820s Arnold, like his neighbor Thomas Clay, stocked whisky as part of his provisions.

Planters, for obvious reasons of discipline, preferred that their slaves remain at home, and therefore visiting off the plantations, although not forbidden, was discouraged and required the master's permission. Favorite slaves were extended visiting privileges as a reward. For example, in 1837 Tom Morel had permission to visit his family at Belfast, a neighboring plantation, and Arnold specifically instructed the overseer Swanston to allow him that privilege during his absence in the North.[75] Eliza Harriet Allen, visiting the slave quarters at White Hall on a Sunday, noted that Kate was entertaining two Negroes from Colonel McAllister's plantation as well as several from White Hall, but then Kate was one of the original twenty-three slaves inherited by Louisa's mother from the estate of Captain James McKay. Mum Phebe herself was absent from White Hall a few Sundays later, visiting at Cherry Hill, and as a result Louisa could not go to church, little Tommy being unwell. Travel by slaves outside the immediate area was strictly controlled, and only very trusted slaves like Amos Morel would be permitted to travel to the city by himself. A pass was required and had to be shown by the slave if challenged by a white man.

To encourage slaves to remain at home and establish a sense of communal identity with the plantation as a whole, the Arnolds upon occasion provided them with a feast on a Saturday night, especially after the planting had been completed (the Arnolds were usually in the North at harvest time). Eliza Harriet Allen described one such feast in detail:

> This evening the negroes all came from Cherry Hill to get supper which had been provided for them. This is occasionally done   a half barrel of beef is boiled   two bushels of rice   bushel of dried peas & of the liquor of beef a soup made. It is all cooked out of doors in the day, & they come in the evening. It is then divided equally amongst the Cherry Hill & Whitehall people according to the number in the family. Those who do not come themselves send representations. and they look more like a gang of gypseys than any thing else. The pots with fire under them in the yard and the negroes with torches form a most singular group. They seem perfectly happy laugh[ing] & shouting—each takes his portion in a large kettle or pail and goes home   those of Cherry Hill stay if they please with the Whitehall people, but most of them prefer to go home four miles—they think nothing of walking that distance when they have no business.[76]

The elaborate ritual devised to ensure a fair and equal share of food is an attention to detail that was symptomatic of the schizophrenic paternalism of slave owners like Arnold who maintained the forms of civilized democratic society while in reality enslaving large numbers of people and living off the fruits of their labor. Even the feast itself was cooked by the White Hall household slaves. But observers like Mrs. Allen with a predisposition to accept slavery as foreordained by God saw it as evidence that the slaves were happy and contented. She could not, therefore, understand why the Cherry Hill slaves would want to walk home four miles that same night: the illusion of freedom is in the feet.

Glowworms as well as feasting slaves entertained the white folk that night when Richard Arnold captured two worms:

> We made the room entirely dark & put them on a book and could read the
> words distinctly round them—I have often read of the "glow worms light" but
> never saw it 'till now—We wish much to preserve them to take to the north
> but fear we cannot. . . . We were watching the negroes until late—& I retired
> to my room but not to bed until 2 minutes past twelve—It began to rain before
> that time . . . & some of the negroes who insisted upon going back must have
> been very wet—[77]

Glowworms do not survive in captivity and none was taken north. As-
sumedly the Cherry Hill slaves survived the soaking rain that night; and God
in his mysterious ways saw to it that a fair and equal share of rain fell upon
the whites after church services the next morning: "Just as we reached home
a most violent shower commenced which must have completely drenched
some of the people who had far to go."[78]

The Bryan Neck Presbyterian Church was the religious center for the
county in the 1830s, and for the Arnolds it was conveniently located on
plantation land only a mile from the manse. Like the house, the church was
in the middle of an idyllic setting. A humble place of worship, it was "a
rough building whitewashed on the inside as well as out," but large enough to
accommodate the planters and their families, about forty white people, some
of whom came from some distance, since it was the only Presbyterian church
in the area.[79] Although the White Hall slaves were generally Baptists, the
Arnolds encouraged their house servants to attend the Presbyterian church
services with them on Sunday mornings, the slaves sitting separately in a
body in the gallery with the servants of other planter families from surrounding plantations. In the afternoon the rest of the Arnold slaves could hear the
sermon preached by the same white minister.

Arnold revealed a typical but profound white planter's ignorance of the
Afro-Baptist faith when he told Olmsted that he had tried unsuccessfully to
prevent his slaves from shouting and jumping at their meetings because he
believed "there was not the slightest element of religious sentiment to it. He
considered it to be engaged in more as an exciting amusement than from any
really religious impulse." On the contrary, shouting and jumping were for
the Afro-Baptist a way of expressing religious ecstasy that had its roots in
African culture, a manifestation of a real religious impulse and not mere
amusement.[80]

Although Richard Arnold was a member of the Bryan Neck Presbyterian
Church while in residence at White Hall, he was also a member in good
standing of the First Baptist Church in Providence, founded by Roger
Williams in 1636, the oldest Baptist church in America. On June 8, 1846, he

was elected moderator of the Charitable Baptist Society, the lay organization which oversaw the legal and financial affairs of the church. Despite the fact that he was absent half the year in Georgia, he remained moderator until June 12, 1854, when he was succeeded by his son-in-law Samuel Greene Arnold.[81]

Arnold himself was never baptized; nonetheless, he was not unfamiliar with individual manifestations of religious ectasy as members declared themselves repentant and reborn, including his own daughter Louisa on October 4, 1857.[82] Still, the barrier between him and the Baptist faith of his slaves was a profound one stemming from New England reticence as well as the difference in race. The deeply conservative tradition of the First Baptist Church in Providence is evident in the fact that like the Quakers the congregation originally condemned music and singing at its services, and it was not until the 1830s, nearly two hundred years after its founding, that an organ was installed in the church.[83] Blacks were received into the congregation, but they were expected to sit in a segregated section. The free blacks of Providence formed their own church in 1820, the African Union Meeting House, built on land purchased and donated by Moses Brown.[84]

Arnold perhaps disapproved of his slaves' emotionalism in religious worship for another unexpressed reason. The spirituals they sang were as much about earthly freedom as they were about spiritual deliverance in the double meanings of the biblical symbols and heroes they celebrated.[85] Although slave owners like Arnold encouraged their slaves to embrace Christianity and paid white preachers to instruct them, it was with the expectation that they could control the blacks' religious experience. The social order of the plantation would be reinforced by inculcating in the slaves the concept that the master-servant relationship was a reflection of the cosmic order of the universe. Obedience to the master by the servant stood in the same relationship, albeit on a temporal level, as obedience to God, for all men are God's servants. The fact that Nat Turner was a preacher further determined the slave owners to control the slaves' religious instruction.

Religion, therefore, was central to the southern planter's rationalization of slavery as a social institution, whatever the economic reasons. By the 1830s southern churches and their clergymen were either enthusiastic defenders of, or apologists for, slavery. White Presbyterian ministers like the Reverend Seagrove William Magill (1810–1884) in the 1830s and the Reverend John Winn (1814–1892) in the 1840s served the Bryan Neck Presbyterian Church congregation of planter families and, as part of their duties, instructed the Arnold slaves in Christian doctrines and preached to them on Sunday afternoons.[86]

Both Magill and Winn were native Georgians who were educated in New England. Both attended Amherst College, but Magill transferred to Yale, graduating in 1831, and continued his theological studies at Yale and Princeton, whereas Winn returned south after graduating from Amherst in 1834 to attend the Columbia (South Carolina) Theological Seminary, where he graduated in 1837. Winn's first parish assignment was in Saint Mary's, Georgia, on the Florida border, Magill's birthplace. Magill's assignment to the Bryan Neck Presbyterian Church from 1835 to 1840 was his first major appointment. In their youthful histories there was nothing to distinguish them from the hundreds of other young southern men of their social class and generation who were educated in the North and returned to the South to fulfill their careers, some as planters, some as pastors. Each, however, was drawn by some sense of missionary zeal to devote his efforts to the "moral elevation" of the slaves (Winn's brother William was a slave-owning planter in Liberty County). Each was ambivalent toward the institution of slavery and the white planters they served. As far as can be determined, neither blamed the masters (Magill remained on friendly terms with Arnold, and Winn named one of his sons after Thomas Clay), but Magill, especially, blamed the institution, finding himself constantly circumscribed by state laws and public sentiment in his efforts to teach the Negroes. It explains, in part, why he left Bryan Neck Church to accept a call in Tallmadge, Ohio, and later in Waterbury, Connecticut, and why he became involved in the work of the American Missionary Association, returning to Georgia in 1865 after the fall of Savannah to organize schools and churches among the freedmen.

Similarly, although not as suddenly, John Winn left the South in 1858 to accept a call in Henry, Illinois. He had served the Bryan Neck church from 1843 to 1851 and subsequently preached to the slaves of Liberty County. Unlike Magill he never returned to the South after the war, retiring instead to Madison, Wisconsin. It was, however, Charles Colcock Jones (1803–1863), known as the "Apostle of the Blacks" for promoting Christianity among the slaves, who was the most complex and well known of this generation of white southern Presbyterian ministers seeking to "elevate" the morality of the slaves and save their souls.[87]

Also a native Georgian, Jones, like Magill and Winn, was educated in the North (Andover Academy and Princeton), but what made his situation different, although by no means unique, among white southern clergymen was that he had been born on his father's plantation in Liberty County and inherited his father's slaves at an early age. He faced a moral dilemma as a southern slave owner studying at a northern theological seminary where, although the

antislavery ideas of his classmates and teachers were quite mildly evolution-
ary for gradual emancipation rather than radically revolutionary for immediate emancipation, slavery itself was considered a great evil. The crisis of
conscience that developed was undoubtedly sincere, but nonetheless, he rejected the solution that his friend J. Leighton Wilson had decided upon, a
solution that at once resolved the crisis and rid Wilson of his burden of
guilt—that is, freeing his slaves, paying for their passage to Liberia, and
helping them settle there.[88] For reasons as much economic and social as well
as religious and moral, Jones decided to keep his slaves and the plantation but
to devote his life to being a white missionary among black slaves, Christianizing them through religious instruction.

Jones's ideal was to create a biracial community of mutual trust, self-disci-
pline, and Christian piety based on the reform of individuals, white and
black, rather than the transformation of society as a whole. The flaw in this
plan was the limitation of his own cultural and social perceptions of the black
man as a passive mold to be shaped into what the white man saw as good for
him; therefore, the idea of a biracial Christian community, aside from the
inequalities of the master-slave relationship, was doomed to failure.[89] The
best that can be said for Jones's efforts was that he encouraged such slave
masters as his uncle William Maxwell, his long time friend Thomas Clay, and
others to improve the living conditions of their slaves. Jones's credentials were
unquestioned, since he was a native Georgian and a slave owner, but what
convinced the planters was that it was in their own enlightened self-interest
to improve the moral and social conditions of their slaves:

> The heart of Jones' argument for self-interest was based upon the axiom that
> "virtue is more profitable than vice." If a planter sought to exercise his "duties"
> toward his slaves with integrity, if he were virtuous and honorable, his planta-
> tion profits "would increase and the quality of life between owner and owned
> would be improved." Cotton would be picked and rice harvested with less loss
> of time, less trouble, and few disciplinary problems. The master would be
> "measurably relieved from perpetual watching, from fault-finding and threat-
> ening and heart-sickening severity"; and he could "begin at least to govern
> somewhat by the law of love." All this would combine to make the plantation
> more profitable.[90]

Thomas Clay was inspired to adopt Jones's methods of inculcating religious principles for the "moral improvement" of his slaves, methods which
Clay, at the request of the Georgia Presbytery, published in *Detail of a Plan for
the Moral Improvement of Negroes on Plantations* (1833). Written from a layman's
and a planter's point of view, the plan is based on the belief that religious

instruction was an effective and pragmatic means of controlling and disciplining the slaves, doing "more for the good order and quiet of the country, than any civil or military patrol we have ever had." For the slaves were taught not only that slavery was sanctioned by God, "the Maker of them all," rich and poor, but also that obedience to the master as God's temporal representative on earth was required of them.[91]

On her first Sunday at her brother Richard's plantation, April 9, 1837, Mrs. Allen heard the Reverend S. W. Magill preach "a fine sermon from the text 'Christ suffered for us leaving us an example that we should follow in his steps.'" Lest the slaves misunderstand the text and literally leave the plantation to follow Christ, Mr. Magill devoted the afternoon to preaching to the White Hall Negroes. The Reverend Mr. Magill may well have used the popular text published by Charles Colcock Jones, his fellow minister, *Catechism . . . for the Oral Instruction of Colored Persons* (1834)—oral, because it was illegal in Georgia as elsewhere in the slave states to teach slaves to read and write. If so, then he might have read them the passage: "It is contrary also to the will of God for servants either to run away, or to harbour a runaway. The servant who always abides at home at faithful service, fares better a thousandfold than he that runs away."[92] To follow in the footsteps of Christ is to stay where you are.

The religious instruction of the slaves in the area was considered part of the regular duties of white ministers of the Bryan Neck Presbyterian Church although it was supplemented by the planter's family, usually his wife. It was, however, quite a different minister whom Thomas Clay and Richard Arnold met on April 10, 1837, as they were coming back from Cherry Hill. The Reverend Edward B. Hall of Providence stayed the night at White Hall and spent the evening conversing with the Arnolds and their guests until two o'clock in the morning. A Congregationalist, Mr. Hall had been "nurtured with Abolition," and so "it was thought best [he] should see all that could be seen."[93] All, presumably, that would reflect favorably on the paternalistic system of providing moral instruction to Negroes on plantations.

Therefore, to show the Reverend Mr. Hall "all that could be seen" at White Hall on Tuesday, April 11, 1837, was to show him the Sunday school class and put its members through their lessons. They were assembled early that morning to exhibit to Mr. Hall. Since Mr. Hall was to spend that night at the Clays, he undoubtedly was shown "all that could be seen" there to improve the moral condition of the slaves. But Mr. Hall had to be in Savannah the next day, and thus he would have missed the school at the Elliott plantation on the opposite bank of the Ogeechee, where Miss Hetty also taught the slaves to sing. She "requested" them to perform for Eliza Harriet Allen: "I never heard music which affected me more than this; some had delightful voices and as she and her sister sing well themselves, they had taken pains in teaching the negroes hymns in addition to those they learned themselves—There was one bass voice which exceeded any I had ever heard except one of the Hermanns, who exhibited some years since; but now dead, a celebrated German singer."[94]

Mrs. Allen saw no irony in the situation. Indeed, the following Sunday, April 16, Bible in hand, she took her sister-in-law's place and walked to the slave quarters at White Hall and read to the slaves from the Bible. She called first at the house of Mum Kate, an old woman who, Mrs. Allen felt, knew more "than I could impart—she is humble contented and cheerful and constantly relies upon her heavenly father for every blessing & feels that she has many." Mum Kate had learned well the text of the Reverend Mr. Magill's sermon that morning: "It is my mind to do the will of him that sent me." Mrs. Allen called at every house, including that of Nan, "who when Anna [Eliza Harriet's daughter] was here was a favorite house servant but having behaved very much amiss was put into the fields and does not now come to the house at all." Mrs. Allen returned to the manse, fatigued but very gratified by these visits. She was inspired to write in her journal that evening an apologia for the plantation slave system:

> The wife of a planter as well as the planter himself is placed in a very responsible situation. So many souls committed to their care. Many think it a very easy situation, but it is from ignorance that they form such an opinion. No one who has not seen, can imagine the constant calls upon their time and patience. No day passes that the attention is not called to some one sick & to many wants which are always freely made known, and always if possible supplied on this plantation at least. I am daily more convinced that every station has its own peculiar cares, and while we think that other than our own wants be easier, and better for us to bear, we ought to be assured that the very station in which each of us is placed by providence is the one for us to fill.[95]

Eliza Harriet had learned her lesson well from the Reverend Mr. Magill, and thus it was without fear or guilt that the next day while walking in the woods she saw "a snake about five feet long, which was the first I have seen while walking."[96]

As a trustee of the Bryan Neck Presbyterian Church, Richard Arnold subscribed and paid his share of the Reverend Mr. Magill's salary, seventy-five dollars in 1837 and eighty dollars in 1838. Mr. Magill's preaching to the White Hall slaves in rotation with meetings at other plantations on successive

Sundays was considered part of his regular ministerial duties. Officiating at weddings at the plantation, however, would be considered beyond his regular duties, and therefore, on March 26, 1838, Arnold recorded as a plantation expense the five dollars he presented to "Rev[d] S W Magill for marrying my man Cato & Girl Lucy 24 Inst."[97]

Although slave marriages had no legal status in Georgia and the other slave states, they were encouraged on southern plantations. More than any other attitude toward human relationships, the problem of marriage revealed the schizophrenic dilemma of paternalistic masters toward their slaves. On the one hand, Christian planters like Thomas Clay and Richard Arnold, believing in the sanctity of marriage and the family, encouraged slave marriages, and indeed provided white ministers to consecrate the ceremony. The master, as paterfamilias, should inquire "into the character of the parties, before giving his consent to their union," Clay suggested in his plan to improve the moral condition of slaves, and the master should "be present at the marriage ceremony, and bestow on the party and their friends, some testimonials of his approbation, and interest in their happiness."[98] On the other hand, the owner's vested interest in his slaves as chattel property was in direct conflict with recognition of the slaves' vested interest in marriage or family. As much as they were willing to follow the Reverend Charles Colcock Jones in his evangelical path of improving the moral condition of slaves through religious instruction, neither Clay nor Arnold would be willing to accept Jones's logic that "because slave marriages were not protected by law the whole fabric of southern society was threatened, for marriage was a divine institution, ordained of God, and first in order of time and importance in human relationships. If the institution of marriage was threatened, the whole society was threatened." In the end, Jones himself could not accept the logic of his argument, and he compromised his principles when he decided in 1857 to sell his runaway slave Jane and her family: the economic investment in property blinded him to "the terror of slavery and his involvement in its inhumanity even when he was tempted to be kind and to give his 'servants that which is just and equal.'" Jane and her family were separated from their friends and other members of their family and from the "home" they had known for years. And the new owner, despite his promise to Jones, broke up the family.[99]

Lesser mortals were saved from the anxieties of such religious crises; Clay and Arnold pragmatically accepted those aspects of Jones's precepts that contributed to the stability of the slave community, encouraging marriages and the raising of families but not worrying too much about the moral and psychological contradictions inherent in the system. Arnold's contempt for "such a woman as Lissy" is evident when he tried to bargain with Colonel Morris over her price, and even if the contempt was merely a ploy to bring down the price, it demeaned the bargainer. Arnold, however, was not troubled. If anything, he would have considered himself righteous, deserving of the Reverend Mr. Jones's praise, in his determination "to unite" Lissy and Cain "as man & wife" regardless of any children or family she left behind. He chose to interpret Colonel Morris's description of Lissy as one of his "most fruitful" women to mean most productive in labor ("strictly prime as you state").

The more mundane practice of hiring out slaves as domestic servants or laborers rather than the dramatic episodes of buying and selling slaves most often underscored the reality of their treatment as chattel even by paternalistic masters like Arnold. On April 19, 1847, Arnold hired Jinny to Willis Ball for six months. It was a common business arrangement, particularly by planters like Arnold, who closed the manse for the summer months and went north, taking only one or two trusted "servants" with them. Perhaps because it was a temporary arrangement, and only to Savannah, where Ball resided, Arnold would not think about the arrangement beyond the financial terms of the contract—eight dollars per month, that is, forty-eight dollars profit for himself, Jinny receiving room and board from Ball and her summer clothing from Arnold. Jinny, fifty-eight years old, had no choice but to go where her master sent her. In 1838 she had been sent for a longer period much farther away, to work in Tallahassee, Florida, where on October 21, 1838, she wrote to Arnold. One has to read between the lines of any letter written by a slave to his or her master, but Jinny's concern for her daughter Nan is direct: "I am very glad Nan I hear you behave well & hope you will serve the Lord. Elsey and Philis must take very great care of Nan. Beg Mistress [Louisa Arnold] member her promise to [take] good care of Nan, according to Nan behave. I know Mistress will mind her."[100]

Whatever it was that Nan had done, it was bad enough for her to be banished from the house to the fields as punishment and to be forbidden to come to the manse where once she was a favorite servant: "She seemed very penitent, but I believe she is much doubted," Eliza Harriet Allen reported on April 16, 1837, and obviously a year and a half later she was still doubted.[101] But between the lines of a mother's anxiety for her daughter is the fear of what may happen to Nan, separated so many miles and for so long a time from her mother. "I will thank master if he will answer my letter."[102] The letter was not answered until January 24, 1839, and then by Dr. Godolphin, the physician Arnold hired to care for the plantation Negroes. It is not known who in Jinny's family was ill or had died, but by March 1847 Nan was still alive and still in disgrace, working as a field hand.

On February 24, immediately on his return from the Morris plantation to fetch Lissy, Cain was back at his task of sawing timber. Lissy, four months pregnant, was listed as a full field hand. Since Lissy and Cain had literally or symbolically "jumped over the broomstick" and into bed "without benefit of clergy," and since Cain had gone against his master's wishes and "married" off the plantation, Arnold did not hold a wedding for them. The plantation, however, had its marriage festivities that spring when Shadwell, age twenty, married Hayer, age sixteen, on Saturday, April 17, shortly before the Arnolds were to leave for the North. Officiating at the wedding was Dr. David Lynn Carroll, former president of Hampden-Sydney College and currently active in the Colonization Society, who was visiting the Arnolds at White Hall. The wedding was held at White Hall even though Shadwell, a favored slave, was a field hand on the Cherry Hill plantation.

A similar wedding six years later was described in detail by Julia Comstock Tolman, wife of William E. Tolman who had been hired to tutor the Arnold boys. Peter, a carpenter, age thirty-two, married Rinah, a field hand, age twenty-three:

> Last week two of Mr. Arnold's negroes from Cherry Hill were married at Whitehall—*Peter* and *Rinah*. We all saw them married, and then they all came upon the east piazza and danced a while for my edification, as I would not go to the house where they were going to dance. They danced to a fiddle and tambourine. Mr. Arnold is going to get a set of new instruments before the next wedding. They had a grand supper after the dance of rice, hominy, potatoes, turkeys, meats, and plain cake, with two good sized loaves of Bride's cake frosted and sprinkled with the gayest sugar plums Mrs. A. could find. Mrs. A. always provides cakes and a supper and a new dress for the Bride and a new suit for the groom, and they looked quite stylish, I can assure you. Their dancing was amusing. Some danced as gracefully as any white person I ever saw and some took all sorts of steps, but they *all* kept the most *perfect time;* they got so excited sometimes, it seemed as though they wouldn't be able to stop. Their singing too is worth hearing; many have melodious voices. The choir at the church where Mr. A's family attend is composed of the negroes. We concluded at the night of the wedding that their performances were equal to the *Chrysties.*[103]

From the point of view of Louisa Arnold, the preparations for the wedding of Carpenter Peter and Rinah were all part of her duties as the mistress of a slave plantation. She and her husband had planned to go into Savannah the morning of February 1, accompanying Olmsted, but the trip was postponed because Richard Arnold had to attend a business meeting at the Bryan Neck church the next morning. "I want to get a few things for the wedding," she wrote her daughter, but there would not be time to do all the errands in Savannah and still return for the church meeting. "I hope it will turn out well," she added, for "Peter has been anxious to marry her [Rinah] for three years past."[104]

The wedding feast itself turned out well, as Julia Tolman reported, and Louisa Arnold, writing to her daughter a few weeks later was enthusiastic:

> [It was] the gayest wedding we have had for a long time. They were married in the wash room—and then danced in the Piazza by a violin until eleven o'clock while they danced Tom [Morel] had the supper table set. The cake looked very pretty and they had a most abundant supper   Turkey ham and tho there were over one hundred to eat they left a quantity which they took the next morning   Amos and Sylvia danced together and looked quite stylish   S [Sylvia] in Harriet's [her daughter, Mrs. William Brenton Greene] Bustle and white Petticoat and A [Amos] in Brent's [her son-in-law, William Brenton Greene] Red plaid Pants and a handsome new coat father brought him   Mr and Mrs Tollman approved   Surprised and delighted it was truly amusing   I wish Sam [her son-in-law, Samuel Greene Arnold] could have seen and heard them calling each other Mr & Mrs   Peter is Mr Blake.[105]

Undoubtedly, the Arnolds hoped also that marrying Rinah would be a stabilizing influence on Peter, who had been in trouble in the past, but five years later he was in trouble again, having been caught by Amos stealing and selling plantation supplies.

Still, whether it was the wedding of Peter and Rinah in 1853 or the wedding of Shadwell and Hayer in the spring of 1847 or any other slave marriage on the plantation, there was no honeymoon for the bride and bridegroom. The newly married couple were back at work early Monday morning, although Shadwell was at least spared the burden of carting out the manure on Monday, April 19, 1847, Charles and Cyrus being given that task. Since it was planting season, work consisted as usual of bedding, trenching, plowing, and planting the rice, cotton, and corn fields. The building of the sugarhouse continued. Even though the Arnolds were leaving for the North in a few days, the plantation work went on at its own pace.

The next day, Tuesday, April 20, was a busy one for Richard Arnold, for it was his last full day at the plantation before his departure for Providence. He supervised the lowering of the water in the first planted rice fields. He saw to it that additional acres of rice, cotton, and corn were planted and that sixteen acres were plowed for corn. He checked to be sure all was going well at the sugarhouse. One of the last things he did was to send his house servant Jinny for hire to Mr. Ball in Savannah; she was to commence work the following night, April 21. It was a sure sign that the Arnolds were leaving for the North and shutting down the manse for the summer. The weather was getting warm, the "miasma" season was approaching, when the decaying vegetation in the swamps supposedly bred the poisons that caused malaria. It would not be safe for the Arnolds to return until after the first frost in autumn.

CHAPTER THREE

Plantation Journal

JANUARY 9, 1847–APRIL 20, 1847

[The journal here is torn down the page, but the information it contains is vital to understanding the context of Arnold's concerns regarding plantation work during this planting season.]

1847	The
Saturday	lime
Jany 9	varies
	70 &
76 Bushels	Adam
	of the force
	1. 18 & 17
C. Peter	when the
on his good	& finished
behavior	Mr Ferguson
from this	with pleurisy &
date	at W Hall all the
	½ of W Hall Square
	about 76 Bushels & put into House

Monday Jan 11   At C Hill Peter & Shadwell with Fisherman Cain & Pompey Sawing   ten ploughs in Rice field—Finished with Oxen No. 14 largest Square & plough 12 acres with mules in No. 13. Oxen went into No 4 this afternoon— ten hands cleaning out ditches in No 19. & 20—& the Small hands with Morris raising low places in dam   Over-

*1½ acres new
ground taken
up this day
144 B Rice*

seer has been Sick with pleurisy the last five days. rec^d on Friday fr Savannah 4000 Brick pr [per] Cotton Plant. At W Hall 4 Hands winnowed & put into Barn 144—Bushels Rice. ten in Cotton House & the balance cleaning up New ground, but made out badly   only took up New tasks 1½ acres

*Friday [sic]
Jany 12*

*66 Bushels Rice
4 Acres new
ground taken
up this day—
In all taken up
41¼ Acre*

At C Hill Peter & Shadwell fishing caught 25 Shad   Cain & Pompey Sawing. Charles ploughed half in day & hauled timbre the other half. Adam & eight mules ploughed all day. finished No 13 Square with mules & went into little 14. Square. 11 Hands cleaning out ditches & small Boys, & two or three old Hands turning ground in ploughed Square at W. Hall   winnowed 66 Bushels Rice & the rest of the hands with 33 C Hill hands cleaned up New ground   took up 4 Acres this day—

[Page torn]

hands cleaned
Small hands
is very ill
Rogers. Two hands
full & Amos
at W Hall all
C Hill 4 Excepted
Have been thrashing
put into Barn 118 Bushels

Jany

*split 600 Rails
winnowed 90
Bushels Rice*

*last of the New
ground cleaned
up   say 2
acres   making*

same work as yesterday including 7 Mule & ten Ox ploughing   the Mules finished No 14 Small Square & went into No. 15. this afternoon   the Oxen ploughing in No 4. Mr Ferguson a little better—met J. P. Maxwell at C. Hill who promised me to buy my Note in about 6 weeks—[1] through T. H. Harden of Savh & I loaned him some more money   At W Hall—12 Hands thrashed Rice & finished all but a little   Say one hands work   also winnowed & put into Barn about 100 Bushels Rice this night   the Ax Hands Split 600 Rails. Carpenters geting

in all about 43
Acres

out White Oak & Sills for negro House & the rest of the people finished cleaning up New ground & loged [logged] up two or three tasks.—

Friday 15th

710 Rails

118 Bushels
Rice

At W Hall finished thrashing Rice & winnowed 118 Bushels & put into Barn. the women cleaned up part of the tasks that had been done badly.—& all men twenty in— number loged up 4 acres of New ground & 5 men Split 710. Rails at C Hill   caught last night 26 Shad. Women cleaned out ditch in No 15 & the little people turned ground after ploughs in Savage Squares—

1847 Saturday
Jany 16.

38 Bushels Rice
put in Barn @
W Hall makg
the whole crops
650 B

750 Rails

At C Hill finished ploughing No 15. with Mules & No 4. with Oxen, excepting 2 days work   Peter caught only 11 Fish last night. ten women cleaning out ditches in No 8. & 14. Squares—three tasks each & a few old & young hands turned ground in No 3 after the plough   Mr Ferguson Still very Sick—at W Hall C Hill & part of W Hall People listed two tasks each in Cotton field & all the Men from both places Fishermen & Plough Boys. excepted loging up New ground. did about 5 Acres to day.—Winnowed last of W Hall Rice   38 Bushels & put four hands to thrash Peoples Rice—also Split with 5 Hands this day 750. Rails   Amos Sold 55 Shad for $8.50—Broke the Axeltree to his Cart. & his own Horse expenses & new Axeltree will about consume the money[2]

Monday
Jan 18th

Split @ W
Hall 670.
Rails

At C Hill caught 15 Shad   five mule ploughs in No 7. & Oxen plough in No 4   The women   26 in number cleaning out main ditches in No. 8, 13, 14, 15. Old Hands & young turning ground in No 3 after the ploughs   Mr Ferguson Still quite Sick. All the Men Carpenters included at W Hall—roling Logs   6 women sorting Cotton & the balance finished listing 12 acre Cotton field   5 Rail Splitters turned out 670 Rails

Tuesday
Jany 19.

At C Hill caught only 6 Shad. Mules   five in number ploughing in No. 7. Oxen two ploughs finished No 4.

Gined 200 lbs
Cotton

Split 740.
Rails

Square. The Women cleaned out large ditches in the forenoon & quarter drains in the afternoon   At W Hall all the
balance of C Hill Men with part of W Hall loging up. & 4
men ditching & five Splitting Rails in New ground women
Started to hoe in do. [ditto] & first day ginned 200 lbs
Cotton—

1847
Wednesday
Jany 20

700 Rails

At C Hill cleaned out ditches & made up dams   Adam
Harrowing No 12   Charles ploughing margin   Mule
ploughs finished No 17   Caught 7 Shad—At W Hall
women beded [bedded] New ground two in a task but did
not finish, turning before beding. Six ditching in do. 5
Split 700 Rails & two Gangs of Eight each Log roling did
6 Tasks to a gang   Ginned 170 pounds of Cotton.

Thursday
Jany 21

700 Rails

At C Hill Same as yesterday   Caught 30 Shad. Amos
gone to Savh to carry letters   Jim Harrowing with two
Mules in No 1. Overseer Still confined to the House—At
White Hall same work as yesterday   Ginned 150^{lbs} Cotton & Split 700 Rails—

Friday Jany 22

Have Split in
all at W Hall
5570= Rails
Took out of
House 1.
Bushel Rice

At C Hill made up dams   turned ground   run two har-
rows in No 1. & No 12   Boston Mending Harrows &
fixing overseer Smoke House—at W Hall Rose & Phoebe
Mouting 20^{lbs} Cotton   first this year. Ginned 150 lbs. two
ditching. three Gangs loging, & a few hands beding in
New ground, Jacob & Sambo ploughing in Rice field at
W Hall this day & yesterday   3 Ploughs in Same field
Stopt Rail Splitters—caught 35 Shad

Saturday
Jany 23

At W Hall Sambo ploughed   Jacob & Ellick cleaned up
leaves in front of House   Ginned 200^{lbs} Sorted 300^{lbs} &
Mouted 200^{lbs} three hands beded one task in new ground
two doing half work. Abraham ditching & three Gangs
loging up doing only five tasks each   Amos gone to
Sav^h—At C Hill turned ground with part of the people &
raised low places on outside dam   Adam & Charles harrowing in No 12   Jim in No 2   Peter & Shadwell fish-

ing   Overseer came out today a little while for the first time   Amos went to Town with 55 Fish—

1847 Monday
Jany 25

Caught 53
Shad but
Fishermen only
a/ced for 33

At W Hall Three Gangs Rolled Logs doing only 4 Tasks each—Abraham dug ditch   King Billy, Gibbs & Cupid beding up New ground   Rose & Critia hoeing after log-ers—7 mouted 175^{lbs} & July Ginned 175^{lbs} Cotton & Sorted 300^{lbs} Seed Cotton.—At C Hill—Same work as Saturday   Fished during the day   caught 50 shad. Amos returned from Savannah & brought a Sack Salt   Jack Split puncheons at C Hill today.

Tuesday
Jany 26

Packed 1st Bag
W Hall Cotton

At C Hill part turned ground after the ploughs & part made up dam. Jim Adam & Charles all Harrowing   Peter & Shadwell fishing   Caught 17 fish. At W Hall Ginned 150^{lbs} Sorted 500^{lbs} Sambo ploughing. Jack Abraham & King Billy ditching & all the rest loging up in new ground   did with three Gangs 12 tasks in the heaviest timber.—Scipio packed first bag W Hall   White Cotton Big [illegible]   lbs

Wednesday
Jany 27.

At W Hall ten men ditching in New Ground & twenty eight others in three gangs roling Logs. Eight mouted 175^{lbs}—five Sorted 500^{lbs} & July ginned 175^{lbs} Sambo ploughed in Ricefield   Charles brought in load potatoes   42 Bushels from C Hill   Peter & Shadwell fishing   Caught 53 Shad—Jim finished Harrowing No 2. & Adam & Charles finished No 12 at Noon   12 Hands Sorted Cotton & the balance raised outside dam to No 14 & turned in Same Square & No 9. after the ploughs

1847 Thursday
Jany 28.

At C Hill Adam Harrowing in 14. Jim in No 3. Charles Carted two loads Cotton to White Hall   Peter & Shadwell Caught 47 Fish. & the rest of the people at C Hill making up outside dam & turning over in No 15. Flora & Eve winnowed 20 Bushels Seed Rice. At W Hall ten men ditching & all the other C Hill hands with W Hall Men loging up New ground   July Ginned 175^{lbs} mouted 175^{lbs}

& Sorted 500^{lbs}—White Hall Cotton   our family dined at Mr Demere's this day in Co. with Mr & Mrs Starr[3]

Friday
Jany 29th

Much work
done this day
for Overseer
ought to be ch.
[charged]

Packed 2ᵈ Bag
W Hall
Cotton.

At W Hall All the Men with a few exceptions from both places roling logs in New ground   Abraham & Billy ditching in do. five Women Sorting 400^{lbs} cotton   7 mouting 170^{lbs} & July ginned 185^{lbs}—100 being the balance of W Hall White Cotton & 85^{lbs} the first of C Hill White ginned this year   Scipio packed 2ᵈ Bag W Hall White Cotton—lbs   & Sambo ploughin in Rice field   At C Hill very little done excepting for overseer   Charles & Buck with Wagon & 3 Yoke of Oxen drawing lightwood from Sans Souci[4] & Adam with Wagon & w Yoke drawing wood from New Ground & Manure to his Garden until 3 Oclock & later probably and Old Johnny huling Rice for him   12 hands Sorting Cotton & the balance hoeing round fence at C Hill Next Silk Hope—no Harrowing done today

1847 Saturday
Jany 30.

At W Hall 12 men loging up New ground   hoped to have finished the loging tonight but did not Succeed, the rest of the men turning in the alley & beding new ground two in a task, have about 4 Acres done this night   Abraham deepened ditches in New ground. Ginned 285^{lbs} of C Hill White Cotton. Mouted 155^{lbs} W Hall Cotton & Sorted 400 C Hill White   Charles brought two loads Seed Cotton for C Hill about 1600^{lbs} each load—has brought 4 loads in all & a half load left to come   At C Hill Adam & Jim harrowing & the rest of the people making up & raising outside dams. Caught fish this night

Monday
Tuesday &
Wednesday
3ᵈ Feby.

Packed 3ᵈ Bag
W Hall Cotton
[blank] lbs

Have been in Sav^h with Mrs Arnold.—during my absence Eight of my Men have been working the Road at W Hall. have ginned 860^{lbs} C Hill White Cotton—Have mouted balance of W Hall White Cotton. 300^{lbs-} & 375^{lbs} C Hill White Cotton & the men have deepened ditches in New ground & to day cleaned up Some of the Cane   tasks in ditto   At C Hill Monday with part of the Hands loged up in New ground & five Split Rails each day. Geo & the women worked in Rice field & yesterday & to day have been thrashing Rice. Carpenters Caulking Boats—& fixing Gates to Trunks. Fishermen Caught the last three days. 150 fish   Scipio packed 3ᵈ Bag W Hall White Cotton.

1847 Thursday Feby 4ᵗʰ

Packed 4ᵗʰ Bag W Hall Cotton [blank] lbs.—

At C Hill five hands Splitting Rails—4 cuting off Logs for Rail Splitters   the Mill hands winnowing the Late Rice that was thrashed by hand. Carpenters mending flat & the balance of the force cleaning out quarter drains in No 12 & 14 Squares—Charles & Adam Harrowing in No 4—Jim in No 3 & Sambo Started to Harrow in No 6. this day—At W Hall men ditching in New ground & Women Sorting & mouting Cotton   9 sorted 800ˡᵇˢ clean cotton & 8 mouted 200 lbs   Ginned 250ˡᵇˢ C Hill White—Scipio packed 4ᵗʰ & last Bag W Hall White Cotton   lbs   caught 40 Fish

Friday Feby 5

Packed 5ᵗʰ Bag White being 1ˢᵗ of C Hill Cotton [blank] lbs.

First days work two Wagons hauling out manure

At C Hill winnowed Rice   No 19 Square   that was thrashed by Hand 510.Bushels—also winnowed about— 50 Bushels of No 12 left when we last Shipt Rice—a part of the Hands cleaned out ditches in Rice field & five men loged off trees in New ground for wood & five Split Rails   four mules ploughing two furroughs each for Sugar Cane   Adam & Charles carting out manure for Cane—At W Hall Scipio packed 5ᵗʰ Bag White Cotton, being the first of C Hill White—Ginned 275ˡᵇˢ & mouted 200ˡᵇˢ   Sorted 800ˡᵇˢ—five men hoeing off the Cane in New ground   Fish 50

Saturday Feby 6

At C Hill Adam & Charles carted Manure half-a-day & then came to W Hall with Cotton & tailing for poultry. 4 mules ploughed for Sugar Cane   Mill winnowed 460 Bushels—Rice—five men Splitting Rails   the rest—loging up in New Ground & listing Corn field.

1847 Saturday Feby 6.

At W Hall mouted 200ˡᵇˢ   Sorted 750ˡᵇˢ   the last of C Hill White Cotton & Ginned 250ˡᵇˢ & the men cleaned up Cane tasks in New ground. Scipio packed 2ᵈ Bag C Hill

Packed 6ᵗʰ Bag   White Cotton   this being the 6ᵗʰ Bag of White packed this
White Cotton   year   Sent to C Hill 30 Bushels Cotton Seed & Bbl Salt.
Caught 26. Fish.

Monday   At C Hill 30 Hands listing in Corn field   four Mules
Feby 8ᵗʰ   ploughing bed. for Sugar Cane. Two Ox Wagons Carting
Rails—five hands Splitting Rails. & the rest of the force
loging up New ground   Overseer & his family gone to
Savʰ. At W Hall two hands cleaning out Creek leading
from New ground to Mount field & Six hands cleaning up
tasks of Cane in new ground   11 Hands mouted 275ˡᵇˢ
C Hill White Cotton   July ginned 140ˡᵇˢ last of C Hill
White & 159ˡᵇˢ C Hill yellow Cotton.—Peter & Shadwell
fishing   caught 119 Fish   Carpenter Peter & Lewis
Caulking flat   Boston making tongue & Harness to mule
Wagons

Tuesday Feby 9   At W Hall mouted 275ˡᵇˢ of W Cotton & put 75ˡᵇˢ in Bag
packed this day of [blank] lbs C Hill White being 3ʳᵈ Bag
Packed 7ᵗʰ Bag   C Hill. Ginned 145ˡᵇˢ balance C Hill yellow Cotton &
of CH [sic]   [blank] lbs W Hall yellow & the balance of W Hall   four
White   cleaning up New ground at C Hill   two ox Harrowing in
No 4. & two mule Harrowing in No 3 & 6   Carpenters
Caught 219   workg on flat. 30 Hands listing, & the balance roling logs.
Shad this &   & Splitting Rails. Overseer returned from Savʰ. Mr & Mrs
last night   Demere passed the night with us

1847   At C Hill caught 102 Shad   Four Harrows running in
Wednesday   Rice field   Women & half hands listing & Men Roling
Feby 10   Logs in New Ground   At W Hall finished Ginning Cot-
ton 190ˡᵇˢ—White Hall Yellow   Mouted 275ˡᵇˢ C Hill
Packed 8ᵗʰ Bag   White Cotton & the rest of the Hands hoed off Cane & in
White cotton   New ground   Mr & Mrs Demere Mr & Mrs Patterson Mr
being 4ᵗʰ of C   C Rogers & family including children Miss C Woodford &
Hill weighing   Revᵈ Mr Rogers from North Hampton passed the day
[blank] lbs   with us—Scipio packed 4ᵗʰ Bag C Hill White Cotton
[blank] lbs

Thursday   At C Hill two gangs roling Logs & four hands Splitting
Feby 11ᵗʰ   Rails in New Ground—Three Harrowing in Rice field

Eight persons making up fence & the balance Listing in cornfield   Peter & Shadwell fishing   Caught 92 Shad   At W Hall Mouted 200ᵗᵇˢ White Cotton   last of C Hill—also mouted 75ᵗᵇˢ W Hall Yellow. Mr Manvill returned this Evg from Darien—⁵

Friday
Feby 12ᵗʰ

At C Hill caught 39 fish by Peter & Shadwell & Brenton, Mr Bukcly & myself caught 30 Rockfish with lines from the Wharf @ C Hill   Adam Carting Rails   Charles Jim & Sambo Harrowing Rice field   four hands making up fence   the Women finished listing Corn field & four Men Splitting Rails & the rest of the Men in two gangs roling Logs in New Ground—At W Hall 7 Mouted 175ᵗᵇˢ W. Hall Yellow Cotton 3 C Hill Yellow & the rest of the force excepting Geo who has been Carting Rails, raising Backwater dam & digging a Short piece of ditch next to it.—Revᵈ Mr Rogers fr North Hampton still on a visit at W Hall

1847 Saturday
Feby 13.

Packed 9ᵗʰ Bag
White Cotton
being the 5ᵗʰ of
C Hill White

At C Hill four Splitting Rails   two Gangs—loging up & four others cutting & Sawing off logs. & Six others clean-ing up Some tasks not finished before   Adam Carting Rails   Charles—with Ox Harrowing in No 7   Sambo finished No 6. & Jim with Mule harrowing in No 18— Peter & Shadwell fishing caught 6 fish & the rest of the force finished listing in Lot next Barns. At W Hall packed 9th Bag of White Cotton [blank] lbs   Mouted 175ᵗᵇˢ C Hill—Yellow. 25ᵗᵇˢ W Hall Yellow & 75ᵗᵇˢ of Yellow taken out of the white when mouting—making all of this years Cotton, expect to mout over a part of it. Miss Maria Habersham has come to make Harriet a visit this day. Mr Rogers still with us.

Monday
Feby 15

Mr Manvill &
son commenced
work @
C. Hill

At C Hill two wagons & one Ox Cart Carting out Cane. five hands Splitting Rails   4 Boys ploughing between Cane beds & opening a trench with trenching ploughs to plant in the Cane   the rest of the force all Cutting [and] planting the Cane next Richmond   finished 5 acres this night   Mr Manvill & his Son commenced work this day at C Hill & the Carpenters with him   I give him Jinny to

Cook & Wash for him & allow him $5 per week in lieu of Bonding him & his Son—At W Hall Sancho gone for Oysters. Geo Carting Rails & the rest of the people making up fence round New ground   Old Amy mouting over Cotton

Tuesday
Feby 16.

thru this night
13 acres Cane
planted

At C Hill five Splitting Rails. 2 Fishing Caught 70 Shad & the rest of the force cutting [and] ploughing   Cutting & planting Cane   planted this day 8 Acres   run five wagons in drawing it out. At W Hall. made up fence round New ground & dug ditch & raise dam in do.

1847
Wednesday
Feby 17

At C Hill only Caught 17 Shad   Carpenters workg with Mr Manvill & his Son framing Sugar Mill   five men Splitting Rails & the rest of the force with Six fr W Hall planting Cane   five wagons & one Cart drawing it out. & the rest Cutting it [and] loading the Carts &c. about Sixty persons employed & we have planted this day Seven & a half Acres—At W Hall Tom & Amos Setting out Box in front yard. Scipio packed first Bag Yellow Cotton C Hill Weighs [blank] lbs   Rose & Amy in Cotton House & the others digging out ditch on outside of dam in New Ground & raising that dam & widening it by carrying part of the dirt from high ground

Thursday
Feby 18

Manvill lost
half a days
work

Finished
planting Cane
@ C Hill
30 Acres
planted.—

At C Hill the Same work as yesterday including Cain & Pompey who are Sawing. Mr Manvill lost half a day in attempting to go to Savannah—Settled yesterday with Capt Bailey of Schr [Schooner] Cotton Plant by receiving $25—for the deficiency in the delivery of his Rice   he should have paid much more—but being a poor man let him off easy.—At White Hall Same work as yesterday & also worked on fence round New ground   Scipio packed White Hall yellow Cotton [blank] lbs   have only 140^{lbs} White left to be put into a packet tomorrow   caught 23 Shad—

1847 Friday *Feby 19.*	At C Hill two Mule Harrows in Rice field two Saw- ing two fishing with Dean caught 27 fish part of the Women—cleaning out quarter drains & part—making up fence round New ground & balance women cleaning up ground that has been loged up four Splitting Rails & the rest loging up. At W Hall four Wagons Carting out Ma- nure for Oats. marked 15 calves & 16 pigs Shipt cotton by Science Eleven Bags & one packet whole Crop of 46.—being 14 Bags of 300^{lbs} two of them Yellow—the rest of the hands levelling back dirt in Rice field, excepting Rose & Amy picking—Burrs out of wool—
Saturday *Feby 20.*	At C Hill fifteen hands cleaning out quarter drains in Rice field two Sawing two fishing caught 16 fish the rest with exception of two Harrows in Rice field are all work- ing in New ground—loging up. Splitting Rails & making fence & cleaning up after the logers. At White Hall Charles Adam Geo & Prince with four wagons Carting out Manure to potatoe lot Rose & Amy burning heaps in New ground & the rest levelling dirt in Rice field Sent Cain after his wife Lizze that I bought of Colo^n Morris for his accommodation giving $600 for her. Maria Habersham Mr & Mrs Winn & children at W Hall Maria has been with us eight days.—
1847 Monday *Feby 22^d*	At C Hill did not fish, Cain gone for his wife two mule & one ox Harrows in Ricefield fifteen hands cleaning out quarter drains fifteen men making fence & toting Rails in New ground Adam Carting Rails—four hands Splitting Rails in New ground a few hoeing one task in do & the rest loging up in New ground, Charles with his Ox team ploughing potatoe field next Barn yard @ W Hall for Oats. Geo doing Same with his Mules—Amy picking Burrs out of Wool & the rest of the White Hall force cleaning out quarter drains turning ground & levelling in Rice field.— caught 50 fish
Tuesday *Feby 23*	At C Hill twenty five hands cleaning out ditches in Corn field ox harrows in No 7 Cain gone for his wife Peter

& Pompey fishing   Carpenters working on Sugar House
Beams & a [*sic*] ten hands making fence   Adam drawing
Rails & the rest cleaning up & laying up in New Ground
At W Hall 4 Split 125 Rails each ten feet long
Geo & Charles finish ploughing for oats   Geo Harrowing
do & Charles with Ox harrow & two Mule Harrows in
White Hall Rice field & the rest leveling dirt toting Rails
& raising low places on dams. at White Hall. Caught 52
fish this night.

Wednesday
Feby 24

At White Hall 3 mule Harrowing & one Ox harrowing in
Rice field   four Splitting Rails & the rest of the force
toting Rails & making up dam next McAllisters. At C Hill
Cain & Pompey Sawing. Peter & Shadwell fishing
Caught 62 Shad   one Ox Harrowing in No 7. Men Roling
Logs in New Ground   Morris & little Gang making fence
next Silk Hope   Geo with a few hands deepening ditches
in Corn field

1847 Thursday
Feby 25.

At C. Hill 22 Hands beded 11 Tasks in New ground eight
roled Logs & heaped up Wood—Morris with Small gang
made fence next Silk Hope   Cain & Pompey
Sawed   Peter & Shadwell fished. Carpenters worked on
Sugar Mill   Bandy Harrowed in Rice field Adam Carted
Rails. Charles Jim Sambo harrowed in White Hall Rice
field   Geo carted Rails to line fence next McAllister & the
balance of White Hall force made up fence & 4 Hands
Split 125 Rails each ten—feet long. Amy & Rose picking
Burrs from Wool.—

Friday Feby 26

Planted Oats
this day 3½
acres   also 3½
acres of Rice in
W Hall Square

At C. Hill Same work as yesterday.—excepting twenty
four hands came to White Hall to work. & only eight
beded in New ground—At W Hall run Six ploughs in
Corn field   Started late & only ploughed 18 Acres instead
of 24 throwing two furroughs in the list, twenty hands
trenched with back trenching hoes in Rice field & Oat
patch doing almost ten tasks to a gang of four instead of
twelve wh [which] is the task & 4 gangs   Covered 3½
acres of Oats—3½ of Rice & chopt clods early in the

morning.—Charles ploughed about ⅔ds of an acre of Bermuda grass next Turnip patch   Expected Mr. Patersons family including the Borelands to dinner, but owing to its being a rainy day they did not come. Mr. Rogers fr North Hampton, Miss M—— Habersham & Mr Buckly are all Staying with us—Hand packed & weighed 187lbs Wool this day.

1847 Saturday Feby 27.

First planted Rice being W Hall Square done this night

At C Hill Charles & Adam drawing—rails & the rest of the force in New ground beding   two hands to a task first turning under the bed. have 7½ Acres of New ground at C Hill beded this night—Carpenters workg on Sugar Mill. At W Hall 6 ploughs did 2¼ acres each two furroughs in Corn field & then the plough Boys went to cover Rice   Rose picking burrs out of Wool & the rest of the force trenching & planting Rice field at W Hall with twelve of the C Hill hands   planted 54 Bushels seed 4½ Bushels more than 3 Bushels to the Acre—

Monday March 1.

At C Hill 13 hands beding in Corn field   Morris with several hands mending break in dam in 18 Square Charles & Bandy harrowing. Adam drawing Rails to Miller field   the men finishing loging up New Ground @ C Hill & the rest of the hands nearly finished the beding in C Hill new ground—no fishing since Friday. At W Hall beded 2½ Acres for Corn & 5 Acres listed in New ground Cotton field   Six ploughs finish Corn field & about 8 Acres of Cotton field   Mr Rogers & Mr Buckley & Miss Habersham left us this day. Miss H was with us 16 days & Mr R 10 days   Mr B. all winter   he returns again on Wednesday   tomorrow my Son in law leaves for north & my Daughter H. goes to Savh to make a visit. Caught last night 26 Shad

1847 Tuesday March 2

At C. Hill Men at last finished loging up New ground, women beded for Corn   two Ox Harrowing   finished No 8 Square.—Carpenters worked on Sugar Mill—& this night two Black Masons came out & will commence work tomorrow   Adam Carting Rails to Miller field   Brenton left for the North & Harriet accompanied him to Sav^h & Essey Sullivant came out to W Hall   At W Hall two ploughs in Cotton field   Geo Carting Rails & the rest beded three tasks each in Corn field and was out early   the plough having run only two furoughs

Wednesday
March 2 [sic]

Shipt per
Science 70 Bags
Oats   about
150
Bushels   to A.
Champion

At C Hill finished Beding the 25 Acres of Corn ground next Cane & planted about ten Acres of it   Charles & Bandy Carting out Manure to Potato field   Sambo & Jacob Harrowing in No 5 Square   Two Black Masons commence workg on foundations for Sugar Mill & I am to pay $2.25 pr m [month]   find them with provisions & tinder to mix Mortar & curing Brick & if I think the care worth 25^cts more per m I am to give it, but not other- wise—To day the Cotton plant arrived at C Hill with 12000 Brick for me—Miss Sullivant came from Town— caught fish. Carpenters all at work on Sugar House. At W Hall five hands minding Birds from Rice field   Geo Carting Rails round pasture fence & the rest beding 3 tasks each for Corn in New ground

1847
March 4th
Thursday

Very Rainy
day.

At C Hill presume they took out the Brick from Cotton Plant & it being a very rainy day do not think the Carpen- ters or Masons did much of anything   At W Hall Same hands in Rice field & the rest beding in New ground Corn field—

Friday
March 5th

Michael Drew
No 74 Penn
St. Phila

Wrote this day R H & Son Accepting their offer of 95 cts for my Rice at Plantation or $1 deliverable in Sav^h at my election   freight is 3½ cts—At C Hill people cleaned out ditches in No 5. & 7.   a few dressed up dams in Rice field   five wagons Carted out Manure for Potatos   two Mule Harrows in Rice field   Masons workg [working] on foundations for Sugar Mill   Carpenters on Frame   Fish- ermen caught only 16 fish & have this day discharged Dean & paid him for 50 days work @$1—& for twine & netting the nets $25.87.—At W Hall all hands excepting Bird Minders listing four Acres for Corn in Meeting House field.—

Saturday
March 6.

First trenching
of Rice at
C Hill this
dy   18 Acres.

At C Hill 24 Hands trenched & tracked 18 Acres for Rice in No 3—the five Harrows in No 9 & 11   two Sawing   two fencing & the rest making up dams in Rice field   Carpenters gone this morning up for ten Cypress Sticks to Canuchee   Masons & White Carpenters Same as yesterday. @ W Hall finished beding 40 Acres for Corn & listed 3½ Acres for Potatoes.

1847 March 6
Saturday

Sold this day to Stephen Habersham all the Corn I have to Spare @ $1—pr Bushel deliverable at Plantation presume I shall have 500 Bushels to deliver him

Monday
March 8

Planted 24
acres Corn
C Hill & 17½
@ W Hall

At C Hill planted 17½ acres of Corn   covering by taking dirt from the alleys with hoes & doing 6 Acres to the Gang of five hands   Should have done Seven Acres—At C Hill five harrows in Rice field   Adam drawing Rails part of the day & Manure on Cotton field part of the day. Peter running out tasks in Rice field   Cain & Pompey Sawing & the weak hands finished planting the 33 Acres of Corn & balance of the force trenching in Rice field excepting Peter Boston Lewis & Abraham gone up Canuchee for Cypress Sticks to Saw for Sugar Mill. two Black Masons, from Sav^h & Mr Manvill & Son workg on Sugar Mill[6]

Tuesday
March 9

Planted 19
Acres Corn @
W Hall.

Recd 2 Rafts
from DeLoatch
one very poor

At C Hill 5 Harrows in Rice field   Adam Carting Manure to Cotton field   Flat returned last night with ten Sticks Cypress fr Canuchee   three hands making up fence next Ways. & the rest of the force trenching Rice field   4 hands doing twelve tasks working backward   Carpenters still on Frame for Sugar Mill & Masons finished foundation & cellar to Sugar Mill this night—At W Hall all hands excepting two minding Birds in Rice field have been planting Corn. done this day 19—Acres making 36½ planted at W Hall   Rec^d fr Wm 11 B 3 Pecks   Battist 3 Bushels Adeus 2 Bushels 3 Pecks. & Geo 3 Bushels 4 quarts.

1847
Wednesday
March 10.

At W Hall finished planting New ground Corn field [blank] Acres planted this day—Sent 7 Hands to C Hill last night   A C Hill paid Mason, for laying 9000 Brick in foundation for Sugar Mill $22.50—being $2.50 per m   I

finding Mortar Mixer & Brick Curing & bonding the Mason—agreed to pay $2.25 they worked only 5½ days. Also
raised the Sugar Mill with 12 Hands including Mr Manvill
& his Son & finished all excepting the Rafters & Rig pole.
the Building is one Story 80 feet by 24 feet. three Harrows
running in Rice field & the balance trenched   almost 30
Acres with Hoes   have tonight 104 Acres trenched fr Rice

Thursday
March 11th

First Rice
planted @
C Hill No 3.
29½
Acres   2½
Bushels pr Acre

At C Hill planted No 3 Square   29½ Acres being the first
Rice planted @ C Hill this year. also trenched with 15
Acres & with 14 trenching ploughs [blank] Acres. Harrowing in No 13, then with two Ox Harrows & Carpenters
took out 2ᵈ Raft from River & worked with Manvill & his
Son in Sugar Mill   at W Hall only 4 Hands in the field
wh. [who] finished planting New ground Corn & deepened main ditch in the Corn field

Monday [sic]
March 12.

planted No 1
& 2 @ C Hill
with 2½
Bushels pr
Acre.—

At C Hill carpenters putting up Rafters & Staging for
Shingling & two Ox Harrows in No 13. Six trenching
ploughs in No 11. four Gangs trenching No. 5 & part of
No. 10. Adam Carting Manure & the rest of the force
planted Nos 1 & 2 & about Six Acres in No. 6. 2½ Bushels the Acre. No. 3 planted with 2½ Bushels to the Acre.
the few hands @ W Hall minding Birds in Rice field

1847 Saturday
March 13.

Sunday night
Ice

Planted No 6
& 7 squares @
C Hill

At W Hall all hands not gone to C Hill Minding birds.—
At C Hill planted No 6 & 7 & part of five Squares, No 7.
3 Bushels to the Acre   the others 2½ Bushels. Six trenching ploughs finish'd 9 & 11 Squares. trenching & a few
hands trenching after ploughs   Charles Harrowing
finished No 13 & worked half a day in little 14 Square.
Adam & Billy Carting Manure to Cotton field

Monday
March 15th

At W Hall Same as Saturday at C Hill   Charles & Adam
Carting Rails to Miller field   Jack & Israel deepening
ditches in Corn field   4 Minding Birds in Corn

Ice

field   Billy Carting Manure to Cotton field   five ploughs trenching   finished No 8 & went into 13 @ 5 oclock

Planted No 5
& 12
Squares.—

[illegible] Bandy trenching margins to Nos. 9. & 5, planted No 12 & 5 & had hard work Breaking clods in 12 Square. Should have been harrowed with More Care. Carpenters Commenced Shingling today. Sugar Mill   planted 12 with 3 Bushels & 5 with 2½ Bushels pr Acre. One gang trenching with hoes in No. 10. Square.

Tuesday
March 16

At White Hall doing nothing but minding Birds   marked the young Lambs. had 12 [illegible] & 19 yews, making 51 Lambs marked & two not marked—also counted Old

C^{td} 170 Sheep

Sheep & found 117 in all   170 Head besides 3 in the fattening Coop—At C. Hill Adam & Charles drawing

planted No. 9.
& 10

Rails   one Ox Lamb died   Six Mules trenching in No 13. Square. five people minding Birds   Carpenter on Mill House—Shingling   four hands trenching after ploughs &

pd $90 for
lumber

the balance planted No 9. & 10 Squares   2½ Bushels the Hand   p^d Deloatch for two Rafts lumber rec^d a few days since at C Hill

White frost.

Wednesday &
Thursday
March 17th &
18th

Absent in Savannah   have planted Nos 11. 13 & 8 Squares of Rice @ C Hill with 3 Bushels each acre, & also beded about 3 acres of the potatoe field   two Harrows finished No 14 Square & part of 15.—two ploughs ploughed Six Acres—fr potatoes. Carpenters working on

Planted 11.
13. & 8
3 Bushels
Have 200
Acres planted
@ C Hill

Sugar mill & wagons drawing manure into Cotton field & what hands at W Hall not minding Birds Carried two hundred Rails out of the new ground & beded garden

Friday
March 19.

At C Hill finished beding & planting Six Acres of Slips twelve hands listed 1½ tasks in Corn field next Silk Hope   a few spread manure in Cotton field   ten Cut & Sorted potatoes   too many entirely   four taking off trash from Rice field   two Mule Wagons & one Ox Cart drawing out Manure into Cotton field   two—Harrows in No

15, & ten Cutting poles 150 each & making up fence with
them at Miller field & the balance making up fence with
rails at Miller field   at W Hall Same work as yesterday
let off the water from Rice field at White Hall that is in the
Sprout flow & was put on a/c/ [account of] frost, we had
frost three nights, in succession   two of them had ice.—

Saturday
March 20ᵗʰ

Handed in Tax
Return this day

At C Hill five Splitting Rails   ten toting rails & making
up fence at Miller field   two levelling dam   Charles Carting Rails   Shadwell Carting Manure   Jacob & Jim harrowing in No 15.   a few taking off trash   Cain & Pompey
sawing & the rest listing Corn ground next Silk Hope
Carpenters in Sugar Mill   at W. Hall Geo carting Cotton
seed & Rails   the others minding Birds &c.

1847 Monday
March 22ᵈ

Hoed off Sugar
Cane beds   one
Acre each hand

At C Hill finished Making New fence round Miller field
with ten men & Charles wagon   thirty hands hoed Sugar
Cane beds on the Sides—to be doing one acre to the hand
two Harrows in No 15 & I presume finished that
Square   two ploughs covering Manure in Cotton field & a
few hands Spreading Manure. Cain & Pompey Sawing &
Carpenters workg on Sugar House   Peter & Henry have
taken fr a task the whole Weather boarding the Outside &
Building Stage fr it & finish it Complete in ten days   have
already worked on it 4 days.—finished one long side & ¼
of the other   Lackleson came to C Hill this day to arrange
for Sugar Mill   He will have to furnish one Shaft & one
five foot wheel & promises to have it done & put up by the
first of June next. At C Hill Six hands Spread Cotton Seed
on the list & beded 1½ tasks each for Potatoes in New
ground Cotton field   two dug ditch & Made up dam one
task length in New Inland Rice field   the rest minded
Birds in Rice & Corn field

Tuesday
March 23

At C Hill ten hands planted Cotton in new ground   three
took off trash from Rice field. Six minding Birds in Corn
field   three running Harrows in Rice field   two Sawing.
Carpenters moving Watchmans House in Barn Yard & the
balance put on board Capt Thompsons Sloop Science 2200

Bushels Rough Rice that I have sold deliverable to Mr
Habersham in Savannah at One dollar pr Bushel I paying
freight & Commission—the hands that put the Rice in
vessel also hoed one task Sugar Cane—

1847 Tuesday
March 23ᵈ

At W Hall four planted two Acres of potatoes   thirty two
Bushels—& force beded 8 tasks Cotton & the rest excepting Rhina [Rinah] & Adeus who were sorting potatoes &
cutting them, have been Minding Birds in Rice field &
Corn field

Wednesday
March 24ᵗʰ

At C Hill ten planted Cotton in New ground & finished
that field about 8—Acres in all   two mules trenching on
No 14   two Wagons drawing out Manure & the rest of the
force cleaning quarter drains in the Savage Squares. took
off covering from No 16 Trunk & covered with new
boards. At W Hall Eight hands beded Cotton field & the
rest of the force—Minding Birds in Rice & Cornfield excepting Geo. who Carted out Manure for the Potatoes &
hauled Rails—

Thursday
March 25ᵗʰ

At C Hill twenty hands cleaned out quarter drains in 14.
& 15 Squares   four took out Old & put in New Trunk to
No 20. five trenching ploughs in No 15. Charles Carted
out Manure to Cotton field   ten hands listed in Corn field
& the balance—trenched Nos 18. & 19 Square. Carpenters on Sugar House.—At W Hall Six hands Spread the
Manure & beded ten tasks for potatoes   two beded for
Cotton & the rest Sick or Minding Birds

Friday
March 26

At C Hill 24 Hands trenched eighteen Acres & finished
No 17 Square   two Mule ploughs in No 14. and about 20
Hands finished cleaning quarter drains in 14. & 15   four
raised check dams & four covered New Trunk in No 20.
Square   Two Ox—Wagons & two Mule Wagons Carted
180 Bushels Rice to C Hill

1847
March 26

At White Hall two Mule Wagons Carted Rails from New
ground to potatoe field & afterwards carrd load Rice to

Friday

Sent 180
Bushels Seed
Rice fr W H to
C Hill

C Hill   five hands planted ten tasks potatoes & three beded two tasks each for cotton   the rest Minding Birds in Corn and Cotton fields   Sent this afternoon from White Hall to C Hill 180 Bushels Seed Rice in four Wagons & one Cart & put down New Trunks in No 20 @ CH

Saturday
March 27

At C Hill Six ploughs in No 14 Square   One wagon Carting out Manure   Manvill gone to Sav^h with Monday & Cart. the other Carpenters workg on Sugar House   part of the hands levelled the holes in 16. & part trenched 10 Square—At W Hall beded fr cotton in New Ground with a few hands   Sancho went for Oysters & the rest Minding Birds.

Monday
March 29

Colo
McAllister put
14 – 2 inch
planking on
Bridge Stirling
Creek &
wagons took
home old planks
1/2 feet
9 oclock A M

At C Hill planted Nos 18. & 19. & a few Acres in No 17. making all planted to day 30 Acres   Six ploughs finished trenching No 14 & went at Noon in No. 4. trenching two wagons—Carting out Manure in Cotton field four trenching after the ploughs—planted Nos 17, 18 & 19 with 2½ Bushels pr Acre—Carpenters all on Sugar House   At W Hall beding for Cotton with all hands not engaged Minding Birds   have 15½ Acres beded this night   Mrs Geo. Jones 3. children 3 servts & two horses came Saturday last on a visit to W Hall

Tuesday
March 30th

At C Hill 4 Hands trenched after ploughs in No 1. 4. Six ploughs finished No 4 trenching   fifteen minding Birds Charles & Sambo Carting out Manure & the rest planted 31 Acres of Rice   finished No 17. planted No 16. & 9 Acres in No 14 Squares.

1847 Tuesday
March 30th.

At W Hall a part of the force beded for Cotton in New Ground & balance Minding Birds in Rice & Corn fields have this night twenty acres ready for planting Cotton—

*Planted 30
Acres Rice @ C
Hill*

Carpenters—with Manvill & Son workg on Sugar House at C Hill—

*Wednesday
March 31.*

*Planted 30
Acres of Rice @
C Hill & sent
80 Bushels Seed
Rice fr W
Hall.*

At C Hill three Wagons Carting out Manure   three ploughs in Cotton field   One in Rice field   four hands opening after trenching ploughs   the rest planted 30 Acres of Rice finishing the two fourteen Squares. 3 Bushels pr acre & doing twelve acres in No. 4.—Carpenters on Sugar Mill   Mrs Jones & family left us this day for Sav^h   Sent—this morning (80) Eighty Bushels Seed Rice to C Hill—At White Hall—Same work as yesterday beded [blank] Acres for Cotton—

*Thursday
April 1/47*

*Finished 2^d
planting
Rice   about
100 Acres
this day @ C
Hill*

At C Hill finished 2^d Planting Rice being 7 or 8 Acres balance No 4 Square 3 Bushels pr Acre & then beded 2 tasks for Cotton back Negro Houses after ploughs & eight hands Spread Manure in Cotton field   Six ploughs finished ploughing the Cotton field & Six hands cleaned out & deepened ditches in Same. Charles & Jim Carted out Manure for Slips—@ W Hall beded about 4 Acres for Cotton   2 tasks ea. without ploughs

*1847 April 2^d
Friday*

*Planted 25
Acres Cotton
@ C Hill*

At C Hill finished beding & planted 25 Acre field back of Negro Houses with Cotton   Six mules finished ploughing cotton field & went at 10 o'clock to Miller Corn field to plough   Charles & Jim Carted out Manure on potatoe field   have this night about 7½ acres Manured Carpenters workg on Sugar House   Sold Dorsey about 10 Bushels Slip potatoes @ 62 cts the Bushel—at White Hall Sancho ploughed three Acres in Cotton field & the rest finished beding 12 acre Cotton field & did Six tasks in 15 acre Cotton field   Peter run out tasks in New Inland Rice field—

*Saturday
April 3^d*

At C Hill a few hands cleaned out and deepened ditches in Cotton field   Jack stopping leaks in Rice field dams. Pompey and Cain Sawing   Carpenters in Sugar Mill

New ground at
W H Contains
35½ acres

House. Six ploughs finished Miller field & the rest of the hands beding three tasks each in Miller field done about Sixteen Acres—at W Hall Sancho ploughed in Cotton field & the hands beded 5 Acres in Same field Peter running out tasks in New ground at W Hall & tracked two— Acres for Rice.—The New ground field Contains 41½ acres in all. 4½ now planted in Corn. about 1½ to be planted in Cotton and 35½ to be planted in Rice.

Monday
April 5ᵗʰ

At C Hill finished beding Miller field & planted 13 acres of it with Corn. two Sawing Jack Stopping leaks to dams Carpenters working on Sugar House & Twenty five hands gone to W Hall to work. Charles & Shadwell Carting out Manure—at W Hall men loging up in new ground women finished beding for Cotton Jim ploughing Sancho went to Kilkenny & exchanged 35 Bushels Cotton Seed

1847 Tuesday
April 6

Planted 25
Acres Cotton
@ W Hall
with five this
day

At C Hill two Sawing two wagons Carting out Manure Carpenters on Sugar House twenty four hands @ W Hall, balance finished planting Miller field with Corn & replanted part of first planted Corn field at W Hall planted 25 Acres Cotton with Mr Rogers Seed Sancho ditching Peter tracking & the balance of the Men heaping up logs in new ground Mrs Champion and her Daughters came this day to W Hall

Wednesday
April 7.

Finished
planting
Cotton @ W
Hall 19.—
Acres this day.
& replanted
20. acres Corn

At C Hill finished replanting Corn & Spread 7 Acres of Manure in Slip field Cain & Pompey Sawed part of the day & tracked in New ground in the Evng Charles & Shadwell Carted out Manure & have 14 Acres Manured this night. Jim also Carted Manure about one dozen Minding Birds & twenty five—hands at W Hall. Jack Stopping leaks to dam. At W Hall finished planting Cotton 19 acres & replanted 20 Acres of Corn. Israel Isaac & Sancho ditching & Sampson leveling dirt in New ground. & ten hands trenching for Rice but did only about half a task each. Should have done One.

Thursday
April 8th

Ten ploughs
covering—
Manure @ C
Hill.

At C Hill Jack stopping leak. two wagons & Cart carrying out Manure   ten hands trenching one task ea in New ground & the balance spreading Manure, at W Hall, twenty two hands trenching one task ea in New ground. Peter tracking 4 Acres   Cain digging ditch   Sampson levelling dirt & the balance   12 in number   finished replanting Corn

1847 Friday
& Saturday
April 9. &
10th

Discover my
Corn House
broken into

Have been absent in Sav^h these two days. at C Hill Carted out Manure two wagons   part of the women Scattering Manure   three ploughs covering it & 12 Hands trenching one task each in New ground Rice field—Have eighty Acres trenched   At W Hall three hands removed about fifteen hundred Rails fr. Rice field New ground & the balance with twenty five C Hill hands trenching one task each in New ground   have this night 19 Acres trenched Stephen Habersham @ W Hall

Monday
April 12

Flowed all of
first planted
Rice this
night.—

At C Hill planted 4 Acres Rice in New ground & trenched three acres   Pompey finished tracking in do & this night put on the water to all of the first planted Rice   200 Acres   four mules trenching in No 15 [illegible]   Charles absent   Cyrus Carting in Manure—At W Hall 25 C Hill hands together with the W Hall force. took up eight Acres trenching in New ground   only 13 finished their task, each was to do one task   had they all finished twenty eight Acres would have been done to-night   five hands Carrying Rails out of New ground   one raking trash, put on the water to night on Rice field at W Hall

Tuesday
April 13th

Mason fr.
Liberty came
but did very
little work this
day

At C Hill planted the balance New Ground 8 Acres with Rice   7 ploughs finished trenching No 15   Jack—Pompey & Peter opened after ploughs   Cyrus carted out manure at W Hall   planted 13 acres Rice in New ground 2 Bushels pr Acre. Mason came today

1847 April 14
Wednesday

Planted No 15.
+ 4½ Acres in
New ground at
W Hall
making 17½ in
all planted in
New Ground to
night

At C Hill Seven ploughs finished No 15. & also No 20. trenching, three Men opened after ploughs, three cleaning up little 2 acre Square & the rest planted No 15 with 3 Bushels Seed to the Acre. Mason worked today.—At W Hall planted 4½ Acres Rice in New ground, the C Hill hands having gone home last Evg. Today Battis two Clarks, Ham. + Sam & two others hunted Cattle in my range & drove off twenty herd of my Cattle & I was obliged to send Ellick, Wm & Jacob. to get them back & notwithstanding they carr^d off four & Ellick & Jacob will have to go tomorrow after them. It was by accident that I discovered them driving off fr I probably would never have seen my Cattle again.

Thursday
April 15.

Finished Rice
planting at C
Hill. & also
planted 4½
Acres Rice at
W Hall Inland
field

At C. Hill five ploughs finished Rice field & nearly finished ploughing the Rattoon Cane, Charles carted out manure & the rest of the force planted No. 20. & the little Square of 2½ Acres making a finish of the Rice plantg at C Hill & listed Some in Corn field—. & the Men put the Kettle into Sugar House, Israel workg with Mason Carpenters all workg on Shutters & door fr do—at W Hall planted 4½ acres of Rice in new ground. Dr Carroll & Daughter came to make a visit this day at W Hall—

1847 April 16
Friday &
Saturday
April 17

Manvill did
not work
Saturday

At C Hill five ploughs finished ploughing 28 Acres next Silk Hope for Corn   a few hands beded the New ground & planted about ten Acres   At W Hall twenty hands nearly finished the trenching [of] the Rice field part of New ground & 8 hands planted 3 Acres Rice. Dr Carroll—& Daughter have been two or three days on a visit @ W Hall. Mr Laws & Son dined with us to day. Also—planted yesterday 3 Acres Rice & trenched four Acres—Have planted in New ground this night 28 Acres of Rice—Shadwell & Hayer are to be married this night by Dr Carroll.

Monday
19th April

At C Hill planted 18 Acres Corn   Charles & Cyrus Carted out Manure   Manvill his Son & my Carpenters

Finished
planting the
Corn field next
Silk Hope   27
Acres in all

worked in Sugar House. Mason with lsrael worked Siting
Kettle   the other hands @ W Hall beding round Rice field
for Cotton   trenching the balance of Inland Rice field &
planting 7 Acres & a half leaving 2 Acres of Rice & about
2 Acres of Cotton yet to plant & the work of three hands
to finish the beding of that field   35½ Acres planted in
Rice this night   Six ploughs ploughed 4 furrows between
the rows & did 2 Acres each plough in New ground Corn
field   Hired my woman Jinny to Mr Ball for Six months
to Commence Wednesday night 21st Inst. He to pay $8 pr.
mo. & find her with everything but clothing.—Sent her
20th April/47

1847 Tuesday
April 20

At C Hill hoed 12 Acres Cane. Charles Carted Manure
part of the day. Carpenters, Mason, Charles Pompey &c
put Sugar Rolls in Mill & also put Kettles in their beds in
Sugar House—lowered the Water in all the first planted
Rice by puting the Leak way to get the Hills out of water,
the water—has been on ten days.—At W Hall listed two
tasks to the hand & did ten Acres in Meeting House Corn
field   9 Hands finished planting Rice about 2 Acres &
planted 5 tasks Cotton in New ground. Eight ploughs. run
four furroughs & did 16 acres in corn field. Sent Jinny this
afternoon to Mr. Ball.—

CHAPTER FOUR

Providence, Rhode Island

When in May 1824 Richard Arnold returned to Rhode Island for the first time as a slave owner, the free blacks of Providence living in Hardscrabble, a ghetto in the northwest section of the city, were seething with anger at being treated as second-class citizens. Arnold had delayed his departure from White Hall in order to establish his white overseer firmly in command of the slaves while their master was absent for six months in the North. On October 18 a group of black residents of Hardscrabble, rebelling against the daily indignities of racial discrimination, refused to get off the sidewalk when approached by whites. The ensuing race riot, "started because whites were angry at the failure of the blacks to show deference to them," led to the destruction of property. Hardscrabble was a poor neighborhood, its residents a mixture of hardworking men like Christopher Hill, who worked at odd jobs gardening, woodcutting, and farming for the whites, and those like Henry T. Wheeler, who was attracted by the cheap rents to open a dance hall. In the riot "the homes of hard-working blacks as well as dance halls were pulled down," including the home of Christopher Hill and the dance hall of Henry Wheeler.[1]

Most Providence blacks were free by the 1820s and had developed a sense of community centered on their newly established church, the African Union Meeting House (1819). Yet they "remained the victims of prejudice and oppression in every sphere of life. They were segregated in the churches, kept out of the public schools, denied employment in the textile mills, and finally, in 1822, denied the right to vote."[2] For Christopher Hill the final blow was the fact that the white men who had destroyed his house and had been arrested in connection with the riot were either found not guilty or the charges against them were dismissed on legal technicalities, the defense argument apparently prevailing that the rioters were ridding the city of "a notorious nuisance." In the spring of 1825, Christopher Hill, a widower, and his three children emigrated to Liberia.[3]

Prince Bent, a free black of Providence, who had earned his freedom by serving in the Rhode Island Black Regiment during the Revolutionary War, also worked at odd jobs gardening, woodcutting, and farming for the whites of Providence. He was one who stayed, and in the spring of 1824 he was hired by Louisa Arnold to put the garden in order. He had authority from Richard Arnold to drive out any white boys who might try to use the garden area, until then a vacant lot, to play ball.[4] Mum Phebe of White Hall, Georgia, property of Richard and Louisa Arnold, was counted in the census as one of the 1,400 blacks living in Providence, nearly 10 percent of the population, but her residence and arrivals and departures depended entirely upon the wishes of her master: Phebe, Richard wrote from White Hall to his wife in Providence, "will probably not arrive [in Providence] as soon as I do, for I cannot part with her before I leave Bryan."[5] Even if Mum Phebe had wished to do so, as a slave she could not become part of the free black community in Providence, although she made the journey back and forth from Georgia every year until her death in 1841.

At the time of the Hardscrabble race riot, Richard Arnold was settling with his brother, Samuel, for his share in their father's estate so that he could obtain the capital for the purchase of Cherry Hill plantation and its sixty-three slaves. By November he felt ready to return to Georgia in order to devote that half of his life to being a rice planter and slave owner. For him, the plantation represented adventurousness, a different way of life as well as a business investment (it was no mere quixoticism that nineteenth-century businessmen called their speculative business enterprises "adventures"). Rhode Island and Providence were the safe haven for the "adventurers," and indeed Arnold's business friends in the North were surprised at what he had done. Eliza Harriet Allen reported that his old friend William Amory of Boston could scarcely believe that Richard had invested in a plantation: "He thought with the rest of us that the money he [Richard] gave for it would in ten years with the interest be *much* greater than the land with all the profits. besides always having it at command. I hope," she added, "he would not get too much attached to the life of a planter."[6] William Amory need not have worried too much about his friend's business acumen because Arnold hedged his bets and continued to invest his property, stocks, and bonds in the North throughout the antebellum period; at no time was he entirely reliant on only

Silhouette of Richard J. Arnold, 1842. (Courtesy of the Arnold-Rogers Collection.)

one source of income. When he purchased Cherry Hill to complement his inheritance of White Hall through marriage, he already owned nearly $5,000 worth of various real-estate properties in the North and a further $3,700 worth of stocks in various companies and banks.

The only response of the Providence Town Council to the Hardscrabble riot was to increase the police force in 1825. Harassment of blacks continued, and in January 1826 an expedition of thirty-two Rhode Island blacks, led by Newport Gardiner, an old man and ex-slave, emigrated to Liberia under the auspices of the American Colonization Society. The group had scarcely settled in Liberia, however, when they were wiped out by a yellow fever epidemic.

The American Colonization Society, to which Richard Arnold later contributed, was founded in 1817 to promote the voluntary transportation of free blacks to Africa and to encourage southern slave owners voluntarily to emancipate slaves through manumission and emigration to Africa. Supporters of the colonization movement did not necessarily sympathize with the slaves, but they viewed slavery "as an economically unsound and dangerous institution, incompatible in the long run with the prosperity, peace, and security of society." Whatever its impact in the South, and scholars like George M. Frederickson admit that colonization had "no real impact on the future of slavery,"[7] by the early 1830s the black community in Providence had rejected the idea of emigration despite the fact that in September 1831 racial tensions in the city exploded into four days of rioting with great loss of life and property.

The riot began as a saloon brawl in Olney's Lane between white sailors on shore leave from ships docked in the port of Providence and local blacks. To the sailors, Olney's Lane was the red-light district, but like Hardscrabble it was also the residence of many hardworking and honest but poor black families. There followed a confrontation as symptomatic of racial conflict in the North as Nat Turner's uprising one month earlier was symbolic of racial conflict in the South:

> By this time [after the brawl in a saloon on the night of September 21, 1831] over a hundred people had gathered, ready for an "affray," and accompanied by the sailors they moved up the lane into the black residential section. There marchers were pelted by stones thrown from some windows, and they replied in kind. Suddenly a black man stepped from one of the buildings. Holding a pistol, he reportedly cried, "Is this the way the blacks are to live, to be obliged to defend themselves from stones?" A shot rang out; exactly who fired is unclear, but one of the white sailors fell, mortally wounded.[8]

The next day the mob, incensed that a white man had been killed by a black man, went on a rampage, making no distinction between the residents, destroying property indiscriminately, and eventually threatening to loot banks and businesses in the area. The mob could not be controlled even by the presence of the militia, the sheriff, and the governor of the state, Lemuel Hastings Arnold (no relation to Richard Arnold). On the following day, September 23, as though temporarily satiated, the mob dispersed. But on Saturday, September 24, "a great crowd" assembled and again sought to invade the black ghetto. This time the militia were ready for them, their guns loaded. Despite an appeal to the mob by Governor Arnold to disperse, the reading of the riot act by William S. Patten, justice of the peace, and warning shots fired by the militia, the mob refused to leave. The troops then fired into the crowd. Four white men were killed and many others wounded.

The next day, September 25, in an extraordinary Sunday session, the town council (Providence was not incorporated as a city until the following year) regretted the loss of life but condemned the mob's attack on private property and its defiance of civil and military authority. "The meeting then appointed a committee of fourteen prominent citizens 'to prepare and publish a correct statement of facts relative to the riots.'"[9] The composition of the committee precluded any finding that racial and economic discrimination was a fact contributing to the riot: Richard Arnold, slave owner and prominent Providence businessman was appointed, as was his brother-in-law, Zachariah Allen, and Allen's brother Crawford, both textile manufacturers who like other mill owners did not hire blacks. Furthermore, William Blodget, Samuel Dexter, and Edward Carrington, also on the committee, became members of the Providence Anti-Abolition Society four years later.[10] They were all honorable men, prominent citizens, men of business and property—and one of them, Richard Arnold, counted black human beings as part of his wealth and property, $38,225 in 1834. Some were bankers, like George Curtis. Some were professional men—lawyers, such as William S. Patten, Charles F. Tillinghast, and John Whipple. Some were clergymen, like William Richmond (Episcopal). Most of them were graduates of Brown University.

The committee report, signed by all fourteen members and dated September 28, 1831, characterized the black ghetto as containing "a number of houses tenanted chiefly by idle blacks, of the lowest stamp," but the committee was mainly concerned with the threat to private property inherent in mob rule. It concluded that "of all the evils that can be inflicted upon a civil society, that of a lawless and ferocious mob is the most capricious in its ob-

jects, the most savage in its means, and the most extensive in its consequences."[11] After all, Olney's Lane was near Zachariah Allen's residence on
South Main Street, and William Blodget's home on Smith Street was close to
where the mob assembled on that fatal Saturday evening. Richard Arnold's
residence was near the wharves where the sailors who started the riot came
ashore. The Edward Carrington mansion, like the mansions of other wealthy
Providence merchants, looked down upon those same wharves from the hill
above. Therefore, although charged only with ascertaining the facts of the
riot, the committee members as individuals recommended that the police
force be more vigilant in enforcing and executing existing laws against "idle
and vagrant persons" in order to protect life and property. As a further result
of the riot, Providence obtained its own charter and incorporated as a city the
following year.

That the protection of private property was foremost in the minds of the
committee is evident in a letter Zachariah Allen wrote Arnold more than a
year after the Providence race riot: commenting to his brother-in-law on the
agitation in South Carolina for state nullification of the federal Tariff Act of
1832, he says, "It seems to me as necessary for the good of the country that
blood should be shed to restore peace and quiet, as it did during our period of
riotous mobs. Civil war must unavoidably ensue, before these men can be
restored to reason."[12] Allen was not a bloodthirsty man, but the "rabble" was
a greater evil to him than state-sponsored violence. The incorporation of
Providence as a city with its own charter, however, did not resolve the issue
of law and order in Rhode Island any more than the tariff compromise of
1833 resolved the issue of states' rights versus the federal government. The
election in Providence was barely over, and Eliza Harriet Allen wrote to her
brother complaining that "our town government was much more efficient
than this will be with the officers as they were chosen."[13] Ten years later,
Rhode Island erupted into civil war over the issue of law and order and
suffrage.

It is doubtful that such a blue-ribbon committee could ever be assembled
again in Providence to ascertain the facts of a race riot, certainly not without
protest at the inclusion of a slave owner and three antiabolitionists. The
white power structure consisting of old families, wealthy merchants, bankers, landowners, textile manufacturers, and professional men retained political as well as social and economic control in Rhode Island throughout the
antebellum period, but by 1833 the lines were being drawn in New England,
and in Rhode Island in particular, on the issue of slavery. The New England
Anti-Slavery Society was formed in 1832 by William Lloyd Garrison and the

American Anti-Slavery Society in 1833. On June 7, 1833, the Providence Anti-Slavery Society was established with Josiah Cady as president; the Reverend Ray Potter, vice-president; John Prentice, treasurer; Gilbert Richmond, corresponding secretary; and Henry E. Benson, recording secretary.

It was a different world across the Providence River and into the shops of the newer section of Providence where Josiah Cady made shoes on Broad Street and lived on Pine Street, the west side of the river. The old families and shipping merchants had mostly settled on the east side where the wharves and warehouses were located, moving up the hill to build their mansions (unless, like Arnold, one already lived in a historic mansion on the main street). Captain Nightingale, for example, who had made his fortune in the slave trade and later the China trade, built his mansion of wood on the hill in 1782. It was purchased in 1814 by Nicholas Brown, Jr., whose father and uncle had likewise made their fortune in the slave and China trades, the uncle building his mansion on the hill in brick and stone. But shoemaking was a humbler trade, as was paperhanging, the trade pursued by Henry Cushing, one of the charter members of the Providence Anti-Slavery Society.

The membership of the antislavery movement in Providence was drawn from these lower-middle-class tradesmen and shopkeepers; men with a conscience, like the tailor John Prentice and the hatter Gilbert Richmond, were officers of the society, and Martin Robinson, owner of a small circulating library and stationer's store, and John Edwin Brown, owner of a bookstore, were its counselors. The Reverend Ray Potter, Baptist minister, and Wilbor Tillinghast, an older student at Brown University and later a Baptist minister, suggest the support the antislavery movement received from clergymen in the early years, and Wyllys Ames, owner of a temperance store, is suggestive of the link between the temperance and antislavery movements in the early 1830s.

The men who rioted in Providence in 1831 came from the same social and economic class as the abolitionists, symptomatic of the deep division in attitudes toward blacks among ordinary citizens of Providence, a division which in microcosm reflected the opposing views of many New England citizens during the antebellum period. Of the four race rioters killed by the militia on September 24, 1831, three were in similar trades as the abolitionists: Cyrus B. Guile, shoemaker; Walter Lawrence, paperhanger; and Samuel A. Whitemore, bookbinder. Only the fourth, Allen Cory, a sailor, belonged to the group who were the original inciters of the mob.

As Leonard L. Richards has pointed out, "Northern anti-abolitionism was both a pervasive and an intensive component of Northern life."[14] The wealthy merchant families of Providence were more homogeneous in their antiabolitionist views than the oridinary citizens, for they considered the abolitionists dangerous radicals and troublemakers who in their way were no more respectful of private property than the mob. For example, although the committee investigating the facts of the 1831 riot did not discover that any of the houses destroyed or damaged in the riot had actually been "occupied by respectable inhabitants," they ascertained that most of the "injured" houses were *owned* by respectable citizens, including three slum dwellings belonging to Nicholas Brown, whose father had been in the slave trade and a business partner of Richard's father, Welcome, in a rum distillery, and who himself was president and director of the Blackstone Canal Bank, where Arnold was a member of the board of directors. As one of the vice-presidents of the Providence Anti-Abolition Society, Nicholas Brown on November 21, 1835, subscribed to a series of resolutions which in part stated that "all coercive measures for the abolition of slavery, by whomever adopted, are in violation of the sacred rights of property."[15]

The resolutions were stated in general, legalistic terms to counter the abolitionists' argument that there can be no inherent property rights in another human being under moral law. Since most of the society's members were long-time business associates and friends of Richard Arnold, they were undoubtedly aware that the argument was more than just an abstract debate about constitutional principles concerning states' rights. The 1830 census listed four slaves residing in Providence. Two of these slaves were the "property" of Arnold, namely Mum Phebe and Mary, whom he had brought from White Hall.[16] Mary was especially needed the summer of 1830 in Providence because the first Mary Cornelia had been born in January at White Hall and thus was still a baby when the trip north was made. She was needed again in the summer of 1833 when the first Richard J. Arnold, Jr., who had been born on March 19, 1832, was ill. He died on June 12, 1833, soon after the family arrived back in Providence, which may have been the reason why the Arnolds decided to send Mary back earlier with the Clays. Instead of returning to Georgia, however, Mary took the opportunity to run away to freedom, and Eliza Harriet Allen writing to her brother suggested that the Negroes in Boston were hiding her.[17] For Arnold, the loss of property was more than the $275 per head he listed in his account book for his 139 slaves on July 29, 1834, because that figure was an average for all the slaves, young and old, and Mary was in her "prime."

Since the Providence Anti-Slavery Society was organized on June 7, 1833, the same day the Arnolds arrived back in Providence together with their slaves Mum Phebe and Mary, and its first public meeting was held on July 4, it is within the realm of possibility that Mary received the message "that no man can have a right of property in human creatures."[18] In 1835, however, the Providence Anti-Abolition Society addressed itself to the more general proposition that antislavery statements tended to incite the slaves to rebellion and at best tended to "exasperate their passions, to agitate their minds with fallacious hopes."[19] These resolutions were signed by the officers of the society, Richmond Bullock, president; James Fenner, vice-president; Walter R. Danforth and Amos D. Smith, secretaries. Richmond Bullock was a merchant with an office near Arnold's in the wharf area, and indeed they were partners in the Screw Dock Company in the port of Providence. Bullock's home was only a short distance up South Main Street from the Arnold residence, and the Commercial Bank, of which he was president and director, was located across the street from his house.

Of the thirty-six people who officiated at the organizational meeting of the Anti-Abolition Society in 1835, twenty-one were chosen vice-presidents; with so many vice-chiefs, one had to be first among equals.[20] Since he had been born into politics, James Fenner was chosen chief among the vice-presidents. Son of Governor Arthur Fenner (1790–1805), Fenner was U.S. senator from 1805 to 1807 and governor of the state from 1807 to 1811 and again from 1824 to 1831. Of an older generation than Richard Arnold, having been born in 1771, James Fenner was by 1835 an elder statesman with a reputation for possessing an "iron will" and an "inflexible resolution." Descendant of an old Rhode Island family prominent in state politics, he belonged to the network of business and professional men who were born in Providence and graduated from Brown, and who, whether they were merchants, lawyers, or manufacturers, were the ruling class, worshiping at the same temples of commerce six days a week and at the same churches on Sundays.[21]

The meeting of the Providence Anti-Abolition Society on November 2, 1835, was only the latest in a series of such meetings organized in the larger cities of the state and in New England, including one in Newport on September 14. Since Richard and Louisa Arnold had been in Newport for three days the week before, they undoubtedly discussed the upcoming meeting with friends. Arnold had only three weeks earlier valued his slaves at nearly $40,000, and therefore their value as property was fresh in his mind.[22]

Whereas the Providence organizers sought to take the high road in their resolutions through legalistic arguments about the Constitution and states' rights, the Newport resolutions were out-and-out racist in content despite disclaimers to the contrary that "we sincerely deplore the evils of slavery."[23]

Newport was openly prosouthern and proslavery in the 1830s, and unlike the Providence resolutions, those passed in Newport were requested and unanimously adopted by "the freemen of this town" at an official town meeting. The committee that drew up the resolutions included Benjamin Hazard, representative in the state legislature from Newport, who along with Virginia-born Richard Randolph, also of Newport, led the proslavery faction in the legislature to obtain adoption of these and other proslavery resolutions, including the so-called Southern Resolutions, which demanded a gag rule against Rhode Island abolitionists.[24] The Newport resolutions were directed against the abolitionists in general and the Providence Anti-Slavery Society in particular rather than the blacks of Rhode Island:

> The chief leaders and officers of their association [the Providence Anti-Slavery Society] have recently published "*a declaration of their principles and objects*," with smooth and plausible "*explanations and assurances*" of their innocence! They declare that they rely wholly upon facts and arguments, and *moral influences* for the attainment of their object [and not upon incitement to insurrection by the slaves against their masters] . . . [yet] those masters are constantly assailed with the foulest abuse, and denounced as robbers and murderers, and threatened with the vengeance of their slaves.[25]

The defense of abolition principles prepared and published by the Providence Anti-Slavery Society in 1835 actually consisted of two parts, the first part being a general statement of abolitionist principles and the second part being the "Declaration of the National Anti-Slavery Convention" held in Philadelphia, December 1833. Of the eight delegates to the national convention, two of the officers of the Providence Anti-Slavery Society attended, the Reverend Ray Potter and John Prentice, vice-president and treasurer; George W. Benson, the younger brother of Henry E. Benson, secretary, also attended. Such national figures as William Lloyd Garrison, Amos A. Phelps, Lewis Tappan, and John Greenleaf Whittier were also delegates, all signing the declaration which asserted among other things that "no man has a right to enslave or imbrute his brother—to hold or acknowledge him, for one moment, as a piece of merchandise—to keep back his hire by fraud—or to brutalize his mind by denying him the means of intellectual, social and moral improvement." Furthermore, "no compensation should be given to the planters emancipating their slaves" because "man cannot hold property in man" and because "SLAVERY IS A CRIME, AND THEREFORE IT IS NOT AN ARTICLE TO BE SOLD."[26]

The general statement of abolitionist principles subscribed to and published by the Providence Anti-Slavery Society combined an attack on racial prejudice against free blacks with an attack on the American Colonization Society for fostering the idea that blacks were an inferior race undeserving of democratic freedoms in America and better off if sent back to Africa. Instead, the Providence society called for the immediate abolition of slavery *as a first step* toward "the improvement of our enslaved population." They agreed that "it will require years of well devised and perservering effort to extirpate the evil consequences of the slave system," but those evil consequences of slavery should not be used as an excuse to say that slaves therefore should not be emancipated. On this point early abolitionists like Lewis Tappan became ambivalent, adhering to a concept that came to be known as "gradual immediation," a position that the Providence Anti-Slavery Society held in 1835:

> If it be true, that the mass of our enslaved population do not possess the qualifications, which are demanded of our free people as the condition of citizenship, and may therefore be immediately admitted to the exercise of all the prerogatives of freemen, this surely is no reason why they should be held one moment as *property*, and treated as if they were brutes. Nor is the ignorance and degradation of the mass of them a valid excuse for withholding from those of them who do possess intelligence and moral worth, any of the privileges which are accorded to other men, who possess the same intelligence and moral worth.[27]

William Lloyd Garrison disagreed with the gradualist concept of postemancipation, second-class citizenship for the large majority of former slaves. As early as January 1, 1831, in the first issue of *The Liberator*, he declared, "I shall strenuously contend for the immediate enfranchisement of our slave population," recanting a previously held view favoring gradual abolition. Garrison's position was simple and direct—immediate and unqualified emancipation for the slaves—and it eventually prevailed in the American Anti-Slavery Society as Garrison gained control of the organization.

The 1836 Constitution of the Rhode Island State Anti-Slavery Convention significantly left out any reference to qualifications "as the condition of citizenship" for the emancipated slaves and instead loftily and abstractly spoke of the need "to raise them to a rank befitting rational, accountable and immortal beings."[28] While this statement stopped short of calling for Garrisonian "immediate immediation," it was a long step away from the patronizing attitude of the 1835 statement of the Providence Anti-Slavery Society. The presence of Garrison himself as a delegate and the fact that he addressed the convention may have had an effect on the delegates. Furthermore, his brother-in-law, George W. Benson (whose brother Henry was an officer of the Providence society), was very active in the organization of the convention, chairing the nominating committee. But more important, the existence of antiabolition societies in the state and their attempts to organize opposition to the antislavery movement in Rhode Island tended to polarize and radicalize the abolitionists. They had to avoid voicing reservations concerning the right of slaves to citizenship and thus unwittingly offer ammunition to the antiabolitionists. Therefore, one of the main documents of the convention, "Declaration and Expose," attacked the institution of slavery as a moral evil, the American Colonization Society as a fraud, and the antiabolition meetings as inspired and sustained by "the Aristocratic classes."[29]

In less than the five years since "the Aristocracy" had reported on the evils of mob rule during the 1831 race riot in Providence, it was, itself, as a class being accused of "*exciting* mobs" against abolitionists in New York and Massachusetts and of attempting to deny abolitionists the rights of assembly and free speech in these states as well as in Rhode Island. In this context the declaration asserted that "we hold that emancipation should be immediate, unconditional, and universal." Garrison's position had been accepted totally by the convention.[30]

2

Eliza Harriet Allen wrote to her brother two weeks after the antislavery convention:

> There has been an anti-slavery meeting here but every thing was so quiet that no one except those at the meeting knew any thing about it   no mobs & no notice taken of the good people who chose to congregate and all that *we* know about it is from the newspapers of *other* states—our own merely mentioned the meeting—Garrison was here but went out of town every night—I suppose fearing a mob—very few knew he was here until it was over—They collected a good many names amongst others a great many students & afterwards headed the paper "we citizens of R I"—when not *one* of the fifty or sixty students who subscribed were of this state—[31]

It would be misleading to suggest that Providence, or even Boston, was an armed camp of Christian soldiers ready to march against the forces of evil. If anything, the abolitionists did battle among themselves, dividing into various factions, depending on whether members believed in gradual or instant immediacy, integration or segregation, moral persuasion or political activism.

There were even heated discussions in various antislavery societies whether blacks should be admitted to membership for fear of alienating some white supporters of the movement! The most radical group of abolitionists, and the one most feared by the southern planters, was the Garrisonians, who believed in full and complete emancipation and integration of the slaves. In a coup, Garrison gained control of the American Anti-Slavery Society in 1840 by packing the convention with pro-Garrison delegates, defeating the proponents of gradual immediacy, who were the followers of the Tappan brothers, the founders of the society. Yet Garrison was not radical enough for former slave Frederick Douglass, who eventually broke with him on the issue of political action, believing that persuasion alone was inadequate. The abolitionists were united in their opposition to the colonization movement. The American Colonization Society was largely discredited in the North by the 1840s, due primarily to the efforts of the American Anti-Slavery Society and various state societies in labeling it as being proslavery in the South. Yet colonization continued to appeal to some northern whites who supported the idea of a Christian colony as an easy solution to the race problem, for it offered a religious justification in solving a social issue by means of total and physical segregation of the races. Even Harriet Beecher Stowe seemed to endorse the idea of colonization at the end of *Uncle Tom's Cabin*. But the Rhode Island Anti-Slavery Convention of 1836 denounced the colonization scheme in no uncertain terms, seeing it as an "excuse for laws forbidding the emancipation of slaves, except on condition of their removal" from the United States and as falsely portraying free blacks "as a degraded class, whom it was desirable to remove from among us, while, with singular inconsistency, their Colonization on the coast of Africa, was to Christianize a heathen continent!"[32]

Politically, the antislavery movement in Rhode Island was ineffectual. A resolution calling for the abolition of slavery and the slave trade in the District of Columbia was overwhelmingly defeated in the state legislature in 1836. Rhode Island politics at the time was dominated by the Whig party, and the Whig party was dominated by conservative Yankees, native-born whites of Anglo-Saxon ancestry like the Allens and the Arnolds who were men of property in commercial or industrial enterprises. Indeed, the textile manufacturers of New England came to be known as the Cotton Whigs, natural political allies of the southern planters at the other end of the Cotton Kingdom (even wool manufacturers were their allies, since most wool cloth manufactured in Rhode Island was the coarse "kersey cloth" sometimes called Negro cloth because it was used to make clothes for the slaves).[33] At best the antislavers were able to maintain the status quo by fighting the pro-slavers in the state legislature to a standstill; no abolitionist resolution could get past the Newport prosouthern representatives, and because of the free-speech doctrine no anti-Garrison gag rule based on resolutions requested by southern slave states was passed. Because of malapportionment in the legislature, Newport had one-third *more* representatives in the assembly even though it had only about one-third of the population of Providence.

At about the same time that the antislavery movement was being formed in Rhode Island in the early 1830s, the movement for constitutional reform began to organize in earnest, and in 1834 the Constitutional party was formed. The two movements were separate and in the end diverged completely, but at the beginning they overlapped on one important issue—their opposition to disenfranchisement. Rhode Island's constitution at this time was still based on the royal charter of 1663, a document which though liberal in its day for emphasizing religious freedom was increasingly undemocratic in its property requirements and native-born qualifications for voting, which disenfranchised the ever-increasing immigrant Irish and French Canadian population working in the factories and mills. Furthermore, those blacks who did qualify were disenfranchised in 1822 by the passage of the law which limited the vote to *white*, native-born adult males who owned at least $134 of freehold property. As if this were not enough, no constitutional bill of rights existed in Rhode Island as in other states, where constitutions had been adopted after the American Revolution and had been modeled on the national document.

Constitutional reform and political leadership in the antislavery movement coalesced in the person of Thomas Wilson Dorr. Dorr was from an old Rhode Island family. Although his father, Sullivan Dorr, was a self-made man who acquired a fortune in shipping and manufacturing, his mother was an Allen, and thus the Allen brothers, Philip, Crawford, and Zachariah, prominent men in political and business circles of Providence and Rhode Island, were his uncles, and Richard Arnold was his uncle by marriage. He was educated at Phillips-Exeter Academy and Harvard (1823), graduating with high honors. He studied law under James Kent in New York and clerked in the Providence office of the conservative lawyer John Whipple, one of the members of the blue-ribbon committee to investigate the facts of the 1831 riot. He seemed destined for an establishment career in law and politics, and indeed when he was first elected to the state legislature in 1834, he seemed more interested in banking reform than the slavery issue or universal suffrage. But there was something of his grandfather Ebenezer Dorr in his makeup (Ebenezer Dorr had been with Paul Revere on that famous ride). Thomas became a rebel against his own social and economic class, working toward political equality with the radical labor leader Seth Luther.

Stymied by the realities of Rhode Island politics in his effort to obtain passage of antislavery resolutions in the state legislature, Dorr concentrated instead on the issue of universal manhood suffrage. In 1840 the Rhode Island Suffrage Association, composed mainly of disenfranchised mechanics and laborers from Providence, was organized, dedicating itself to obtaining the extension of suffrage to all *white* male adults. As a result of the association's agitation for reform, the general assembly agreed to call a constitutional convention for November 1841. But since the official call made no mention of suffrage extension and delegates were to be chosen under the old qualifications, the association decided to hold its own constitutional convention, a "People's Convention." Thus two rival conventions were held in the fall of 1841. Dorr had actually been elected to both of them, but it was the People's Convention, held in October, that he attended. This convention easily agreed to the extension of suffrage to all adult white male citizens after a year's residence in the state and to equalized apportionment of legislative seats so that the northern industrial towns of the state would be better represented. The only issue which split the convention was whether blacks would also be given the vote. The motion to strike the word white from the description of who was qualified to vote was defeated overwhelmingly by a vote of eighteen to forty-six, despite the efforts of Thomas Dorr and Benjamin Arnold (no relation to Richard Arnold) to persuade the convention to accept universal adult male suffrage. This vote split the movement, and Rhode Island blacks withdrew their support. Garrison denounced it, and Douglass actively campaigned against it. Dorr accepted the vote as the will of the convention and became the declared gubernatorial candidate of the People's party under the new constitution.[34]

In February 1842 the Law and Order party, a temporary coalition of conservative Whigs and Democrats led by former governors Fenner, Francis, and Gibbs and by merchants such as Carrington, Brown, and Ives, reconvened the Landholders' Convention, as it came to be known. The conservative delegates, as Marvin Gettleman suggests in *The Dorr Rebellion*, calculated "the minimum amount of reform that would calm the discontents and still leave political power in the hands of those manufacturing and landed interests who traditionally rule the state."[35] The Landholders' constitution kept the white, native-born voting qualifications and retained the malapportionment of legislative seats favorable to the rural southern part of the state.

Although the People's constitution was approved by a large majority of Rhode Island citizens (the Law and Order party boycotted the election) and the Landholders' constitution was narrowly defeated (the Dorrites voted against it), the main constitutional issue by March 1842 had shifted from suffrage to the question of where the locus of ultimate sovereignty was to be found in the community. Did it reside in the people, as the Dorrites contended, or in the authority of the existing government, whereby any new constitutional convention would require prior sanction from the old government, as the Law and Order party contended?[36] Early in March, three judges of the Rhode Island Supreme Court offered the view ex cathedra that the People's constitution was a mere expression of public opinion and had no "binding force" in law. They went further to state that any attempt to put it into effect would be treason against the state.

The stage was set for a conflict between the two factions; the rupture was inevitable, since early in April, shortly before the Dorrites held an election, the general assembly had enacted a law providing for heavy fines and imprisonment for "anyone presuming to run for unauthorized office . . . and those who actually dared to exercise such office were deemed guilty of treason and could be jailed for life."[37] Dorr was declared the "People's Governor," and he and those elected with him set up a rival government in violation of the law passed by the old regime, or charter government as it was called. The Dorrites did not wait for the charter government to act. On May 17 they seized the old Revolutionary War cannons on display at the mall in the center of Providence and decided to march on the state arsenal on the west side of the river. The charter governor, Samuel Ward King, a former physician and bank official who had been elected as a Whig in 1840 under the old charter, immediately called on the citizens of Providence to take up arms and defend the arsenal. Rhode Island was on the verge of a civil war to be fought over broad constitutional issues.

Richard Arnold and his family were still in Georgia on May 17, not leaving for the North until later that month. For the first time since 1837 weather conditions were favorable for an early blooming of cotton, and Arnold preferred to remain in the South. On the same day that Dorr attempted to seize the arsenal—his father, his younger brother, his brother-in-law Samuel Ames, and his uncle Zachariah Allen, all inside the arsenal, defending it against him—the cotton bloomed at White Hall. Dorr's assault on the arsenal failed, and he had to flee the state. The establishment, however, took care of its own, no matter how rebellious. Just as family and influential friends rallied around the Arnolds when their son became a Union prisoner of war during the Civil War twenty-two years later, so family rescued Dorr when he was about to be arrested for his "act of insurrection." According to Zachariah Allen, Governor King and members of his council "were ready to get rid of him [Dorr] without any further struggle, on Napoleon's maxim, 'make a bridge of gold for a retreating enemy' "; his uncle Crawford Allen thereupon provided Dorr with his own carriage for the retreat.[38]

Leaders of lost causes are sometimes lured back to the scene of their defeat, and Dorr returned to Rhode Island the following month, still hoping to establish his own government by force, since he considered himself the legitimate governor of the state. This time the members of the establishment showed him no mercy and took no chances. On June 25 they declared martial law and sent 2,500 troops of the state militia after him, holding the militia of Connecticut and Massachusetts and federal troops stationed at Newport in reserve. They sent all the gold and silver from the banks to Boston and New York, just in case, and on second thought, sent their families also. All business was suspended, so "the undivided attention of the population was devoted to arms."[39] Dr. Francis Wayland, president of Brown University and a Baptist minister, was appointed chaplain of the Providence regiment, and Richard J. Arnold (who held the rank of colonel in the state militia) was appointed assistant commissary general to feed the army poised on June 27 to advance on Dorr's army of rebels assembled at Chepachet, seventeen miles from Providence.[40]

If an army travels on its stomach, seventeen miles is a long way to go empty. Arnold ordered 600 pounds of beef and ham, 9 barrels of hard bread, 3 barrels of soft bread, 100 pounds of smoked beef, 1 demijohn of vinegar, ½ dozen mustard, 19¼ pounds of tobacco, 12 pails, and 12 dippers to feed the army.[41] Among the many men who assisted the assistant commissary general was Tristam Burges, Jr., Arnold's nephew, who was taken on at the behest of his father: "In the day time we feel safe & he might come into the city & assist in the commissary department & come out at night. In this way he may aid the cause of R. Island more efficiently than if he marched out with the troops in pursuit of Dorr & his traitors; & at the same time he would not neglect the perils of his family at home."[42] Arnold sent young Tristam to Woonsocket, in the middle of Dorrite territory, to be commissary to the troops stationed there.

Finally, so as to leave no door unopened, Dorr's father and some of his friends were sent to Chepachet "to induce him to desist from further hopeless resistance. Their representations, and the more powerful argument of an overwhelming array of martial force, convinced him of his rashness."[43] Dorr again fled the state and all armed resistance ceased.

Although the war ended in a decisive and humiliating military defeat for Dorr and his followers, the cause of political reform advocated by the Dorrites was not entirely lost in the end. The new state constitution adopted in November 1842, to take effect the following year, incorporated some of the specific reforms in modified form, such as reapportionment of the House of Representatives, the inclusion of a bill of rights, and provision for an independent judiciary; but on suffrage the conservatives were less liberal, adopting a $134 freehold qualification for naturalized citizens, whereas native American citizens qualified on payment of $1 either of property or poll tax. Ironically, on one aspect of suffrage the new constitution was more liberal than the People's constitution—in recognition of the active support by Providence's black community during the June crisis, 200 men having volunteered to join the Home Guard, the adjective "white" was deleted from the definition of elector. Furthermore, slavery was specifically prohibited in the state. Since most of the blacks in Rhode Island were native-born, they were re-enfranchised. A newly instituted poll tax of $1 would discourage the "undesirable" poor, black and white. Dorr's archrival in politics and antiabolitionist James Fenner was elected governor under the new constitution as the candidate of the Law and Order party.

Although the Dorr War was over by June 28, the charter government continued to enforce martial law until August 8, when Governor King suspended it. More than three hundred arrests were made during this period as various Dorrites were rounded up by the militia.[44] Arnold continued as assistant commissary general, but his main duty consisted in paying bills, closing the books, and returning unexpended funds to the state treasury.[45] The political and military situation in Rhode Island had so calmed down by the end of August that Arnold could turn his full attention to the financial status of an institution entirely different from the state militia, Brown University.

The Brown University Corporation appointed a committee from among the trustees at its annual meeting in 1842, consisting of Richard Arnold, John Carter Brown, and Thomas Burgess, chairman, "to consider the subject of the salaries of the officers of the Institution—including the Librarian and Steward."[46] As behooved a committee consisting of two businessmen and a lawyer, they decided first to find out what exactly the faculty members did for the salaries they were paid before considering what to do about their salaries. Even Dr. Francis Wayland, president of the university, was queried on his duties, for he held the position of professor of moral and intellectual philosophy, for which dual duties he was paid $1,500 annually, the rent of the president's house, and the use of the college lands to grow vegetables and pasture his cow. Of the regular faculty (there were only four at the time), each received $1,000 annually except that Alexis Caswell, professor of mathematics and natural philosophy, was paid $1,100, presumably in recognition of the fact that he was senior professor and had acted as president pro tempore in 1840–1841 during Wayland's sabbatical leave.[47] In comparison, Arnold at about this time (for the year 1844) paid his overseer in Georgia, J. B. Gross, $800 annually, the rent of a house, the use of two cows and three slaves. On the other hand, George Chace, professor of chemistry, was expected to teach *all* of the physical sciences and did not have the use of cow or slave. Nonetheless, it was a shock to the committee members to learn that professors were occupied "in the immediate duties" of their professorships for as little as five hours a day and that they were responsible for only one lecture and one recitation a day for a total of eleven for the week. Therefore, their recommendation to the Brown University Corporation was that the work loads, not the salaries, be increased, namely, that except for the president, the professors be required to attend "two recitations each day, or perform a duty equivalent to it together with the necessary lectures."[48] Richard Arnold could return to his plantation in Georgia that fall satisfied that he had done his part in saving the citizens of Rhode Island from overzealous democrats and Brown University students from overpaid professors.

The apparent peace and quiet of the groves of academe were shattered late in the summer of 1848 when three of the senior professors officially complained to the Corporation "that they could not support their families on their salaries, the cost of living having increased twelve or fifteen per cent in recent years; that other professional salaried men in the city got from fifty to a hundred per cent more than they did; and that while their salaries had remained the same, their work had been increased by the reduction of the teaching staff, so that they now had three or four recitations instead of two." This action by the professors was the mid-nineteenth-century equivalent of a mid-nineteen-eighties threat of a teacher's strike, using much the same arguments and about as effective. Only the resignation of President Wayland on September 2, 1849, the day after commencement, galvanized the Corporation into appointing a new committee on salaries. One of the first acts of this new committee was to recommend that Wayland's salary be increased to $1,600, Professor Caswell's to $1,250, and the rest to $1,200, not exactly what other professional salaried men in the city were getting nor as much as comparable senior professors earned at Harvard (up to $2,000) but more than professors were paid at Amherst College and even at Yale University.[49]

President Wayland withdrew his resignation and continued as president until his retirement in 1855. In the 1840s he was at the height of his reputation as a moral philosopher, and in March 1845, both as a Baptist minister and as a moral philosopher, he engaged in an epistolary debate with the Reverend Dr. Richard Fuller of Beaufort, South Carolina, also a Baptist minister. These letters were published in book form that same year and constituted a restatement of traditional proslavery and antislavery positions held by Christian clergymen, North and South, rather than new ideas or fresh approaches.

From the beginning of the debate, Wayland made it clear that he belonged to no political party and no abolition society, and therefore, he had no secular ax to grind. His opposition to slavery was on moral and religious grounds:

> Slavery is, from the very nature of the case, essentially a moral evil—. . . a violation of the rights of man, and a transgression of that law under which all human beings are created. "Thou shalt love thy neighbor as thyself," and . . . the moral character of the relation is the same, whether the master be the captor or the purchaser of the slave; whether his power be upheld by his own individual prowess, or by the combined authority of society.[50]

For these reasons he favored the abolition of slavery, but he made a distinction as to the *degree* of moral guilt among slaveholders. If the slaveholder teaches his slaves "self-reliance and profitable industry," if he cultivates their intellects and improves their morals," and if he emancipates them "as soon as he is able," then Wayland concludes, the slaveholder "seems to me innocent of the guilt of slavery." Such gradualism harked back to the old paternalism of the defunct Providence Abolition Society formed by Moses Brown. It was a lofty moral position that the Garrisonians considered anathema, and a solution, if it ever was one, soon overtaken by events. Yet Wayland persisted in his praise of the paternalistic, benevolent slaveholder:

> I have known Christian slaveholders who have devoted themselves through life to the welfare, temporal and spiritual, of their slaves, with the spirit of the most self-denying missionaries; and who, I confidently believe, if they could do it with a reasonable prospect of improving the condition of their slaves, would gladly manumit them and support themselves by daily labor at the North.[51]

Certainly the Reverend Dr. Richard Fuller saw himself as a Christian slaveholder: "With reference to my own servants, their condition is as good as I can make it." There follows a litany of all that he provides his slaves—clothes, provisions, fuel, home, land to plant for themselves, a missionary to teach their children, medical attention, profits of labor completed on their own time, protection of them as a guardian, and administration to their wants—even though they "perform not one half the work done by free laborers." In short he provides everything but their freedom. Nor did he feel guilty of any sin or crime, since slavery is not "a moral evil and a great crime in the sight of God" because it is an institution handed down by previous generations: and if "there is no sin . . . in being the heir or legatee of this power [slaveholding], then the use of it, may be most virtuous."[52] Richard Arnold would not have quarreled with either man's position on the humane slave owner who had inherited his slaves, for that was exactly his image of himself.

Even so mild-mannered a disagreement between President Wayland and the Reverend Dr. Fuller over the slavery issue could not cover over the fundamental division within the Baptist church on slavery. Despite efforts by President Wayland—president of the Baptist General Convention as well as president of Brown University—the Triennial Convention, which was due to be held in Providence late in 1845, was dissolved, and the Baptists split between North and South over the issue of appointing a foreign missionary who was also a slaveholder. President Wayland had sent a message to the Southern Baptist Convention, which convened in Augusta, Georgia, on May 8, 1845: "Your rights have been infringed. . . . We [of the North] have shown how Christians *ought not* to act. It remains for you to show us how they *ought* to act."[53] The message back from Georgia was that the Southern Baptist Convention had formed a new missionary organization with the same name and with power to appoint missionaries whether they were slaveholders or not.

A copy of *Domestic Slavery* (listed as *Fuller & Wayland on Slavery* in the inventory) was kept in Arnold's library at his Providence residence. There was little in President Wayland's concluding remarks with which Arnold dissented: "We [Fuller and Wayland] both affirm that to hold slaves is not of necessity a guilt, and under peculiar circumstances it may not be wrong."[54] Commencement Day at Brown University, which in those days fell on September 1, was no occasion for embarrassment for either President Wayland or Trustee Arnold. They had known each other in their respective roles for twenty years. If the subject of slavery ever came up between them, Richard Arnold needed only to remind Francis Wayland of his peroration to Richard Fuller: "If we have been enabled without bitterness to express our views to each other on a subject which is so liable to arouse the worst passions of our fallen nature, let us ascribe it all to that love of God shed abroad in our hearts, which teaches us to treat as a brother every disciple of our common Lord, though he may embrace opinions in many respects differing from our own."[55]

3

When Arnold and his family arrived back in Providence on April 28, 1848, it was to a relatively peaceful, politically stable and, on the surface at least, socially calm city, so different from his arrival six years earlier in the middle of a civil war. True, at the beginning of February the general assembly had passed a law forbidding state officers to enforce the Fugitive Slave Law of 1793, but the local scene itself was placid, the antislavery movement within the state all but dead, and the business establishment more concerned with the tariff on cotton goods than the economic and social well-being of blacks, free or enslaved.

The Arnolds had been making their transition from one way of life in the South to another in the North for a quarter of a century, so by 1848 there was little adjustment necessary for the family. Arnold entered easily into his second life, that of Rhode Island citizen, prominent businessman, civic and social leader, descendant of two leading Rhode Island families, the Arnolds and the Greenes—in short, a "gentlemen of property and standing," in the phrase of the day. There would be no problem of change for him from one life as a southern planter and slave owner to the other as a New England man of wealth and property, since he and his family, his wife a southerner who had grown up in the North, were readily accepted socially in both worlds. It was national events and political and social forces beyond his control that ultimately forced Arnold to choose between the two worlds.

Yet what was Richard Arnold's life in Rhode Island six months of the year, and was it so similar to being a southern man of property the other six months? It was one thing to be *master* in Georgia: he could ride all day making the rounds of his plantation lands, inspecting the work being done, the physical plant, the crops, the fences, the cattle, the horses, the mules, the carriages, the plows, the slaves—*all* his property, owned and managed by him. The barrels of rice and the bales of cotton were the real and tangible products of his southern enterprise. One of the last acts he performed before leaving Savannah on April 21 was to pay Aaron Champion $123.95 for groceries purchased for family use during the past winter; one of his first acts after arriving in Providence was to pay at market $5.25 for family provisions. It was an act of continuity so commonplace as to suggest the continuity of life itself, and yet there was all the world of difference between paying $5.25 at market in the city of Providence and paying $5.00 two weeks before to his slave Harriet for her pigs on the plantation, as different as paying $2.35 for shoes in Charleston for his sons and paying $153.47 for shoes for his two hundred slaves left behind in Georgia.[56]

White Hall, the mansion house in Georgia, was closed down, and the master and his family returned to Sabin Tavern, the mansion house in Providence. The Providence house had been rented furnished for the winter months for $500, collected by Zachariah Allen, who acted as Arnold's agent and trustee for his northern property. Arnold owned a store and other commercial buildings in Providence, but he did not go to work at the store or even check the accounts. Allen, as trustee, collected the rents and paid the taxes and insurance on the buildings and saw to the repairs, if needed, while Arnold was in Georgia. Allen had, for example, overseen the work of the firm of Andrews and Palmer, which had built a new cistern the previous fall, had repaired the range, and had completed other small tasks at the mansion house in Providence after the Arnolds had left for Georgia earlier than usual in 1847, sailing from New York on October 29. Allen paid the firm's bill of $139.72, and on May 27, 1848, Arnold duly recorded the amount in his account books as a debit to his account with Z. Allen, "Trustee."[57]

In the past Arnold had listed himself in the Providence city directory as a merchant with offices on the waterfront, but that was in the days when he was still active in the shipping business, having inherited ships from his father and brother. As a merchant he viewed a ship, though real enough, as a means to an end rather than as a career, making a profit from trade. Besides, his ship the *Louisa*, home port Savannah, had sailed the Caribbean until it was confiscated by the Mexicans during the war, for which loss Arnold was compensated in October 1848 by the American government in the settlement of his claim on Mexico.[58]

Arnold had inherited a farm, just outside Providence, but instead of living on it or working it himself, he rented the land to tenants until he sold it in 1841. In short he was a businessman while residing in the North, but he had no place to go where he was "master," giving orders and receiving reports, no work force to manage, no overseer to direct. He was an investor, not a manufacturer like Zachariah Allen, and as such his life in the North was without the usual visible signs of industriousness, of a factory or an office with his name on the door. Yet, in temperament he was more like Zachariah Allen than George Noble Jones, absentee planter; he needed to be busy all the time—doing, planning, accounting. The Protestant work ethic was strong in him, and the need to be constantly active in business may explain the extent and diversity of his investments in the North as well as in the South.

In the North as in the South, Arnold invested heavily in real estate. With the breakup of the family shipping business after the death of his brother, Samuel, in 1826, Arnold expanded his holdings in warehouse and wharf property along the Providence River near his residence on South Main Street. There was, however, an essential difference between his acquisition of new land in Georgia and in Rhode Island. His land acquisitions in Georgia tended to be large expanses in the immediate plantation area, such as the recently purchased Sedgefield Plantation, consisting of 240 acres of rice land and 1,200 acres of pine woods. Those in Rhode Island tended to be small lots of commercial or residential property in the city of Providence, although he occasionally bought rural lots in outlying sections adjacent to the city in the expectation that they would eventually be developed into suburban housing. Thus, for example, on June 1, 1848, he paid $2.50 in taxes on his lots in Cranston, to the south of Providence, in which direction the city was expanding. Since the tax rate was only $0.25 per $100.00 and the land only valued at $1,000.00, he could afford to wait for his property to appreciate in value.[59]

Closer to home and more directly related to his northern business enterprises was the lot on the Providence River which he purchased on June 5, 1848, for $1,600.00; it was a small but valuable piece of commercial property, doubly valuable to him because it adjoined the stone store he had inherited more than twenty years earlier. It was one-fifth of the price he had paid for more than 1,500 acres of land in Bryan County, Georgia, just two months previously, but it was worth it to him, and he paid the first installment of $800.00 in cash, thus saving himself $4.40 interest charges on a thirty-day note.[60]

It is apparent from Arnold's business records that once he was back in Providence he took over full responsiblity from Zachariah Allen for keeping the accounts, settling with him any outstanding bills and receiving credit for any dividends that had accrued during his absence, as for example, the $130.00 dividend on stock belonging to Mrs. Arnold from the National Bank, which more or less equaled the bill owed to the firm of Andrews and Palmer that had been paid by Allen. Money came at regular intervals, payments of dividends and rents, not large amounts as in Georgia after the harvest, but steadily—a $280.00 semiannual bank stock dividend; $144.00 in stock dividends from the Providence and Pawcatuck Turnpike; even a $10.00 stock dividend from pews owned in the First Baptist Meeting House and $9.00 from stock in the Broad Street Hotel; $108.66 from stock in the new

Swan Point Cemetery; $31.25 in quarterly rent of a North Providence store; $100.00 in rent from the house he had inherited from his uncle Jonathan Arnold.

As he did in Georgia, he kept strict, personal records of family expenses; there was no separate housekeeping account into which he might contribute a regular, if parsimonious, allowance. Every disbursement of money, no matter how small, was duly paid and recorded, and although he himself might not always have personally handed over the hard cash to its ultimate recipient, there was never any doubt from whose pocket it came. For example, on May 10, 1848, he disbursed $24.25: $3.00 to Mr. McCullen for three days' work done in the garden; $3.50 at market that day and the day before; $1.50 presented to his children and $6.25 to his wife for her own use; and finally, a $10.00 charitable contribution to the Reverend Mr. Hall for the Seaman's Bethel. Two days later he debited "Family Expenses" $7.50, paid to the family's colored cook. There were the usual day-to-day expenses, although $229.65 paid George W. Gladding and Company on May 24 for dry goods purchased during the previous year for family use was not exactly a small amount to pay out at once. More typical of such expenditures was the $5.25 paid the same day for leather to cover the library chair.[61]

A regular expense at this time was the education of his eldest son, Richard, and on May 22 Richard Senior paid Matthew Meigs, principal of the academy at Newark, Delaware, $70.00 for board and tuition during the term ending September 21, and handed Richard Junior $5.00 pocket money. So that his son might be in style, he was outfitted with shoes, hat, and umbrella for $6.50. More unusual, for Richard Senior did not usually indulge himself, was the $150.00 he paid that same day to have his portrait painted by G. P. A. Healy and $23.25 a few days later to have it framed. It is unclear whether he liked what he saw, for he paid another painter, Charles C. Ingham, $100.00 on account to begin a portrait of Mrs. Arnold.

Louisa Arnold provided a capsule critique of the two portraits when she wrote her husband on August 13 from New York: "I think he [Ingham] will try to have a fine picture   I told him you had just had yours done by Healy   he says H. paints very fine portraits but he does not like that course [sic] style as a Portrait ought not to be hung high." The "fineness" of Louisa's portrait was achieved by several sittings for the head with "the rest" being completed after she left: "He now says he will take my figure and borrow a velvet dress to paint from but that it must be *velvet*." Louisa took time while in New York to visit Greenwood Cemetery and was "fully rewarded for it is without exception the most beautiful spot I ever visited." Reality, however, is in the figure of "poor Buckley," a White Hall visitor, who "had been very sick and had not been out for a long time before   I really pity him   he says he had not been outside of the city since he left Whitehall."[62] Reality is also coping with servant problems upon returning to Providence:

> Elisa told me this morning that Mrs Duncan would give her 2 dollars for doing chamber work and that she was coming to see me about her. I told her I knew she would be required to sew or to wash and iron but she thinks it is merely for chamber work. I do not know how it will end   I told her I was not willing to give more than I do   I liked her and would like to keep her but she seems to think it too little   her work is very light and is not worth more.[63]

Louisa was not unused to paying wages to servants; obviously, she knew the going rate for chamber work by white servants in the North. But "they" were not grateful like black servants in Savannah, to whom Richard Arnold gave $3.50 on April 21, the day they had sailed for Providence.

The buying and selling of real estate occupied whatever time, energy, and resources Arnold devoted to business matters in the North, for it involved considerable planning and commitment of money as well as balancing assets against the opportunity to make a profit. For example, on July 19, 1848, he committed himself to purchasing two lots in a planned housing development in the northeastern part of Providence for $1,717.00. The following week he sold five lots of land in the commercial area on the Providence River to the Providence Gas Company for $4,200.00. Similarly, on September 26, he purchased thirty-seven house lots in Providence at auction for $3,650.00. To finance this and other real-estate transactions he renewed his note for $10,000.00 at the Providence Institution for Savings for another year, paying $600.00 interest on September 30. On the same day he recorded a net credit of $326.23 from his "adventure" in lands on or near the Maumee River, Ohio, and in New York City. All told, the assessed value of his property in Providence as of October 2, 1848, was $39,700.00, for which he paid $173.29 in taxes.[64]

It was not a huge estate, but it was certainly respectable and gave him high social standing among the men of property in Providence. His wealth was large enough to require a certain style of life while he was in residence in Providence—servants, carriages and horses, tutors for his sons' education, shopping trips to Boston and New York, and vacations at fashionable watering spas like Saratoga Springs and Newport. Arnold's style of life was not as cosmopolitan and sophisticated as that indulged in by George Noble and Mary Nuttall Jones, but it was ostentatious enough to cause comment from his prospective son-in-law, Samuel Greene Arnold, who wrote to his mother in 1847 that Richard and Louisa Arnold "are too fond of display" and that his fiancée, their daughter, "takes the same view of the matter" and "sees this great defect in her parents and sets herself firmly against it."[65]

Richard Arnold, like Zachariah Allen, was active in many civic and cultural organizations. He was a founding member of the Providence Athenaeum and the Rhode Island Historical Society; and he supported the founding of Butler Hospital for the Insane, as did Allen, for both were paternalistic men of the nineteenth century. And if Allen involved himself in the landscaping of the Old North Burial Ground, Arnold concerned himself with the development of the newly opened Swan Point Cemetery, both exhibiting a normal Victorian interest in cemeteries as parks rather than as morbid subjects for abnormal interest. There were meetings to attend, including the meetings of the board of trustees of Brown University and the annual commencement exercises held on September 1. There was a tutor to hire, and Arnold hired the best, Silas Axtell Crane, an older man of experience (class of 1823), Phi Beta Kappa like himself but an Episcopal clergyman, rather than a Baptist, who had received his master's degree at Middlebury College in 1832 and served as president of Kemper College from 1837 to 1839. While the oldest son, Richard, Jr., was sent to Mathew Meig's School in Delaware, the two younger sons, Thomas and William Eliot, were enrolled in Silas Crane's school closer to home for the summer term. They later joined Richard, Jr., for the winter term when the family journeyed south in late November, first dropping off daughter Mary Cornelia at Miss Haines's School in New York.

The Arnolds no longer brought "servants" with them to Providence from the plantation. Mum Phebe was the last one—she was included in the 1840 census as one of the five remaining slaves residing in Rhode Island, thus distorting the figures—but she died in 1841. There was some discussion about whether Louisa Arnold would bring her slave Fanny as a cook for the summer of 1842, but the 1842 Rhode Island Constitution prohibited slavery in Rhode Island, presumably ending the practice of bringing in slaves as servants.[66] Furthermore, the political turmoil in Rhode Island during the Dorr War and the changed political atmosphere over the issue of admitting Texas as a slave state made it the better part of discretion to hire Irish servants or local blacks as cooks and handymen.

Whereas in Georgia the Arnolds were part of a small circle of friends and neighbors, slaveholding planters who were like-minded in their defense of slavery and their attitudes toward blacks, in Rhode Island they were members of a wide circle of family and friends of differing views on the slavery issue. The family as a whole accepted that Richard Arnold owned "property" in the South which required his attention six months out of the year. True, their nephew by marriage, Thomas Wilson Dorr, was against slavery, but he could be dismissed as an eccentric maverick, and besides he was no longer a factor in Rhode Island politics. His views were more than balanced by the staunch loyalty of Eliza Harriet and Zachariah Allen. True also, it could have been embarrassing when his niece Mary Allen announced in March 1843 that she was engaged to Andrew Robeson, Jr. Robeson was the son of an abolitionist and, what was worse from Arnold's point of view, a Garrisonian, Andrew Robeson, Sr., of New Bedford, a Quaker who had made his fortune in whaling, banking, and calico printing and contributed a share of Garrison's salary as editor of *The Liberator*. But any embarrassment was defused by the Arnolds' invitation to the newlyweds to stay with them at White Hall on their wedding trip to the South, an invitation which was readily accepted.[67] Since Mary Allen had come to White Hall in the winter of 1837–1838, soon after her mother's visit, and apparently had enjoyed it so much that she paid the Arnolds a return visit in the winter of 1838–1839, there was little risk of being rebuffed. The Allens, the Arnolds, and the Robesons remained on the best of terms throughout the antebellum period, whatever their individual beliefs on the slavery issue.

Eliza Harriet Allen summed up the family attitude, for she had nothing but fond memories of her stay at White Hall in the spring of 1837. Upon the Arnolds' return to Georgia that fall, she wrote, "I often think of you at the South and imagine you walking over the fields or seated in the dining or drawing room—or on the piazza talking to the negroes—and feel glad that I can see you at least in my minds eye occupied in your various duties."[68] The Allens accepted the image of Arnold as a humane master who had been forced into that role by circumstances, having married Louisa Caroline Gindrat, who herself had been forced to become a slave owner by reason of inheritance. Within these limitations, Arnold was viewed as a benevolent, kind Christian who treated his servants well and humanely and who was doing the Lord's work by Christianizing and civilizing the slaves on his plantations.

None of the Arnold daughters was destined to be a plantation mistress. Except for the youngest, Susan, who married a Savannah doctor after the war, they all married northerners, conservative men of business or professionals, rather than sons of southern planters as was often the custom among daughters of the planter class. None of the sons-in-law was an abolitionist.

Although the three older Arnold daughters were born at White Hall (only the youngest, Susan, was born in Providence), they all married in Rhode Island. The plantation was a place to visit; for example, William Brenton and Harriet Greene came south in February 1847 and again in December 1848, but it was not their way of life. They all made a life for themselves in New York or Rhode Island, accepting that their parents owned slaves in Georgia and that they had themselves been raised with the help of slaves at White Hall. The first two daughters had married their cousins—William Brenton Greene and Samuel Greene Arnold. It was not until the marriage of Mary Cornelia, the third daughter, that events overwhelmed the family and threatened to split them apart. Indeed, William Talbot had rushed down to Georgia after the outbreak of war to rescue his fiancée, and they were married in Newport on June 27, 1861. But in the summer of 1848, war was a remote campaign recently ended by a treaty with Mexico, and all that remained was to await the settlement of Arnold's claim for indemnity against Mexico for confiscating his ship *Louisa*. The big event that summer was the forthcoming marriage of their daughter Louisa to Samuel Greene Arnold.

Samuel and Louisa may have wanted a simple wedding without ostentatious display, but the father of the bride was paying the bills. A local architectural firm, Tallman and Bucklin, was hired that summer to renovate the mansion house in Providence from top to bottom, inside and out. There was one last shopping trip to New York in October before the wedding while the house was being painted. The wedding itself took place on November 23, and on the 26th the bride and groom stood on the dock in Providence waving goodbye to Richard and Louisa Arnold and the rest of the family who were sailing for New York. The newlyweds then returned to the newly refurbished mansion house to live until they joined the family later that winter at White Hall.

Although the summer and fall of 1848 were unusual for the Arnolds because of the renovation of the house and the wedding of their daughter Louisa, their social life in Rhode Island followed the same general pattern as in Georgia—visits to and from close friends and relatives. There would be almost daily visits between the Richard Arnold family and the Zachariah Allen family, especially the mothers and daughters, and between the twins Eliza Harriet Allen and Richard Arnold. Other members of the family circle, the Philip Allens and the Crawford Allens, were an integral part of the Arnolds' northern social life, for they all lived in Providence. Arnold's first cousins, the James Arnolds of New Bedford, however, were quite different from the conservative Cotton Whig Allens of Providence. James Arnold was a birthright Quaker, son of Thomas Arnold, Richard's uncle and, like his father, active in the antislavery movement. He married Sarah Rotch, the daughter of William Rotch, who was also active in the abolitionist movement; both the William Rotches and the James Arnolds supported the Underground Railroad in New Bedford. Eliza Harriet and Zachariah Allen remained on the best of terms with the James Arnolds—they had traveled together the previous summer to the "far west" of Wisconsin territory, coming back with tales of meeting a scalping party of Indians in the wilderness. But the James Arnolds and the Richard Arnolds stood at opposite poles of that divided world of North and South over the issue of slavery. They were a world apart in their perception of the fugitive slave as either a human being who had escaped to freedom or a piece of lost property that was recoverable under the 1793 Fugitive Slave Law and later under the 1850 Fugitive Slave Law; only a year separated Thomas Rotch's (Sarah Rotch Arnold's brother) rescue of a fugitive slave from a Virginia agent in Philadelphia in 1840 and Richard Arnold's letter in 1841 to Thomas Butler King informing him that Arnold's overseer had caught his runaway slave Larkin.

Among Arnold's close Providence friends was Robert Hale Ives. Like Arnold he too graduated from Brown University, Phi Beta Kappa (class of 1816); both made the grand tour of Europe, and both became trustees of the university in the same year, 1826. By the time he joined the family business, Brown and Ives, in 1826, the firm was divesting itself of shipping and investing capital in cotton manufacturing. These two friends, each at opposite ends of the Cotton Kingdom, were together at White Hall in April 1849, where Ives and his two daughters were guests of the Arnolds.

The Arnolds, however, did not need to go outside the extended family circle for their social life while living in Providence. The extended family circle encompassed the high society of Rhode Island in the antebellum period, for such were the interconnecting links of family and friends that to touch one life was to touch them all. Even the friendship with Robert Hale Ives, for example, was not without its connection to the family network, since Ives's older brother Moses had married Ann Dorr, Zachariah Allen's niece, and the Iveses were the epitome of the establishment family. Similarly, Candace Dorr, Ann's younger sister, married Edward Carrington, Jr., only child of Arnold's old friend and business associate. Thus too, years later in 1860, when Arnold's oldest son, Richard, Jr., married, it was to Minnie Clarke, daughter of John H. Clarke, an old family friend who had studied law under Tristam Burges, Arnold's brother-in-law, and who had served on the Resolutions Committee of the Providence Anti-Abolition Meeting in 1835. He began his full six-year term as United States senator from Rhode Island on March 4, 1847. As a manufacturer, he was naturally a conservative politician, a Cotton Whig who supported high tariffs but who nonetheless, under instructions from the Rhode Island legislature, opposed the Fugitive Slave Act of 1850.[69]

Living in Providence the Arnolds could not easily avoid or at least be aware of others who did not share their social and racial views. The Reverend Dr. Edward Brooks Hall, for example, who had visited White Hall in 1837, lived a few blocks away. Pastor of the First Congregational Church in Providence since 1832, and "nurtured in Abolition," as Eliza Harriet Allen had described him, he and Arnold were a world apart on the slavery issue. He was active in the peace movement, attending the World's Peace Convention at Frankfurt, Germany, in 1850, as well as in the antislavery movement. In 1841 he joined Arnold on the board of trustees of Brown University. Although they shared an interest in education, they were at opposite ends of the issue of whether to educate slaves beyond oral lessons in Sunday school. The reason that the Clays and the Arnolds had been so eager in the spring of 1837 to exhibit their "black scholars" was to show this northern abolitionist and clergyman that the slaves on their plantations were not denied a Christian education even though they were forbidden by law to learn how to read and write.[70]

It was no mere chance that the Reverend Dr. Hall was in Georgia in 1837; he had been advised by his doctor to go south for his health. The Clays undoubtedly knew him from earlier days, for he had been born in Medford, Massachusetts, where they too had lived and still maintained a summer residence. And if Louisa Gindrat did not know him from those days when she lived with the Clays in Medford, the Arnolds would have met him in Providence, even though they were not Congregationalists but Baptists in the North and Presbyterians in the South. Since the Halls and the Arnolds lived in the same Providence neighborhood, it would have been difficult for them to avoid each other, even if they had wished to do so. The safest ground for the Arnolds was to take an interest in the various charitable organizations and projects that engaged the Reverend Dr. Hall and his wife, such as the Seaman's Bethel in Providence, to which Arnold contributed $10 on May 10, 1848.

As members of the upper middle class, the Arnolds would have little occasion to meet socially the original organizers of the Providence Anti-Slavery Society, who belonged to the low middle or artisan class, but as the antislavery movement spread and the artisans and mechanics who were the backbone

of the movement gained social and financial status, it became more difficult
for the Arnolds to be unaware of their activities. For example, one of the
delegates from Providence to the convention of the Rhode Island Anti-Slavery Society in February 1836 was Nicholas Arnold Fenner (no relation to
Governor James Fenner). He was at the time a mechanic and draftsman,
forming a partnership in 1835 with his brother John to build machinery for
cotton mills. In the 1840s, he made his fortune manufacturing a new kind of
butt-hinge, expanding the business, the New England Butt Company, into
one of the largest in the country. He did not become directly involved in local
politics until after the Civil War, but his advocacy of abolition in the antebellum period was indicative of the widespread support the antislavery
movement received among artisans and mechanics in Rhode Island.

It would have been difficult for Arnold to avoid Amos Chafee Barstow,
Providence delegate to the Rhode Island Anti-Slavery Convention in 1836,
for he was involved in so many different activities. Anyone who needed an
iron stove, a furnace, or a range purchased it from the Barstow Stove Company or else from Amos Barstow's father-in-law, James Eames, who was also
an abolitionist. Anyone who went to Roger Williams Hall for a concert or
lecture or to the grander Music Hall sat in buildings built by Barstow and
Company. Barstow was also the president of the City Bank and the founder
of the Mechanics' Savings Bank. Amos Barstow was in the center of the
temperance movement, which the Arnolds supported, running for mayor of
Providence as the candidate of the Temperance party in May 1847. He succeeded in becoming mayor with the next election in May 1852, at which time
the whole state went dry. Arnold and Barstow presumably met at board
meetings of the Butler Hospital for the Insane, for not only were they both
on the board but Barstow was president. Similarly, they presumably met at
meetings of the Mechanics' and Manufacturers' Association, since they were
both members and Barstow eventually became president. Arnold, however,
would have missed Barstow's speech dedicating the library and reading room
of the Mechanics' and Manufacturers' Association on February 6, 1861, for
the Arnolds were in Georgia. One speech by Barstow that Arnold presumably was glad he missed (he was again in Georgia) was the one Barstow made
at a public meeting on December 2, 1859, the day John Brown was executed.
In that speech Barstow drew a parallel between the contemporary John
Brown and the eighteenth-century John Brown of Rhode Island, who was a
slave trader; Barstow predicted the end of slavery as surely as the slave trade
itself ended.[71]

While Louisa Arnold was in New York early in August having her portrait painted and visiting her daughter Harriet, Richard Arnold was in Newport visiting southern friends who had arrived for the summer season—the Middletons, the Izards, the Pinckneys, and especially the Joneses. Admittedly, nothing quite so splendid was occurring in Newport the week of August 9 as had occurred the previous August: the fancy ball held in the ballroom of the Ocean House in late August 1847, attended by close to seven hundred costumed dancers in which Mary Nuttall Jones "appeared as a Spanish Donna, in a robe of the most costly and beautiful black lace over a rose-colored silk . . . the richly embroidered veil falling in graceful folds almost to her feet, veiling, not concealing, her magnificent form." And Miss Louisa Arnold's costume was singled out as the most perfect in conception and most becoming to the lovely wearer:

> The soft folds of a crimson cashmere fell in drapery which seemed to have been modelled on that of some antique statue, over white muslin. Her hair drawn back from her face fell in rich, waving masses low over the ears and at the back of the head. Her turban of crimson and white was modelled on that of the sybil she represented, and whose likeness in a beautiful cameo confined it to the head in front.[72]

It would have been socially awkward if the Joneses had inadvertently asked about Thomas Clay in passing, because that winter Arnold, a very litigious man who began his career as a planter suing John Miller over the ownership of some slaves, was involved in a boundary dispute with Clay. It was apparently a sore point between them because Eliza Harriet Allen discreetly referred to it as a "family difficulty": "Family I call it for you [and the Clays] used to appear as one."[73] Death ended the "difficulty"; Thomas Clay died suddenly on October 24, 1849, at the age of forty-eight.

The Arnolds usually spent the month of August in Newport, but by September 1, if not earlier, Arnold was always back for the commencement exercises at Brown University. In the summer of 1848, because of the forthcoming wedding and the remodeling of the mansion house, to say nothing of the building of a new stone wall at the wharf, Arnold was back in Providence by mid-August. On the day after commencement, the same day that he purchased a hat for himself for $4.50, he handed at the door $10.00 to one Pinckney Middleton of Bryan County, Georgia, and honored his subscription to pay $5.00 "to a poor man who lost his horse." It was entirely within keeping of his image as a humane man of charity that such evidence of random giving should be a commonplace in his account books, whether it was $0.50 "presented to a negro" or $3.00 to "blind children" or just plain "charity to a man" ($2.00). But more long range yet personal and individual charity appealed to his paternalism: thus, for example, on May 3, 1848, he paid J. O. A. Clarke of Savannah, Georgia, $60.00 "towards defraying your expense in obtaining a liberal education [at Yale] & which you are to refund when able." Clarke might possibly have been related to Mrs. Arnold, whose mother, Barbara Clark, had been the widow of William Clark when she married Abraham Gindrat. By January, however, he had sent only $40.00 cash. Arnold apparently decided that it pays to be more precise with words, and therefore on October 17 he changed the imprecise proviso that J. O. A. Clarke would repay him "when able" to "previous to your becoming of age."[74]

Charity at home, however, was quite another matter, and Arnold's "loan" on July 22 of $20.00 to his nephew Tristam Burges was "on demand," which demand was made a month later. Since Burges was always in and out of financial difficulties it was best not to loan money to him on the understanding he would repay "when able." The loan of $20.00 may come under the heading of charity, but the loan of $2,339.42 on September 22 to his son-in-law William Brenton Greene was a matter of business. Arnold loaned the money to enable Greene to get a discharge from his creditor, but Greene was able to arrange his business affairs to the satisfaction of his creditors so that he was able on September 30 to return Arnold's note unused. Certainly, there was no lessening of cooperation between two businessmen, and as in the past Arnold continued to use his son-in-law's good offices; for example, Greene paid daughter Louisa's bill in New York from Stewart and Company ($100.63), and Arnold repaid him on October 23 when Greene and his wife and Louisa returned to Providence, charging Louisa's dividend account for the full amount.[75]

Arnold did not put his trust in acts of God, and on October 27 he paid the American Insurance Company a premium of $25 to insure for one year his household furniture, "including Paintings Pictures Ornaments Musical Instruments Books etc contained in my dwelling house."[76] The paintings were new, the paint hardly dry, but the books had been accumulated over the years. One of the last things Arnold completed before leaving Providence in the fall of 1847 was a list of the 838 volumes in his home library.[77] The inventory was as much for insurance purposes as for personal reasons, for the Arnolds had rented their house furnished during the winter season ever since the winter of 1841, when the caretaker, Mr. Bailey, reported that there was something wrong with the door lock and he could not open it to check the premises. Fearing that there had been a burglary, Arnold asked Zachariah Allen to investigate. Zachariah had discovered that the door was stuck "from being swollen by dampness" and that "everything appeared in its proper

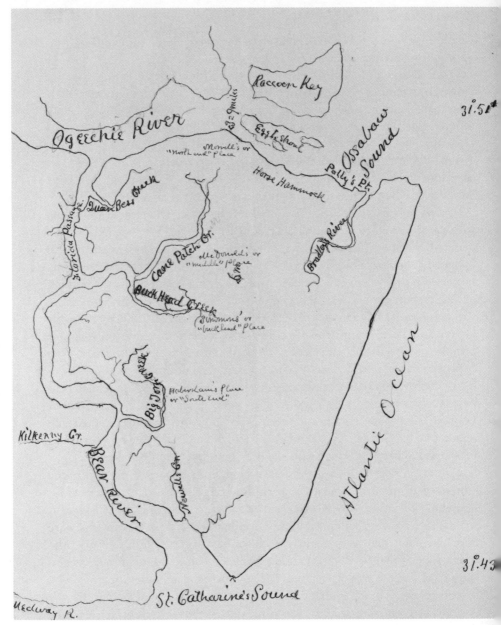

31°.51′

31°.43′

Samuel Arnold's "marooning" map of the Ogeechee River area before 1860. A maroon originally was a runaway slave, and marooning was the search for fugitive slaves organized by white slave owners. This map, however, indicates the area near the plantations where Arnold's family and northern guests hunted wild game. (Courtesy of the Arnold-Rogers Collection.)

place and in good order." But, Allen warned his brother-in-law, "There is much risk in leaving your wines &c so much exposed, without any person to occupy the house," especially during the winter months.[78] Dampness is as bad for books as for doors. Implicit, however, was a concern for the safety of the property. Not only was the political turmoil of the Dorr era beginning, but the unrest represented by the facts and figures was all too evident to the upper middle class still living in the heart of the city—by 1840, Providence had a population of 23,000, a 38 percent increase since the last census, most of that increase accounted for by the foreign-born immigrants working in the textile mills and the now-thriving and expanding jewelry industry.

Book lists are an inventory of the mind, and while Arnold did not have the intellectual pretensions of Zachariah Allen, his library reflected the tastes of an 1814 Phi Beta Kappa graduate of Brown University. Besides the copy of the Wayland-Fuller debate, Arnold's library included a copy of Zachariah Allen's *The Science of Mechanics*, a technical study Allen published in 1829 after his European trip "to examine," as he explained in his preface, "the effects of the important improvements in machinery upon the state of society at the present day."[79] The library also contained two copies of Allen's version of this same trip for the general reader, entitled *Practical Tourist* (1832). Presumably at least one of the copies was a presentation copy from the author. It was in this work that Allen revealed his nineteenth-century faith in material progress, asserting that America would progress culturally as it progressed materially: "The Useful Arts are the handmaids to the Fine Arts. They spring up, flourish and decline together."[80] Undoubtedly, Arnold obtained a copy of Allen's later work, a textbook entitled *Philosophy of the Mechanics of Nature* (1850).

The copy of Maria McIntosh's *Two Lives, To Seem and To Be* (1846) in Arnold's library may also have been a presentation copy from the author, for he had invested for her the money she obtained from the sale of her slaves in 1834. Some of that money was lost in the Panic of 1837, so she fell back on writing and teaching to support herself at Miss Haines's School, which Mary Cornelia and, later, Susan attended. Arnold also obtained a copy of her novel, *The Lofty and the Lowly* (1852), which portrays an idealized slaveholding southern planter, much in his own image.

Arnold's library was that of a cultivated gentleman of the time. It ranged from the classics—Tacitus (complete), Horace's *Satires*, four volumes of Homer from an original set of eight—to the latest novels—Dickens's *Nicholas Nickleby* (1838–1839) and his *The Battle of Life* (1846) and the *Works of Maria Edgeworth* (complete in thirteen volumes). The standard classics of English literature were well represented from Shakespeare's *Plays and Poems* in eight volumes (Collier's Edition) to the romantic poets, including Byron's *Works* in seventeen volumes. The eighteenth-century poets were well represented also, including, among others, Burns (complete in five volumes), Gray, Thompson, Goldsmith, and Crabbe. Pope's translations of the *Iliad* and the *Odyssey* as well as his poems, complete in nine volumes, were in the library. Sir Walter Scott occupied an honored as well as lengthy space on the shelves—all the Waverley Novels, fifty-three volumes, to say nothing of individual volumes such as his *Life of Napoleon*. Modern French classics were also well represented—the works of Molière, Racine, Corneille, Mme de Staël. A smattering of books on philosophy were included, perhaps reminders of his college days—Locke's *On Understanding* (abridged), Watt's *Logic*, Voltaire's *Philosophical Dictionary*—but Schlegel's *Lectures* and Channing's *Works* were probably more recent acquisitions. The various European travel guides were certainly mementos of his European sojourn, but the history and current affairs books reflected Arnold's own personal interests—a *Life of Nathanael Greene*, Hamilton's *Works*, Warren's *American Revolution*, Webster's *Speeches*, *De Tocqueville on America*, the *Rhode Island Suffrage Question* by Jacob Frieze, an anti-Dorrite. The library also contained a rare book which Arnold might have acquired while in Europe—a fourteenth-century illuminated manuscript volume.

Sometimes libraries are suggestive of the collector's mind by what they do not contain: despite his obvious special interest in the subject, no book or pamphlet on the slavery issue either pro or con was included in the inventory list other than the Wayland-Fuller debate, and its inclusion reflected more the fact that Arnold knew Wayland than it revealed his interest in the topic. For example, although one would not expect Arnold to keep copies of Garrison's *The Liberator* in his library, one might expect to see a copy of Theodore Weld's *The Bible Against Slavery* (1837), if for no other reason than that Weld inspired the Rhode Island Anti-Slavery Society in its arguments against slavery on biblical grounds, his letter to the 1836 convention accusing Rhode Island of being "the summer resort of thousands who hold slaves at the South."[81]

By the same token, to balance the argument Arnold might have but did not include in his library the proslavery polemic by Thornton Stringfellow, *A Brief Examination of Scripture Testimony on the Institution of Slavery* (1841). But all the known biblical arguments between Christians were contained in the Wayland-Fuller debate, both of them ordained ministers whose avowed purpose was to examine domestic slavery "as a scriptural institution," and they both wrote two letters each examining the arguments for and against slavery as it appeared to them from the Old Testament and from the New Testament. Fuller's main argument was stated in capital letters and bold type: "WHAT GOD SANCTIONED IN THE OLD TESTAMENT, AND PERMITTED IN THE NEW, CANNOT BE SIN." Richard Arnold would presumably be satisfied with that premise as opposed to Wayland's argument that slavery is a "transgression of the law of our Creator, *Thou shalt love thy neighbor as thyself*."[82] These were the standard arguments used for and against slavery; abolitionists and antiabolitionists in Rhode Island and elsewhere had used these same arguments pro and con a decade earlier.

The Bible itself, of course, was in the Arnold library: the family Bible of Welcome Arnold was originally on the list but then crossed off; perhaps the Arnolds decided to take it with them to Georgia or else left it with the Allens for safekeeping within the family. The family Bible was originally published in Oxford, England, in 1770 and purchased at the cost of eleven shillings, three pence. A printed label on the inside front cover identifies it as "The Property of Welcome Arnold" and on this same label is the signature of Richard J. Arnold, who probably acquired it after the death of his brother, Samuel, in 1826. On a blank page following the Book of Prophets and continued on the verso of the title page of the New Testament is the family record— Welcome and Patience Arnold and their fourteen children, only four of whom survived them. It includes Richard James Arnold's and Eliza Harriet's birth date (October 5, 1796) and his death date (March 10, 1873) but not his twin's (August 30, 1873).[83]

Did Richard Arnold turn the pages and heed Christ's warning in the Gospel according to Matthew, the first book of the New Testament: "No man can serve two masters. . . . Ye cannot serve God and mammon"? The signs were ambiguous, for although the journey south that fall was very smooth in passage, being "much favored by the weather," Arnold worried all the way from Wilmington, Delaware, where he boarded the steamer *Northerner* to Charleston, South Carolina, where he disembarked, for he considered the ship unseaworthy.

CHAPTER FIVE

Plantation Journal

NOVEMBER 4, 1847–APRIL 19, 1848

Thursday Nov 4th. I arrived at the Plantation with Mr Howe   the family arrived the day before, we left Saturday @ 4 o'clock N York in the Northerner & reached Charleston @ 8 o'clock—Tuesday morning   the same Evg at 10 o'clock reached Savannah. by the Wm Seabrook. Our staterooms in the Northerner were 26 & 27—our passage rough & attendance bad   people picking peas @ C Hill   have made but few this year

1847
Octo [sic] 5

At C Hill people picking Cotton   at White Hall doing the Same thing   Mr Ferguson thinks we have at C Hill this night 7 Bags. & at White Hall 6½ Bags in the House—

Saturday
Nov. 6

At C Hill Women picking Cotton & Men ditching & making Road to Miller field from C Hill   at W Hall all hands picking Cotton   picked a half bag this day.—

Monday
Nov 8th

made Contract
for the year
1848 with my
overseer Mr.
Ferguson to

At C Hill all the men ditching & making road to Miller field   Women   35 in all   gleaning Rice for the first time this year   five Baskets to the hand   At W Hall, men raising back water dam in Inland Rice field. Women picking peas. for the first time this year   12 Baskets to the hand.—This day made a bargain for another year with Mr. Ferguson I agreeing to give him Eight Hundred dollars to allow him to keep a Horse & I to furnish him four

pay in money
$800.—

quarts of Corn pr day to feed him with, & to furnish him with a Summer residence by building a log House in my pine Wood or hewing a House for him   the Contract in every other respect the Same as last year & the year 1845.—See Agree^t of these years

1847 Tuesday
Nov 9th

At C Hill Women gleaned 4 Baskets Ear Rice   Men working in road leading to Miller field   Charles & Pompey drawing light wood from Sans Souci—At W Hall Geo drawing in [illegible] & Ash   also peas. Sancho gone for Oysters & the other people picking peas.—

Wednesday
Nov 10th

Cut 3 Acres
New ground

at C Hill started Mill to thrash Dorseys Rice but did but little owing to the windfan   about 16 Hands picked the Rice & 16 more Cut down New ground   part—doing one task & part two in a task cut down about three Acres next Miller field. At White Hall fifteen hands picked peas. about 112 Baskets   Carpenters made Bridge on Causeway leading to Miller field & put fence into flat @ C Hill   four hands with two Ox Wagons carting lightwood from Sans Souci—

Thursday
Nov 11.

Cut 4 Acres
New ground

At C Hill part of the hands picking ear Rice   Sixteen at the Mill thrashing Mr Dorseys Rice. & 21. Cutting down New ground next Miller field   four Carting Lightwood from Sans Souci—At White Hall Geo Carting wood to House & the rest of the people picking peas. 105 Baskets picked this night The Carpenters brought a flat load of paling posts & Laths from the Barn Yard C Hill to White Hall. for Poultry Yard.—

Friday
Nov 12.

3 Acres of
Wood cut down

At C Hill 21 men Cutting down New ground   Cut about 3 Acres. fifteen gathering ear Rice & balance of the people   Say 21 Hands   thrashing Rice for Mr Dorsey   He to pay 8 pr ct. toll & furnish hands to run the Mill   the Rice—having been injured by the freshet Could not thrash half the usual quantity—At White Hall picked 120 Baskets peas.—

Saturday
Nov 13ᵗʰ

2 Acres Wood
cut

At C Hill thrashed Mr Dorseys Rice   cut down New
ground & picked ear Rice Same as yesterday At W Hall
picked peas 116 Bushels,—in the pod—2 Acres of Wood.
finished cutting & a number of tasks half done. Two wagons drawing Lightwood all the week fr Sans Souci—

Monday
15ᵗʰ Nov 1847

Dorseys Rice
turned out 670
Bushels.

Dug eating
potatoes   at
least 300.
Bushels

At C Hill 40 Hands dug potatos two in a task. finished five
Acres & banked 7 Banks potatos   thirty five baskets in
each bank. & one bank Slips—thirty baskets—the Mill
finished Dorseys Rice in the forenoon. having thrashed
670 Bushels in all which took four days to thrash, also
thrashed the ear Rice & Small Rice of No 4   in all 125
Bushels & part of the large Rice to No 4   150 Bushels—
At W Hall picked 115 Baskets peas, & Carpenters Worked
on fence round poultry House   Charles & Billy drawing
Light wood fr Sans Souci   Gibbs burning Coals fr
Blacksmith

Tuesday
Nov 16

Light frost first
this fall

At C Hill dug 7 Acres Slips with 60 hands & they yielded
only 350.Bushels & two or three hands picked a little Cotton   at W Hall picked 105.Baskets peas & Carpenters
worked on Poultry Yard. <u>Frost</u>

Wednesday
Nov 17

At C Hill dug 7½ Acres Slips   yielded only 200 Bushels.
& at W Hall Carpenters Same as yesterday & finished
picking peas. 87.Baskets. have in all @ W.H.900 Baskets
also picked 30ˡᵇˢ Cotton—

1847   Thursday
Nov 18.

At C Hill dug 8 Acres potatos   only yielded 4 Bank   Say
200 Bushels   eating potatos & one Bank seed. a few hands
picked Cotton—Boston mending Cart Wheels and Amos
Seting tires in do—at W Hall dug one & a half Acres of
potatos   only yielded 40 Baskets   Say 55 Bushels   &
part of a Bank of Seed   two picked Cotton & Carpenters
getting puncheons fr Cowpen fence.—

Friday
Nov. 19.

Last night Scipio at W Hall died & Quality at C Hill had a
Child Born.—At C Hill 28 Acres Cut down New ground

Cut down
about 4 Acres
New Ground

24 Hands finished digging potatos   only—dug fifty Bushels eating & one Small Bank of planting potatos   11 hands
picked about 100^lbs Cotton   at W Hall dug a few potatos
& listed one task Cotton field

Slight frost

Saturday
Nov 20

Cut & dug up
12 Acres of
Cane &
Mattressed it
today

At C Hill eighty picked Cotton & fifty four Cut & Mattressed Cane   each hand doing one task   finished very
late   Amos workg on Thrasher. Boston on Wheels
Charles Billy & two Boys Cutting Lightwood
Ferguson absent yesterday & to day in Town   At W Hall
dug 56 Bushels potatoes & part of a Bank of Slips. two
picked Cotton. Carpenters making fence to Cow pen
Tom white washing

Monday
Nov 22^d

At C Hill 38 dug up & Matrressed the balance of the Cane
& the rest of the force picked Cotton in New ground   at
White Hall two picked Cotton & the rest dug potatoes in
New ground   about fifty Bushels. Carpenters made up
fence round Cowpen and fr Science 3 Boxes 10 lbs 1
Keg—

Tuesday
Nov. 23

At C Hill 22 men Cutting down New ground   5 Splitting
Rails   Billy & Buck Carting Rails   twenty hands Sent to
W Hall & the balance picking ear Rice. At W Hall dug 2¼
Acres of Potatoes   turned out 200 Bushels. & picked
about 200^lbs Cotton.

Wednesday
Nov. 24/47

At C Hill Same work & Same hands as Yesterday & at
W Hall all hands—including twenty fr C Hill have been
listing in New Ground Corn field doing one task & 1¼
tasks to the hand the Grass being very thick—Carpenters
getting out Stuff of Cowpen Racks   Daddy John Killed a
deer this day.[1]

Thursday
Nov 25th

At C Hill Six hands Split Rails   have this night 1600-
Split   Billy Carting them home   about fifteen other

First heavy
White frost this
Season

hands gleaning Rice & the balance of the C Hill force at
W Hall listing   At W Hall five picking Cotton & the
balance with 20 from C Hill listing 1½ tasks each in New
ground Cornfield which has a very heavy growth—on it &
not as yet injured by frost. have finished listing this night
19 Acres

Friday
Nov 26.

At C Hill Billy Carting Rails & Gibbs & Moses Making
fence round potatos. fifteen hands puting Grass to Sugar
Cane & listing in Corn field   the rest at W Hall including
Rail Splitters   Same at W Hall, have 35 Acres finished
listing tonight   Carpenter jobbing @ W H

1847 Saturday
Nov 27

At W Hall finished listing Corn field   84 Acres with
C Hill hands   have 44 Acres listed this night & dug potatoes near Barn Yard   finished all but 2½ Tasks. dug
about 150 Bushels & one Bank planting Slips—

Monday &
Tuesday
29 & 30th
Nov.

Have been absent with Mrs Arnold in—Savh   Qualitys
Child died last night   the Infant. Men at C Hill not
workg on the Road   have been cutting down New
ground   Women listing. At W Hall Women picking Cotton & Men listing.

Wednesday
Dec 1st

At C Hill eight Sorting Cotton   eight Sick   13 working
on Road   ten Cutting down New ground & balance listing
in Corn field   At W Hall four listing in Cotton field 1½
tasks each. Seven picking Cotton about 30lbs each   three
making Clothes for people. Geo. Carting wood   Carpenters part on road & part getting rack fr W Hall Cowpen.—
Yesterday recd by the Cotton Plant Bbl Hams less one.
wet & damaged. 2 Kegs Butter & ½ Bbl Tongues. &
should have recd a Bbl of Cider, which did not come to
hand.

Thursday
Dec 2d

At C Hill the Same work as yesterday & Amos Battist &
Boston Setting Tire to Timber Wheels &c. All hands at
White Hall listing in Cotton field that was not planted last
year 1½ tasks to the hand, have nearly 8 Acres listed this
night—

Friday Dec 3ᵈ

Engaged
Mulbery Hill
for two years of
J. Bailey

At C Hill 12 Men On the Road   twelve Cutting down
New ground   Women listing Corn field   Amos & Battist
in Blacksmith Shop   Boston Working Mending Wheels—
At W Hall finished digging potatoes   made two—have
now twelve Banks eating & three of planting Slips.—This
day agreed with J Bailey to plant his part of Mulbery
Hill—I am to have it for two years. to clean up the Square
nearest the river that has not been planted & put whatever
ditches I may think proper in it & a new trunk & also to
clean & plant the Second uncleared Square from the high
ground Should I wish to do it, & the clearing up these two
Squares to be the rent for the two years use of the Plantation   Should I fail to clean up & plant the Second Square,
I am in that case to allow as rent the Sum of one dollar pr
Acre for the Amount of Acres that Square contains—the
four Buildings I am to look after but take no responsibility
fr them being in good order when my lease expires, if
Stolen or burnt it is to be Mr Baileys loss.—

Saturday
Dec 4/47

At C Hill Men work Same as Yesterday   13 Women at
W H.   the rest cleaned near pens. At W Hall 18 picked
350ˡᵇˢ Cotton   2 Hands listing. have 8 Acres done—Bot
Hog of Kit/ Dr Eliots man   weight 180ˡᵇˢ   pd him in a/c
$3— ²

Monday 6 Dec
1847

Thrashed @ C
Hill 160
Bushels Rice

At C Hill 19 men Cutting down New Ground   21 People
in Mill thrashing Rice—Abby Sorting Cotton   12 gone to
W Hall   At White Hall 17 picked about 300ˡᵇˢ Cotton &
four worked Cleaning up round the House, & 4 listed 1½
tasks in New ground Cotton field   gave out Shoes &
Coarse Pantaloons Saturday.—Today 7 Women Sewing
Making Shirts &c   viz. Lissy. Eve. Elsay. Sue. Jacky Polly
& Harriot   Mary Ann Cutting out.—

Tuesday
7ᵗʰ Dec

111 B
W. Hall Rice

At C Hill 19 Cutting down New Ground   22 in Mill &
the balance at W Hall   thrashed @ C Hill [blank] Bushels
Rice   At W Hall all hands thrashed Rice   Winnowed &
put into Barn 64.Bushels Rice—had previously put
50.Bushels in Barn—Carpenters at C Hill getting out Stuff

for Wheels   Hubbs. Spokes &c from Live oak & White Oak out of the New ground—

Wednesday Dec 8

Bushels 72. W.H. Rice

Brenton & Harriet arrived this day

At C Hill 20 Cutting down New Ground   twenty two in thrashing Mill & twelve at W Hall. Carpenters getting Live & White oak New ground for Wagon Hubbs &c Thrashed this day 300 Bushels Rice at C Hill. At White Hall thrashed with twenty hands & winnowed & put into Barn 72 Bushels Rice   my Son & Daughter arrived this day fr. N. York

Thursday Dec. 9

Bushels 83. W H Rice

At C Hill Same work as Yesterday and thrashed with Engine 255 Bushels   Little Scipio thrown & badly hurt from Horse Big Philly—at W Hall Same work as Yesterday   thrashed 83 Bushels Rice

Friday 10th Dec.

89 Bushels W Hall Rice put in Barn

At C. Hill thrashed 400 Bushels Rice   twenty Men Cutting down New ground but progress very Slowly   the timber is large & Some men have been four days Cuttin down One task—the Women not employed at the Mill are at W Hall.—Carpenters part Making Trunk for Sedgefield & part getting out White Oak for Waggons &c. at W Hall thrashed & Winnowed 89 Bushels Rice & finished thrashing all the Rice from the River Square tho did not finish Winnowing it.—

Saturday Dec 11.

W Hall Square turned out only 413. Bushels wh is only 25 Bushels pr Acre

At C Hill thrashed 390 Bushels Rice & Men Cut down New ground   Carpenters workg in trunk fr Mulbery Hill. At White Hall—Seven Women have been making Clothes the past week fr the people   the rest of the White Hall force/excepting three/ that have been winnowing Rice. 80 Bushels. Have been pickg Cotton together with twelve of the C Hill—Women—gave out this Evg cloth to the— Women & Blankets to the people.—

Monday
Dec 13ᵗʰ

Commenced
ploughing Rice
field @ W Hall

Recᵈ 9 Bbls.
Grits fr CH

At C Hill thrashed 360 Bushels & put about 80 Bushels from the winnowing House into the Barn, 22 Men Cut down New ground & the rest cleaned round fence.—At W Hall three men Cut down potatoe ground one task each   Geo commenced ploughing in Rice field & the balance listed 1/2 tasks in New ground Cotton field excepting two Sorting Cotton & Seven making clothes. Bot Hog of Wm   120ˡᵇˢ   also of Adam. 184ˡᵇˢ

Tuesday
Dec 14ᵗʰ

Killed Hogs
this day

At C Hill Mr Arkwright came @ 1 o'clock with his Horse & Gig this day to put up Sugar Mill   thrashed 280 Bushels. winnowed [blank] Bushels   6 Hands picked Cotton & 19 Cut down New ground   @ W Hall 6 picked & Sorted Cotton   3 Cut New ground & Jim & Geo. ploughed in Rice field   Double ploughs

1847
Wednesday
Dec. 15

At C Hill twenty one men Cutting down New ground. a few hands cleaning up—round the Mill. All the Carpenters with Arkwright workg on Sugar Mill—Amos in Blacksmith Shop   Pompey & Cain Sawing & the balance picking Cotton in New ground—at C Hill—did not thrash to day   have in Mill about 3000 Bushels Rice thrashed At W Hall 6 picked Cotton   4 finished listing Cotton field   two Sorted Cotton—7 worked making Clothes fr people. three Cut down trees near Rice field
Geo. & Jim ploughing Rice field with two Mules each turning in Stubble—

Thursday
Dec 16

Covered Seed
Cane with
dirt—

At C Hill Pompey & Cain Sawing boards   Billy & Buck Carting wood & the rest of the men Cutting down New ground   Women listed half a day in Miller field & then Covered Seed Cane with dirt—Carpenters working with Aukwright on Sugar Mill   At W Hall Geo & Jim ploughed in Rice field   Sancho Sampson & Battist Cutting down near Rice field & the rest cleaned round New ground fence 100 Panels each   two Sorted Cotton.—

Friday
Dec. 17.

At C Hill Women listed in Miller field 1½ tasks to the hand   Men & Carpenters Same work as yesterday & the Same work done at W Hall this day. Called at Mr Rogers with Mrs Arnold—³

Saturday
18 Dec/47

At C Hill Men Cutting down New ground   Women listing in Miller field   Carpenters workg at mill   at W Hall two plough in Rice field   two men Cutting & the rest Cleaning round New ground fence.

Monday
Dec 20/47

At C Hill Twenty two hands Cutting down New ground   Women listing in Miller field & Geo & Bandy ploughing with double plough in No 12 Square Carpenters working with Aukwright in Sugar Mill—At W Hall Geo. & Jim ploughing in Stubble in Rice field— Sancho & Battist Cutting down potatoe field next Rice field & the rest of the force Cleaning Round New ground—fence.—Mr Law left us this day.—

Tuesday &
Wednesday

Have been in Savʰ   during my absence finished ploughing White Hall Rice field   two Cutting down at W Hall Wood. Seven Sewing fr People & balance finished the Cotton & hoeing Round New ground fence & cleaning out ditches in Rice field   At C Hill men & women cleaned out quarter drains Tuesday   two ploughs in No 12. Carpenters & Amos working with Aukwright at Mill Wednesday   Men—Cutting down New ground & Carpenters & Women Same work as yesterday.—

Thursday
23ᵈ Dec.

At C Hill Carpenters & Blacksmiths Workg with Arkwright on Sugar Mill   Women in quarter drains and Burning Stubble, Men Cutting down New ground except Neptune & Jim who did ploughing in No 12 Square. Yesterday Daddy John Killed his third deer this Season & today his eighth Turkey Since the 1ˢᵗ November last.—We expect Mr Sam Howland & Peleg Hall of N.Y. tomorrow⁴

1847 Dec. 24

At C Hill All hands/except two plough Boys in No 12 Square & carpenters with Arkwright in Sugar Mill until

Arkwright went to Sav^b @ 1 o'clock this day.

1 o'clock when he broke off to go to Sav^h/ cleaning out ditches & hoeing Stubble—at—W Hall 7 Sewing & the balance cleaning out drains in Rice field & cleaning out round the House,   this night had—1000. Rails in Meeting House field fence burnt.

Saturday Monday & Tuesday

These three days   Holy days   Killed three Boars for the people & had Dancing at W Hall all the time—Jim & Venus married. Mr Howland & Peleg Hall passed the Holy days here

Wednesday 29th Dec.

Mr Arkwright came from Town & arrived @ 2 o'clock just in time to eat his dinner & do no work. Carpenters work-ing at Mill   Jim Prince & Shadwell ploughing with one Mule each in No 6—Neptune finishing No 12 with two Mules   Science came today & brought 80 Bbls empty for Syrup. & will take Rice for me. At W Hall Geo. drawing wood   Battist, Sancho & Sampson Cuting down New ground   the others cleaning round Meeting House field fence.—

Thursday 30 Dec.

Put on Science 2000. Bushels Rice in my a/c/ at C Hill & 600 in a/c Dorsey 5 ploughs running in No 6. Carpenters workg on Sugar Mill. At W Hall men cutting down New ground   Women cleaning ditches Corn field

Friday Dec 31st

Mr Arkwright left off work this day @ 12 o'clock

Thrashed 200 Bushels Rice @ C H half a day

At C Hill about twenty five hands making ditch outside of dam to Nos 11 & 12 & the rest at the Mill part of the day trying the Sugar Mill & the other part thrashd Rice No 12 Square. Mr Arkwright left at 12 o'clock & went to Mr. Heyward having finished his work @ C Hill   four ploughs running in No 6 Square   Israel coopering the Empty Bbls that Came from Savannah—Sent four hogs of my own to C Hill this Evening.—Yesterday Bot Hog of Morris weighs 200^lbs & one from Boston weighing 164^lbs—At W Hall hoed fence part of the day & put on board of the Science 410—Bushels Rice—Shipped by her this trip 2410. Bushels Rice in my own a/c^t—

Saturday
Jany 1, 1848.

Thrashed 350
Bushels at C
Hill

At C Hill part of the hands dug ditch outside Nos 11. & 12 Squares. & part centered these dams   4 mules ploughs running in No 6 & Carpenters making Spouts for Sugar Mill & the balance of the force thrashing Rice, rec^d one fish from Dean today the 2^d only rec^d this Year   At White Hall Rose Sorting Cotton & all the rest of the people cleaning out & deepening ditches in Corn field   All our family except the Boys & Susan dined with Mr. Winn at Tivoli this day.—

1848 Monday
Jany 3^d

At C Hill thrashed 350 Bushels Rice and the rest of the force dug Center ditch to outside dam in Nos 11 & 12 & filled it up   7 ploughs running in Nos 2 & 1—at W Hall—all hands Cleaning out & deeping ditches in New ground Corn field

Tuesday
Jany 4/47 [sic]

At C Hill thrashed 405.Bushels Rice—ploughed No 1. with 7 Ploughs. Carpenters making Axeltree, & Hubs for Cart Wheel & the Women part Cleaning up quarter drains & the others Centering & filling up dam in No 12 Square. At W Hall all hands ditching in New ground Corn field   expect to Send to Mr King tomorrow morning for Sugar Bales—

Wednesday
Jan 5.

Mr Kings
George came to
C. Hill.

At C Hill thrashed 545 Bushels Rice   7 Ploughs running in No 1. part of the hands raising dam & stopping leaks to No 11. & 12 Squares. This night Geo. Mr King's man Came to C. Hill to assist in making Syrup & Sugar   he left home @ 2 o'clock   at W Hall two Sorted Cotton & balance—dug ditches in New ground.

Thursday
Jany 6.

At C Hill thrashed 500 Bushels Rice & all the force not employed in the Rice Stripping Cutting Carting Cane & cleaning Kettles & preparing to grind Cane. At W Hall Same work as yesterday. Carpenters fixing Wagons

Friday Jany 7.

At C Hill undertook to grind Cane & the mill trembled as much   also interfered in one thrashing of Rice, only thrashed 315.Bushels. Sent ten hands from W Hall &

Made first
Syrup @
C Hill

these together with all the C Hill force not thrashing Cut, Carted, Striped & ground & boiled Cane. Made about two barrels of Syrup. Carpenters fixing different things in the Mill—the few hands that remained @ W Hall Sorted Cotton—.

Saturday
Jany 8.

515 Bushels
Rice—
8 Bbls Syrup

At C Hill thrashed 515 Bushels Rice & cut Stripped & ground Cane & boiled Syrup & Bbls off   8 Bbls of Syrup— the White Hall hands & all the—Wagons & Carts put in requisition to haul Cane. excepting 4 Hands at W Hall that were Sorting Cotton.

Monday
10ᵗʰ Jany

At C Hill thrashed 300 Bushels Rice & made four bbls Syrup too dark   not fit for market, owing in part of leakg between the Kettles, Stopped boiling in the Middle of the day & Sent to Savʰ for Sheet lead to finish the Kettles.— the rest of the hands workg in the Cane excepting ten on the Road.—

Tuesday
11ᵗʰ Jan

Lost this juice
by souring

At C Hill thrashed 240 Bushels Rice but did not Start Sugar Mill   have 800 Gallons juice ready to boil & fear it will be Sour waiting for the Kettles to be fixed   all hands—working in Sugar Cane including all from W Hall   excepting 4 that are Sorting Cotton—

Wednesday
Jany 12.

At C Hill thrashed 120 Bushels Rice   14 Hands cleaning out quarter drains 3 ploughing   ten hands employed about Sugar Mill & the balance employed Cutting Carting Stripping Cane including 9 from W Hall. At White Hall 5 Hands Sorting Cotton & two Carpenters making up Rack in Cowpen   Mrs Mangin died at the House today   The Sugar Mill Worked badly   Halliday Says it ought to be coupled to the upper rollers & the Shaft moved 18 inches back would do it. or use the old wheels & move 9 Inches back would do it & add nearly double the Speed of the rollers   Say 7 to 8 pr minute instead of 3⅔ the present rate & he offers to make pattern to fit—into my Old Wheels & grind them on to the Shafts for $20—I paying

for the Castings & furnishing wedges   The way the mill is
now gears Cannot Keep the Mill in its place

Thursday
Jany 13ᵗʰ

At C Hill 19 Hands cleaning out quarter drains in Nos 7
& 17. three ploughing—& the balance including 9 fr
White Hall all engaged in Stripping Cutting Carting grinding & boiling Sugar Cane   4 Cutting & 6 Stripping to
each Cutter. all the Carts & wagons either carry Cane to
Mill or carrying of the Cane that way as finished. At
W Hall same as yesterday—Have this night 13 Barrels of
best Syrup—about 40 Gallons each & 8 Bbls that is Sweet
but too dark coloured for market. & have five coolers filled
part for Sugar & part for Syrup exclusive of 800 Gallons
lost by Souring in Keeping one day & night in the
Reservoir

Friday Jany 14

At C Hill filled 5 Bbls Best Syrup & ten Gallon Keg for
Mr Winn. also one Bbl dark Syrup when Mill broke
down. carrying away 3 Cogs. in Lower—Wheel. Cleaned
up Mill House & discharged Mr Kings man George paying
$11—for his services.—Have four Coolers filled hoping to
Granulate.—they hold about Six bbls. which makes in all
that I have made say about 43 Bbls. of all kinds. not
including 800 Gallons Juice thrown away by Souring.—
Also had Seven ploughs running in Rice field & had 19
Hands cleaning out ditches   Carpenters working on
Trunks & Wagons   Mr Fergu[s]on Sick with Measles—
Winnowed 55 Bushels Market Rice & thrashed the Upland
Rice wh yielded only 25. Bushels—

Saturday
Jany 15

100 Acres only
ploughd @
C Hill—very
backward

At C Hill five men Stopping leaks in outside dam. Carpenters workg on Trunks   thirty five hands Cleaning out
quarter drains & the balance cleaning large ditches   three
tasks to each hand. Nine ploughs finished No 3. &
ploughed No. 18.—Square. have 100 Acres Rice field
ploughed @ C Hill

1848 Monday
Jany 17

At C Hill 9 Ploughs nearly finished ploughg No 19
Square   five hands continuing outside dam in No. 11 &

12—thirty hands cleaning out quarter drains & twenty five hands—cleaning out large ditch & Savage Canal Carpenters getting punchons with Israel & Charles Carting White Oak to Carpenters Shop   the few hands @ White Hall Sorting Cotton, Scipio making baskets. Rec^d 100 Bushels Flour at C Hill this—day from Capt Thompson

Tuesday
Jany 18

At C Hill 8 Hands Stopping leaks in No 12 Square twenty five Cleaning out large ditches   30 do [ditto] quarter drains   Carpenters getting White Oak from New Ground & Charles drawing it in. Arkwright came out to see Sugar Mill & returned Same day & Says he will guarantee that he can fix the Mill to run well as it is now geared. I consented he should try   Lackleson agreeing to take the risk   At W Hall five hands Sorting Cotton

Wednesday
Jany 19

Sent Amos to Sav^h with the broken—Wheel. People doing Same work as Yesterday   Mr Ferguson has been Confined eight days with measles   this day he went to Chatham to bring his Sister   rec^d this night 50 Bags Supposed to contain 100 Bushels Rice flour at W Hall frm Thompson. Phoebe, Mary Ann, Charlotte, Sylvia & Sylvias youngest child. sick with Measles & at C Hill little Nero   All our family dined @ Pynchons today.

1848 Thursday
Jany 20

At C Hill Same work as yesterday & the day before in every respect. Overseer—Came into the field for the first time since his attack of Measles—have nearly finished Cleaning out all the ditches excepting two Squares at C Hill   Eight ploughs running yesterday & today & have finished ploughg No. 11 & possibly 16. tonight which will make about 130 Acres already ploughed there.—At W Hall w[e]ighed off the Cotton—Sorted up to this night 5250^lbs—written Mr Pynchon about Sedgefield today & sent to the Stage for Wm Dexter.—[5]

Friday
Jany 21st

At C Hill 9 ploughs finished No 16. & part of 5. Carpenters workg on Trunk for Mulbery Hill   Charles Carting White Oak & the rest of the force ditching in Nos 20. &

No 5. & making up dams   At White Hall Sorting Cotton.—

Saturday
Jany 22

At C Hill part of the hands raising dam in Rice field & forty thrashing Seed Rice   Adam & Charles Harrowing in No 12. finish harrowing this Season. 9 Ploughs in No 5 Square. Carpenters puting trunk together for Mulbery Hill   Same work @ W Hall. as Yesterday

1848 Monday
Jany 24

About forty hands from C Hill Commenced Cleaning up Square at Mulberry Hill   Carpenters Carried up the Trunk to Mulberry Hill—The balance of C Hill force raising Cross dams in Low places at C Hill & 9 ploughs finished 5. & about half of No. 4 Square. Peter Making pattern for bushing Sugar Mill Wheels.—at White Hall Commenced thrashing Rice for Seed.—This day William A. Dexter. from Boston Came to White Hall to make a Visit.—

Tuesday
Jany 25

107 Bushels
Seed Rice put
into Barn @
W.H.

At W Hall all hands thrashed Rice & Winnowed & put into Barn 107.Bushels.Seed   at C Hill 9 ploughs finished No 4 & went into No. 7 Square   Adam & Charles harrowed with Oxen in No 12 & a few hands—making up dam & raising low places in C Hill Rice field. the rest about forty hands   ditching out Square at Mulberry Hill that has not been planted for twenty years—Dined with Penny

Wednesday
Jany 26

At White Hall rainy day   Men in Corn House & Women in Cotton House   at C Hill 9 mules ploughing in No 7— & Oxen harrowing in 12—a few hands Making up dam & the balance   40 in number   working at Mulberry Hill ditching out New Squares.

1848 Thursday
Jany 27

At C Hill Amos gone to Savannah for Wheel to Sugar Mill. 8 ploughs finished—No 7 & went into No 9   Adam & Charles finished harrowing No 12 & went into No 19. Peter has been workg for Several days. on patterns to bush Sugar Mill Wheels. Boston on Trunk @ Mulberry Hill   a

few hands Making up dams & the rest   40 in
Number   cleaning out ditches   Cutting out Stumps &
throwing back dirt from ditches & puting down Trunk in
New Square @ Mulberry Hill.—At W Hall three in Cotton House   ten cutting down trees & the rest listing 1½
tasks in Cotton field—Had a party to dine this day. The
Demeres, Footmans & Pennys.—

Friday Jany 28

133 Bushels
Rice

At C Hill 8 Ploughs in No 9. two Harrows in 19. Peter
workg on pattern   Boston Cutting Cypress trees @
Mulberry Hill   Peter & Cain ditching @ do & the rest of
the force @ C Hill cleaning out ditches in Nos 9 & 10. &
deepening & cleaning out Canal next high ground   At
W Hall thrashed & winnowed with all hands at W Hall
put into Barn 137 Bushels Seed Rice   rec^d last Evg from
Mr. Habershams Schooner 2000 Bricks & 4 Casks lime

Saturday
Jany 29

63 Bu[s]hls
Rice

At C Hill cleaned out ditches in No. 5 & finished cleaning
out Canal next High ground & ploughed No 10 & finished
No 9. Harrowed in No 19. with Ox Harrows. At
W Hall—all hands thrashed Rice & winnowed 63 Bushels
& put in Barn   all dined @ Mr Starrs.—

1848 Monday
Jany 31.

141. Bushels
Seed Rice @
W Hall

At C Hill all hands thrashed Rice & winnowed & put into
Barn 141 Bushels   at C Hill five ploughs in No 20
two—Mule harrows in No 5 & two Ox ones finished No
19 & at 12 Oclock went—into No. 18 Square   about ten
hands raising Bank between 4 & 15. & the rest of the
force   Say 40 Hands   at—Mulberry Hill ditching & Mr
Aukwright came today at 1 o'clock to put Wheel in to
Sugar Mill—

Friday [sic]
Feby 1.

85. Bushels
Rice @ W Hall

At W Hall all hands thrashed Rice & winnowed & put
into Barn 85.Bushels. At C Hill four harrows run half a
day & two the—whole day in No 5 & 18. people turned
ground in No 5. after the plough half a day &·then Stript
Cane   Arkwright finished Sugar Mill about Noon when
they—Started to grind & boiled in the afternoon & Eve-

ning   Family dined with Mr Rogers at Kilkenny. William Dexter with us.

Wednesday
Feby 2ᵈ

Wrote
Lackleson

At White Hall a few hands Sorted Cotton & what are not tending the Sick are at C Hill where 3 Harrows are running in the Rice field & one plough & twenty—hands turning ground after the ploughs & the rest of the force all employed—about the Cane Grinding & Boiling

Thursday
Feby 3ᵈ

Wrote
Lackleson

At White Hall children Sick with measles & woman at home   missing ten hands @ C Hill   mill broke down @ 3 oclock   have barreled off the last 3 days   13 Bbls Syrup should have been done in one day

Friday
Feby 4/48

At C Hill 3 Mule Harrows in No 6. 2 Ox—harrows in No. 1.—3 Ploughs in No. 8. afternoon   part of the hands raising low places in the dams. & making up other dams part—turning ground after ploughs. & about 20—hands half a day digging ditch outside No 15 dam to get dirt to raise it. Amos & Davy mending Cogs. to Sugar mill   Peter fixing trunk in No 15. Boston & Lewis mending harrows & trenching ploughs—William & Henry Cleaning Sugar House   ten of White Hall hands workg @ C Hill & the others either Sick or nursing the children that are down with measles.

Saturday
Feby 5.

At W Hall nothing done except to attend on the Sick   fifteen being down with Measles   at C Hill broke down the Sugar Mill being the third time this week   four cogs broke this day. three harrows finished No. 6. & two Ox harrows finished No 1. & went into No 2 Square   ten hands raising low places in dam near gate. fifteen dressing dam & levelling Margin next 4. & 15.—& the rest turning after ploughs in Nos 16 17. & 18 Squares   three ploughs in No. 8. Mr Habersham & Dr. Turner dined with us today—

Monday
Feby 7ᵗʰ
Tuesday 8ᵗʰ

Went to Savʰ with Mr & Mrs Greene who left us for N York by the Wilmington rout[e]. Monday night, during my absence have been harrowing with 5 Harrows @

C Hill & ploughing with 3 Ploughs in No 8 & raising dams & cleaning out ditches with the others   Carpenters getting out Timber @ W Hall   dug ditches in New Ground & listed 2½ Acres

1848
Wednesday
Feby 9ᵗʰ

At C Hill Carpenters getting timber for Sugar Mill. 3 Mule Harrows in No. 3—& 2 Ox harrows in No. 7. three ploughs in No. 8. part of the hands raising low places in dam in No 13. & check dams & part Stopping leaks. & raising low places on outside dams. Charles drawing timbre & Billy puncheons. This Evening two—Carpenters came to C Hill by order of Lackleson to fix Mill—At W Hall have been beding in New Ground that was planted last year in Rice   did only half a task to the hand—have fifteen Sick with Measles & four nursing them at W Hall.

Thursday
Feby 10

Lacklesons
2 Carpenters
worked for the
first time this
day—

At C Hill Charles & Adam drawing timbre from Sans Souci   Billy puncheons from New Ground   three Mule Harrows nearly finished No 3   part of the hands raising Cross Banks—part filling holes & raising Corners in No 11 & 12 Square next Rice   also throwing up line Bank next Silk Hope & the Men driving pilings & puncheons to stop brake [sic] in little New Square—Two Negro Carpenters came last Evg from Savannah & did no work yesterday today they have done very little   then together with my three Carpenters Squared a twenty foot thick one foot Square—& from 11 oclock until night the two fr Savʰ only planed this Stick—at ½ past 3 P.M. Aukwright had not arrived at C Hill   at W Hall beded in New ground Rice field ½ a task to the hand   ought to have done ¾ each.—

Friday Feby 11

At C Hill Men employed Stopping dam next little Square & stopping leak in No. 20. Trunk, Women raising dam next Silk Hope & cleaning out ditches   Same place half a day & then went into Corn field cleaning ditches after ploughs   two harrows finished No 3 & then went in the high ground to plough for Cane   Adam & Charles drawing timbre for Mill   Lacklesons two Black Carpenters &

my three workg on Sugar Mill   Arkwright came out to
C Hill & Staid about one hour but did not see either
Myself or Overseer. At W Hall bed New ground two
hands in a task

Saturday
Feby 12.

At C Hill five Carpenters at Mill Overseer. & all the men
workg until 10 Oclock getting off wheels & prapering for
Carpenters. 8 Ploughs throwing—two furoughs for Sugar
Cane   Adam drawing Sticks for puncheons & Charles a
Stick of timbre in the forenoon   in the afternoon both
harrowing in Rice field. All the other hands (excepting 4
men with Flat hauling mud) cleaning out & deepening
ditches for Sugar Cane planting. Cyrus.—Shadwell. &
two of Georges Children sick with Measles @ C Hill—&
six at White Hall—

1848 Monday
Feby 14

54 Bushels Seed
Rice Winnowed
makes in all at
W Hall of Seed
Rice 582
Bushels

At White Hall trenched out field   winnowed & put into
Barn the balance of the Seed Rice. 54 Bushels   &
thrashed & winnowed about 8 Bushels Oats   Sancho
went for Oysters.—At C Hill run eight ploughs in Cane
land ploughg 4 furroughs & calculate tomorrow to run
trenching plough through it in wh to plant Cane. Part of
the force listing   part—deepening & cleaning out ditches
in Cane field & Corn field adjoining & part Stripping the
leaves off of Seed Cane. 4 Hands flating [flatting] dirt to
little Square & two—throwing it into center ditch.—Peter
laying out tasks   Carpenters workg on Sugar Mill.
Charles & Adam Carting Light wood from Sans Souci.—
Marion McAllister & Mott Francis came to W Hall today
on a visit—

Tuesday
Feby 15

Planted Oats
@ W Hall 3
Acres

C Hill 6 Acres
Cane

At W Hall planted 3 acres of Oats & burnt New ground
near House for Slips—at C Hill five persons employed
flating mud to little Square   Eight ploughs running in
Cane   part trenching ploughs   three—Wagons Carting
out Cane   twenty hands Striping Seed Cane & balance of
the force. laying, Cuting & beding Cane—one task to the
hand   did about Six Acres this night   Sam setting out
Box

Wednesday
Feby 16

planted @
C Hill 5 Acres
Cane.

At C Hill four Wagons Carting out Cane   five hands with
flat & all the rest of the force Stripping & planting Cane
have planted this day all double 5 Acres—Carpenters
workg on Sugar Mill.—At W Hall listed 1½ tasks in Cotton field

Thursday
Feby 17

Planted 5
Acres Sugar
Cane @ C Hill

At C Hill two harrows running in Rice field   four wagons
Carting out Cane   five hands flating mud for little Square
Carpenters with the two from Sav^h working on Sugar Mill
& all the force not in Sick house stripping & planting
Cane   only planted five acres   the great labour is in
Stripping.—At White Hall the few hands here listing in
Cotton field—Geo H. Timmins from Boston came to
W Hall this morning

Friday Feby 18

planted 6 Acres
Cane

At C Hill Carpenters   5 in all   work on Sugar Mill   the
rest of the force with two Ox & three Mule wagons Carting out Stripping & planting cane   all double planted only
6 Acres   White Hall listing

Saturday
Feby 19

5 Acres Cane
planted today.

At C Hill five men flatting dirt to little Square
Carpenters   5 in number   workg on Sugar Mill   also 5
other men—⅔ of a day workg with them getting mill in its
place—The rest of the force Stripping & planting Cane
about—27.Acres of Cane planted this Night   At W Hall
Sam has been working all the week planting Box in front
yard—the few hands not at C Hill listing in Cotton field—
Dr Carroll & his Son came yesterday to make us a visit at
W Hall. Marion McAllister & Mott Francis went to Col.
McAllisters

Monday
Feby 20th [sic]

At C Hill finished planting Cane   have planted in all 30
Acres. And I believe I have put double the quantity of
Seed necessary in the ground & quadruple the amount of
labor on it, having run 4 furroughs with ploughs & then
run one through the middle of the four

1848 Monday
Feby 21.

With trenching plough in this furough I put the Cane all
double thus = & then covered it with a good bed with

Read this before
planting Cane
in 1849—
Have planted
in all this night
30 Acres Cane

hoes. 3 Acres on the hill next Richmond Avenue are an exception in the quantity of Cane put in. that being Single. —. & 3 tasks nearest Negro Houses which was put in half Single only   Cut with knives leaving only 3 Eyes in each piece & planted thus — — — —. Now I am inclined to think I could have Saved ¾ of the Seed & planted it in the—last named way & realized as much from it. & I also think I could have save ¾th of the labour—for I think by running one furrough in the alley with the plough puting the Seed Cane in to that furrough & then—turning two furroughs one on each Side over it, it would be better—planted than I have done it &—the roots would be lower in the ground   by the experiments tried mentioned—above, I shall next year be able to judge if I am right—After—finishing planting all hands Cut &—wagons Carted Cane to Mill to be ground as soon as mill is finished. two black Carpenters left off work Saturday @ 3 Oclock   my own working on frame for mill to day & Amos on bolts for do—

1848 Monday
Feby 21

five men at the flat Carrying Mud to little Square & Scipio Harrowing with two Mules—about ten hands in Sick House with Measles.—at W Hall Sam fixing garden & the few people not at C Hill listing in Cotton field for Corn

Tuesday
Feby 22

Split 750 Rails

At C Hill five hands with flat carry mud to little Square my own Carpenters workg on Sugar Mill & the rest excepting 4 Rail Splitters gone to W Hall. have been Cutting Stripping & Carrying Sugar Cane to Mill—excepting one hand Harrowing in Rice field at W Hall   five hands Split 150 Rails each near House & the rest listed 1½ tasks & Cut Cotton Stalks—Have about fifteen hands Confined Sick   ⅔d the number with Measles—Mr How[e] this day punished Richd by whipping him which I did not approve of   This is the first time either Mrs A or myself have in any way interfered with his management of the children altho we have not been Satisfied with him as a teacher—He takes too much time with his own Studdies & has not fulfilled his Contract with me, never having spent the hour

he agreed too [*sic*] with the Boys out of School or attended
to them at all on Sunday. and as the Boys dislike him & he
them. & has requested me to give him up I have consented
to do it holding him however to the Contract as made in
Prov^e [Providence] with regard to his Wages   He is also in
love. which I presume is at the bottom of the whole business.—

Wednesday
Feby 23 1848

Split 750 Rails

At C Hill finished carrying the Sugar Cane into Mill &
made up dam next Silk Hope, & part of the men drove
pilings at another place against little Square. & five Men
with flat & throwing mud & part Cutting & heaping Cotton Stalks. Hannah Miscarried day before yesterday at
C Hill—At White Hall five Men Split 150 Rails each &
the rest listed in Cotton field

Thursday
Feby 24

Rain

Split 750 Rails

At C Hill two Women planted Bermuda Grass in dam
next Silk Hope   two finished Cuting & heaping Cotton
Stalks in New Ground & the rest listed two tasks each in
Cotton field back of Negro Houses   run Eight ploughs in
Corn field   four hands Cut & carr^d [illegible] in New
Ground   three hands in flat carryg Mud & four tracking
in Rice field   Peter laying out tasks. At W Hall five Splitting Rails   three toting Rails & making fence to New
ground & three listing in potatoe field one task each.

Friday Feby 25

Rain

First trenching
for Rice.

Split 750 Rails

At C Hill raising part of dam next Silk Hope   digging
ditch in Cotton field   listing in do. & part of the Hands
trenchg in Rice field   two wagons Carting out first Manure in Corn field   five ploughs in Corn field   five men
with flat. At W Hall five Splitting 150 Rails each. four
making fence & the rest listing in Same ground. Marion
McAllister & Mott Francis left for Savannah. Also Rev^d
Mr Benning who passed the night with us.

1848 Saturday
Feby 26.

Rain

At W Hall four making fence   five—Splitting Rails 150
each   two Shelling Corn. & the balance listing One task
each in field nearest House.—At C Hill made up fence
next—Richmond. Also dug ditches in Corn field near

Split 750 Rails

Negro Houses &—raised Some dams in Rice field & part of the force trenched with back trenching hoes No 6. Square in Rice field   five hands tracking & each hand doing one Acre each.—

Monday
Feby 28

First planted
Corn at C Hill
25. Acres

Split 300.
Rails

At C Hill twenty five hands planted 25 Acres Corn between Cane & New ground. One Wagon Carted out Manure   One Mule Harrow in No 17. & two ploughs in high ground preparing for Corn   17 trenching with back hoes in Nos one & 2 Squares & Six tracking in No 3. each doing 4 tasks   Several new Cases of Measles—At W Hall Geo with wagon drawing Rails for fence   two Splitting Rails & the rest cleaning up ground near House one task to the hand,   Had a long talk with Mr Pynchon about buying his place & I think it probable tomorrow we may close a bargain

Tuesday
Feby 29th

Planted 14
Acres Corn @
C Hill

300 Rails

At C Hill planted 14 Acres Corn & 21 Hands trenched for Rice   have Nos 1, 2, & 6 finished trenching & 12 Acres in No 3. Arkwright came @ 1 o'clock to C Hill today   6 ploughs in W Hall Corn field & the hands listed balance of old Corn field   Geo. carted Rails

1848 March 1
Wednesday

At C Hill planted No 6. Square & finished trenching No. 3. & 3 Acres in No 7   Aukwright at C Hill with Carpenters & Amos—also Eight hands fr. W Hall   fifteen Sick in the House with Measles   Winnowed 120 Bushels seed Rice at C Hill. At W Hall Six ploughs ploughed yesterday & to day fifty Acres for Corn running two furroughs & four hands listed 1½ tasks each in Cotton field & George drawing out Rails. Sent Tony to Savh this night.

Thursday
March 2d

At C Hill twelve Gangs planted three Acres to a Gang of four persons & finished No 1 & 2 Squares, three hands trenched Canal Margin & Several trenched in No 7 Square   planted 2½ Bushels to the Acre   have planted

Planted No 1
& 2 Squares
Rice @ C Hill
this day.

this night, 44—Acres Rice. At W Hall finished Making up fence round potatoe field & also piece of fence next Sylvias Garden   Geo. Drawing Rails & Neptune finished plough-ing Corn field   almost fifty Six acres ploughed tonight @ W Hall   Mr Arkwright playing the Gentleman today waiting for the Wheel by the Science. Sent flat [boat] after the wheel today.—And Spent one hour with Mr Pynchon & agreed to take Sedgefield Jany 1 1849. & to pay $8000 provided he does not trade with Way tomorrow

1848 Friday
March 3ᵈ

Rice 74 Acres
planted at
C Hill

At C Hill planted No 3 Square of Rice 2½ Bushels the Acre. 29 Acres   three hands trenched in No 7. & also planted about Six Acres in No 7.—ten men Worked half a day on Sugar Mill   the three Squares & Canal Margin contain 74 Acres   No. 7. when finished will add Acres 19½   At W Hall made up fence round potatoe field Carried the Oats into Stable loft & also made up part of fence round Meeting House field   Geo Carted Rails to fence   Arkwright puting wheels on Sugar Mill—

Saturday
March 4ᵗʰ

Finished first
planting of
Rice   in all 94
Acres   & also
finished
Grinding
Cane—

At C Hill started Sugar Mill & finished grinding the Cane which turned out only 4 Bbls from about 8 Acres   it was very Sour & dry & yielded very little   the rest of the people excepting three that were harrowing finished plant-ing No 7 Square   2½ Bushels the Acre. Two Ox harrows commenced in No 16   two mule Harrows in No 8 & one Mule harrow in No 5.—finished Winnowing Seed Rice 81 Bushels at W Hall   Geo. drew out Rails & one hand in Cotton house & three listing in Cotton field   Arkwright left for Savannah about 11 Oclock this day.—

1848 Monday
March 6ᵗʰ

At C Hill loaded Capt Thompson with 3170 Bushels Rough Rice—Sold A Low Co @ 85 cts   also Sent by him 25 Barrels [illegible] Syrup—WRH & Son. a few hands burnt Cotton Stalks   four men Harrowed two Oxen & two double Mule Harrows in 16. & 18. Squares. four men gone to W Hall & Split 600 Rails—The White Hall force there Shelling Seed Corn & Geo. Carting Rails & plough-ing two acres in potatoe field & the rest cleaned up one task each in potatoe field.—

Tuesday
March 7ᵗʰ

Planted
@ W Hall
22 Acres Corn

At White Hall four hands Split 600 Rails. Geo drawing out Rails round the fences. two hands Shelling Seed Corn. & 22 planted as many Acres in New ground. At C Hill finished—loading the Science   she took in 3170 Bushels & 24 Bbls Syrup & after finishing with the Vessel they listed ground for potatoes—two Mule & two ox Harrows in Nos 8. & 16. Squares. Carpenters Jobbing

Wednesday
March 8ᵗʰ

Planted @
W Hall 28½
Acres Corn.

At W Hall planted 28½ Acres of Corn & George drawing out Rails fr. Potatoe field. At C Hill finished listing & beded part of the New Ground for potatoes & Seven hands Commenced tracking in Rice field @ C Hill

March 9ᵗʰ
1848 Thursday

Bought
Sedgefield &
Pine lands of
Pychon this day

Consideration
$8000 to be
paid
Jany 1/1848—

Planted 6
Acres Corn
W.H.

At W Hall twenty two hands beded in the New part of Corn field 1½ tasks each & Seven hands planted Six— Acres of Corn.—At C Hill two Mule & 2 Ox Harrows running in Rice field   the Ox Harrows finished Nos 16. & 20. & the Mule Harrows finished Eight & part of No 4 Squares. Six men tracking & have finished Nos 16, 17 & 18   Carpenters working in Trunk & three trenching— ploughs. Started for the first time today in No 13 Square. Mr. Pynchon Came to C Hill & agreed to Sell me Sedge- field together with his two tracks of Pine Land   1200 Acres   & His flat & Plantation tools   Windfan &c that are used in Rice Planting for the sum of $8000—the Plan- tation Flat & tools to be delᵈ Jany 1, 1849 & Pine lands as soon as the papers are executed & I am to pay the money on the delivery of the—property for Interest from that date next week papers to be executed—part of the hands at C Hill finished beding Six Acres fr Potatoes in New Ground.—Sent 10 Hands home to C Hill   Mr Pynchon represents Sedgefield as Containing 240. Acres river Swamp. In the purchase of Sedgefield I have bought all the timbre, Trunks & fencing laths & post. in the place

1848 Friday
March 10

At White Hall planted ten acres of Corn   Nine of it New ground—with fifteen Hands—At C Hill planted with part

*Planted 10
Acres Corn at
White Hall &
Potatoes @
C Hill*

of the hands potatoes & part trenched with hoes   three
trenching ploughs in No. 13. & four Harrows two Oxen &
one Mule Harrows in No 3 & 9—Carpenters Working on
Trunks   Amos painting Machinery.—Mrs Winn & family
came to stay @ W Hall today.—

*Saturday
March 11.*

*Have planted
in all at
W Hall 68
Acres Corn &
at C Hall 6½
Acres Potatoes.*

At C Hill 7 Hands tracking   Six Gangs trenching three
Acres each   three Harrows finished the Harrowing No 9
& 10.—Amos Setting tire to timbre wheels & Ox cart &
part of the force finished beding & planting 6½ Acres
potatoes   Overseer gone to Savannah on Kate   At
W Hall finished planting Corn 2½ Acres. making in all
planted at White [Hall] between 68 & 69 Acres &—
afterwards listed Cotton field & Cut & burnt Cotton
Stalks   also at C H run Seven trenching ploughs in Nos
12 & 13 Squares—

*Monday
March 13*

*Planted No
18—12 Acres
Rice C.H.*

At C Hill Eight ploughs trenchg in No 13 & 12 Squares.
Eight Gangs trenching with Hoes & finished No 18 & 19
& trenched 12 Acres in 16—7 Hands tracking in No 4 & 5
Squares & five Gangs planted No. 18 Square   2½ Bushels. the two Ox Wagons Carted out Manure in Potatoe field
@ W Hall   all hands cleaning up New ground for potatoes near House

*1848 Tuesday
March 14*

Ice this night

At C Hill Six Gangs of 4 Each planted No 18 Square &
part of 17. Eight Gangs of three each trenched balance of
No 4 & all of 20 Squares   Seven hands finished tracking
No 5 & 8 Squares. Eight trenching ploughs finished No 12
& part of 11 Square & trenched round the Margins of No
17 & 19 Squares.—Two Ox Wagons drawing out Manure
in potatoe field that was planted in Cane last year—Dr
Carroll & his Son will have been with us one month on
Friday. Mrs Winn & her two Children came last . . . friday to stay ten days.—

*Wednesday
March 15*

At C Hill Six gangs finished trenching No 8 & part of No
5. Six tracking & two wagons drawing out manure   Eight

*Ball worked
half a day with
his man but
was at C Hill
the whole day*

ploughs trenching Margins to 16 & 18 & finished No 12 &
11 Squares & part of No 9. Six Gangs finished planting
No 17 & 20 Squares & Six Acres in No 16 Square. also
Carried from W Hall two loads of Rice   Say 60 Bushels.—This day Ball & his Black man packed Corn mill   if
it grinds as much in few motions to the Size of Stones as
Mr Haywards & as well I am to pay him for fixing it, but
not otherwise—the few hands @ W Hall listed Cotton
field—Mrs Gray & Daughters & Geo & Stephen Habersham & Miss Habersham dined here

*1848 Thursday
March 16.*

*Have Sent Seed
Rice in all fr.
W Hall 212
Bushels*

Ice this night

At C Hill Eight trenching ploughs—finished No 12 & part
of No 9 & hoed margins in 4, & part of 8 & 4 Hands
opened after trenching ploughs in No 13 & 11   Gangs
covered 3 Acres each finishing No 20. Also No 4. & doing
2 Acres in No 8. Two Mule Carts & one Wagon & 2 Ox—
Wagons Carted to C Hill from W Hall 155 Bushels Seed
Rice & the two Ox Wagons afterwards Carted out Manure   Carpenters workg with [illegible]   twenty Sick
with Measles including—children—The few hands @
W Hall listed for Cotton   4 Cut Cotton Stalks.

*Friday
March 17*

*Ice this night
Orange trees
Injured*

At C Hill Eight trenching ploughs—in Rice field   Six of
them in No 9—two Wagons Carting out Manure   Six
hands opening after the ploughs in No 12   about a dozen
minding off the birds from Corn field & Rice & the balance Eleven Gangs planted 33 Acres Rice   2½ Bushels to
the Acre. finished No 9 & 13. & planted about 2 Acres in
No 12 Square—At W Hall four hands in Cotton field &
by their carelessness let five hundred feet of fence—get
burnt in New Ground.

*Saturday
March 18*

*made return of
Taxes to
Strickland*

At C Hill planted No 12 Square & 4 Acres in Eleven.
Eight ploughs—finished trenching No 9 Square & two
Wagons Carted out 12 loads all today   Made my Tax return to Mr Strickland Tax Receiver & at White Hall repaired fence burnt yesterday

1848 Monday
March 20

At C Hill finished planting No 11   also planted 9 & 10 Squares   all with 2½ Bushels Seed to the Acre—four men opened trenches   After the ploughs   two Wagons Carted out Manure & the rest of the force Minding Birds/at White Hall   three double Mule Harrows in Rice field & the few hands in Cotton field listing   Geo drawing out Rails from New Ground   the tides have been very Short & we have No 13, 12 & 20 Squares not half covered & yesterday ought to have been the highest tide.—

Tuesday
March 21

Finished 2ᵈ
planting Rice
@ C H

At C Hill finished planting No 5. Square & wagons Carted out manure   the rest of the force went to W. Hall   four hands there Split 150 Rails ea   three double Harrows in W Hall Rice field & the rest trenching in New ground less than a task to the hand. I went to Savʰ today.

Wednesday
March 22ᵈ

Returned this Evg from Savʰ   at C Hill cleaned & loged up in New ground   Carted out Manure Same as yesterday   At W Hall hoed off Stubbel & trenched ½ a task to the hand Inland Rice field   four hands Split Rails & Geo. carted them out of the field

Thursday
March 23ᵈ

At C Hill three wagons Carting out—manure. three men Flating mud & part of the force trenching & loging up New Ground   the rest @ W Hall trenching in New ground   Geo. Carting Rails   Scipio & Peter Splitting Rails—Mrs McAllister & Mrs Ward arrived this Evening at W Hall.—

1848
March 24
Friday

At C Hill three hands with flat   three Wagons Carting out Manure & Sixteen in New Ground trenching for Rice & loging up & balance went to W. Hall

Saturday
March 25ᵗʰ

At C Hill 3 men with flat   Six—with Wagons Carting out Manure   four loging up in New Ground & about ten Minding Birds & taking off trash   Sixteen trenching in New Ground & the rest of W Hall   five trenching with

Mules in the Rice field & the balance with White Hall
hands excepting Geo. who is Carting Rails & the bird
minders, cleaning up & trenching inland Rice field—doing
about ¾ of a task to the hand

Monday
27 March

5½ Acres of
Inland Rice
field planted
this day—

At C Hill trenching in New ground   Carting out manure
& Six trenching ploughs in No. 14 Square   At W Hall 16
Hands only planted about 5½ Acres of Rice—19 Hands
finished trenching Inland Rice field excepting two tasks
doing one task to the hand   Mr & Mrs Brown Mr & Mrs
Winn Mrs Gray & Anne—Mr Patterson Miss Borland &
little Patterson—

Tuesday 28ᵗʰ

Settled with Mr Howe & he left for the North after passing the winter not very profitably for our children.—

Wednesday
March 29

Planted 14½
Acres of Rice in
New Ground
2½ Bushels the
Acre

At C Hill finished planting the Inland Rice field, excepting
only the inside, three wagons Carting out Manure & Six
trenchg ploughs in Rice field & the rest of the force at
W Hall—where together with the White Hall hands they
Covered fifteen Acres of New ground Rice field. Geo
Carted Rails   Peter & Cain finished the trenching in that
field.

Thursday
March 30ᵗʰ

Finished
planting
Inland Rice
9 Acres   the
whole field
29 Acres
@ W Hall

At C Hill finished planting New ground Rice & then
cleaned up   trenched & made up dam to little Square. Six
trenching ploughs running in No 15. & three Wagons
Carted out Manure. /Overseer Sick/   At W Hall finished
planting Inland Rice field   the whole being 29 Acres. One
hand trenching after ploughs & 12 Hands—loging up &
burning New Ground near House for potatoes.—

Friday
March 31

At C Hill cleaned up & trenched little Square & opened
after the ploughs in No 15   Six ploughs finished trenching
No 15   three Wagons carting out Manure—At W Hall

Planted W
Hall Rice field
16. Acres
Rice all planted
@ C Hill
29 Acres. Rice
W.H. Inland

three hands listed & beded one task for potatoes   four
hands finished loging up potatoe field   Geo. drawing Rails
to New ground fence. Celia & Rose Sorting potatoes for
planting & the balance with C Hill force—planted Rice
field @ W Hall 2½ Bushels per Acre.—

Saturday
April 1

Planted 1 Acre
of potatoes 16
Bushels also
planted 28
Acre field
@ C Hill

At C Hill five ploughs run one furrough each side of List
in Corn field back Negro Houses   did 22¾ Acres. two
Wagons Carting out Manure, two hands hoed margins to
first planted Rice which I ordered flowed today & the rest
planted little Square & No 15 & 4 Acres in No 14.—2½
Bushels pr Acre @ W Hall beded 5 tasks for potatoes &
planted one Acre

1848 April 3
Monday

Finished Rice
planting at C
Hill this
night have
planted in all
@ C Hill
356 acres

At C Hill two wagons Carting out Manure, ten hands
opening after the ploughs in No 14. the balance of the
force planting Rice & finished the Rice planting at C Hill
this night   planted Saturday & today 135 Bushels Seed
28 Acres planted this day—At W Hall planted 3¼ Acres
potatoes   16 Bushels to the Acre   & beded one Acre for
potatoes   Six ploughs running four furroughs in Cotton
field   George went to Kilkenny with a load of Cotton
Seed to exchange with Mr Rodgers   Ferguson very ill
with Pleurisy.—

Tuesday
April 4th

At C Hill planted 16 Acres Corn in—field rear of Negro
houses & finished listing Same field. three wagons also—
Carting out Manure. Had Cattle driven to W Hall this
day. Sent 20 men to—Mulberry Hill to trench & cut
out—Stumps from ditches   trenched between 8 & 9
Acres in Square nearest high ground   At W Hall ten
hands listed two tasks each in Cotton field & three Cut
heaped & burnt Cotton Stalks   7 ploughs run four furroughs each in Cotton field & did 14 Acres. two hands

beded the balance of 4 Acres for potatoes & one task for ground nuts—

Wednesday
April 5

Put on water
for point flow
to 2ᵈ planting
this day.

At C Hill finished planting 25 Acre field of Corn back of Negro Houses & half a day worked replanting Corn with 19 hands. Adam Carted out Manure & a few hands took off trash from Rice field, turned the gates to let in Water on part of 2ᵈ planting Rice. viz. Nos 4. 8. 13. 16. 17. 18. 19. twenty left dry as we must take out the Trunk. No 12. & 10 shall let in water this night, flowed the first planted Rice on the 31ˢᵗ ulto   At White Hall listed in Cotton field with fifteen hands & five ploughs. run four furroughs in Cotton field doing two Acres each   Billy commenced Carting out Manure at W Hall into potatoe field. Rose & Celia finished planting potatoes   have in all planted @ W Hall 4 Acres potatoes. At Mulberry Hill twenty five Men trenched about Eleven Acres & two hands cut out Stumps from quarter drains

Thursday
April 6.

At C Hill replanted Corn with 19 Hands & took off treash from Rice field with ten more, 28 Hands at Mulberry Hill 21 of them trenching for Rice   the balance levelling dirt over   At W Hall listed 9 Acres for Cotton   have fifty Acres Cotton lands listed & three quarters of it ploughed with four furroughs for beding—This day Mrs Harper & Daughter   Maria Champion   Young Carroll & Dr Mc-Queen—arrived W Hall & My Daughter Louisa returned from Savannah

1848 Friday
April 7ᵗʰ

Planted first
Square 17
Acres @
Mulberry
Hill 3
Bushels to the
Acre.

At C Hill did nothing   all the hands either at W Hall or Mulberry Hill, at Mulberry Hill planted One Square 17 Acres nearest high ground & 2 Acres in rough Square & twenty one hands finished trenching 2ᵈ Square & leveled back dirt in 4ᵗʰ—Square from quarter drains   Peter Stopping leaks. At W Hall beded 12 Acres for Cotton & 7 Ploughs in Corn field doing 3 Acres with three furroughs each   Dr. McQueen very ill at W Hall—Catharine also & Young Carroll bleeding at the Lungs & Mrs Harper quite—indisposed—[6]

Saturday
April 8

First planted
Cotton @
W Hall fifteen
Acres

At Mulberry Hill planted 2ᵈ Square   19¼ Acres   3
Bushels to the Acre & 9—men digging ditch to make dam
back side of 4ᵗʰ Square at Mulberry Hill, at C Hill 5 hands
Spreading Manure on Potatoe ground and Billy Carting
out manure. At W Hall planted fifteen Acres Cotton &
beded 4 Acres for Cotton   7 ploughs in Corn field—
planted 6 Tasks each hand of Cotton.

Monday
April 10

planted 5 Acres
Cotton.

At C Hill Billy finished hauling out Manure & with the
exception of Bird minders all the people either at Mulberry
Hill or White Hall   at Mulberry Hill dug ditch & made
up dam next Hines   also levelled back dirt from quarter
drains & hoed off Stubble to No 4   At W Hall planted 5
Acres Cotton & beded 16 Acres for Cotton & 7 ploughs
finished ploughing Corn field

Tuesday
April 11

Planted 5
Acres Cotton

At C Hill a few hands shelling Corn & a few Minding
Birds   forty hands @ Mulberry Hill making up dam &
trenching in No 4 Square which Contains 23 Acres—8
Acres yet to be—trenched in that Square. At White Hall
planted five Acres Cotton, & beded about 9 Acres for
Cotton, & the ploughs finished Cotton field. Mrs Harper
& her daughter went to Savannah this day.—

Wednesday
April 12

Planted @
White Hall 16
Acres Cotton
this day

At C Hill eight hands hoed Sugar Cane & 7 ploughs run
three furroughs in Corn & Cane fields & ploughed three
Acres each   about 40 Hands @ Mulberry Hill   men
finished trenching No 4 Square & also cut down what
Bushes were left in No 3 & Women cleaned off & heaped
part of the rushes &c in Same Square doing 2 tasks each—
At W Hall finished beding Cotton field & planted 16
Acres Cotton.

Thursday
April 13

Planted 11
Acres Cotton

At C Hill a few hands hoed Cane & 7 ploughs run in Corn
& Cane. ten Minding Birds   40 at Mulberry Hill   24
trenching each one task in No. 3 Square   balance cleaning
up & hoeing off Rushes &c in Same Square doing three
tasks each   No 3 contains 20 Acres   At W Hall finished

*which makes
53 Acres in
all. finished
planting
Cotton*

planting Cotton 12 Acres & hoed after ploughs 13¾ Acres of Corn

*Friday
14ᵗʰ April*

At W Hall hoed 18½ acres Corn & at C Hill hoed Cane part of the day & 7 ploughs—running part of the day & afterward put into Cotton Plant. 735 Bushels best & 115 Bushels Inferior Rice. at Mulbery Hill trenched 5¼ Acres in Rough Square one task to a hand

*1848 Saturday
April 15*

*Shipped from
C H & W. H
1500 Bushels
Rice pr [per]
Cotton Plant
and also
finished hoeing
52 Acres Corn
@ W Hall—.*

At C Hill finished puting Rice on board Cotton Plant   in all 1335 Bushels—735 of the best & 600 Bushels Inferior— 165 Bushels best added at W Hall makg the whole ship- ment 1500 Bushels—after puting the Rice in vessel at C Hill the People hoed two tasks Sugar Cane & twenty three men trenched one task ea & 21 men trenched one task each at Mulberry Hill in rough Square which I call No 3—The ploughs   7 in number   running in Corn & finished the Same this Evg—At White Hall twenty one hands hoed 20 Acres Corn making in all Corn hoed @ W Hall this night fifty two Acres.—

*Monday
April 17*

*Planted No 4
Square at
Mulbery Hill
23 Acres.*

At C Hill 7 Ploughs in Corn & Cane field and the rest of the force at Mulberry Hill with part of the W Hall hands—& have planted No 4. Square next Clays Canal also finished cleaning up No 3—Square & planted about 2 Acres in that Square   have put 3 Bushels to the Acre to both—Squares—At W Hall all hands replanting Corn in New ground. Mr Champion Came out this Evng for his Daughter.—Recᵈ this day from Savʰ 18 Bbls Syrup that was returned to me on a/c being Sour—

*Tuesday
April 18*

At C Hill Six hands hoed Cane & two ploughs finished ploughing Corn & Cane, & five ploughs ploughed 2 Acres each 4 furroughs in Miller field   the rest of the people @ Mulberry Hill finished trenching No 3. Rice & planted two thirds of it—At W Hall. 7 Hands replanted 22 Acres of Corn—

Wednesday
April 19th

At C Hill Eighteen Hands hoed Sugar Cane   7 ploughs ploughed Miller field & the balance of the people at Mulberry Hill finishing the planting of the Rough Square—have Sowed at Mulberry Hill. 360 Bushels Seed Rice & planted Eighty two Acres. At White Hall replanted all of the old ground Corn   about Sixty Acres with eight hands in three days.—Rose & Celia hoed three tasks each in Corn field. Sent Catharine to Savannah this day with Amos & Jinny to take care of her.—

CHAPTER SIX

Bryan County, Georgia

It was a measure of the Arnolds' wealth and status that while in residence at White Hall they could afford to bring a tutor with them from the North to teach their children, but it was also indicative of the dual nature of their lives divided between the North and South that the children's education was disrupted as the family journeyed back and forth according to the seasons. For example, the older Arnold girls, Eliza Harriet and Louisa Caroline, were tutored by Charlotte H. Bradley for several years in the early 1830s, the teacher going back and forth with the family between Georgia and Rhode Island. Later, before they married, the girls were sent to finishing schools in the North. Louisa, for example, went to the Beacon Hill School in Boston in 1845, spending her seventeenth birthday reading a book in the company of her cousin, Samuel Greene Arnold.[1] The daughters of the middle and upper classes, although they attended private schools, did not go to college.

All three of the Arnold sons went to private preparatory schools in the North, even during the winter season, so that they could enter their father's alma mater, Brown University. In 1846 both Richard, Jr., and Thomas were in the same school in Jamaica Plains, outside Boston, run by Charles W. Greene, a cousin of the Arnolds. Their dual life as they journeyed back and forth according to the seasons in their early formative years apparently caused problems, however, as reflected in Mr. Greene's letter to Arnold assuring him that his son Thomas, then ten years old, was getting special help with his reading difficulties: "Tom is taking the most unwearied pains to read & Mrs. G. [Greene] pays daily attention to him down stairs. She feels a R. I. [Rhode Island] pride to make him equal to boys younger than himself and she keeps him with her an hour in the morning & afternoon & intends to surprise his class, by his reappearance, as equal to the best."[2] None of the Arnold children, male or female, attended public school in Rhode Island and certainly not in rural Georgia, where public education was practically nonexistent at the time.

Rhode Island had pioneered in state aid to public education, passing a law in 1800 which not only established free schools in every township in the state but also provided money to support them. It then lost the chance to establish the best public school system in New England by repealing the law three years later. It was not until 1828 that state support for public education was again established by law, and not until 1845 was a state superintendent of education, Henry Barnard, hired to coordinate and standardize public education throughout the state. Illiteracy remained high in Rhode Island until after the Civil War because attendance at schools was not enforced until 1883 and as many as 45 percent of school-age children worked in the mills or at other jobs and thus did not attend school regularly.[3]

Yet, even if the Arnold children had attended public schools in Providence, they would not have been in the same schools with blacks, since segregation existed in the city throughout the antebellum period. There were no schools and no funds for educating blacks beyond grammar school, and an attempt to integrate the public schools in Rhode Island in 1859 lost by two votes in the state legislature. So unpopular among whites was the idea of integrating the schools that Amos Barstow, who had declared himself in favor of integration, withdrew from running as a candidate for the general assembly in 1858 "rather than jeopardize the chances of those running with him."[4] A black leader in Newport, George Downing, argued that segregation "wars against the principles of the state" and in an argument that anticipated the U.S. Supreme Court decision of 1954 by nearly one hundred years declared that to believe separate schools provided equal educational opportunity was nonsense.[5] It was not until March 7, 1866, that the public schools of Rhode Island were integrated by law. At about the same time, President Barnas Sears, Wayland's successor at Brown University, went to Washington and successfully argued against the inclusion of an integration clause in the Civil Rights Act of 1866. He succeeded in persuading several senators to substitute instead the idea of "equal privileges" of education for whites and blacks; "separate but equal facilities" thus became enshrined in national law.[6]

An effective common school system of public education was not established in Georgia until 1859 despite the fact that in 1850 there was a 20 percent illiteracy rate among Georgia whites. Until the late 1850s half of the small public education funds went to support private academies for the middle and upper classes. Public education in the rural areas was badly neglected throughout the antebellum period. The ideal of public education espoused by Governor Joseph Brown, under whose administration the new reform law was passed, was that every "free white child" would have an equal right to attend school and that there would be "no aristocracy but that of color and conduct."[7] The Civil War ended even that small advance for public education of whites in Georgia. Blacks, free or enslaved, were denied any education.

Since public education was so backward in antebellum Georgia and the other slave states in general, especially in the rural plantation areas, there was no adequate pool of teachers to tutor the children of the planter aristocracy and to prepare the sons for college in the North. Therefore, many northerners went south as tutors, including Eli Whitney and William Ellery Channing, to name only the most famous, as well as Arnold's contemporary, Wilbur Fisk, a graduate of Brown University in 1815 and the president of Wesleyan University from 1831 until his death in 1839.[8] There was, therefore, nothing unusual about Arnold's arrangement with Phineas Howe (1823–1852). Attending commencement exercises on September 1, 1847, he was on the lookout for a bright young man to tutor his sons. Howe, a Phi Beta Kappa graduate, probably came highly recommended as a serious student, and Arnold, having also been Phi Beta Kappa, appeared to be partial to its members. Since he was available, Howe seemed the best choice among the graduates of the class of 1847.

On February 22, 1848, the arrangement with Phineas Howe came apart, and although Arnold insisted that Howe fulfill his contract and complete his term as tutor, Howe's disciplinary control over the Arnold sons was undermined from that point. Although Arnold indicated he had been dissatisfied with Howe as a teacher for some time, the whipping of Richard, Jr., on that day led to Arnold's firing him, "holding him however to the Contract as made in Providence with regard to his Wages"; thus Howe forfeited approximately $100.00 of his contracted wages of $450.00 per annum. The sum of $350.74 was paid him on his day of departure, March 28, $11.00 of which was paid him even though, according to Arnold, "he had no claim." Arnold did not, however, pay for his return passage.[9] Banished from the Garden of Eden, Phineas Howe left for the North burdened with the ultimate curse that a practical businessman could hurl at a teacher who "takes too much time with his own studies": his pedagogical efforts had not been "very profitable for our children."

Howe's transgression was that he literally usurped the role of father and whipped Richard J. Arnold, Jr., like a slave. Phineas's being in love seems to have been the real cause "of the whole business," according to Arnold. If by any chance Howe had fallen in love with Arnold's second daughter, Louisa, who was nineteen when they arrived at the plantation early in November 1847, he would have been teased unmercifully by the Arnold boys. And Richard, Jr., the oldest at thirteen, would have led the teasing. Undoubtedly, Richard Arnold, Sr., considered Phineas Howe, newly graduated from college and without any prospects beyond lowly paid teaching or ministerial positions, an unsuitable son-in-law. Arnold had strong views on the propriety of young men courting his daughters, and in 1842 had told his neighbor and fellow planter John P. Hines, who owned Silk Hope plantation, that his daughter Harriet was too young at seventeen to be entertaining proposals of marriage. On May 2, 1843, he wrote Hines that "the same reasons that existed last year, now exist to prevent your addressing my Daughter," one of those reasons, besides her age, being that she was not in love with him. "I therefore recommend to you as a friend to abandon all idea of the thing, & not allow yourself one moment to think it can be accomplished."[10] If Phineas Howe had fallen in love with Louisa, he was out of luck because she was in love with her first cousin Samuel Greene Arnold, whom she married the following fall. Phineas Howe left the Arnold plantation the day before Louisa's twentieth birthday.

By the winter term of 1848–1849, Arnold's sons, including the youngest, ten-year-old William Eliot, were in the North at a private school again. It was the Newark Academy in Delaware, run by Richard Mathew Meigs. At the same time Arnold's daughter Mary Cornelia, age eight, was placed in Miss Haines's School in New York City while the Arnolds went South. Only the youngest child, Susan, accompanied them to White Hall in December 1848.

Maria McIntosh, attempting to justify the system of slavery in the South, wrote in *Woman in America* (1850) that not only was there for the slaves the advantage of "partial civilization and Christianization of the race" but also that slavery was "the means of promoting the intellectual cultural and social refinement of those forced into the position of their masters." It was all a blessing in disguise because northerners, lacking the leisure of slave labor and thus unable to send their sons to England for an education, established their own colleges where "Southern youth have come to receive an education, for the last fifty years" instead of going off to England for their education! Southern woman was twice blessed, for "she is a missionary to whose own door God has brought the Pagans to be instructed," and she has learned the virtues of charity, gentility, love, and patience "to interpose the shield of her charity between the weak and the strong, to watch beside the sick, to soothe the sorrowing, to teach the ignorant, to soften by her influence the haughty master, and to elevate the debased slave."[11]

Both Mary Cornelia and Susan Arnold, who also went to Miss Haines's School in the 1850s, did not need to learn these lessons directly from Maria McIntosh, who began teaching at the school after her return from Europe in 1859. Their mother Louisa was the kind of southern woman Maria McIntosh idealized in her book.

Arnold's sons had neither the talent nor the ambition to become scholars. Richard, Jr., was admitted to Brown on July 10, 1851, with the class of 1855, to pursue the new degree program of bachelor of philosophy; Thomas was admitted as a special student on September 17, 1855, as a candidate for the bachelor of arts degree with the class of 1859. Neither Richard, Jr., nor Thomas graduated. Richard, Jr., left college after a year and a half on February 20, 1853, in time to travel west with his father that spring but too late to meet Olmsted at White Hall. Thomas left college after only one term.[12] They knew they would inherit the plantations one day, as Thomas and William Eliot did in fact, or be fitted into Arnold's northern business interests, as Richard, Jr., eventually was. They were the sons of a wealthy man who in the South was the literal master of two hundred human beings by whose labor he prospered and in the North was a respected businessman. Richard, Jr., and Thomas were in no mood to settle down and lead a disciplined life in the groves of academe. They were young, they were wealthy (or at least their father was), and they wanted to enjoy themselves before taking life seriously.

Thomas went south to join his family in Georgia after leaving college in January 1856, but by April he was back in Providence seeking advice from his cousin and brother-in-law, Samuel Greene Arnold, the intellectual in the family:

> He did not like to advise me as you [Richard Arnold, Sr.] and he differed so
> much upon matters of education, but he said if I wished it he would give me
> his advice and it was this, to leave college and pay strict attention to my
> english study French and read history; to follow this up until fall and then go
> to Burlin and studdy for one or two years, and he says that when I return, I
> would be better educated than I would by remaining here, for he says people
> have got the idear that I do not know much; and no matter how hard I study
> here it will be a long time before they will alter there minds   besids I will
> learn the modern languages which I can not do in this country. I hope you will
> approve of this plan. Dr Sears [president of Brown at the time] says there is
> nothing like a german education and advises every boddy that can be educated
> there. So I did not return to college but I am following out these plans.[13]

An indulgent father granted his son's wish to study in Germany, but the real reason for Thomas's poor showing in college and for his father's willing-

ness to send him to Europe is revealed in Thomas's letter to his father from
Heidelberg, Germany, dated July 18, 1856:

> I have received your letter and am very much surprised to see how kindly you
> write me after the outrageous manner in which I have treated you, and dis-
> grased myself, but I do not suppose that you can ever trust me again, with the
> same freedom that you did at one time; but I do not pretend to give any excuse
> for my conduct & I acknowledge that I have led a most sentual and disipated
> life for the last two years. The reason that I did not tell you of these enormous
> debts before I left America was because I knew you would not let me go. (and
> justly too) for you would not have confidence in me; but I felt it was better for
> me to leave Providence and the sooner the better, and when I left Providence I
> left it with new rezolutions   among them was the rezolution that I would not
> drink ardent spirits and another that I would never gamble again.[14]

Thomas was probably jealous of his older brother, who had gone to Europe for the year while he remained in Providence studying, and so he had
welcomed his cousin's advice to study in Germany. As it was, Thomas joined
his brother Richard, Jr., in Germany in July. On July 3 they sent their father
a bottle of 230-year-old wine from Bremen for which they paid "a little over
two English dollars" and which Tom tasted ("it is a strong wine").[15] Tom,
however, was not breaking his resolution by tasting the wine, for wine, no
matter how strong, is not ardent spirits. Ultimately, of course, Papa paid for
the wine. On November 28, 1856, he recorded in his account book:

R. J Arnold, Jr. by this sum to be allowed for your expenses first yr in Europe	[$] 1200.
Thomas C. Arnold For this sum to be allowed 1st yr in Europe	1100
to this sum allowed my 2 sons 1st yr in Europe	2300[16]

The sum allowed each was $100 per month, but apparently Thomas was to
have one month less.

Arnold received a double shock when he learned a few weeks later just
how well his son Richard, Jr., was enjoying himself in Paris. Thomas could
be forgiven his peccadillos, having not yet reached his majority and being on
his own for the first time. Besides, his debts were not that enormous, although Thomas admitted in his letter from Heidelberg that there were six
additional small debts he had forgotten to mention, totaling $71. The eldest
son, now twenty-two years of age, should have known better. True, Thomas
had practiced deception by not revealing his debts until he was safely in

Europe, but Richard had promised before going to Europe to mend his extravagant ways. More upsetting was that others were involved—Richard, Jr., had written to his cousin Tristam Burges begging him and his uncle Zachariah Allen for money so that he could pay his debts in Paris without his father knowing. Cousin Tristam forwarded the letter to Richard's father, who received it just in time "to turn the festivities of Christmas into a day of mourning."[17]

Arnold's letter to his son, which he carefully copied for his records, was sent "not in anger but in deep sorrow." It vacillated between scolding him for having "spent as much in five months as I allowed you for the whole time you were to remain abroad consequently there is no other alternative than for you to come home," and indulgently forgiving him in the hope that he could still salvage something of his grand tour—"if the amount you wrote Tristam for will pay all you owe in Paris & leave you enough with the addition of 3 or 4 hundred dollars to allow you to go into Italy & return by the middle of March or first of April to England you may go but if your debts in Paris will require much more you must return home at once." Having said all this by way of forgiveness, Arnold made sure his son would never forget what he had done:

> I had a plan drawn and estimates made to build a house in Newport early in the Spring but in consequence of the many calls for money and the extreme shortness of my crop and a loss that I heard of the same day your letter was received of the Knoxville Steamer at N Y I have concluded to give up the Building of the house and am not certain that I shall not sell the lot and abandon Newport altogether.[18]

Richard, Jr., did not return home on the next steamer. One may assume he made it to Italy, for the summer found him in Heidelberg again, describing his grand tour of Switzerland and the Alps, a copy of Byron's poems in hand: "His Poems are very interesting to read while you are at the very places," including Interlocken, "site of what is supposed to be Manfreds Castle, Byrons Philanthropist." A reformed Richard, Jr., now wrote to his father of his future plans, both immediate and long-range:

> I again take up my pen to acquaint you with my future plans which are viz 1st To come home by if not before the first week of September. 2nd Not to stop twenty-four hours in Paris but go directly on to London   3rd to write once every week while in Europe   4th Immediately on my arrival in America to go into some business & stick to that business whatever it may be & with the *Blessing* of God to compensate for past miscomings.[19]

Still, Richard, Jr., need not have worried, if indeed he had, that his father might have to sell the land in Newport to keep him in Europe in the style to which he was accustomed. On February 17, 1857, Arnold recorded in his account book the sum of $11,000 paid to John P. Hines for tracts of land, being "the whole of Orange Grove Plantation and one half each of the Mulbery Hill and Sans Souci plantations," the other half of each being already owned by Arnold. This purchase rounded out his antebellum plantation holdings. He continued to send money to Thomas and Richard, Jr., in Europe, and on July 3, 1857, perhaps in return for the wine sent him the year before, mailed a box of books to Germany, paying three American dollars for the freight.[20] By the following summer the family was able to move into their new house in Newport, designed by Russell Warren, a prominent Rhode Island architect.

While Richard, Jr., was still enrolled at Brown in the fall of 1852, his father hired William E. Tolman, an 1849 Phi Beta Kappa graduate of Brown, to tutor his younger sons. Arnold made sure this time there would be no difficulty with lovelorn tutors who were still involved in their studies. Tolman was a newly married man who had previous teaching experience. The original idea, however, had been that Tom and William Eliot would enroll in Tolman's school in Providence, and thus all three Arnolds boys would remain in the North. But Tolman wrote to the Arnolds in the late fall that his wife Julia was very ill and that the doctor had advised her to go to the sanatorium in Philadelphia, in which case he would have to give up his school for some months in order to be near her. Arnold thought "it would be a great disadvantage to Tom to change his teacher," and Louisa Arnold feared that no one else would "take as much pains with Eliot." The Arnolds' solution was to invite William Tolman "to bring his wife out here [White Hall] and let the boys come with him," an arrangement which was mutually advantageous.[21] The Tolmans agreed, and William Tolman was paid $136 to tutor the boys for the term January through April 1853.[22]

Arnold, secure in his image of the benevolent and kind slave master, had no qualms about hiring a man who had chosen the subject "Can the Institution of Domestic Slavery be defended on the principles of Political Economy?" for his graduation oration in 1849. By 1853 there was a messianic undertone to Arnold's defense of himself as a slave owner to the Tolmans and to Olmsted, who was there at the same time. He was convinced that the moral education of the Negroes instituted on plantations by owners like himself and Thomas Clay was so beneficial as to justify slavery itself. Tolman, however, saw slavery as having a harmful effect on the education of whites as well as blacks in the South:

> In point of *education*, too, if we may instance the case of Virginia as our criterion, we learn that over and above the number of uneducated blacks in the slave states the number of whites, who can neither read nor write, is four times the number of the same class in the free; while the number of students and scholars in colleges and schools in the slave states is but one thirteenth of the number of the same class in the free.[23]

Arnold may not have known that Julia Comstock Tolman was the daughter of Christopher Comstock, an abolitionist and a leader in a local antislavery society, which as early as 1837 was raising questions about the propriety of southern planters' bringing their slaves as servants into the free state of Rhode Island. Her abolitionist heritage, however, was compromised by the fact that her maternal grandfather, Asa Potter of Kingston, Rhode Island, and Rhinebeck, New York, had purchased and owned slaves as late as 1803.

Like Olmsted, Julia's first impression of White Hall was that she had arrived in paradise:

> We are delightfully situated—everything is green and beautiful; flowers are blooming around us, and we can almost imagine ourselves in Fairy land. . . . the house is surrounded with trees, indeed it seems as though the house had dropped into the midst of a forest, but of such fine cultivation that you fancy yourself in the midst of a beautiful garden rather than a forest.[24]

Snakes, however, were everywhere in this paradise, snakes of all kinds, including rattlesnakes, "and I expect you'll almost hear my screams of terror in New York some of these times," she only half-jokingly wrote to her cousin, Frank Hagadorn.

On the other hand, for all the paternalism of the Arnolds observed by the Tolmans and confirmed by Olmsted, it was the denial of education that Julia Tolman especially cited as an evil consequence of slavery, no matter how benevolent the master:

> We see slavery in its very best form here. Mr. A. never sells his slaves; among his 150, there is scarcely one who was not raised on the plantation. Their wants are all supplied, and Mrs. A. is very careful in ascertaining their wants and in providing flannel for the old people every year. The house servants have much less to do than our Northern servants, for each one has only one thing to do. I mean one kind of work. They think everything of Mr. and Mrs. Arnold. But with however great kindness they are treated, the wrong of the system is not in the least altered. Only a few of them can read and that only a little. One or two have begged Mr. T [Tolman] to teach them which he does with pleasure. Mrs. A. always teaches the children at Whitehall on Sundays, and she spoke to William about his doing the same at Cherry Hill.[25]

It is true that teaching slaves to read and write was forbidden by law, but as in the case of manumitting and freeing slaves, it merely begged the question, because the laws pertaining to slaves were made for and by slave owners. Undoubtedly, Arnold's answer was that the Negroes were not capable of much learning and that was why only a few of them could read and that only a little. Throughout Thomas Clay's *Detail of a Plan for the Moral Improvement of Negroes on Plantations* there is a patronizing attitude toward their intelligence: white planters considered their slaves incapable of learning anything but the most simple lesson:

> After reading and explaining the selection, read distinctly and emphatically, one verse, or a part of one [from the Bible], then ask some question on the verse, and let it be as simple as possible, containing but one thought or proposition, and pointing directly to the answer. Take, for example, this verse,—"Blessed are the poor in spirit, for theirs is the kingdom of heaven." First explain what it is to be blessed. Next describe the poor in spirit, and what is meant by the kingdom of heaven. The teacher will then repeat the first clause of the verse—"Blessed are the poor in spirit," and ask, "Who does the Lord say are blessed?" The answer is too obvious to be mistaken by them. He will likewise read the last clause and ask, "What does the Lord say shall be theirs?" This method will spare them the embarrassment of calling too many faculties of the mind into exercise at once. It demands only attention and memory, which, in the order of nature, must always precede *thinking;* the last, most difficult, and highest exercise of the human kind.[26]

And as for the *children*—since the *adults* were to be so treated—their lessons "should be taught and repeated in a fixed order; this will aid the memory in recalling them. . . . The constant repetition of the lesson deepens the impression on their memories, and especially assists the younger children whose progress has been slow."[27]

In the mid-1840s Arnold hired the Reverend Mr. Williams, a missionary, as "a teacher to my negroes," paying him $100 per annum.[28] Whether the morality of Arnold's slaves improved or not as a result is unknown, but the literacy would have remained the same. On large, paternalistic plantations like Arnold's, however, there was usually a "showpiece" Negro who had benefited from the system—literate, privileged, rewarded with money or possessions—who was shown with "fatherly" pride to northern visitors as proof that the slaves were well treated and could even thrive under the system. Admittedly, such evidence was contrary to the usual portrait of the slave as lazy, immoral, and intellectually inferior. But (a planter might explain with a nudge to the ribs among males) the privileged ones were often mulattoes, favored and favorite house servants. Even George Noble Jones, absentee owner and therefore not involved to any extent in paternalistic feelings toward his slaves, had his showpiece on the plantation in the person of William Nuttall, bastard son of his wife's first husband. William Nuttall, according to Ulrich Bonnell Phillips in *Florida Plantation Records* (1927), "moved on the fringes of high society, and practised at least one [drinking ardent spirits] and perhaps all of the genteel vices."[29] Miscegenation, however, was not considered one of the "genteel vices."

The showpiece slave on Arnold's plantations was Amos Morel, a mulatto, son of Mum Phebe. His brother, Tom, also a mulatto, was head house servant at the time of Olmsted's visit. Olmsted, impressed with the appearance of authority exhibited by Amos Morel in marked contrast to the overseer, inquired of Arnold about him: "Being the son of a favorite house-servant, he had been, as a child, associated with the white family, and received by chance something of the early education of the white children."[30] Amos Morel, born in 1819 or 1820, probably learned some of the rudiments of reading and writing in the 1830s while the two oldest Arnold children, Eliza Harriet (born 1825) and Louisa Caroline (born 1828) were being tutored on the plantation by Charlotte Bradley. There is no evidence he ever accompanied his mother on her trips north with the Arnold family, but there would have been opportunity for him as a house servant's son to pick up the basic skills while the Arnold girls were "in school" at White Hall. As Olmsted indicated, however, it was by chance rather than by design.

Normally a house servant, which would have been Amos Morel's position on the plantation, did not do field or shop work. Therefore, it was probably at his own request, as Olmsted reported, that he was "allowed to learn the blacksmith's trade" on the plantation, where he also learned to make and repair cotton gins with considerable skill and ingenuity.[31] Late in 1836, when he was sixteen or seventeen, Amos Morel's life changed drastically, albeit still within the slave system. It was at this point that the mythology of slavery as a benevolent institution came into conflict with the reality of the true social and economic relationship of a slave to his master. The reality of Amos Morel, "my engineer," as Arnold was fond of naming him in his account books, was not quite the idealized "rags to riches" story described to Olmsted. The discrepancy between the reality of Amos Morel as a slave and his appearance as "a gentleman of good-breeding and fortune," which was Olmsted's first impression, was simply too much for the myth to bear.

Having learned the basic skills of the blacksmith trade on the plantation, Amos was hired out to Mr. Robinson, a Savannah blacksmith, in 1836.

Whether he wanted to go or not—Amos very likely welcomed the less super-vised life in the city, but he was also being separated from his family and friends—he had no choice. As a slave he *had* to go. He had a marketable skill, and he was hired out for money as surely as Jinny and others were hired out by Arnold all the time. For hiring Amos Morel, "Robinson has the privilege of keeping him until my return in the fall by paying me $18 per mo. & Amos $2 [the $2 went to Arnold to pay Amos], but he has also the privilege of discharging at any time giving my agent Mr. Habersham one Months Notice, in the event of his being discharged he pays me $20 & Amos $2 per Mo until discharged." The next entry in Arnold's account book was for $15 charged to T. R. Bond of Savannah "for Services of Barefoot to his Mare."[32] Above all else, Arnold was a farmer-businessman who ran the plantation as a profit-making enterprise.

Certainly Amos's services brought in money—by May 1839 Arnold was collecting $1.25 a day for the plantation account from Amos's employment in Savannah. Although forbidden by law, the hired slave in practice could keep some of the money earned. Thus, Amos wrote to Arnold on August 22, 1841, "Master I wants to beg you to get me a watch for about ten or twelve dollars if you please to get me a good one and when you return I will settle with you."[33] Amos by this time must have built up some credit in his account with Arnold, for the watch represented a half year's wage at the original rate of what he was to keep for himself. On October 16, just before returning to the plantation, Arnold recorded in his account book under "Family Ex-penses" that he had paid George Baker of Providence $14.50 for a watch and key.[34]

At some point, according to Olmsted, it is not clear exactly when, Arnold took Amos Morel "to a steam-engine builder, and paid $500 to have him instructed as a machinist."[35] It was probably early in 1843 because that is when Arnold considered building a rice mill operated by a steam engine so that he could grind and polish his own rice before shipping it to market instead of paying someone else to do so. Although the context in which Olmsted reported Amos's apprenticeship to the steam-engine builder sug-gests the benevolent paternalism of Richard Arnold, Olmsted's information came entirely from Arnold himself. Arnold would, of course, place the ar-rangement in its best light. Thus, Olmsted reported, "after Morel had be-come a skilled workman, he obtained employment, and was allowed to spend his wages for himself."[36] The context almost suggests that Amos Morel was a free man working for himself, but he lived and worked in Savannah only by his master's consent, and his "wages" were the amount left after Arnold deducted his lion's share. Since Arnold had to pay an engineer $2.00 a day to come down from Providence to set up the engine at the rice mill in early 1844, and good engineers were getting as much as $2.50 a day, the idea must have occurred to him then, if not from the beginning, that "Amos, my engineer," would be needed back on the plantation.[37] Whether or not Arnold recouped the $500.00 he supposedly invested in Amos while the slave was still in Savannah, it was money well spent from a business point of view, regardless of any paternalistic motivation.

It is true, as Olmsted reported, that Amos settled into his life in Savannah, for in July 1843, he wrote to Arnold, "Dear Master I have made up my mind to take a wife and partner for life and I would ask your consent. I have the consent of both the girl and her Mistress   Mrs Ward is the lady to whom she belongs   her name is Mary." As though she would have any choice in the matter, Amos had asked Mary "if she was willing to live with you if you would buy her   she is a good house made and a very good seamstress and she says she is willing to live with you."[38] The master's consent was required for a slave "marriage" to take place even though such marriages had no force under the law. Marriages between slaves belonging to different masters were discouraged because of the complication recognized by Morel in his plea to Arnold that the partner would have to be bought or at least hired if the couple were to live together.

Consent costs little, except for providing the food for a wedding reception and paying for the minister to perform the ceremony. But buying the slave would require an outlay of capital, approximately $600 at current market prices. In keeping with Arnold's image of himself as a benevolent master he granted the "great favor" of his consent to his favorite slave. But apparently Arnold did not purchase Mary from Mrs. Ward, hiring her occasionally instead. Thus he entered in his account book on August 11, 1844, payment for "Amos Wife's wages . . . $13.60."[39] What Arnold bought with this arrangement was Amos's undying loyalty.

There never was any question, however, of Amos Morel's being allowed to remain in Savannah, his own man. On August 29, 1845, he wrote a pleading letter to Arnold in Providence asking to remain in Savannah: "Mr. Groce [John B. Gross, the overseer] has sent word to me this week which comes very inconvenient to me at this time   I should rather not go providing you would please for to make some arrangement for me, for Dear Master if I was for to go out in the Country I would have no chance whatever Dear Master for to provide for myself and family." Bad habits were not the reason for Amos Morel's return to the plantation, as Olmsted mistakenly supposed,

*Miniature of Welcome Arnold (1745–1798),
Richard's father. (Courtesy of Mrs. Burges
Green.)*

*Miniature of Richard J. Arnold, 1819.
(Courtesy of the Arnold-Rogers Collection.)*

Portrait of Louisa Gindrat Arnold (1804–1871), by Charles C. Ingham, 1848. (Courtesy of the Arnold-Rogers family.)

Portrait of Richard J. Arnold, by G. P. A. Healy, 1848. (Courtesy of the Arnold-Rogers family.)

A view of Providence from Smith's Hill, 1827. (Courtesy of the Rhode Island Historical Society.)

View of Newport from the harbor, c. 1870.

Bellevue Avenue, Newport, c. 1860. Arnold's family spent summers in Newport near his business. To the right is the rebuilt Ocean House; behind the fences on the left are the "cottages" of George Noble Jones and Andrew Robeson, Jr. (From View of Newport, *1860. Courtesy of the Rhode Island Historical Society.)*

Sabin Tavern during the 1880s, on the corner of South Main and Planet streets, Providence, Arnold's birthplace and boyhood home. (From Welcome Arnold Greene, Providence Plantations for 250 Years, *1886. Courtesy of the Rhode Island Historical Society.)*

Drawing of White Hall mansion by the Reverend M. A. H. Niles (1842), who passed the winter of 1841–1842 at the plantation seeking to recover his health. (Courtesy of the Arnold-Rogers Collection.)

Drawing of Bryan Neck Presbyterian Church, by the Reverend M. A. H. Niles, 1842. (Courtesy of the Arnold-Rogers Collection.)

Richard J. Arnold, undated, probably early 1860s. (Courtesy of the Arnold-Rogers Collection.)

The children's nursery at Cherry Hill, Richard Arnold's plantation in Bryan County, Georgia, 1853. Drawing by Frederick Law Olmsted appeared in A Journey in the Seaboard States, *1856. (Courtesy of the Rhode Island Historical Society.)*

White Hall mansion, Arnold's home in Bryan County, Georgia, late nineteenth century. (Courtesy of the Arnold-Rogers Collection.)

although Amos's suggestion that he did not want to leave Savannah because it was inconvenient bordered on insurrection. The fact was that Morel's skill with steam engines was needed. Arnold had too much time and money invested in Amos's training to tolerate such independence and ignored his plea that "Cousin Sam is capable of running the mill as I am unless something gives way and then I know I am compelled for to go out."[40]

In the same letter Amos Morel revealed that he had visited his brother, Tom, who had been jailed, accused of stealing money from Arnold: "I talked to him outside [the jail] and asked him if he knew anything about the money you lost   he declared to me he knew nothing about the money and I think if he did know he would lead me into the secret." Whether or not Arnold believed Tom innocent on the basis of Amos's word, Tom was eventually forgiven, if not exonerated, because by February 1853, as reported by Olmsted, he was serving as headwaiter at White Hall. A slave who served a jail sentence for stealing money from the master would very likely be sold as being untrustworthy. Amos himself risked being jailed for going to see his brother at the jail: "I was to Mr. Habersham on the 4 day of July for to ask him for a Ticket to go and see him [Tom] and he refused me, and I did went to the Jail."[41] Amos could have been arrested for traveling without a ticket. In Georgia, as in the other slave states, a slave had to have the written permission of the master or his agent to travel anywhere by himself. Arnold may have been more impressed by this risk taken by Amos than by his reasoning about Tom's innocence. Twenty years later in January 1865, Arnold himself had to apply for a travel permit to visit his plantations and return to New York accompanied by black servants (formerly his slaves). Although Savannah had surrendered by then, the war was still going on.

In the seven years between the time Amos Morel reluctantly returned to the plantation and the time Olmsted met him, his skills were put to advantageous use: "He had made," Olmsted wrote, "all the alterations and repairs necessary in running a steam-engine and extensive machinery . . . and his work was admirable, both in contrivance and execution."[42] Having been away from the plantation for so long, however, and being kept busy working in the blacksmith shop and on the steam engine and the new sugar mill machinery, Morel had not consolidated his authority over the field hands when the head driver and watchman, Harrington, died sometime in 1847. Arnold designated Israel, who was nine years older than Amos, as head driver. When and for what reason Arnold replaced Israel with Amos Morel is not known. Israel may have died, for his name no longer appeared on Arnold's slave list of January 1858, but definitely by the summer of 1852 Morel was head driver. The nature of his authority and duties over the rest of the slaves and drivers inevitably would bring Amos Morel into conflict with the overseer, particularly in the absence of the master.

On June 20, 1852, he wrote to Arnold in Providence:

> I am sorry to inform you that I have had to break William of his driver ship and have gevin him his hoe, since you have left William has got into debt to the other driver 35 days and gets along very badly with his work on account of having too many favorits in the field. I have put big Peter in his place to drive and would be glad to hear from you if you approve of what I have done.

Amos had chosen well the situation in which to assert his authority, because if William in fact was in debt to the other drivers for the equivalent of thirty-five task-days for his work force, he had indeed been negligent in his duty and playing favorites, since Arnold had left the plantation only seven weeks earlier, on May 1. Furthermore, Amos continued: "the Carpenters are getting along badly with their work."[43] While he does not mention the overseer, Charles Ferguson, the implication is clear: the overseer is overlooking the laziness of some of the slaves, "indulging them foolishly," as Arnold complained to Olmsted a few months later about overseers in general, "in their disposition to idleness, or in other ways to curry favor with them, so they may not inform the proprietor of their own misconduct or neglect."[44] Ultimately, Richard Arnold indulged Amos Morel in his privileges and responsibilities because he wanted a check on his overseer's authority. As master he could manipulate the system and play favorites: on December 6, 1852, back again on the plantation, he presented his "head man Amos" $75 for "good management."[45]

Amos Morel had thus reached the pinnacle of his power and privilege on the plantation by the time Olmsted met him several months later. Indeed, Mrs. Arnold wrote to her daughter Louisa less than three weeks after Olmsted's visit, that her husband "would do any thing for Amos he is so attached to him," including buying his wife and child from the Waters family "which we do not wish to do for they would be of no use to us."[46]

Amos always worked within the system. He used it to his advantage, but he also knew his welfare depended on the master's favor. Like his horses and guns, the keys and the watch, the trappings of power and privilege were Amos's only insofar as they were tolerated by Arnold and served Arnold's purpose of playing Amos Morel against Charles Ferguson so that in his absence he would have better knowledge and control over what was really happening at the plantation. The overseer could be fired at any time, and such a provision was a standard feature of overseer agreements. But the head driver could not be discharged, only broken like William, made a field hand or else sold. Amos's authority depended on his ability to please Arnold and remain in favor. He instinctively recognized this dependence, for he wrote again to Arnold two days later, June 22, 1852, a conflict of authority having developed between him and Ferguson, presumably over the "breaking of Driver William" and replacing him with Big Peter: "Ples to rite mr fougason and Tell him the man that Cannte Pleze my Boy Amos Cannte Pleze me Cepote my Law dear master and it will Bringe the People in good Order."[47]

Writing to Arnold four weeks later, on July 16, Ferguson does not refer to the breaking of William and his replacement with Big Peter. Instead, he asserted his authority decisively. He had his own solution on how to bring the people to good order—the whip. Illness on the plantation resulted in some of the slaves refusing to work, and Ferguson suspected they were feigning illness: "I have whiped some of them to make them work but had to give way," presumably because the illnesses were real. Perhaps to reassure his employer that his favorite slave was neither ill nor whipped, Ferguson added, "Amos and his wife is quite well and begs me to tell you all howdy for them." But Ferguson makes it clear that it is his law of the whip that keeps the slaves disciplined: "The People has behaved quite well so far   they all beg to tell you all howdy for them."[48]

Amos Morel's feud with Charles Ferguson came to a head in early June 1853, just four months after Olmsted's visit. Amos wrote to Arnold, then back in Providence for the summer, "I think you will fall out with Mr. Ferguson before long, for he is hard to keep your orders, for he take Maria to wait for him." Furthermore, when Amos's wife took Maria back to stay with her, "Mr. Ferguson take Prince to wait on him."[49] This kind of tale bearing was common on plantations and sometimes was encouraged by the planter as a means of checking on what the overseer had done in the planter's absence. Overseer's agreements spelled out specifically what servants they were allowed, and Ferguson was to have a cook, and a small boy and girl to wait on him. Obviously Morel was convinced that Ferguson had exceeded his rightful number of slaves.

However, Morel's tattling on Ferguson was only a prelude to the climax of his personal quarrel with the overseer in a struggle for dominance. The confrontation was symbolic, but like many such conflicts it revolved around an ordinary but very real incident: Ferguson's hog, turned out to root for itself, ate all but thirty-seven of Amos's ninety-five turkeys. These turkeys represented money as well as food to Amos because of the long-standing custom

A letter to Richard Arnold from his slave Amos Morel, June 22, 1852, asking Arnold to write the overseer "and Tell him the man that Cannte Pleze my Boy Amos Cannte Pleze me." (Courtesy of the Rhode Island Historical Society.)

on the plantation that he and the other slaves could sell their excess produce and fowl to Arnold for credit in the books. Amos wrote, "I take my Gun to kill it," but when he found out it belonged to Ferguson, he "caught the hog and put [it] in pen." Ferguson, on hearing that Amos had threatened to kill his hog, "come down to give me 100 stripes [of] bear hide." The confrontation was as symbolic of slavery itself as the bear-hide whip Ferguson held in his hand. But it was a confrontation *within* the system between two men, one white, one black. The fact that Amos had a gun underscored the symbolic relationship of these two rivals within the plantation hierarchy: Amos might kill the hog that ate his turkeys, but he did not threaten, let alone kill, the white man who wielded the whip. Conditioned to be a part of the system and loyal to it, Amos Morel backed down from challenging Charles Ferguson: he told the overseer, "I did not know the hog is his."[50]

Ferguson backed down too and did not whip Amos. He knew that if he whipped the master's favorite slave, particularly if, as Amos complained to Arnold, he had "broke your law much," he might be fired on the spot. Ferguson may have been free and white, but his livelihood depended on pleasing his employer as much as Amos's privileges depended on pleasing his master. Sitting in judgment hundreds of miles away, Richard Arnold decided to arrange an accommodation between his overseer and head driver, dividing their duties so that they would not be in conflict. Separate they could be, but not equal, and already the following spring Amos was complaining that Ferguson was not living up to his promise and was undermining Amos's authority.

Arnold neither fired Ferguson nor stripped Morel of his authority, however, and the situation continued as before for several more years, both men reporting to Arnold by letter during the summer, thus keeping a check one on the other. For example, in August 1856, Morel complained to his master that Ferguson was spending so much time building his own house and barn that there was now more grass in the rice because the driver, left unsupervised, was neglectful and it was almost too late to save the crop. While there seemed to be a stalemate between Amos Morel and Charles Ferguson, apparently Amos was biding his time. On July 29, 1858, the feud broke out again. This time, instead of attacking Ferguson directly, Morel got at him through the very man he had broken to assert his authority six years earlier, ex-driver William. William, possibly hoping to regain favor, told Amos that Carpenter Peter (called so not only because of his job but also to distinguish him from Big Peter) had stolen molasses and sold it to the slaves at a neighboring plantation, saying he was selling it for Amos. Since Carpenter Peter was directly under Ferguson's control, Morel informed Ferguson and asked him to search

A letter to Richard Arnold from his slave Amos Morel, June 2, 1853, recounting the latest episode in his feud with the overseer Ferguson. (Courtesy of the Rhode Island Historical Society.)

i think dare maßter we will make a good
Crop ~~make~~ more then laßyare if god pleß to help ~~us~~ ous
To get it in gorge iß tenßull to hiß horßeß
And all of the horßeiß in good order now
i think you will fall out with mr fugazan be
Long for hx iß hard to keß you order
fore he take maria to wate on him and
i inform you that my wife hav take ~~mare~~
mary to flae She and Seny that mr
fugazon take Prince to wate on him
All So but you will not Rite to him a
But that for i Charge the time to
him when he woß maven oup to the
Summer houßes ngh him abote tom
Carrige home he Sa you iled not til
hime bring him don to work or nat
William houße iß don but adeug iß not
Dogton and henry workinge it now for
Peter monday Sinng Darky workinge to ~~i~~
Summer Shouge this date make 3 week
To the 6 June he Sole hiß horge take
Stoppin to Ride and i tell him you
~~tole~~ me to make gonge fed ~~him~~ but he
Sa nat it to much trubel to Sen for
him So far avil you charge me that
ße one to write the Sharge an i tell
him and this make 2 time he wich
Donnyßante to wite hall i hav 4 B
and one P of corn Chage him now

I Recived 200 ℔ Rice flour from Savannah
And i Charge when to take to fede the hog
I thort that to lef the Plase teli have from
you for when he move to the Summer
hauge turn out his hog eat all of my
Juky all to 37 i turn out 95 an i take the
gun to hel it and fine out the hog
is his So corte the hog and Put in
Pen So the hog when't an tel him
All So eat Som of yors he com don to
ger me 100 lef Stripe have hide So when
he Storn at me the i wod hil and Pay
And him Pass for the hog eat Som
maggten then i tol him I did not
Nol the hog is his i expet him to
fol out whith me before longe for i
Stringe him brake your law much Plez
To geti my lov to all the People Pag you
To yer lob Plez maggten you borte the
molarcis you borte te Savannah
for we hav nan On the Place for i
Fininge Children out af the barn
And i l be glad to have how i will
get Som &c my Spellige dear
maggten Plez t I Write me as my litter
Recived no Bemore at this time i
Ramene your Reblige Sarent
Amos Morell

Peter's house for the key to the supply barn: they could not find the key "but found about 4 B [Bushels] corn in his house."[51]

Morel was able to place the blame on Ferguson's laxity because Ferguson had accepted Peter's story that Stephen Hines of Savannah had purchased the molasses. In the meantime, ten more bushels of corn were stolen from the barn. As if this neglect of Arnold's interests were not enough, apparently Ferguson had allowed Peter to feign illness: "I then told Mr. Ferguson that if Peter well [enough] to see he is well [enough] to work for you so he come but did not work." Instead, Carpenter Peter used this time to sell molasses again.[52] Whether the reason was this particular incident or the feud, Arnold apparently was finally through with Ferguson. He did not renew his contract the following year, even though Ferguson had worked for Arnold for thirteen years, an unusually long tenure.

Amos Morel had won, and his archenemy was banished from the land. In March 1859 Ferguson wrote to Arnold from a plantation in Camden County, Georgia, near the Florida border, and although it was not a great distance from White Hall, it was a world apart: "I am in a strange part of the world and amongst strangers and with a new employer." An odd letter, it alternates between hurt pride and obsequiousness, a mixture of self-justification and begging for forgiveness:

> [it] being Planting time it is out of my power to leave [Arnold had asked him to testify in a court case] or I would do it with all the Pleasure in the world to serve you and when you receive this if you think I will be of any import advantage to you I will risk all things to serve you although I know that I am the last one in your estamation at this time but thank God I have one Consolation that I have done you justis while I was in your employment treated your negroes kindly and made them do there duty to wards you and I have always spoken very highly of you and your kind treatment to wards me also of your kind family but alas I suppose all things is at an end.

He did not mention Amos Morel directly, but he alludes unmistakably to their difficulties in terms Arnold would clearly have understood: "I would of went any length to surv you or anyone of yours but they have been hard things tole on me which I hope may Come out right One of these days." He hopes Arnold is well satisfied with his present overseer, but if "you Should want an Overseer for a nother year you can consider me as an applicant for it."[53]

Amos Morel's triumph was short-lived, however. The system required a white overseer, and from Morel's point of view, Ferguson's successor was even worse. By June 1860 Amos Morel wrote to his master complaining in even stronger terms about the new overseer, Edward M. Bailey. The increasing frustration of the situation to Amos notwithstanding, one of the lessons he had to learn was that no matter how far he had risen within the system, no matter how much he might be favored by the master, as a slave he was at the mercy of any white man in authority: "I am constrained to write to you about my getting along, for I discouraged in doing for mr Baly do not like me to superintend as a head driver for I have not been to White Hall Sedgfield Mulberry nor San Souci [all the plantations belonging to Arnold] from the time I plant the rice   All I can say the people say we have a good crop of rice."[54] Good crop or not, it was the last one to be harvested before the outbreak of the Civil War.

2

If one were looking for portents, the almost simultaneous breakdown of the sugar mill and the outbreak of a measles epidemic at White Hall in February 1848 might serve as well as any, unless it be the arrival of the two Negro carpenters from Savannah who did not work and infected three of Arnold's carpenters with the laziness bug, or Phineas Howe's extraordinary behavior in whipping Richard, Jr., with Hannah's miscarriage having occurred the previous day. To top it off, Ferguson came down with pleurisy again. All that was needed was for the house guests to fall ill, and sure enough on April 7, Dr. McQueen was very ill, young Carroll bleeding at the lungs, Mrs. Harper quite indisposed, and Catharine, the children's nurse, so ill that she had to be accompanied by Amos and Jinny to Savannah. Richard Arnold, however, in twenty-five years of running the plantation had seen or known almost everything that could affect the health of the community. The Arnolds themselves had lost two children in their infancy, both born at White Hall, but one dying in Georgia in 1832 and the other in Rhode Island in 1833.

Life and death as an ironic juxtaposition was to be expected in so large a community—on November 19, 1847, Arnold recorded without comment the death of Scipio in his prime and the birth of Quality's child. If anything, he was impressed by the longevity of his slaves, particularly those slaves who formed part of his wife's original inheritance, suggesting of course how well he had cared for them. The fact that Quality's child died ten days later while the Arnolds were absent in Savannah would be considered part of the natural course of events. Charles Ferguson reported to Arnold on July 16, 1852, that another child of Quality's was born dead: "I cannot account for it." Polly, on the other hand, had a fine baby, "both doing well."[55]

The *good* slave master took good care of his slaves in sickness and in health, from birth to death. If nothing else, the Arnolds prided themselves on the personal care of their slaves when they became ill. Eliza Harriet Allen, Julia Tolman, Frederick Law Olmsted—all commented on this quality of concern and care, and indeed Mrs. Allen used the occasion of an epidemic among the slaves during her visit to comment on how both her brother and his wife took time each day to visit the sick, a responsibility they accepted as master and mistress of the plantation. It was a standard clause in the overseer contracts from the beginning that the overseer attend to the sick, and by Ferguson's time the overseer's duty "to take good care of the negroes in Sickness & in health" is spelled out in more detail in the contract: "In case of any epidemic such as Dysentery, Cholera &c he is to remain with the People & to remove them if necessary to the Pine land, & attend on them there."[56]

Supplementing the general charge to the overseer to take good care of the Negroes, particularly in case of an epidemic, were the specific duties spelled out in the detailed and elaborate instructions Arnold wrote out for newly hired overseers. For example, on May 22, 1837, shortly before leaving for the North with his family and guests, he left specific instructions with his then overseer, J. Swanston:

> Should the measles get among the children give them sassafras tea warm & gruel & endeavor to keep them from exposure to a draft & not give anything cold—give them rice allowance & as soon as you finish planting please give out half pease each week until they are gone & then give half rice & half corn until the dirty rice is consumed then give the [illegible] rice—the fish give out whenever they want them until the cholera come, if it should come either of our places or any other on the river you may give rice allowance, no fish—& cut off all the watermelon vines as they are bad in cholera. . . . Should you have occasion to call in a physician and Dr. Sanders should be at D'Lyons, you may send for him at C. Hill & Doctor Golphin at W. Hall . . . but I hope you may be so fortunate as not to have occasion for a Physician at either place— Make the nurse at both places send the child minders into the field every day with a pail of water, morning & afternoon & she can make them take turns in carrying it—and if you ascertain there is any one who drinks dirty water, have them punished for there is no way the dysentery is brought upon a place so soon as by drinking ditch water.[57]

Again, in 1839, Arnold, fearful of an outbreak of smallpox in the area left elaborate instructions for the vaccination of the slave children: "If the scab falls from my child before leaving I will send it to you in a letter which open carefully so as not to lose it. If you do not get it in this way take some from the healthy children at Colo^n Morris' place just nine days from the day before he left as he vaccinated them on that day & make a list of all you do & of all that take—if they do not take the first time try them a second time."[58]

During the summer of 1849, Arnold's fears of an epidemic among the slaves was almost realized, and Ferguson took drastic measures to remove the slaves from their quarters on the plantation and put "them all out in the Pine land" for safety, where they camped out until the threat of the cholera epidemic was over. The doctor was called for the very sick. As a remedy, or at least nostrum, the overseer placed "around Every Negroes neck little and big a small bag of Asaphelaton Camphor and Sulpher which I hope will be a preventattive in some measure." More to the point he used chloride of lime around the camp. "The worst thing is the feeding of the Negroes   they must have such things as will Prevent them from Running away from the Camps at Night."[59] Whether it was the camphor and sulphur bags or the lime, the sickness apparently worked itself out and the community was saved.

Was Arnold's concern for the health of his slaves motivated by compassion and humaneness or was it a calculated attempt by a businessman to protect his capital investment? The difficulty with the idealized image of the good Christian master as portrayed, for example, by Mrs. Allen in her journal is that he was absent from his plantations and care of the slaves for six months out of the year. The clause "to take care of the Negroes on said plantation in sickness and health" was so standard a part of overseer contracts as to be almost meaningless legal jargon. This clause appeared in George Noble Jones's contracts with his overseers in 1849, and he was absent from his plantations most of the time.[60] The real difficulty with the image, whether the master was present or absent on the plantation, was that when a human being is considered *property* with an attached monetary value, it is a loss when the owner is deprived of his property's labor because of illness, and there is a total loss when death liquidates the assets. Neither Arnold nor Jones would have been so crude as to debit his account book the fair market price every time one of his slaves died, but such an accounting is implicit in Arnold's reckoning for any given year the total worth of all the *living* slaves at so much per head according to the market price, averaged out between the young and the old, the sick and the healthy, the prime field hands and the house servants.[61]

Whether or not Arnold in his concern for the health of his slaves was motivated by economics or compassion or both, he was careful not to allow illness to become a means of malingering. Olmsted, accompanying Arnold on his daily round of inspection, related the incident of the Negro youth who had gone to the nursery, which also served as a kind of hospital, complaining of a stomachache, but who the nurse, a black woman, suspected of malingering, a diagnosis which Arnold confirmed on the spot, upon which he ordered the youth back to work.[62] Such casual doctoring stemmed from the belief prevalent among planters that the aches and pains that the flesh is heir to were often an excuse to get off work. Serious contagious diseases that could wipe out a sizable portion of the labor force were another matter and had to be taken seriously, but their symptoms were supposedly known.

The ambiguity of southern planters like Arnold toward illness among the slaves was summed up by Thomas Clay many years earlier:

> The diseases of negros are generally simple in their nature, and only require good nursing to remove them. . . . The master should see the sick every day, visiting them at their houses or at the hospital and however unacquainted with the science of medicine he will soon be able to detect the cases of feigned sickness, and to ascertain for whom the aid of a physician is necessary. Such kindness will exert a good moral influence.[63]

On the other hand, the easy assumption is made that somehow blacks, unlike other people, have only "simple" diseases and that all that was required was a bit of experience to detect the difference between the genuine simple disease and the vague complaint of a stomachache used to feign illness. A medical dictionary might be consulted to supplement the probing hand, but it depended on who did the probing and the consulting.

At about the same time that Ferguson wrote Arnold about sickness among the slaves at White Hall, John Evans, George Noble Jones's overseer, wrote to him from Chemonie, one of his two plantations in Florida:

> I am glad to See that your Family Continues Well. I have bin quite Sick of Late myself but have Not Losed any time by being Sick. I have bin able to attend to My business all the While. Old ben dont seem to get any better. I sent up for Dr. Randolph to Prescribe for him and since Drs. Randolph and Gamble have both bin out to Chemonie to see ben. they Now Say ben has Dropsy and I think so My Self for he is Swoolen Verry bad. I don't think ben Can Live Long. I did all I New for him before I sent him to Dr. Randolph. the balance of the people Enjoy Pretty good health at this time.[64]

In the absence of the owner, the care the cases received depended to a great extent on the practical experience of the overseer—Evans knew enough to call the doctor when the case was serious—and on his humaneness. On August 6, 1854, while Jones was enjoying the cool ocean breezes at Newport, the overseer at El Destino, D. N. Moxley, wrote to him:

> I thaut this morning that I should loose Coatney. Yesterday Coatney Filles Veanus Elise all fainted in the field from over heeat it being the hotes day wee have had hear but all the rest of them seamed to gained strength very fast except Cotney. She seam to caep Sinking till this morning   She can walk about now   all so Lin and Di was over heated but not so much onley just to weaken them. those other cases is feavor tho modriet [moderate]. the rest of the people are all in fine health aspeseley [especially] the children.
>
> Polley has got a case of the whites [leucorrhoea, a vaginal infection] and has had it ever since the case of fever she had in June but she kept it consealed till Wednesday last. She Seames to be mending.
>
> Mealer [Amelia] Seames to be lingriñ for som tim also so Mari[a]h   wee have had a few days of the hotes wether that I have ever experienced. I have had a fine rain this afternoon and the wether has changed. . . .
>
> P.S. The people ar all better this morning and now new cases today. Mr. Jones pleas send me Webersters Medical Dictionary as I cant git one hear.[65]

Cooling rains and breezes do more for Polly and Venus and Nan than all the "Webersters" dictionaries.

The care of slaves varied widely from plantation to plantation even when owned by the same absentee master, and the contrast between Evans and Moxley serves as a paradigm of the different treatment they received. Sometime in the autumn of that same year Evans wrote to Jones that Die [Di] picked 210 pounds of cotton yesterday, a good day's work: "Mr. Moxley sent Die up here because he could not get her to work. I have not had the Cause to strike her a Lick. I wish he would let her stay hear   She will work for me without any trouble."[66] But Evans's "humaneness" was subordinate to what he considered his main purpose—to get as much work out of the slaves as possible and to whip them as much as necessary to get the maximum work from them. He defended Moxley's treatment of the slaves at El Destino when the situation exploded in October 1854. Aberdeen, one of the slaves working in the saw mill, grabbed an ax and threatened to kill Moxley when the overseer caught Aberdeen's sister either to flog or to put in jail. The driver prevented Aberdeen from using the ax on Moxley. In the meantime, four of the women slaves ran away but were caught in Tallahassee and put in jail. As a result, town gossip reported that the four women had been badly whipped by Moxley, which Evans denied, having "examined their backs Myself and I did not see any thing that was cruel about them."

I dont think that Mr. Moxley treats the negroes on Eldesteno Cruely When they don't deserve it. you noe that the negroes on Eldesteno have not bin at work for the Last 4 years so Moxly had to be pretty strict on them to get any thing out of them. I think Moxley is a good planter and would treat the negroes well if they would behave themselves. they is but one thing I see in Mr. Moxleys Management that I dont Like and it is this, I think when he Flogs he puts it on in two Large doses. I think moderate Flogings the best. When Ever I See that I have Convinced a negro I always turns him Losse. I always punish according to the crime, if it is a Large one I give him a genteel Floging with a strop, about 75 Lashes I think is a good Whipping.

Aberdeen, according to Evans, who witnessed it, was given "a genteel Flog-ing," adding gratuitously, "which I think he deserved."[67] To make seventy-five lashes a "genteel" punishment lies only in the arms of the flogger.

Although it was in the best economic self-interest of a slaveholder to treat his slaves well and keep them physically fit for work, the image of happy, healthy, hard-working "darkies" was a myth found only in the self-serving propaganda of the proslavers and in novels like Maria McIntosh's *The Lofty and the Lowly* (1853), a copy of which arrived for the Arnolds on February 1, 1853), the day Olmsted left the plantation. Part of the myth, which continues to this day, was that the Negro was somehow by his racial constitution better fitted physically to work in the cotton and rice fields of the South:

> The survival of frontier conditions, the inadequate medical facilities typical of rural areas, the super-abundance of undrained swamps and ponds, and the long summers and mild winters which enabled insects to thrive and increased the difficulty of preserving foods, all helped to make Southerners exceptionally vulnerable to epidemic and endemic diseases. These, however, were the very conditions which Negroes presumably could endure without injurious effects; and one would therefore expect to find much lower morbidity and mortality rates among them than among the whites. The slave of tradition was a phys-ically robust specimen who suffered from few of the ailments which beset the white man. A tradition with less substance to it has seldom existed. In the South, disease did not discriminate among men because of the color of their skins; wherever it was unhealthful for whites to live it was also unhealthful for Negroes.[68]

Between July 29, 1834, and August 17, 1835, Arnold had a net loss of six slaves over and above any births that occurred during that time. Since he did not buy or sell any slaves in that period, in all probability at least a dozen slaves died and an unknown number were sick. It was Arnold's practice to have two doctors on call to attend to the slaves if necessary in his judgment or, in his absence, the overseer's judgment. In 1834–1835 Drs. Mitchell and Charlton were on call, and usually one attended the Cherry Hill slaves (the latter) and the other the White Hall slaves. Thus, when a neighbor, Mrs. Matilda Harden, wrote Arnold in Providence on July 19, 1834, that she had seen Dr. Charlton and "he said there were a few cases of fever among the Negroes" he was presumably reporting on the Cherry Hill slaves.[69] And on April 10, 1835, Arnold paid $26.50 to Dr. Mitchell for "attending on Tom & Amos," at White Hall.[70] Tom and Amos survived, but others may not have been so fortunate. The duality of the paternalistic slave owner is dramatically underlined in the dry figures of plantation account books: the net loss of six lives was balanced in the books as a $1,675 capital gain because the net worth of each slave averaged out had risen from $275 each in 1834 to $300 each in 1835.[71]

Although healing the slave was Christian and economic, the physician was not always able to heal his own man or for that matter himself. On September 10, 1835, Dr. Charlton, a planter as well as a physician, wrote from Bryan County to Arnold in Providence that Arnold's slaves were well, but "I have had the misfortune to lose my *primest* negro man who was taken ill with syphylis at the time I was too ill to attend him and before I was aware of his danger he was brought up dying." Dr. Charlton assured Arnold that though he himself had had a severe attack of the fever, he was well now.[72] Arnold received the letter on September 21. The next day Dr. Charlton was dead: "What a lesson," Arnold wrote on the envelope, "this is to me to be prepared to meet my God?" It was also a lesson in the vagaries of the weather, for when the Arnolds returned to the plantations on November 3, they discovered that there had been "very little frost & have some apprehension that we have come too soon."[73] The lesson could but be reinforced, for Dr. Charlton was buried in White Hall cemetery, his grave not far from that of Abraham and Barbara Gindrat, Louisa's parents.

Olmsted observed in general that "the negroes do not enjoy as good health on rice plantations as elsewhere; and the greater difficulty with which their lives are preserved, through infancy especially, shows that the subtle poison of the miasma is not innocuous to them."[74] Besides malaria, yellow fever, cholera, dysentery, small pox, measles, and other diseases that were endemic or epidemic in the area and a threat to the slave community—to say nothing of pleurisy, pneumonia, and pleuropneumonia in the winter—slaves who worked in the rice fields were vulnerable to foot rot as an occupational disease, and those who worked in the cotton fields were prone to infected fingers from picking cotton. Tuberculosis, sometimes called Negro consumption, was also prevalent.

Even on a plantation as paternalistic as Arnold's, the overseer in the absence of the master might not send for the doctor except in cases of very serious illness. Ferguson, who, like Jones's overseer Evans, prided himself on his doctoring abilities, wrote to Arnold in July 1849: "Sorry to inform you that I have three cases of Sick which I consider very sick so much so that I have just this morning sent off for the Dr for two of them these two is Tamer and Sallys little Diannah but I hope they will get well yet but a very poor hope at this time and the other Case is Polly White   She is very sick but I think I can manage hers my self."[75] Given the state of medical practice in the antebellum South, in which "bleeding, cathartics, emetics and diluents" were prescribed for fevers, the sick slaves were, as Stampp suggested, "fortunate if the remedies did not retard recovery or hasten death."[76] Whether the remedies of the doctor or the overseer were preferable was a toss-up: Tamer survived and was still alive when Arnold prepared a slave list on January 1, 1858. Sally's little Diannah and Polly White were, however, not on the list and presumably died either in 1849 or, weakened by that illness, at some subsequent time before 1858.

It was not that southern planters like Arnold sought medical advice from charlatans for their slaves. As Stampp points out, "Many masters employed trained physicians, often the same ones who treated the white families."[77] Physicians North and South, however, beset by rival theories of medicine in the 1840s and 1850s—homeopathy, hydropathy, Thompsonianism—seemed to be in a kill-or-cure mood. C. W. Greene, headmaster of the school the Arnold boys attended, described one such drastic remedy to Arnold, one fortunately that cured rather than killed. Nowadays the incident may seem amusing, but to Greene in April 1845 it was a miracle:

> The fact is that Franklin Greenes little boy of 5 years of age, was dreadfully attacked by the croup. We were obliged to send for a Homoepathic Dr (Providence rage) and the child was soon at extremity—when a consultation of Homoes & Hydropaths—decreed that he should be put into a tub. scrubbed with cold water & that eight pitchers of water should be poured from an elevation of 3 feet upon his head & neck. Mrs G & I held him in the tub. and I expected to see him expire under my hands. & felt like one of King Herod's murderers of "the innocent." The child was—from a state of suffocation before—smiling in a sheet in Mrs Gs lap—& when his mother came in. said to her—"I have had a proper hard wash."[78]

Young Greene's miraculous recovery may well have induced the Arnolds' daughter Louisa to take the water cure the following year when she was ill. She survived the treatment, also.

It was sound medical practice at the time for southern physicians to advise planters, particularly rice planters, to migrate north during the malaria season. As late as 1879 Zachariah Allen stated authoritatively in his book *Solar Light and Heat* that nitrogen "from decomposing animal or vegetable substances, constitutes the real miasma, or *malaria*." Frost "brings a cessation of yellow fever and other diseases springing from such decomposition."[79] Only then, he should have added, is it safe for his in-laws to return to the swampy rice fields of Georgia. In late November 1852 the Arnolds arrived in Georgia too soon, before the first killing frost, and they remained in Savannah with John Elliott Ward until December 6. An outbreak of cholera at the plantations on the Chatham County side of the Ogeechee was subsiding, and although there had not been a single case or even symptom of cholera at either White Hall or Cherry Hill, the Arnolds were taking no chances. Arnold checked the plantations but always returned to Savannah by eight o'clock. Their neighbors, the Clays and the McAllisters, had all moved to high ground in the pine woods, working at their plantations only during the day. Ferguson, the Arnold overseer, kept lightwood fires burning "all up the street all the time which the Drs. say purified the air."[80]

The winter migration from North to South by planters like Richard Arnold and George Noble Jones and their families was augmented by northern consumptives who were advised by their doctors to seek the warmer southern climate during the harsh New England winter. As early as the 1830s the Arnolds extended their hospitality to northern friends who suffered from tuberculosis or who had been advised by their doctors to go south for their health. For example, in February 1836 Joseph Bridgham, youngest son of Samuel Bridgham, first mayor of Providence, accompanied by his mother, was in Savannah for his health. The Bridghams were part of that network of family and friends to which the Arnolds belonged, and therefore it was only natural that Richard Arnold should invite Joseph Bridgham, a recent graduate of Brown (class of 1834), and his mother to visit White Hall—"re-visit" as Joseph described it, since they had been there earlier in the winter.[81]

Joseph Bridgham found the hospitality at White Hall congenial, agreeable, and kind. Nothing he saw disturbed his enjoyment, but he sympathized with Arnold that "serious indisposition" had broken out among the slaves:

> It really seems to me as a *Northerner* that the care & anxiety attending the possession of slave property far exceed the profits. I understand that there is a disease now prevalent among the negroes, which has, thus far, defied the skill of the physician. It is something like the pleurisy, but beware how you make use of *Daddy John's lancet*. Tis s^d. that bleeding kills instead of cures. Mr. Habersham, I believe, has lost a number of negroes by the disease.

But he did not hold it against them for being so troublesome to their master: "Remembrance to my friends, the sable descendants of Ham."[82]

Eliza Harriet Allen, who herself had almost died of pleuropneumonia in the winter of 1822 (an experience that left her with a deep sense of mortality even in the midst of youth), described in her journal the ups and downs of William Dorrance's health during the spring of 1837, when he accompanied her to White Hall. William Tully Dorrance, born in Providence in December 1809, graduated from Brown University in 1829. He made the grand tour of Europe like other sons of the middle class, accompanied by his mother and sister, and returned to Providence in 1832, destined for a career in law. But poor health, later diagnosed as tuberculosis, ended his law studies, and he went to Florida for his health. When he returned to Providence, he changed to the study of medicine, perhaps following the advice "physician heal thyself." Again, his studies were interrupted by poor health, and this time he accepted the invitation of the Arnolds to stay with them and Mrs. Allen at White Hall.

At first, Dorrance's health seemed to improve at the plantation, but that may have been only in contrast to the voyage down, when he felt so poorly that Mrs. Allen commented on Easter Sunday, March 26, while they were still at sea, that "his time on earth is evidently short." By May 13, only a fortnight before they were all to return to Providence, he confided to Mrs. Allen that he thought himself "much more unwell than when he left home . . . he was fully aware of what awaited him & sometimes felt willing to go." Two days later, Mrs. Allen reported "He is very cheerful . . . and seems quite happy."[83] William Dorrance, convinced he was going to die, lived to the ripe old age of seventy-one, achieving his biblical threescore and ten and surviving his wife by thirty-two years. Julia Tolman, on the other hand, also suffering from tuberculosis and also at White Hall for her health, believed that she had regained her health and was practically cured. She died a few months after returning with her husband to Rhode Island in the summer of 1853.

Olmsted himself was convinced of the efficacy of the southern climate for northern consumptives, citing the experience of a northern friend who had migrated to Georgia, purchased several rice plantations, and regained his health. There is, however, some medical ambiguity, in that Olmsted's friend also believed that "malaria operates as an antidote to the consumptive tendency" and, vice versa, that a predisposition to consumption "renders the poison of malaria innocuous." In actuality, the only evidence offered by the friend was that he was ill neither with consumption nor malaria, whereas one of his neighbors, who had no predisposition to consumption, was dead within the week upon exposing himself to malaria![84]

The visiting consumptive did not always return alive to his native land in the North. Timothy Green, married to Arnold's niece Cornelia, came to White Hall for his health in the winter of 1840 when he became seriously ill in New York. Mrs. Allen wrote to her brother on February 11, 1840, "I regretted very much to hear of cousin Timothys illness and cannot yet give up the hope that he may return improved in health to his home."[85] He died on March 16, 1840, his thirty-fourth birthday, and was buried at White Hall. Eventually he did return to his native land. His widow wrote to her uncle two years later:

> I shall ever feel deeply grateful to you & your household for touching & unremitted tenderness, & I now express my thanks for your late act of sympathy & love. I am grateful for the kindness, care & labour which have brought my dear husband's remains so near me. While I love to think of him in heaven my heart clings to the poor mouldering dust, & with all the sense of bereavement, there was a solace in seeing it laid safely in my father's vault. I know our graveyard is not to the eye an attractive spot, bleak & barren, the pines stint [stunted] & grass withered, it is a contrast to the verdue & beauty of the little enclosure at White Hall; still I expect to rest here, & my children as they go to their father's tomb may be reminded of his christian life on earth & of his home with Christ above.[86]

Another member of the Arnold family network, Susan Aborn Allen, daughter of Philip and niece of Zachariah, was at White Hall in the spring of 1842, seeking to recover her health. But she died that fall, age twenty, deeply mourned. The Arnolds named their youngest daughter, born in 1843, Susan Allen Arnold.

The death of a slave, however, was the wiping out of an asset as far as the master was concerned, and the slave's name disappeared from the plantation records. Dawn, a field hand, was pregnant in the spring of 1839, and Arnold left instructions with his overseer that she was to be given the task of picking the burrs out of the wool "if she cannot go into the field," but she did "little or nothing all Summer," apparently using the excuse that she was pregnant and later that the child was sickly. What was worse from Arnold's point of view was that her attitude infected others: "Last summer [1839] there was some gross misconduct in W. Hall & C. Hill between Morris & Jane, Wm & Dawn. I wish you to have an eye to these things & should you discern any more between any of the People make a serious example by punishing them—and when you visit W Hall let the different people shew you their own tasks, so that none need escape from doing their full proportion."[87]

Dawn, however, was on good behavior, because "since the Death of her child she has done as much as any one in the field." Therefore, in 1841 she was listed as a full field hand entitled to the full food allowance ration of 8 quarts of corn per week. Sometime between 1841 and 1844 Dawn presumably died, her name disappearing from the Arnold slave list as though she had never existed.[88]

But such is the ambivalence of human interaction hidden beneath the stereotype patterns of behavior in the master-servant relationship that the death of Daddy John in mid-December 1852 becomes a paradigm of the ambiguities inherent in the "peculiar institution." There is no reason to doubt Louisa Arnold's sincerity when she wrote to her daughter Louisa that "we shall miss the old man sadly," but conscious of the growing political and social divisions between the North and South, she added, "I dare say some Northern people would think we would be glad to get rid of such old people but they little know how stronly [sic] attached we are to them   his death seems to have cast a gloom over the place."[89] Certainly, Mrs. Allen was not one of the northern people who would think so, for she wrote to her brother that she "regretted that you were called to part with good old daddy John whom you must miss daily," offering the time-honored consolation appropriate for such occasions that Daddy John's age and "increasing infirmities must have warned you long ago, that this [Daddy John's death] must be expected & therefore it could not have overtaken you suddenly."[90]

For Daddy John (sometimes called Old John, sometimes Yellow John in Arnold's slave lists), the end was not so sudden that he had not put his house in order: "He told Tom what he wanted done with all his things and how to divide his Hives and Fowls   he has about forty Bee Hives and a quantity of Fowls."[91] Part of the hives and part of the fowl were to go to his mistress. To the end he fulfilled his role of the faithful, loyal servant, acting out the expected behavior of a "Sambo."[92] Louisa Arnold played her expected role of the kind, benevolent mistress who would not profit from her slave's death: "I intend to pay for them [the hives and the fowl] and give the money to Sambo and those to whom he left his things."[93]

Daddy John was a hunter, and his master, Richard Arnold, permitted him the privilege of keeping a gun for hunting deer and wild fowl. Probably there never was a moment that Daddy John thought to turn the gun on his master; and although Olmsted was amazed that Arnold allowed his slaves to purchase firearms and ammunition, this arrangement would never have been permitted if a slave had ever turned a gun on master or mistress. Yet in his younger days when he was not quite so old and infirm, say fifteen years earlier, on Tuesday, May 16, 1837, to be precise, did he look at the wildcat that he had caught in a steel trap in the poultry yard, to look beyond the anger he had felt against the animal for destroying his poultry and to see in the wildcat's eyes the anger and pain of *his* captivity? Better to play the role expected of him and leave part of his hives and fowl to his mistress so that she would in her compassion and benevolence be kind to his family. The gift of the hives and the fowl was a symbolic gesture which Louisa Arnold understood.

Two weeks after the death of Daddy John, on Christmas morning, Richard and Louisa Arnold went to Cherry Hill "and gave out the Calico," the traditional Christmas gift to the slaves: "They were very much pleased   it was very pretty." Since it was Christmas, Arnold "gave the children about four dollars in five cent peices [*sic*] which delighted them very much."[94] "Father" Christmas kept his children happy. The only sour note in this happy family was Mrs. Ferguson's piano, evidence that she was "uppity": "I do feel sorry for him she is so extravagant," for not only did she buy a piano, she expects "to have a teacher in their family when they return" from their holiday. Still, a Christmas carol should have a happy ending, and so along with the traditional turkey and ham for Christmas dinner, the slave Sylvia "treated father to a very nice omlette souffle which you know he is very fond of."[95]

CHAPTER SEVEN

Plantation Journal

DECEMBER 5, 1848–APRIL 21, 1849

We arrived in Bryan County   Myself Lady & youngest Child Susan Tuesday Dec. 5ᵗʰ 1848. Having come by the Wilmington rout[e].[1]

Wednesday
Dec 6

All hands @ C Hill raising river bank in No 13 Square excepting 6—ploughs that commenced this day in No 3 first ploughg in Rice field this Season   At W Hall picked Cotton   have about 8 Bags in all picked in—

Thursday
Dec. 7

Bushels 300

Went to Court to attend a Summons as Witness in case G.W. McAllister & J.F. Maxwell. Case did not come on— Thrashed about 300 Bushels Rice & the balance made up dam at C Hill   At W Hall finished picking Cotton   say 500ˡᵇˢ—

Friday Dec. 8ᵗʰ

Rice 500.

At C Hill Men dug ditch outside dam in 13 in order to get dirt to raise & widen that dam   five—ploughs doing two acres each in Rice field   Six women hoeing Stubble before the ploughs & the rest in the Mill. threashed this day 500 Bushels   At W Hall 18 Hands hoed round New ground fence   thirty pannells each hoeing both sides—Had a talk with Overseer about Wages another year   He wants me to pay him $1000—& he will agree to live for that Sum as long as I choose to employ him   I have not Come to any decision as yet on the Subject.—[2]

Saturday *Dec. 9* *Bushels 550*	Went to Mr Harden, & Mr Winn, to call this morning, afternoon went to C Hill. Have thrashed this day 550 Bushels Rice & made up dam next to No 13 Square at W Hall hoed round fence. Carpenters workg on Wharf & mending Carts.
Monday 11th	Went to Sav^h. all the Men from both places
Tuesday 12th	Workg on the Road to Canuchee Women & Boys @ C Hill raising dam in No. 10. & at W Hall listing & hoeing round fence Corn ficld
Wednesday *Dec 13th*	Men on Road finished Work this night—Women & Boys raising dam to No 10. & 12—5 ploughs running all the week in No. 2 & finished 3 Geo two days gone to Sav^h
Thursday *Dec. 14* *500 B.*	part of the Men & Women raising dam @ C Hill part working in Mill thrashed 500 Bushels—@ W Hall listed one task in Corn field each & hoed the fence—
Thursday *Dec. 14th*	Dr Carroll & his Daughter Mary Came to W Hall to make a visit—Sue's child Born this day—a Boy.
Friday Dec. 15 *4500—in all* *in Barn.*	At W Hall listing one task to the hand in Corn field have about 7 Acres done 3 hands Sorted Cotton for C Hill At C Hill thrashed about 500 Bushels have in Barn according to Mr Ferguson Calculating about 4500—Bushels this night—this days thrashing broke my most [blank] thirty hands cleaning off dam & margin between Sedgefield and Mulberry Hill preparatory to cleaning out Canal three men with flat raising low place in Canal dam at Sedgefield—
Saturday *Dec 16*	At C Hill thrashed 500 Bushels Rice & the rest of the force worked @ Sedgefield at W Hall listed One task to

500 Bush^s
Rice.

the hand & hoed the fence in the field Side—Young Pynchon & his Sister dined with us this day.—

Monday
Dec 18

At C Hill a few hands stopped break between 16. & 17. Square & Six hands—listed in New Ground @ C Hill. Six mules ploughing @ C Hill—& all the rest of the force except Carpenters at Sedgefield digging out Trunk bed at the mouth of Canal Next to Mulberry Hill & found an old Floodgate & had to remove further in   part of the people dug 30 feet in height of Canal   part worked Old dam part raised low—places in Canal & Cleaned out grass from old ditches.—

1848 Tuesday
Dec 19th

At W Hall people listing 1¼ tasks in Corn field   three Sewing for people   At C Hill Six ploughs in Rice field   five Women listing in Corn field   Peter Mending ploughs   Watchman & Amos about Mill, & all the rest gone to Sedgefield puting down Trunk in line Canal next Mulberry Hill & clearing out the Same Canal, the Rushes have been so long undisturbed & the land So full of Water, it is with great difficulty we can clean it out. I would— prefer to dig a New Canal   Carpenters fixing trunk for Square not planted last year.

Wednesday
Dec 20

At W Hall listed 3 Acres Corn land   five Sewing for peo ple & at C Hill   Amos & Henry workg in Blacksmith Shop   Peter mending ploughs   Six ploughs in Rice field five people listing Corn field & all the rest gone to Sedge- field   five digging out old Trunk in Square not planted next Mulberry Hill & high ground. fifteen hoeing Stubble in No [blank] & the balanced [*sic*] diging out old Canal between Sedgefield & Mulbery Hill—

Thursday 21st

At C Hill Same as yesterday & also Same work at Sedge- field & also @ W Hall

Friday 22^d

At W Hall listing Corn field   have 22 Acres done   Sev- eral Women Sewing. At C Hill eight hoeing Stubble.

Eight ploughs in Rice field & at Sedgefield ten hoeing Stubble   Six cleaning out old ditches & balance   40 Hands   dug 7 Tasks of old Canal

Saturday
Dec 23ᵈ

At C Hill ten hands hoed & burnt Stubble   Eight ploughs in Rice field   Amos & Henry workg in Blacksmith Shop Peter makg Ox Yokes &c   the rest @ Sedgefield   Say thirty hands   finished after a fashion—cleaning out Canal having put on Said Canal in labour about 400 days work   twenty hands dug ditch & made up bank next high ground & a few burnt Stubble & made up dam on Canal Trunk at Sedgefield.—Bot this day of Mr Pynchon his five Mules $87 ea   his nine Oxen at $15 each & his Stock Cattle about 65. to 70 in all at $4.75 each head, little & big—

Sunday Dec 24

Mary Anns child a Daughter was—born this day—

25,26&27

Christmas. Holy days. We dined on Christmas day at Revᵈ Mr Rogers & at home the other two days   Ellick & Charlotte were married on the 26. Instant³   have written to Wᵐ M. Bailey & my son Richᵈ.

Thursday
28ᵗʰ Dec.

At C Hill run Eleven ploughs in 18. & 19 Squares   five others hoeing Stubble & the rest of the force at Sedgefield   Carpenters working on Trunks. ten hands hoeing Stubble & the rest dug New ditch nex[t] to high ground & cleaned out & deepened Old ditch in Square not planted last year   Sent this Evng 4 plough lines for a ditch line & 2 to Shadwell   one for himself the other Prince

1848 Friday
Dec 29

At C Hill Eleven ploughs running in Rice field   unloaded the Science   took out 100 Bushels Rice flour   7000 feet of lumber   three Bbls Lime   one of tar & one of Water Cement.—Scipio Splitting Rails   Israel made Watchman—⁴ Carpenters workg on Trunk @ C Hill; Eighteen hands digging quarter drains two tasks each 1½ feet wide & two feet deep   ten hands hoeing & burning Stubble & the rest cleaning out Main ditches in Square not planted last year at Sedgefield.—

Saturday
Dec 30

The few hands @ W Hall listing Corn field   ten hands @ C Hill hoeing Stubble before the ploughs   Eleven ploughs running @ C Hill   Scipio Splitting Rails & all the rest at Sedgefield   Some digging quarter drains two tasks length each hand   2 feet deep   18 Inches Broad. Some cleaning out old ditches & Small gang hoeing Stubble.

1849
Monday 1ˢᵗ
Tuesday 2ᵈ

Same work @ all three places as on Saturday.—

Wednesday
Jany 3

Same work as yesterday. Carpenters—all workg on New Trunk for Canal at Sedgefield   This day made a bargain with OBrian a Fisherman to allow him to Build Shanty @ C Hill & fish fr that   He is to give me 2 Shad each day. & to take them when I think proper & to select. give Mr Ferguson one a week & all the offal fish to the people.—[5]

Tuesday
Jany 4

At C Hill Eleven ploughs finished No 7 & Canal Margins & some part of 13 Square   ten hoeing Stubble finished No 13. Two Boys Carting posts for Avenue fence & taking Slats out of flat brought from Sedgefield   Carpenters start on fence @ C Hill & the other three on Canal Trunk Sedgefield   bought 360 Bushels Corn for Habersham of Pynchon @ 65 cts pr Bushel—At Sedgefield Same work as the whole of this week. the ditchers dug two quarter drains & levelled back the dirt & finished by 2 oclock.

Friday Jany 5

At C Hill ten hoed Stubble   Six ploughs finished No 13 Square. Peter & Henry making fence in Avenue at C Hill   Boston Lewis & Monday workg on big Trunk @ Sedgefield   the rest of the force at Sedgefield   part hoeing Stubble   part cleaning out quarter drains & part digging new quarter drains & Six ploughs Commenced at Sedgefield in No 4 Square this day—[6]

Saturday
Jany 6

Bot Pynchons

At C Hill Same work as yesterday in every respect. & also Same at Sedgefield   This day Mr Ferguson Marked & Branded with letter *A*   All of the Cattle, I purchased of Mr Pynchon except 4 Red & White Oxen

Stock @$4.75
pr Head
Oxen $15 each.
9 in number—

branded **Ꞵ Ꞵ** & have Mr Baker of Liberty County
mark, them—[illegible] by Ferguson, Counting 60 Head of
Stock Cattle & five Oxen besides the Baker Oxen, in all
69. I made but 68, & one of them will die before morning   two cows & calves left with Pynchon

1849 Monday
Jany 8th

At C Hill Six ploughs finished No 13 Square   ten hands
mostly Small ones hoeing off Stubble fr No 9. for ploughs.
Carpenters puting up fence in Avenue   five ploughs
finished No 4   first Square ploughed at Sedgefield   Several hoed Stubble & ten men widened & deepened quarter drains in No 7. at Sedgefield & Women
cleaned out all the quarter drains in No 8. having all the
quarter drains—in Eight Squares @ Sedgefield either dug
New or old drains cleaned out this night   Three Wagon
made one turn to Sans Souci this d[a]y & brought [blank]
Bushels Seed Rice bought of—Ham @65 cts pr Bushel
Measured @ Plantation

Tuesday Jany 9

At C Hill retained all hands except teamers & five plough
Boys. the three wagons drawing Rice from Sans Souci &
the five ploughs—workg at Sedgefield   forty hands Cleaning out ditches quarter drains in Nos 1. 2. 3. Squares—
ten & twelve tasks to each hand   Six ploughs in No 9.
which is nearly finished ploughg and all the light hands
hoeing round fence @ C Hill   Carpenters half on trunk &
half on fence @ C Hill   Made a visit to Mr Winns this
afternoon with Mrs Arnold.—At W Hall listed corn land
with a few hands & five Sewing.—Have this night forty
Six Acres Corn land listed—

Wednesday
Jany 10

At Sedgefield Eleven ploughs running & Carpenters part
hewing posts & part workg on large Trunk for Canal—All
the others except three ox Teams drawing Rice from Sans
Souci. at C Hill, made up fence part of the day & part
levelled old dam between one & two & part took boards
off of Wharf & carried three Small ricks of Rice into Barn.

Thursday
Jany 12 [sic]

The coldest day this year   Thermometer as low as 30
above Zero. early in the Morning and a little thin ice in the

W. Hall Seed
Rice 47 B.

Bot Hams Rice
490 B @ 65 cts
for Seed for
Sedgefield

ditches all day.—Eleven Mules ploughing at Sedgefield & three Carpenters working in big Trunk there. at C Hill Thrashed about 450 Bushels Rice & Charles Carting timbre for Trunk from Sans Souci to Sedgefield having finished Carting Rice bought of Ham Yesterday   Whole Amot recd of him about 490 Bushels—@ 65 cts & Carting. Thirteen of the C Hill hands at W Hall & the rest all working about the Mill not doing much on a/c of the Cold weather   attempted to burn Stubble but did not Succeed recd a letter fr Sam & one from Harriet this day. At White Hall thrashed Rice & Winnowed & put into Barn 47. Bushels—[7]

Friday
Jany 13 [sic]

135 Bush^s
W. Hall Rice

At W Hall Eleven of the C Hill hands with the White Hall hands finished thrashing Inland Rice   turned out about 200 Bushels only. Winnowed & put into Barn this night 135 Bushels. At C Hill thrashed about 505 Bushels. & the rest of the Hands Carrd Rice into Barn, & tried to burn Stubble at Sedgefield   11 Ploughs in Rice field   three Carpenters workg in Trunk & two Carpenters at C Hill workg on fence   a few hands passing Rice through Windfan @ C Hill—

Saturday
Jany 14 [sic]

66 B. W. Hall
Rice In Barn
6500 B.

At C Hill thrashed 550 Bushels Rice & winnowed in Pynchon fan 350. a few hands hoeing Stubble & a few cleaning out—quarter drains, or ploughed field   Some Carried Rice into Thrasher   Eleven ploughed @ Sedgefield

1849 Jany 15.

At C Hill Amos & Henry in Blacksmith Shop   Morris with ten hands hoeing Stubble   Peter workg on fence in Avenue. Three—Carpenters on Canal Trunk @ Sedgefield Seven burning Stubble   nine cleaning out quarter drains   ten cleaning out large ditches in Nos 7. & 8. & the balance of the men widening Main ditches next Canal in 7 & 8 & deepening the Same as low as the Trunk will drain   ten ploughs running in No 8 Square—little Boys levelling dirt back from—quarter drains.—Geo. came from Town this night   Overseer in Town—At C Hill

winnowed balance of Gold Rice   4 Bushels & 9 Bushels
my White Rice.—& have—listed tonight 53 Acres Corn @
W H

[No entries in journal from January 16 through January 22]

Tuesday
23ᵈ Jany

Returned this day from Savannah having passed a week
there with G. Jones with Susan & Mrs Arnold   during
my absence a few hands have been hoeing Stubble at
C Hill   Amos in Blacksmith Shop with Henry   Carpenters part @ Sedgefield & part in av[enue] fence at C Hill.
Eleven ploughs workg every day @ Sedgefield & Men
deepening main ditchcs & women Cleaning out quarter
drains @ do. also put down New trunk to Canal @ Sedgefield & dug out & fixed bed for Trunk & put it back @
Mulberry Hill—At W Hall finished listing Corn
ground   in all 68 Acres.

Jany 24
Wednesday

At C Hill a few hands hoeing Stubble   Amos & Henry
makg Harrow teeth   Boston wooden part of Harrows
three other Carpenters in C Hill Avenue fence   all the
other force at Sedgefield   Men with 4 of Bailey[s] deepening & cuting out Stumps in Canal next Mulberry
Hill   Women & Boys cleaning out large & Small ditches
on the Island. two Ox ploughs have been running all the
Week in Square not planted last year @ Sedgefield   Eleven ploughs on the lsland @ do.

Thursday 25ᵗʰ

Work Same as yesterday in every respect except that ten
instead of Eleven ploughs on the Isl @ Sedgefield Geo.
being Sick—this day offered Dr. Eliots Overseer for him
two yoke Oxen for $60—hope he will not take them.—At
W Hall the last two days have been hoeing round fence to
Meeting House field.—

Friday 26

At C Hill men workg on Canal next Mulberry Hill
Women & Small hands cleaning out ditches on Isl. at
Sedgefield & Mulberry Hill Square   Eleven ploughs on
Same Island. Ten Ox plough half a day in No 6. & half do

[ditto] in 7. Boston making Harrows & Swindle tires.
Amos & Henry in Blacksmith Shop—Peter Lewis & Monday in Avenue fence @ C Hill   ten hands hoeing Stubble
@ C Hill   at W Hall finished hoeing round Meeting
House field   Tom & Jacob Whitewashing. Adam Sorting
potatoes   Have this day 30. Lambs @ W. Hall   Scipio
rail Splitting

1849 Jany 27
Saturday

At C Hill Same Work as yesterday   at Sedgefield finished
digging & Cutting out Stumps at Canal Next Mulberry
Hill   also finished cleaning out ditches in the Island
fifteen hands Cleaning out old ditches & digging New
quarter drains in Mulberry Hill & part of the women
cleaned out ditches in No 1.—ten ploughs finished Iland.
& did Some in No 8 Square at Sedgefield. Jim & Shadwell
both broke their ploughs. Baily had 4 men three days &
three Men one day in all. 15 days work he did on Canal
whereas I did 460 days work on it & put down a new
Trunk at my own expense—

Monday
Jany 29

Finish
Harrowing

At C Hill Same work as Saturday   at W Hall Cutting
Poles Carting Rails & Making up fence to Meeting House
field & hoeing fence next McAllisters.—at Sedgefield making up dam between 5 & 6 Squares. digging quarter drain
in 6. Cleaning out ditches in No 1. & making up Canal
dam. with most of the C Hill hands—Two Ox harrows in
No 3.   two double Mule Harrows in No 4. & Six Mules
ploughing in No 7 Square. Carpenters making fence @
C Hill & also Harrows.

Tuesday
Jany 30.

At White Hall Same work as Yesterday @ C Hill   Same
at Sedgefield   Harrows & Ploughs   Same People—a few
cleaning out quarter drains in No 2. & the rest cleaning
out Canal   two in a task. at Mulberry Hill yesterday dug
quarter drains & today Cain is Cutting out Stumps in
Same. Visited Starr & Demere this afternoon—

Wednesday
Jany. 31

At C Hill Six ploughs finished No 9 & half of No 10
Square. Morris with few hands hoeing Stubble

Carpenters on fence & makg Harrows   the other hands at Sedgefield   four harrows two Oxen & two Mules Harrowed twenty Acres   Cain Cutting Stumps @ Mulberry Hill   all the rest in Canal   finished Canal this night

Thursday Feby 1/49

At C Hill hoeing Stubble   ploughing with 6 Mule ploughs   finished No 10 & a little in 11 Square. Carpenters puting up fence in Avenue & making Harrows. Blacksmiths Ironing Ox Yoke & Swindle trees & Making Harrow teeth. At Sedgefield 4 Harrows two Oxen & two double Mule ones   Men dug ditch in No. 6 Square & widened ditch Next Mulberry Hill in 6. & 7 Squares   White Hall made fence.

Friday Feby 2ᵈ

At W Hall finished Meeting House field fence & made up part next McAllister. At C Hill a few hands hoed round Miller field fence   Scipio Splitting Rails all the week   this night Married by Mr Winn Davy & Matilda   Carpenters Same work as yesterday at Sedgefield   Same Harrows running—three hands digging Center ditch & ditch for dam on Small piece to be taken into No 9 Square. the rest of the Hands all turning ground with hoe in Baileys field @ Mulberry Hill one task the hand but which was not finished.

Saturday Feby 3ᵈ

At W Hall finished making fence next McAllisters—at C Hill finished hoeing round fence to Miller field   Scipio Split Rails   Carpenters Same work   Six ploughs finished No 11 Square & Margin to No 9—5 Squares at Sedgefield   One hauling dirt from—ditches thrown in by Harrows   4 Harrows have nearly finished this Night 4 Squares   Say 85 Acres   & the rest of the force all turning ground @ Mulberry Hill   will not average more than ¾ of a task to the hand—Miss Elliott the Misses Footman Miss Pynchon & A. Cuthbert dined @ W Hall

1849 Monday Feby 5.

At W Hall Making pasture fence   at C Hill hoeing round fence   Scipio Splitting Rails   Boston Makg timber

Miss C. Lean
fr Boston
arrived @
W Hall this
morning.

Wheels   Henry & Monday on Avenue fence   Peter &
Lewis gone up Canuchee for timber   Six ploughs in No
14. The rest @ Sedgefield   Adam ploughg in No 7.
Charles & Billy harrowing   finished No 1 with Oxen   Jim
& Sam with Mule Harrows finished No 2 & went into
Island Square   The rest of the force   about 35 Hands—
turning in Mulberry Hill New Square ¾ of a task
each   did not quite finish the Square   been in it three
days—the Road Commissioners met this day.—

Tuesday Feby 6

450 Bushels

At W Hall makg fence   at C Hill Started Thrasher and
thrashed 450 Bushels Rice   the other hands Cleaned out
quarter drains   Carpenters part on fence   part gone to
Canuchee for lumber & part mending Timbre Wheels. Six
ploughs in No 14—two Mules Carrying off Straw at
Sedgefield   4 Harrows on Island & Adam with Buck
ploughing No 6.—Old Tom White Washing @ Sedgefield
& Gibbs Commenced to W Wash at C Hill

Wednesday
Feby 7

450 Bushels

Same work every where as Yesterday & thrashed 450
Bushels Rice @ C H   Amos & Henry workg in Blacksmith Shop fixing Tire to timber wheels   Charles gone
this Evg to Canuchee for lumber for large Trunk.

Thursday
Feby 8.

500 B.

At W Hall made fence round pasture   Sancho drawing
Rails. at C Hill Thrashed 500 Bushels Rice. 5 ploughs in
14 Squares. Carpenters part on fence & part up Canuchee.
at Sedgefield one Ox & two Mule Harrows on Island.
Adam hauling.

Friday Feby 9

500 Bushels

At W Hall making fence round New ground.   at C Hill
thrashed 500 Bushels Rice   part of the Hands cleaning out
quarter drains   Carpenters Same work as Yesterday, 5
ploughs in 14 at Sedgefield   two Mule Harrows and
Adam ploughg   Charles drawing timbre   Billy wood for
mill.

Saturday
Feby 10

At W Hall finished puting up all the Rails at W Hall. at
C Hill thrashed 470 Bushels Rice & the rest of the people

470 Bushels
Rice

cleaned out large ditches   five ploughs in No 4.—at Sedgefield Adam ploughing & two Mule Harrows on Island   Charles at Canuchee drawing Lumber to Landing   Peter & Boston Rafting it—

Monday
Feby 12

At W Hall nothing doing   people gone either to Sedgfield or C Hill—at C Hill Six ploughs in No 4. Two Mule Harrows in No 7 & all the people cleaning out quarter drains   Carpenters on fence near dwelling House. at Sedgefield Charles Harrowing part of the day—& his Oxen broke the Bridge & fell into Creek   got out without injury   Adam Harrowing all day   moved Williams family to Sedgefield   Elsay, Sancho Maria & little Rose to C Hill. Peter & Cain brought flat fr. Sedgefield   Billy the last three days drawing light wood for Mill.

1849 Feby 13
Tuesday

500 Bushels
Rice

At W Hall four men Splitting Rails   At C Hill Charles getting timbre out of Canal   Billy at Sedgefield Harrowg   Adam Harrowing @ do.—At C Hill Thrashed 500 Bushels Rice. Two Mule Harrows finished No 7. 5 ploughs in No 4. & the force not in Mill turng the ground left by the ploughs.—Carpenters on fence round House This day agree with Mr [blank] to get me straight fat lightwood posts 9 feet long hewed Square 6 Inches for which I am to pay 17 cts a piece delvd at my landing.— Mr Ferguson thinks 12½ cts each was enough for them.— Mrs Rockwell left us today

Wednesday
Feby 14

Ice

At C Hill thrashed 350 Bushels Rice & part of the people hoed Stubble & part cleaned out quarter drains   five ploughs in No 4. 2 Harrows in No 3   at Sedgefield Two Ox Harrows running

Thursday
Feby 15

400 B. Rice

Cold.

At C Hill Carpenters on Avenue fence & getting out timbre   Cain & Pompey Sawing. Six ploughs finished No 4 & two Harrows in No 3. Thrashed this day 400 Bushels Rice & finished thrashing with Engine. Have in Mill almost 10,000 Bushels Rice   part of the Hands turning after ploughs & heaping logs in Rice field @ Sedgefield   two

Harrows & One Ox plough Running & people made up
dam

[Page torn in half]

	a
Sa	No
Feby	Miller
	fence next
Orange	with a few do
Trees	No 15. at Sedgefi
very much	ploughg Billy Ha
Injured	& Celia planting
by the	on dam next Mulberry H
Cold & Ice	three days previous been planting
	Same grass on dam in No 13 @ C Hill
	Carpenters @ W Hall Building Shed Rear
	to Sylvia's House—

Monday	Geo Drawing Rails @ W H, at C Hill 5 ploughs in Rice
Feby 20 [sic]	field Charles getting out timbre fr Canal a few hands
	hoeing Stubble & two Sawing & the balance all thrashing
Ice.	Seed Rice @ Sedgefield two Mule Harrows one Ox Har-
	row & two Ox ploughs in Rice field a few leveling dirt &
	2 Setting net grass on dam

[Pages torn out. Entries lost from Tuesday, February 21, to Wednesday, March 27]

[Page torn in half]

a
& Charles
ine & Shadwell
ploughs in No 17
on High ground
funeral of Rich[d]
of J.F. Maxwell at the
ploughs running One furrough
for Cane. Cain & Pompey Sawing

Frank getting Trunk out of
Charles & Adam ploughg at
Neptune & Shadwell Harrowing
Carpenters getting out Arms &c for New trunk for Irish
Canal out of Cypress at Mulberry Hill & all the other
Planted force—planting Cane   8 Acres at C Hill. The Seed Cane
Cane—badly very much rotted & Sprouted by being Covered to[o] deep
& the winter having been very warm. Should have planted
much earlier Inland if I were to plant Seed Cane Soon
after the potatoes are dug off the land—Enquire how Seed
Cane is put up in Louisiana & when planted[8]

1849 Thursday At C Hill Six ploughs finished No 16. Two Ox Harrows
March 29 & two Mule Harrows in No. 19 & 20. a few hands listing
Corn field or minding Birds & taking off Trash. The rest
of the force at Sedgefield   Scipio Splitting Rails & balance
Chopping & levelling One task each in No. 6 Square.
Carpenters at White Hall fixing Bridge over the Creek &
mending Stable—Boston making New steps for Cottage at
C Hill   Israel & Gibbs White Washing @ C Hill   about a
dozen little & big Minding Birds @ W Hall   Made a call
at Starrs this Evng with Mrs Arnold

Friday At C Hill five Harrows in Savage Squares & Six ploughs
March 30 finished No. 16. & in the afternoon went into No 12. A
few hands listing Corn field   Minding Birds & taking off
trash   let off the Water from No 1 & 2. 3 5. & 6. from
Sprout flow. At Sedgefield Scipio Splitting Rails & Several
Minding Birds & taking off trash & the rest chopping &
levelling in No 6. Square one task each. preparatory to
planting. Mr Ferguson seemed to be aware he had put the
Stretch Water on too Soon on Nos 8. & 9. & this Evg
ordered it off, on the plea the Rice was Suffering from
Worms. a thing not known when fields were flowed.—

Saturday At C Hill Same as yesterday   Harrows finished in Savage
March 31. Squares. & Eleven hands cleaning Quarter drains in No
19. Ploughs Six in Number in No 12. Boston & Henry
mending Steps to Negro Houses & fixing Stable. Peter &
Lewis at W Hall the last three days replacing Bridges

&c   at Sedgefield Same work as yesterday   My family passed the day at Mr Winns.

Monday
April 2ᵈ

Planted 3
Acres Potatoes
@ C Hill

At C Hill 24 Hands planted Potatoes   Six—Mules ploughed the potatoe land. & then went into No 12.— Two Ox Harrows finished No. 16. & then with two Mule Harrows went into No 9. Carpenters two Sick & two workg on Stable.—Nine hands tracking in No 6 @ Sedgefield   two raising dam in No 1 Trunk @ do. Eight hands Chopping Clods in No 5. @ Sedgefield & the balance of the force Minding Birds at White Hall. C Hill & Sedgefield

1849 April 3ᵈ
Tuesday

This day
finished
ploughing all
the Rice land
both at
Sedgefield &
C Hill

At C Hill 9 Hands tracking   five Harrows finished No 9. & part of No 12 Squares. three listing in Corn field Boston Mending Trunk in No 16. ten or twelve Minding Birds Scipio Split 500. Task Stakes & the rest of the force at Sedgefield   Nine Gangs planted No 6 Square 20½ Acres three Bushels to the Acre & also two acres in No 5. three hands finished the trenching   Geo Hawling Rails & the balance Minding Birds   two ploughs finished ploughing No 12. which makes a finish of all C Hill & Sedgefield Rice lands   Expect Mr / R H Ives & his two Daughters tomorrow @ W.H.⁹

Wednesday
April 4

The above is the work of Wednesday. Tuesday all hands trenched

Thursday
April 5

At C Hill Six Harrows in No 12 Square & most of the people either trenching with back hoes doing fourteen tasks to the Gang of three or else tracking 12 tasks each in Savage Square   at Sedgefield three gangs finished plantg No 5 Square which finishes the whole planting of Rice at Sedgefield, the rest Minding Birds at both places—Mr R. H. Ives & his two—Daughters arrived this morning at W Hall.

Friday
April 6.

At C Hill trenched with five Gangs. tracked with Nine men & Six ploughs. planted with Seven Gangs doing four-

teen tasks to the Gang   five Harrows finished No 12. &
part of 11—Square   the rest Minding Birds—Have ordered the water leaked down at Sedgefield from the first
planted Rice & very fearful it has been flowed to[o] Soon
before the Rice was well out in the Sprint & afterwards
kept on too long & Altho it was against my judg^t I allowed
my Overseer to do it   He examined the rice & ordered
the water put on without my Seeing it, tho' at my request.—tomorrow I shall know its Condition

Saturday
April 7

Lissys Child
Born @
Sedgefield

At C Hill planted with Twelve Gangs 42 acres   trenched
with thirteen hands & finished planting the Sixty five
Acres purchased of Silk Hope. Six—ploughs finished No
9 & part of 11 Square   two Mule Harrows I presume
finished Eleven Square. the rest of the force—Minding
Birds at Sedgefield or C Hill   This night Prince & Polly
White—were Married   Mr R.H. Ives & his two
Daughters present at the ceremony   Mr Winn officiating.—

Monday
April 9

Planted 35
Acres Rice @
C Hill

At Sedgefield a few hands replanting Some missing places
in Squares on Island and a few Minding Birds at C Hill
Six Mules trenching in No 11. five Harrows in 11 & 10—
Squares. four Gangs trenching with Hoes in 12 Square &
the balance planted No 9 & the larger part of No 11
Squares—a large Number of Bird Minders in the field as
the tides are so Short we cannot get water over the last
planted Rice.—Scipio Splitting Rails & Geo drawing them
to fence at Sedgefield   Charles Carting timbre to Secure
New Trunk for Irish Canal & Carpenters hewing it
Smaller

Tuesday
April 10

At Sedgefield Same as Yesterday   at C Hill finished Har-
rowing trenching & nearly—finished the balance of the
C Hill planting   all but the Margins to No. 10. & 12
Squares & planted all the Seed Rice & used 70 Bushels in
No 12. of the Rice thrashed by the Machine.—Mr. Ives &
his two Daughters we Sent to Savannah by our Carriage
this afternoon   the[y] came to W Hall. on Thursday
Morning last.

1849
Wednesday
April 11

Finished
planting Rice
at C Hill this
morning

At Sedgefield Same work as yesterday   at C Hill Geo
drawing Rails   two Mule Wagons drawing out Manure &
three Ox Wagons doing the Same work. This being the
first day we have drawn out Manure entirely too late. but
could not be helped as we had so much work to do at
Sedgefield   Carpenters workg with most of the Men taking out old Trunk & preparing the bed for New one in
Irish Canal & which I hope to get well put down by
tomorrow night   three in flat carrying mud to put over the
Trunk. the other hands almost thirty in Number
finished—planting the Margins & then listed 1½ tasks
each in Corn field   John Hines & his wife dined with us
this day.—

Thursday
April 12th

At C Hill four men with flat Carrying mud to Canal
Trunk. twenty Men taking out Old Trunk & puting in
New One to Irish Canal. Boston Making body for Mule
Wagon   Six listing Corn field   Six Wagons Carting out
Manure & the balance of the force not Minding Birds
hoeing off Stubble at Mulberry Hill & replanting Margins
at Sedgefield—

Friday
April 13.

At C Hill Carpenters Commenced to Make Trunk for Savage Canal. five wagons Carting out Manure   four men
with flat & a few listing   two helping teamers load Manure   a few listing & many Minding Birds both at Sedgefield & at C Hill

Friday
April 13

Took Ferguson
Deposition this
day

At Mulberry Hill 7 Hands finished hoeing off Stubble &
about thirty choped up the Clods that had been turned in
Mulberry Hill field two tasks each   William with three
hands replanted Margins   At W Hall Started four ploughs
two furroughs in Corn field & did fifteen Acres   Geo.
Carted out Manure at W Hall for potatoes.—This day
C H Starr J. F. Maxwell & Charles H. Harden took Mr
Fergusons deposition in my case with Lackleson & J. F.
Maxwell is to carry it to Sav^h & hand it to the Clerk

Saturday
April 14

At W hall four ploug[hs] in Corn field running one furrow
each Side of bed   did 16 Acres   Sam carted out Manure

& three hands listed for potatoes. At C Hill four hands
with flat   five hoeing Margins in Rice field   two listing in
Corn field   five Wagons Carting out Manure   two extra
hands loading   ten or more Minding Birds in Rice field
Carpenters working on Trunks for Savage Canal & No 16
Square.—At Sedgefield   say 30 hands   Chopping Clods
in Bailey Squares   4 replanting margins   last night let off
all the water from 1, 2, 3 & 4 Squares.—No 2 & 3
[illegible] by puting on Sprout flow too long very deep &
then puting on Stretch flow too soon for the point   had I
kept these Squares dry would have had a beautiful
Stand   Now have to replant 3 & patch 2 very much.

1849 Sunday
April 15

Frost this night   Thermometer down to 36°   Ice killed 70
Acres of Corn at W Hall & 20 Acres @ C Hill—

Monday
April 16

Frost & Ice

at C Hill five Wagons Carting out Manure   three extra
hands helping load. a few hands listing in Corn field &
Minding Birds   last night put on all the water we could
get to the first C Hill planted Rice on a/c Cold &—altho
the fields were not covered it—prevented the Rice from
being injured by frost, whereas the Rice on the other Side
of the River was Seriously injured from being dry—At
Sedgefield planted outside Margin next Way & choped
Clods in Bailey Square—doing 1½ tasks to the hand—
Ploughed at W Hall & flat Carried mud.—

Tuesday
April 17

Went over the
River to See
Crops this day.

At White Hall 4 Ploughs in Corn field   4 Hands in do.
hoeing Bermuda Grass. Sam Carting out Manure at
C Hill   Carpenters Making Trunk for Savage Canal. five
Carts Same as Yesterday Carrying out Manure—at Mulberry Hill   hoeing off No 1. @ Mulberry Hill   averaged
only 1½—tasks to the hand. Mr Pynchons Old Woman
died This day @ Sedgefield

Wednesday
April 18

Twenty eight hands @ W Hall—beding after the ploughs
4 tasks each   7 Ploughs breaking up the ground two Acres
each   two hands Spreading Manure for Potatoes—the rest

Dined with
Wilkins this
day

of the hands not Carting Manure @ Mulberry Hill hoeing
off No 1 Square & 4 with flat.—

Frost

Thursday
April 19

Frost this
Night

At W Hall four ploughs finished the Corn field @ W Hall
& Six persons beded & planted Six tasks of Potatoes—At
C Hill a few listed Corn field   five Wagons Carted out
Manure & four Men with flat Carting Mud to Savage
Canal for Trunk. Carpenters workg on Trunk that is going
into that Canal   been trying all the week to flow first
planted Rice at C Hill but have not Succeeded altho the
water put on has prevented the Rice from being injured by
the frost. Whereas the dry Squares have been Cut down
by it tho' I do not think the Rice is killed at Sedgefield.
Most of the people worked & finished hoeing off Baileys
Square next River doing a little more than one task to the
hand & the rest tracked in Same Square—went to court as
Witness for J. F. Maxwell

Friday
April 20

Planted No 2
Square at
Mulberry Hill
23 Acres with
3 Bushels pr
Acre   have
used all the
W Hall &
C Hill Seed
Rice & taken
up to this time
110 Bushels pr
Crop Rice—

At W Hall beded & planted One task of potatoes & have
17 Bushels left to Send to Sedgefield   also beded One task
for Ground Nuts. At C Hill four Wagons—Carting out
Manure   Charles getting logs for Trunk to Savage Canal
& drawing them home. Sent 25 Bushels Rice from W Hall
& 40 Bushels from C Hill for Seed to Mulberry Hill
Geo. Carting Rails to Sedgefield fence   a few hands
Minding Birds & taking trash off of Nos 5 & 6 at Sedgefield   five hands tracking in Baileys Square next river &
four Gangs trenched 12 Acres in Same Square & the balance of the force planted Second Square 23 Acres at
Mulberry Hill & one Acre in No 1. this day rec^d the Cart
& mule from Pynchon & got entire possession of Sedgefield & Wrote him to Send his a/c to me by Stage on
Monday.

1849 Saturday
April 21

Finished
planting
Mulberry Hill
Rice

At C Hill four Wagons Carting out Manure   One Carried
two loads Seed Rice to Sedgefield   80 Bushels   Geo
Carted out Manure for Potatoes @ Sedgefield   two hands
[blank] 4 Tasks for Potatoes. Charles—Cut & Carted Eight
pieces for Trunk for Irish Canal & the rest of the force
finished track[in]g trenching & planting No 1.   @ Mulberry Hill the two Squares that contain 46 Acres   Have
planted ten Bushels over three to the Acre in these
Squares—Gave out Summer clothing this Evg—taken for
Seed out of the [illegible] including 40 Bushels Now at
Sedgefield to replant No 2 & patch No 3 with. 200 B

Grist Mill Prov^e
Two & a half feet stones ground each about a half
inch   fourteen groves on one & 15 on the other Surface of
both flat—the Under Stone turning yields every day ten
Bushels of fine meal pr hour & twenty five bushels of fine
Hominy pr hour & has Ground 30 Bushels pr hour.—

CHAPTER EIGHT

$\mathcal{N}$ewport:
$\mathcal{A}$ $\mathcal{S}$outhern $\mathcal{E}$nclave

On August 1, 1857, Richard Arnold, casting up his accounts for the past fiscal year, recorded his holdings in Georgia, which totaled nearly 11,000 acres of land and buildings worth nearly $100,000, and $96,950 in "Stock": namely, 200 head of cattle, 150 sheep, 12 horses, 11 mules, 3 carriages and carryall, 10 wagons and drays, carts and 10 drays, ploughs and other agri-utensils, and "200 People old & young @ $450" per head.[1] On the same day, he worked out the cost of having purchased 8⅝ acres of land in the northern outskirts of Newport, the estate which he called Sunny Lawn, where he was to build his new house—$11,356.97, or more than $1300.00 per acre compared with the $4.00 per acre estimated value of 2,000 acres at White Hall, the home plantation. His net financial worth on that day, North and South, was over $500,000.

It was a good time to be taking stock of his life, an inventory of his assets and liabilities, for he was in a period of transition, having just purchased land in Newport. Arnold's life was summed up in his account books, and its duality was permanently inscribed in the heading of each page. On page 414, headed "Bryan County Georgia April 17th 1857," he debited the amount he paid his overseer, C. W. Ferguson, $17.50 less $7.50 paid by Ferguson to the railroad "for passages of himself and six negroes sent to Doct Schley for Estate of D M Rogers." On page 538, headed "Providence Rhode Island August 1st 1857," he credited the amount received from Doctor Schley of Savannah to the "Estate of D M Rogers" account $3,200 "in settlement for six Negroes sold him vis. John & his wife Annie—their three children, Jane, Ellen & Nancy—and Charity all belonging to the Estate D M Rogers & sold him April 16/57 for $3200." The Rogers estate account was debited $7.50

that same day in April for the railroad transportation of overseer and six slaves; but the $4.12 he paid his "boy" Derry for ducks, eggs, and poultry, and the $3.50 he presented Amos were listed under "Family Expenses," Bryan County, just as the $12.50 paid the Providence Club on August 1 was listed under "Family Expenses," Providence, "with the understanding that I am to pay for only 6 Mos assessments—being absent from Providence much more than that time."[2] The two worlds were as separate as ever despite their seeming to come together in the balancing of the accounts, but at least he saved $12.50 by not having to pay a full year's assessment to his social club in Providence.

The two worlds of Richard Arnold could not be kept separate, however, in the complicated infighting of Rhode Island politics in the 1850s, which at times seemed more like a family feud than a debate about issues of the day. Arnold stayed out of politics, but his son-in-law Samuel Greene Arnold was in the thick of it, becoming lieutenant governor of Rhode Island in 1852 and again in 1861. In the public arena of partisan attack the two halves of Richard Arnold's private life met. The March 1, 1855, issue of the *Providence Daily Tribune* included a letter to the editor signed "Sam, Jr.," the pseudonym for a political opponent of Samuel G. Arnold, and warning the voters of Rhode Island that there were rumors "that the son of a slaveholder is to take the place of Hon. Thomas Davis in the next Congress." Better Davis with all his faults, the writer continued,

> than to send a pro-slavery man there, who would unite with the enemies of free territory and the rights of man—To this a great majority of the voters in this district will say AMEN, and the voters will be backed up by all the real conscientious men and women of true principle. This principle has taken such deep root among the people, as to render futile any attempt to smuggle a man into Congress from any district, I trust, in New England, who is not thoroughly anti-slavery, as well as anti-papist and anti-jesuit. Thomas Davis we know where to find, but who knows where to find the son or son-in-law of a wealthy slave owner. Freemen and free mechanics and laborers of Rhode Island be on your guard! Down with slave labor, with its whips and chains, thumb-screws and iron collars! You will vote for no man to represent you in Congress who is not a decided enemy to human chattelism.[3]

H. B. Anthony himself, editor of the *Providence Journal* and a family friend, felt called upon to write that "Mr. Arnold has no more connection with slavery than the editor of the Tribune," but this denial was not published at Samuel Arnold's request. The attacks continued so that on December 28, 1859, R. M. Larned, as a friend of Samuel Arnold, wrote to the editor of the

Providence Journal that he was authorized "by [Lt.] Gov. Arnold to say that he is not—never was—and never shall be with his consent, either directly or indirectly, interested in slave property anywhere," a rather disingenuous answer since Samuel's wife, Louisa, had been born at White Hall and was one of the potential heirs to the property.[4]

National politics, of which Rhode Island politics after all was a reflection, intensified into sectional division, North and South. The civil war in Kansas in 1856 over whether that state would be free or slave and the Dred Scott decision in 1857, in which the United States Supreme Court held that slavery could not be excluded from the territories, divided the nation into two hostile camps over the issue of expanding slavery into new states, to say nothing of its existence in the old states of the South. The conservative wing of the Republican party in Rhode Island, to which Samuel Arnold belonged, was strong enough to elect a governor three years in a row beginning in 1857. Although conservative Rhode Island Republicans opposed the extension of slavery into the territories, at the same time they disclaimed any intention to abolish slavery in the states where it already existed.[5]

Richard Arnold, because he belonged to both worlds and had everything to gain financially from the status quo, had no real quarrel with his son-in-law's position. On August 10 he recorded $547.00 in his account with Robert Habersham and Sons "for corn forwarded to Plantations" from their warehouse, and on the same day he presented to his daughter Mary Cornelia ten shares of Blackstone Canal Bank Stock worth $267.50, a northern institution devoted to serving the textile manufacturing interests.[6] Still, being a cautious businessman, Richard Arnold, soon after returning to Georgia that winter, took no chances on the political scene and made a comprehensive list of his 199 slaves as of January 1, 1858, "should Congress ever pay for freeing slaves."[7]

The property Arnold purchased in Newport was in the opposite direction from the fashionable Bellevue area where George Noble Jones, Andrew Robeson, and others had built their villas. But the developed land available in that area was even more expensive than the cost of the land he did buy, being either small subdivisions of larger estates—Jones, for example, sold off a small parcel of his land for $18,000 in 1856—or house lots off the extension of Bellevue Avenue to the south, selling for $5,226 an acre in 1853.[8] Arnold, however, missed out on one real estate opportunity at that time: William Beach Lawrence purchased Ochre Point for $12,000, about what Arnold paid for his land. Lawrence's tract was undeveloped farm land, inaccessible except for primitive tracks, bordered by cliffs on the ocean side. Less than

A list of persons belonging to Richard J. Arnold and their ages, January 1, 1858. A note on the back says, "valuable, should Congress ever pay for freeing slaves." (Courtesy of the Rhode Island Historical Society.)

twenty years later, Lawrence became a millionaire by selling the land to multimillionaires like the Vanderbilts and the Belmonts for their mansions.[9]

Arnold's needs, however, were more modest. He wanted privacy, away from the crowds of tourists filling the hotels—the Ocean House was opposite the Jones "cottage"—a place where his family and grandchildren could enjoy themselves and not feel like transients staying at hotels and boardinghouses as the Arnolds themselves had done in past Newport summers. He was used to *space* in Georgia. True, he could not duplicate the manorial expanse of White Hall, but neither did he want to duplicate the crowded, urban life of Providence. The family home, Sabin Tavern, had served its purpose in the past, but South Main Street was now even more commercial, the city more and more crowded with foreign-born workers (22 percent of the population by 1855). It was not surprising, either, that Arnold's new estate overlooked the edges of the harbor, as did the mansion house in Providence, but farther inland and at great height—as though he had moved "up the hill" but with more land surrounding his house.

More than anything else, what Arnold presumably wanted, besides the cool ocean breezes and the miasma-free air of Newport, was the congenial social and political atmosphere provided to slave owners since colonial times when the first southern planters from South Carolina arrived to escape the threat of malaria and yellow fever indigenous to the swamps of the tideland.[10] Newport remained a haven for slave owners throughout the antebellum period, long after the end of the slave trade and slavery in Rhode Island. As early as the summer of 1830, Eliza Clay wrote to her "brother" Richard Arnold extolling the "purer air of Newport" over Providence:

> I do not think Mrs. Savage's party would be disposed to board in Providence; Newport you know was very *fashionable* last summer & full of Southerners, & as they were much pleased, it will probably be still more *au fait* this season— and as Mary S. has a powerful voice in the councils of her party, I think she would strongly favour Newport. . . . Newport air has such a reputation that it would be preferred by most persons who come on for health.[11]

The southern slaveholders found the political atmosphere of Newport in the 1830s and 1840s as healthy and refreshing as the sea breezes, dominated as it was by the prosouthern attitudes of Benjamin Hazard and Richard Randolph, who himself had been born in Virginia on a tobacco plantation where his father owned slaves. The Joneses, Balls, Middletons, Izards, and Pinckneys formed the nucleus of a summer colony which became an enclave of slave owners. Although at times their extended families seemed to be large, they never numbered in the hundreds, let alone the thousands alleged by Theodore Weld in his letter to the Rhode Island Anti-Slavery Convention in February 1836, but they certainly held among them thousands of slaves. They stayed in boardinghouses and later the hotels (the Ocean House, 1840, and the Atlantic House, 1844) that were built to accommodate the ever-increasing number of summer visitors to Newport. Eventually, some of them built their own homes, summer residences called cottages, which although impressive even today are not to be confused with the opulent mansions built in Newport during the Gilded Age after the Civil War. They were, these more modest dwellings, intended as family residences, even though some were occupied only part of the year.

When the Arnolds began to build their house in Newport a few years before the outbreak of the Civil War, it was at the end of a social era, not the beginning. The era of the "cottage" set began in the 1830s and ended with the Civil War, for the southern slave owners were an integral part of the social scene, intermingling socially and intermarrying with themselves and with the upper-middle-class families of Philadelphia, New York, and New England who found Newport an alternative summer resort to the fashionable watering spas like Saratoga Springs. For example, Hugh S. Ball, whose family, like the Middletons and Izards, owned plantations in the tidewater region of South Carolina near Charleston, married into the prominent Channing family of Boston, who originally came from Newport. The Balls were one of the first of this social set to build their own house, beginning construction in 1836, but they had scarcely settled into their new summer home when they and most of the 150 other New York–bound passengers lost their lives in the wreck of the steamship *Pulaski*, which sank off the coast of South Carolina in 1838 when one of its boilers exploded.

The Balls, like the Izards and the Middletons and other southern slave owners, brought with them to Newport their "servants," that is their personal slaves, but because they were citizens of southern slave states, they, unlike Arnold, did not include their slaves in any northern census. Under the Constitution, representation in Congress was apportioned "by adding to the whole number of free persons . . . three fifths of all other persons," meaning slaves, and therefore slaves were counted in the census of the southern slave states. Furthermore, since slaves were deemed taxable property in the slave states, local census figures were maintained. But the Balls' slave who perished with them in the wreck of the *Pulaski* never appeared in any Rhode Island census as, for example, Mum Phebe did in 1830 and again in 1840 because she belonged to a Rhode Island citizen.

Visitors to Newport from the South in the 1830s and 1840s included Savannah-based planters as well as the Charleston families. For example, in July 1832 William B. Nuttall and his new bride, the former Mary Wallace Savage, accompanied by her mother, arrived in Providence on their way to Newport. But because of an outbreak of cholera in Savannah the day they had left for New York, having been married in Savannah on June 20, they were quarantined while in Providence and could not go immediately to Newport. Admittedly, they lived in style at the City Hotel, but Providence was not Newport, and the Arnolds were unavailable, since they were visiting the Clays in Medford, accompanied by their slave-servants Mum Phebe and Mary. Zachariah and Eliza Harriet Allen visited them at the hotel to cheer them. Eliza Harriet's impression of the newlyweds was highly favorable: "Mary looks very well & pretty & I think Mr. N. an uncommonly fine looking man. he reminds me much of Mr. Clay," and again a week later she wrote to her brother, "I am much pleased with Mr. Nuttall. he appears an amiable man." But she admitted that although she had done "what I could to entertain them . . . I fear they have found it very dull."[12]

The Nuttalls finally made it to Newport, but whether they ever returned to Providence is unrecorded. William Nuttall kept his amiability but not his money. He died of apoplexy on April 10, 1836, heavily in debt, having mortgaged not only his own property, El Destino plantation in Florida, but also his wife's and his mother-in-law's slaves. Mary Nuttall was visiting in Newport at the time of her husband's death in Florida.

In the meantime, visiting in Newport, George Noble Jones had met Delia Gardiner, daughter of Robert E. Gardiner of Gardiner, Maine. They were married in 1834, but only two years later, Delia died. Within the interconnecting network that existed between planter families in Newport and Savannah, George Noble Jones and Mary Savage Nuttall, who had lost their spouses in the same year, met and eventually married, May 18, 1840. Construction of Jones's house in Newport, designed by Richard Upjohn in the Carpenter Gothic style, had already begun, and the Joneses were able to move into it the following summer.

George Noble and Mary Nuttall Jones settled into a second life in Newport as part of the southern enclave, putting down roots in the community that went far beyond being mere tourists or casual visitors to a summer resort. Neither were strangers to Newport: the Savage and Jones families had been frequent visitors in the 1830s, and indeed George Noble Jones had originally planned his house as a summer residence for himself and a year-round residence for his mother and sister. Both Mrs. Mary Savage and Mrs. Sarah

Jones, mothers of Mary and George, respectively, were eventually buried in Trinity Church cemetery, Newport. The Joneses maintained their family connection with Trinity Church, being communicants and baptizing their children there.[13]

The Joneses entertained lavishly by the standards of the day, but their parties were essentially *family* affairs. On August 15, 1842, Jones wrote to his cousin and fellow planter, George Jones Kollock, who spent his summers in upland Georgia:

> Newport has become one of the gaiest watering places. A band of music has been imported from New York and balls, picnics etc. etc. are the constant themes of day and night. My Sister Mary, to diversify the amusements, has engaged in a Fancy party which is to come off this evening. There are many pretty women in this place, who I have no doubt will make a very brilliant appearance. I presume however these affairs do not interest you as much as the crops, fat legacies and plenty of children![14]

Others also had discovered Newport as a summer resort. On July 12, 1844, Jones complained to Kollock that Newport was full of visitors that summer, but few from the South: "This place is becoming like Saratoga on a small scale; several public houses have been opened since you were here, and a large Hotel has been erected opposite to our residence. This is rather annoying but we must endeavour to exclude the view by Trees etc."[15]

Congenial neighbors more than trees helped exclude the transient summer visitors from the mind's eye. The Balls' house was purchased by Dr. David King, a popular Newport physician. Henry Middleton purchased a stone house already standing just north of Jones's cottage. A trend had started, and on October 6, 1849, Jones, still in Newport, wrote to Kollock in Georgia: "Newport as usual has had her crowd of visiters [*sic*] amounting at one time to near four thousand, but strange to say we scarcely know whether the place is more or less crowded as we are entirely independent of transient visiters. Our society consist mainly of the Cottagers of whom there are at present nearly twenty families of which I wish you composed one."[16] Many more of these cottages and villas were built in the early 1850s, including the house of Arnold's nephew, Andrew Robeson, Jr.

One "transient" visitor to Newport in the summer of 1849 whom the Joneses welcomed with open arms and southern hospitality was Richard Arnold and daugher, who stayed at the Atlantic House to attend a ball on August 13. Throughout the 1840s the Arnolds spent part of the summer, usually August, in Newport to escape the heat of the city and to enjoy the beaches and cool breezes, visiting friends and relatives. Presumably, Mrs. Arnold was busy that summer of 1849 helping her daughter Louisa who was in her last month of pregnancy and therefore confined to Lazy Lawn, her home in Middletown just outside Newport, where her first daughter, Louisa Caroline (Luly), was born on September 18.

In the early 1840s the Arnolds stayed at boardinghouses in Newport, but a dispute over a bill from Miss Mumford in 1843 probably soured them on that kind of arrangement.[17] In August 1845 they took rooms in the Ocean House, opposite the Joneses, placing their sons Thomas and Richard, Jr., in C. W. Greene's school in Jamaica Plains, near Boston. There was no chance to argue over the bill this time. The hotel burned to the ground! Greene wrote congratulating Arnold: "We rejoice in your escape, and we have endeavoured to impress the boys with a sense of the gratitude due to God for so great an act of mercy. If the conflagration had been by night, the whole country would have been shrouded in sorrow, as every one of any respectability must have mourned a relative, a friend or acquaintance."[18] Such a near escape did not deter the Arnolds from continuing to visit Newport and to take rooms in hotels, although it must be noted that at least in 1849 Arnold chose the Atlantic House rather than the newly rebuilt Ocean House.

The Arnolds did not attempt to entertain as lavishly as the Joneses—their background was a bit too puritanical to seek rivaling Jones's cellar of French wines, and living in hotel rooms in Newport was not conducive to elaborate entertaining. They undoubtedly engaged in the main social activity of their social class, whether it was winter or summer—the paying of social calls. Their friends were all within short walking distance of each other and from the hotels. More and more the Arnolds were drawn into the social life of Newport in the summer season. It was inevitable that they would eventually build a house there.[19]

Many years later, Henry James, who as a youth had been in and out of these same houses in the late 1850s, described the carefree lives of the summer residents in Newport:

> For nine persons out of ten, among its visitors, its purchasers of sites and builders of (in the old parlance) cottages, there had never been anything in it all—except of course an opportunity: an opportunity for escaping the summer heat of other places, for bathing, for boating, for riding and driving, and for many sorts of more or less expensive riot.[20]

A Jamesian appreciation of social manners is required to suggest that charades performed by the guests, one of the popular means of entertainment among the cottage set in the mid-1850s in Newport, were "expensive riot," but the nuances and reverberations of such evenings were rich in meaning. A delicate balance was needed to pick one's way through the mine fields of conflicting attitudes without committing a faux pas or gaffe, given the tensions underneath the surface of polite social conversation and innocent games. On one such evening at the Joneses', Duncan Pell was Jupiter, and Andrew Robeson, Jr., "perched on a piano stool Slowly revolved with one foot in air—and arm uplifted was Mercury.—Both Gentlemen enveloped in sheets, Mr Pell brandishing poker and tongs for thunder bolts and Mr Robeson the shovel for a caduceus."[21] But what was Mercury's message? Were Jove's thunderbolts the advance warnings of an angry god whose truth was inexorably marching from Lawton's Valley only a few miles away, where Samuel Gridley and Julia Ward Howe spent their summers?

The Pells lived in the hill section of Newport in the Cheseborough house, a colonial structure described by Henry James as possessing "an inward charm that refined even on its outward."[22] Here James in 1858 first met "Archie," the Pells' son, and Thomas Sargent Perry, who became his lifelong friend. Henry James and his brothers William and Wilky along with Perry and Pell, joined by others of the junior cottage set—Andrew Robeson III among them—explored the island that summer and many of them studied together at the Reverend Mr. Leverett's school in Newport, the Berkeley Institute. It is not likely that the Arnold boys were part of this group, for they were older.

Mercury was also god of commerce as well as messenger to the gods, and perhaps in this guise the host understood the message, for Jones, like Arnold, considered himself above all else a businessman. Mercury's message may have been a warning of the impending financial crisis and panic (Andrew Robeson, Jr., himself was a man of commerce, managing his father's textile factory, which printed the calico so popular in the South). In 1855 and 1856 Jones sold off some of his Newport land to finance improvements on his Florida plantations, and in the spring of 1856 he rented his cottage to finance an extended trip to Europe for himself and his family.[23] The messenger himself had sped to Europe even before the Joneses, and on September 13, 1855, Zachariah Allen went to Newport to bid goodbye to the Robesons, who would be gone for two years, traveling part of the time with the Joneses. *His* message, as recorded in his diary on that day, was that "no one can foretell what a single day may bring forth—much less can we imagine what series of events may occur in the period of two years."[24] By the time the Robesons came back from Europe, Zachariah Allen was bankrupt, a victim of the Panic of 1857.

Such were the interrelationships of the cottagers, many of whom lived in Newport year round, that the list of charter members of the Queen of Clubs, a social club organized by the ladies on November 20, 1854, as their answer to the exclusively male preserve of the Newport Reading Room, was a roll call of the political, social, and cultural establishment of the time. It included Mrs. George Cadwalader, wife of General Cadwalader, Union officer. She was the sister of Pierce Butler, who often stayed with her in Newport. His divorce from Fanny Kemble who fled his plantation in horror from slavery was no bar to Newport society, nor apparently was the fact that in 1859 Butler sold 460 slaves in the largest, most notorious sale of slaves belonging to a single owner ever held in Savannah. So large was the "gang" of slaves that they were shipped to Savannah in railroad freight cars and then driven out to the race course where the auction itself was held. The atmosphere was closer to that of a cattle show than a horse race.[25]

Mary Nuttall Jones was a member, living in Newport at the time the club was formed, as was her daughter Mary Nuttall, who had married G. Wymberley Jones (George Noble Jones's uncle) at Trinity Church, Newport, on October 21, 1852. Mary Powel, wife of Samuel Powel of Philadelphia and a neighbor of the Joneses and the Robesons, joined the club. Mary Robeson was a member, as was Mary Tweedy, wife of Edmund Tweedy, close friend of Henry James, Sr., and one of the reasons James chose to live in Newport. Other members included Fanny Perry, widow of Christopher Grant Perry and mother of Thomas Sargent Perry, Henry James's close friend. The mother of Archie Pell, another of James's friends, Mrs. Duncan Pell, was also a charter member, as was Mrs. J. Prescott Hall, the wife of a New York lawyer, who rebuilt Malbone Hall in 1848–1849; she was a de Wolfe, the Rhode Island family deeply involved in the slave trade in the late eighteenth and early nineteenth centuries. To balance the scales was Mrs. Albert Sumner, sister-in-law of the abolitionist senator from Massachusetts. The social organizer behind this seemingly diverse if not opposing group of women was Sarah King, wife of Dr. David King and close friend of the Joneses.[26]

The Queen of Clubs met once a week at the home of one of the members, presumably in rotation. There were few rules and regulations, but one was "all men to be excluded" and another stated that "no lady is allowed to converse of servants or scandal at this Club. An original composition to be the fine for an infringement of this Rule."[27] Since the group was composed of diverse personalities, some of whom would be gone during the winter season, the temptation to break the latter rule must have been overwhelming. Indeed, according to one of its members, Katharine Prescott Wormeley, "The 'original compositions' became rather a burden on the souls of the Queen of Clubs."[28]

The Newport Reading Room, incorporated in January 1854, was the men's social club of the Newport elite, whether they were summer or year-round residents. The purpose of the club as stated at its incorporation was to promote "literary and social intercourse among its members." In practice, the intercourse was more social than literary, but the incorporators had an abiding sense of literature as property: "No member shall take away from the Reading Room, upon any pretence whatever, any book, pamphlet, newspaper, or other article, the property of the Corporation, under penalty of expulsion."[29] Unlike the Queen of Clubs, the Newport Reading Room did not specifically exclude the opposite sex; it simply defined a member as *he*. Dogs, however, of either sex were prohibited under the bylaws. Gambling games such as "Pharo Bank, Hazard, Rouge et Noir, Roulette Table, or any round game of Cards or Dice" were forbidden. Chess, backgammon, billiards, and card games not in the round were permitted, however, and a maximum stake of $5.00 was established (later reduced to $2.50) "on any game of cards or billiards under the penalty of expulsion." In the summer of 1854, a resolution was proposed that "ladies should be admitted to the club"; but the resolution was tabled and not heard from again for thirty years.[30]

Among the original incorporators of the club was Arnold's nephew, Andrew Robeson, Jr. The first officers were William S. Wetmore, president; Albert Sumner, treasurer; and William Beach Lawrence, secretary. There were no vice-presidents, and for practical reasons the officers and the incorporators were drawn from the permanent winter colony. Summer residents, however, were welcome and exempt from the restrictions placed on nonresidents as long as they owned and occupied "houses at Newport during part of the year"; properly vetted nonresidents could be admitted as temporary members. On September 1, 1854, Richard Arnold, although a nonresident at the time, became a stockholder of the Newport Reading Room, joining such southern planters among the summer residents as George Noble Jones and G. Wymberley Jones, Henry A. Middleton, and Ralph S. Izard, all of whom had joined earlier that summer.[31]

The social world represented by the Newport Reading Room and its counterpart, the Queen of Clubs, was a cross section of that upper-middle-class network of family, friends, and business acquaintances that had similarly formed the pattern of the white power structure of Providence; but Newport, being a resort, tended to be more cosmopolitan than Providence, for even its permanent residents among the cottage set more often than not had made their fortunes elsewhere and came to Newport to retire. William Wetmore, for example, began his business career with Edward Carrington of Providence, where his uncle was a partner, but he made his fortune in the China trade, as did the King family, through Russell and Company of Boston, trading in tea, silk, cotton, and opium. Wetmore established his own mercantile house in New York about 1841 before retiring to Newport in 1851 with his family, where he built one of the largest of the wooden cottages on farm land beyond the Joneses, the Robesons, and the Powels. It was perhaps a measure of their cosmopolitanism that the Wetmores' son, George Peabody Wetmore, future friend and schoolmate of the James boys (and future president of the Newport Reading Room) was born in London on August 2, 1846, while they were on an extended visit.

Neither abolitionism nor slaveholding was a bar to membership in the Newport Reading Room, and Samuel Gridley Howe purchased Stock Certificate number 17 on June 1, 1854, followed on the same day by George Noble Jones and G. Wymberley Jones, numbers 18 and 19. Certainly the China trade with its opium traffic was no bar either, for not only was William Wetmore among the organizing members but also Edward King, who built his brick and stone villa in 1845 on land adjacent to Jones. Both Edward and his brother William (who purchased Jones's house in 1864 and named it Kingscote) were deeply involved in the China trade, as were their nephews David and William, Dr. David King's sons. William King purchased Certificate number 50 on July 2, 1854, and Dr. David King purchased number 62 on February 22, 1855. The King brothers were native Newporters, educated at Brown University, but because of their professional and mercantile life they were cosmopolitan in their outlook, fitting in well as local leaders of Newport society, both socially and culturally.

Yet tensions existed just beneath the surface of Newport society. What, after all, could Samuel Gridley Howe have to say to Richard Arnold, his wife's cousin, beyond polite conversation. There would seem to be no greater gulf than existed between the two ways of life represented by Howe and Arnold, two New Englanders, both graduates of Brown University (Howe, being younger, graduated in 1821, seven years after Arnold), both Phi Beta Kappa. Arnold for personal and business reasons became a slave owner; Howe for philosophical reasons devoted himself to idealistic causes. If Richard Arnold, Jr., toured Europe in 1857 shortly after leaving Brown, a copy of Byron's poems in hand, Howe literally followed in the footsteps of his poet-hero after graduating from Harvard Medical School, offering his services as a surgeon to the Greeks in their war for independence against the Turks.

It was consistent with his idealism that instead of going into private practice Dr. Howe accepted the directorship of the New England Asylum for the Blind after his return to Boston. The blind, the deaf, and the insane were to be lifelong concerns to him, both as a doctor and as a humanitarian. But not until a visit South, including a stay at a Georgia plantation, in 1841–1842, when he saw slavery first hand, did he take up abolition as a cause. The passage of the Fugitive Slave Act of 1850 made him an activist. One of his first acts as chairman of the Vigilance Committee in Boston, formed to prevent the recapture of fugitive slaves and consisting of such prominent abolitionists as Theodore Parker and Wendell Phillips, was to arrange the escape to England of Ellen and William Craft, two fugitive slaves from Georgia.

Howe's involvement with the antislavery hero John Brown most directly and dramatically distinguished him not only from the slaveholding members of the Newport Reading Room but also from all the other members of that social club, whatever their attitudes toward slavery. He was a member of a group of radical abolitionists who became known as the Secret Six. Besides himself and Theodore Parker of the Vigilance Committee, they were George L. Stearns, a businessman from Medford, Massachusetts, where the Clays still resided during the summer when they were in the North; Thomas Wentworth Higginson, then a Unitarian minister in Worcester, Massachusetts, the most radical of the group, who often spent summers in Newport; Gerrit Smith, a wealthy New York landowner; and young Franklin Sanborn, to whose experimental school in Concord Henry James, Sr., was to send his two youngest sons, Wilky and Robertson, in 1860. The Secret Six financed John Brown's fighting the proslavery forces in Kansas in 1857. And they financed John Brown's ill-fated raid on Harpers Ferry, which was conceived in February 1858 but not executed until October 16, 1859. Ironically, the first casualty of the raid, Hayward Shepherd, baggage master, was a free black man, accidentally shot dead by Brown's men.[32]

In Georgia, as elsewhere in the South, the impact of John Brown's raid on Harpers Ferry was immediate and strong: "It far exceeded most previous insurrection scares in duration and intensity. As time passed and whites began to ponder the raid's broad implications, initial panic and hysteria solidified into cold fear."[33] Vigilante committees were formed to ferret out "'abolition emissaries,' enforce racial orthodoxy among whites, and suppress unrest among blacks."[34] Arnold must be numbered among those planters who believed in the innate docility of their slaves, however, for his wife, answering an earlier letter of his from White Hall (she had stayed in Newport for the birth of their granddaughter Cornelia on December 29, 1859), seemed concerned on January 2, 1860, only for the orange trees and japonicas that were killed at White Hall by a hard frost. Nonetheless, Richard Arnold again made an up-to-date slave list in April 1860 as he had in April 1859, in case Congress ever compensated owners for freeing slaves.

Meanwhile the party continued in Newport. On August 24, 1859, Mary Cornelia Arnold wrote to her brother Thomas, still in Europe, that

> last week I went to a ball, given by Mrs. Edward King. It was a splendid affair. The grounds were all illuminated with Turkish lamps and a part of the lawn carpeted for the ladies to walk on. The supper was splendid—& a band of music played—for dancing. . . . Yesterday was a great day here, all the Newporters returned home. Flags were hung in every street, & a long procession passed in the morning. The sons of Rhode Island dined in a large tent where speeches were made. Cousin Sam [Arnold] made one, which they say was very good.[35]

"The Re-Union of the Sons and Daughters of Newport, Rhode Island," was a city affair in which all those who had been born in Newport but were absent from the city were invited to join the local residents in a day of celebration. The gathering was like a college reunion, and native Newporters came from all over the country, some of them arriving a week or two in advance, and on the day itself, thousands arrived to join in the festivities, but no actual count was made of the "absent Sons of Newport." An exclusively white affair had been arranged by the mayor, William H. Cranston, the board of aldermen, and the common council, and former mayor William J. Swinburne was chief marshal of the parade. The reunion was strictly a local celebration; the summer residents and even the winter residents among the cottage set were conspicuous by their absence, since most of them were not native Newporters.

Two individuals importantly involved and vital to the success of the festivities were not on any arrangement committee: George T. Downing and Isaac Rice had contracted "to furnish refreshments for twenty-five hundred persons at dinner, and also for the evening's entertainment." They were local caterers, and they were black. Isaac Rice was not a son of Newport, having been born free in the southern part of the state in 1792, but his family moved to Newport when he was very young, and he had lived there ever since. He began work as a gardener, one of the few occupations open to blacks in Newport, working for some of the leading families in the area, including Governor William Channing Gibbs, a cousin of both the late Mrs. Hugh Ball and William Ellery Channing. Rice's hatred of slavery and his knowledge of its evils were learned directly "from the testimony of servants who accompanied their masters in Newport to spend the summer months." His friendship with Frederick Douglass helped radicalize him, and his home, according to Charles A. Battle, became a station of the Underground Railroad in Newport. In the 1840s and 1850s he joined with George T. Downing in the struggle to integrate the Newport schools.[36]

George Thomas Downing was born in 1819 in New York City, where his father had made a fortune in the restaurant and catering business, some of the most prominent white politicians and businessmen of New York being his customers. Because his father was wealthy, he belonged to the black elite, but "out on the street George was just another black boy subject to what one of his contemporaries at the Mulberry Street Colored School called 'the ever-present, ever-crushing Negro-hate' of early nineteenth-century New York." He and his fellow classmates were subjected to the physical violence of white street gangs and the psychological humiliation of white visitors to the school who doubted "the capacity of a colored boy to produce a composition."[37]

As a middle-class, free black whose family had "made it," Downing could aspire "to the status of a refined, well-bred American gentleman, and sought no association with lower classes of either race."[38] He arrived in Newport in 1846, where he established a catering business for the summer colony. He also later established a catering business in Providence, and in 1854 he erected the Sea Girt Hotel in Newport. He had a dream: that his children were the equal of any children, white or black. Doubtless, George Downing never applied for membership in the Newport Reading Room; for though a firm believer in class distinctions, as opposed to racial discrimination, he was not naive. He chose his issue: soon after arriving in Newport, he sent his children to enroll in the white schools. "They were promptly sent away and told to enter the colored schools."[39] Thus began a twenty-year struggle to integrate the public schools of Rhode Island, and in particular those of Newport and Providence.

Downing had learned a hard lesson—that the white power structure of Newport and Providence would continue to do business with him, but they would not invite him into their homes and clubs nor his children into their schools. In 1855 he wrote to Charles Sumner, "You are aware that a certain class in the city of Providence rule it. This is generally so in cities, but particularly so in this city. This class, the wealthy, send their children to private schools, more so even than in Boston. This class are your associates and would favour your sympathy in the matter, if for no nobler reason, because they are not affected thereby."[40]

An attempt was made in February 1860 by his supporters to elect Downing a trustee of the State Normal School, presumably in the belief that he would then be in a position to improve the quality of teaching in the Negro schools. On the first ballot cast by the legislators he received twenty of seventy-eight votes, 50 percent of the votes needed for election, but his name dropped out of the running on the second ballot when Samuel Arnold was nominated and received forty votes of a total of eighty-five, only three short of election. On the third ballot, Samuel Arnold was elected. But Mr. Stevens of Newport then "moved that the roll of the Grand Committee be called, and that each member who voted for Geo. T. Downing (a colored man) be requested to make it manifest when his name was reached. He thought the information would be useful during the pending campaign. Motion was not seconded."[41] Racism and partisan politics were intertwined in that election year of 1860. Later, with the help of Senator Charles Sumner and Thomas Wentworth Higginson, Downing and other leaders of the black community, like Isaac Rice, finally succeeded in integrating the schools. In 1865 Higginson, by then a resident of Newport and a member of the school committee, was able to persuade the committee to remove all restrictions of race or color in public education effective with the beginning of the fall term in 1866. Providence was the last Rhode Island city to desegregate its schools.[42]

In Newport, the wealthy class in these antebellum, pregilded days, showed their wealth, if not always their class, by the amount of "horse-flesh" at their command during the summer social season. Every afternoon, weather permitting, they drove up and down the avenue in elaborate carriages supposedly commensurate with the wealth of the occupants. The not-so-well-kept secret of this social event was that "very few of these [horses] are owned by the parties for whom they are driven, but with the carriages are hired for 'the season' from the proprietors of large stables in Newport. . . . Some of these are magnificent affairs being got up in a style commensurate with the means of the parties by whom engaged." These "turnouts" as they were called ranged from "nice" to "magnificent" in the hierarchy of social prominence. Thus, on September 7, 1859, the *Newport Daily News* scored the turnouts of the current season: Count Fountinelile rated only a nice turnout, but then as an aristocrat, he was already there, whereas August Belmont, being new money, required "4 in hand, black and brown." The South was represented by John Julius Pringle's "pair of blacks" from the local stable, not from his South Carolina plantation, just as Mrs. Porter's "pair of roans" came from the same stable, not her sugar plantation in Louisiana. Politicians love a parade, and so Governor Fish of New York was represented by a "beautiful turnout from Cleary's stables" and Governor Lawrence of Massachusetts by a "pair on wagon." Hotel residents were not barred from the procession if they had the means, and thus the best of the parade was a "magnificent six horses turnout belonging to a well known gentleman, a boarder at the Atlantic."[43]

But naturally it was the cottage set, which had grown to 111 by 1859, that dominated the drive by their numbers if not always by the splendor of their equippage. Besides Edward King and his brother William ("pair bays on wagon"), Thomas Hunter, William Wetmore, Samuel Powel, Prescott Hall, among others, were all to be seen on the avenue. In this distinguished company the Arnold family did itself proud, for Richard Arnold's was a "very nice turnout," and Andrew Robeson's was "A, No. 1."[44] Such was the richness of the social rituals involved in these regular afternoon drives that they not only survived the war but became institutionalized in the postbellum period when Edith Wharton as a young girl was spending her summers in Newport in the 1870s.[45]

Happiness is not knowing the ride is over. On March 1, 1860, Mary Cornelia Arnold, writing to her cousin Samuel Arnold, exclaimed,

> I cannot tell you what a delightful time I have been having since I returned home [to White Hall, where she was born]. Bessie has been with me & a Mr Lee of New York has been staying with Tom [her brother]   Every day we have had some frolick. *Tom & Bessie drive in the buggy, landau, &c. Mr Lee & I on horseback.* . . . Mother & Susie are going to Richmond in the carriage to make a call   The McAllisters are in Bryan & will remain the rest of this season—They talk of going to Europe, in the Spring of eighteen sixty one . . . it is a most perfect day   I am sitting with my windows open—how I wish you were all here, that you might enjoy White Hall & its pleasures with us—Next year however—if nothing happens—I hope the whole family will meet here.[46]

The coy invitation to Cousin Sam that he join the whole family at White Hall the following year was probably her way of suggesting that she would be marrying William Talbot in early summer of 1861. But the only wedding she explicitly mentioned was that "Amos is to be married on Saturday night to Cretia his fourth wife, & he but forty"![47]

The party in Newport was not yet over. That summer of 1860 Newport was host to the American Association for the Advancement of Science. Zachariah Allen attended, staying with the Robesons, who had also invited the eminent physicist Joseph Henry as their guest. It was not all science and no soirée:

There was a general invitation given to the members of the Association to a soiree at the splendid mansion of Mr. Parish [Daniel Parrish] on the cliffs by the sea shore. The moon shone brightly on the sea beneath the piazza, giving to it the appearance of molten silver, while the lights in the grounds, the melody of a band of music, and the beauty of numerous ladies assembled there produced an enchanting effect on the Scientifics.[48]

For the Arnolds, the party extended well into the fall of 1860. They were busy all summer preparing for the wedding of their son Richard, Jr., and Mary S. Clarke, which was to take place on October 11, 1860, in Providence. Zachariah Allen describing the wedding wrote, "There were many children at the wedding, who were apparently happier than those of riper years, who are prone to view such affairs more seriously as grave and decisive act[s] in the drama of life." Andrew Robeson III came down from Cambridge to attend the wedding, as did his mother from Newport. The Arnolds and their son Thomas and daughter Susan stayed with the Allens. "These family visits," Allen wrote on October 17, "have been pleasant, and afford many pleasant reminiscences."[49]

It was, however, past tense, almost as though Allen recognized at the time that the party was over. Three days later the Arnolds and the Robesons departed and "the house seems 'like a banquet hall deserted.' "[50] Andrew Robeson III returned to Cambridge, where he attended the Lawrence Scientific School at Harvard. Andrew Robeson, Jr., and his wife, Mary, returned to Newport accompanied by Thomas Arnold. Richard and Louisa Arnold with their two daughters Mary Cornelia and Susan had one last fling. They went to Boston "to attend the prince's ball" before preparing to return to the plantation in Georgia. The next time they returned to Newport war had already broken out.

2

The contrast in the setting of the two weddings, that of Richard Arnold, Jr., and Mary Clarke on October 11, 1860, and William Talbot and Mary Cornelia Arnold on June 27, 1861, was the difference between peace and war. The former was a leisurely celebration, a family affair; to be sure somewhat dampened by the death only the week before of Mrs. James Arnold of New Bedford, the wife of their cousin James Arnold, but still a happy occasion with all the family present. The latter was a hasty affair; at first it seemed that if it were to take place at all it would have to be at

White Hall rather than Newport as planned. Although there was a wedding finally in Newport, the family was divided, with Thomas and William Eliot, the bride's brothers, conspicuously absent. The event went unrecorded in Zachariah Allen's diary, but Mary Rotch Hunter of Newport wrote on July 2, 1861, to her husband Charles on blockade duty with the United States Navy off the southern coast that "Corneila [sic] Arnold was married last Thursday eveg. to Mr. William Talbot. A card & piece of cake was sent to us yesterday."[51]

Georgia seceded from the Union in January 1861. Arnold had opposed secession, but he was a Rhode Island citizen and his "noble stand," as his daughter Louisa loyally characterized it, would be suspect to the secessionists in Georgia. His own ambivalence toward the fast-moving political developments was reflected in his subscription on February 25, 1861, of seventy-five dollars in his name and that of his son Thomas "to uniform the Bryan County Troops."[52] The donation was made after Georgia had seceded but before it had officially joined the Confederacy on March 7. Yet on March 29, just two weeks before the outbreak of the war, Arnold wrote to his granddaughter Luly, who at age ten had visited White Hall two years earlier, that all was well and the same as ever at White Hall: the slave Sylvia to whom Luly had given a stuffed dog named Sissy "is quite a Queen on Sunday afternoons, in her New House" surrounded by the Arnolds' castoff furniture—the large looking glass from Susan Arnold's room, "& on the opposite side of the room is the clock your mother sent her, & on the floor the carpet Aunt Addie sent & one of the divans that used to be in the Parlour six chairs & a mahogany bureau that she uses as a Side Board & her chamber opposite is 18 x 14 feet & as well & comfortably furnished as Aunt Susy's room." In the midst of all this luxury, Sylvia the queen holds court: "The *Nobility* among the blacks from all the neighboring plantations call & pay her their respects."[53] Admittedly, he would not discuss the ins and outs of the political situation in Georgia with his twelve-year-old granddaughter, but her father, Samuel Arnold, would know that time had run out for the Arnolds. Shortly after Luly received the letter, the firing on Fort Sumter took place, on April 12. It was a clear *act* of rebellion against the Union, and the Civil War had begun. The two lives of Richard Arnold had split apart.

The Arnolds were a family divided, a microcosm of the nation as a whole. The two married daughters were in the North with their families, and Richard Arnold, Jr., and his wife were in Providence, expecting their first child in July. The two unmarried daughters, Mary Cornelia and Susan, and the other two sons, Thomas and William Eliot, however, were all with their parents at

White Hall. William Talbot was in Providence, expecting the return of his fiancée to Newport. On May 7, William Brenton Greene, Arnold's son-in-law and a businessman in New York City, wrote to Talbot enclosing a copy of a letter dated April 25 from Richard Arnold:

> If you see Willy Talbot, and he has a desire to come, he will run no risk of being interfered with by coming, should he come he had better take the upper route. now taken by the Express, and if he comes at all—he should come as soon as possible, and if he does come, it may be wise not to put his name in the books at the Hotel after he gets into the Confederate States as *from the North*—but Whitehall Georgia—and when he arrives at Savannah come out by the first train, without waiting to hear from us "to Ways Station." and we most always have a conveyance there, but if not he can reach our house without any difficulty. by some of our neighbors vehicles.

William Greene added, "From what Mr. Arnold writes me, I think it is doubtful if he, or any of the family come North this summer—they will probably pass the warm season in the upper part of Georgia."[54]

Armed with letters of introduction from business friends in the North to their business friends in the South, William Talbot rushed down to Georgia to rescue Mary Cornelia. In the meantime, the situation had changed drastically for the Arnolds: the two younger sons were determined to stay in Georgia and defend the land and "the people" against the Union army. On May 7, 1861, the same day William Brenton Greene wrote to Talbot, precipitating his hurried trip South, Arnold executed an indenture with his son Thomas, granting him all the plantation lands in Bryan County, Georgia, for the sum of $75,000, and including "the Cattle, Stock, Horses, Mills, and Farming Utensils" thereon, said stock including all the slaves.[55]

The Arnold family, except for Thomas and William Eliot, returned north. The Arnolds remained in Newport for the duration of the war, Arnold insisting that he supported the Union and had opposed secession in the South. Thomas enlisted briefly as a private in Company B, Oglethorpe Siege Artillery, but mainly he ran the plantations. His brother William Eliot joined the Seventh Regiment Georgia Cavalry, led by Colonel Joseph McAllister, their neighbor and the largest slaveholder in the county. Since the Arnold brothers considered themselves Georgians first, there was little danger the land would be expropriated, as might be the case if it was still owned by a Yankee, a Union man who had opposed secession and had kept his Rhode Island citizenship. Richard and Louisa Arnold remained in Newport during the war, maintaining a low profile.

Zachariah Allen kept his distance. He could proclaim in his diary two days after the firing on Fort Sumter that it would be a blessing for the free states to break away from the slave states entirely because "all history demonstrates that the existence of slavery has first corrupted and then destroyed every republic in which it has been admitted." But there was not a single mention of the Arnolds in his diary throughout the war. His own family was divided on the issue of slavery: two of his nephews—Thomas and William Eliot Arnold—were about to join the Confederate forces in defense of slavery, and Thomas now legally owned slaves; two other nephews, Crawford Allen, Jr., and Tristam Burges, and his grandson Andrew Robeson III joined the Union army, Crawford rushing back from San Francisco to enlist later that year. Allen blamed "a desperate slaveholding aristocracy" for the war, but he never seemed to connect his brother-in-law with that aristocracy because Richard Arnold had opposed secession. By the time he wrote those words, September 15, 1862, Thomas and William Eliot Arnold were deeply involved in defending that aristocracy of which they were a part.[56]

Eliza Harriet Allen had an even more difficult choice to make. She wanted to be loyal both to her husband and to her twin brother. She was probably closer to Thomas and William Eliot Arnold than to her nephews Crawford Allen and Tristam Burges. But undoubtedly she was closest to her grandson, Andrew Robeson III. She continued to visit both the Robesons and the Arnolds in Newport. On June 11, 1861, Mary Rotch Hunter wrote to her husband, "Richard Arnold is home, with his wife and daughters. he voted against Secession and is a Union man, but his wife's property & sympathy are altogether South, and their son Tom belongs to a Home Guard in Savannah—Mrs. Allen says, they never mention these subjects, to Mr. Arnold, that he is very unpleasantly situated, and has lost all his friends at the South, by not voting with them."[57] The "property," including more than two hundred slaves, was no longer technically Richard Arnold's under law, and certainly not his wife's, but belonged to his son Thomas. Property as a euphemism for owning slaves was such a prevalent code word in the South as well as a legal term that the United States Army adopted in the early years of the war the term "contraband" as a legal way of "confiscating" any slaves who came under its jurisdiction without having to deal with the political issue of emancipation.[58]

The situation of southern planters in the North, accustomed to spending the summer season in Newport, was so exactly the opposite of the Arnolds that their dilemma was ultimately the same. Although citizens of the rebellious states and owning "property" there, they also owned property in the

North and often by reason of family and friends had close ties with the North. George Noble and Mary Nuttall Jones were typical of the southern enclave in Newport, where South mixed with North, citizens of Georgia owning slaves in both Georgia and Florida but with strong family ties in the North. Shortage of cash in consequence of the Panic of 1857 rather than prescience of the coming war prompted Jones on January 13, 1860, to sell fifty-three slaves to Joseph Bryan of Savannah for $44,200. Since Bryan had arranged the infamous sale of Pierce Butler's slaves the year before, this did not augur well for the slave families that Mary Nuttall Jones had inherited from her uncle William Savage and that Arnold had shipped to her in 1839. The slaves had been at Chemonie plantation for more than twenty years, but Jones not only needed the money; he was "confirmed in his decision by the fact that these slaves had displayed no increase for some time while, on the other hand, there were more laborers at El Destino than could be profitably employed."[59]

Like Arnold, Jones feared expropriation of his property when the war broke out. Like Arnold, Jones was in Georgia that spring of 1861, but Mary and the children were in Paris. Like Arnold, Jones made legal arrangements to prevent his property from being confiscated. He arranged for his brother-in-law, Robert Hallowell Gardiner II, to sell the Newport cottage to Gardiner's brother-in-law, Richard Sullivan of Boston, on November 2, 1861. "Ten days later, Sullivan transferred the property to Sarah Fenwick Gardiner," Gardiner's wife and Jones's sister.[60] The house was at first rented but eventually sold outright to William King, brother of Edward and Dr. David King. William named the cottage Kingscote, and it was as though George Noble and Mary Nuttall Jones, summer visitors, had departed for a long winter, leaving no trace of themselves: "Their nostalgia, however exquisite, was, I none the less gather, sterile, for they appear to have left no seed. They must have died, some of them, in order to 'go back'—to go back, that is, to Paris."[61] Mary died in exile in France, long after signing the necessary legal papers relinquishing her dower rights to the house. George remained in the South throughout the war.

Some members of the southern planter families living in Newport during the winter were cut off from their families in the South. One such southerner, old Mrs. Pinckney, who declared herself "entirely Union," had three grandsons and a son-in-law in the Confederate army. Her niece and companion, Mrs. Izard of the South Carolina planter family, was also in Newport at the outbreak of the war. Her son applied for a commission in the Union army. "These families," Mary Rotch Hunter observed, "are divided in this dreadful war which is the saddest part of the history." Mrs. Mary Porter, like Mrs. Izard and Mrs. Pinckney, was also separated from her family in the South, but unlike them she was also "evidently very anxious about her property," for she owned a large sugar plantation in southern Louisiana, which, according to the 1860 Census was worked by 407 slaves, an integral part of the "property" inherited from her late husband.[62] This plantation was Oak Lawn, which Thomas Sargent Perry, Henry James's closest Newport friend, had visited in the winter of 1859–1860. Perry's attempt to teach one of the slave girls was stopped by Mrs. Porter when her neighbors complained that he was illegally "educating the negroes." Such was the web of friendship in Newport at the time that young Mary and Annie Porter, Mrs. Porter's daughters, were close friends of the James children and their cousins, the Temples, while Alex Porter, her son, belonged to the circle of friends that included the James boys.[63]

Many southerners in Newport walked a tightrope between the appearance of support for the Union cause and the reality of their southern sympathies. John Julius Pringle, for example, expressed his strong Union sympathies to Mary Hunter, complaining to her that "he expects to lose all his property" in the South and had already lost $60,000 by the war. "He takes his family to Europe, and returns" alone.[64] In Europe, Mrs. Pringle made clear her allegiance: when introduced at the court of Prussia, she insisted that she not be presented as "Mrs. Pringle of America," but as "Mrs. Pringle of *South Carolina*, if you please."[65] Mrs. Izard, Mary Hunter reported, "looks sad, but does not say much" but "old Mrs. Pinckey [*sic*], however, cannot keep quiet, she is for the Union."[66] There is perhaps an implication in Mary Hunter's comment that "the lady doth protest too much," for while Mrs. Izard's dilemma seemed genuine, Mrs. Pinckney had assured Mrs. Hunter only the week before that she was pro-Union. In January 1862, Mrs. Pinckney made it back to the South, "very happy . . . to be on southern soil again" where she no longer needed to pretend to people like Mary Hunter that she supported the Union. Her description to friends and relatives of how she and other southern women in Newport vented their real feelings was as dramatic as it was emetic: "We used to get together, shut all the doors and windows and then *vomit* secession."[67] Whether Louisa Arnold joined Mrs. Pinckney and the others is not certain, but it is known that within the privacy of the family she made "violent attacks upon the government" during the war.[68] Mrs. Pinckney, however, felt more at ease among the shopkeepers in Newport: "All the rich people are violent against the South, but the shopkeepers are much opposed to it [the war]."[69] Patriotism and tourism were at war in Newport.

Providence and Newport had been on a war-footing several weeks before the Arnolds returned to Rhode Island, ever since President Lincoln called for 75,000 volunteers from the Union states on April 15, 1861. Rhode Island exceeded its quota of volunteers as Providence and Newport in friendly rivalry raced to be the first to form a unit. Newport won the race by *forming* the Newport Volunteers (later called Company F) on April 16, composed mainly of men from the Newport Artillery. But Providence won the race by *sending* the first volunteer unit; the First Light Battery Rhode Island Volunteers, composed mainly of men from the Marine Artillery in Providence, were the first troops to leave the state for the front, embarking on the steamer *Empire State* on April 18. As the steamer moved from the wharf in the port of Providence, "cheers from the multitude assembled to witness the departure rent the air, to which response was made on board by the discharge of several guns."[70] Whether the ship sailed from a wharf owned by Richard Arnold is not known, but the commanding officer was Samuel Greene Arnold, Lieutenant governor elect of Rhode Island, appointed by Governor William Sprague to his staff with the rank of colonel and given general command of the battery until it reached its destination to become part of the Army of the Potomac. The *Empire State* reached Jersey City the morning of April 19, where the battery transferred to another ship; the *Empire State* then returned immediately to pick up the rest of the regiment, including Company F, the Newport contingent, on April 20.

En route "Colonel Arnold issued a patriotic address, in which he spoke of the great peril of the hour, and of the willing sacrifice that should be made to sustain the government."[71] It is unlikely that Richard Arnold would have approved of his son-in-law's words, but it is almost certain that he disapproved of his daughter Louisa's *action* in helping to sustain the government of Abraham Lincoln:

> Fears were entertained of being fired into in passing Alexandria Virginia,
> which was then in the hands of secessionists. To avoid provoking an attack, the
> men of the battery and all appliances of war were concealed from view, and a
> few persons in citizen's dress, among them Mrs. Samuel G. Arnold, who
> joined her husband at Philadelphia, courageously promenaded the upper deck
> of the steamer, giving it the appearance of a mere passenger boat. The menacing
> point was passed without molestation, the intrepid human targets failing to
> draw the fire of treason.[72]

Meanwhile in Newport patriotic fever ran high on April 17 as the recruits marched down to the Long Wharf, escorted by the Old Guard and 250 citizens marching four abreast, to embark on the steamer *Perry* to join the rest of the regiment in Providence. The scene might have come from *The Red Badge of Courage;* church bells tolled, flags waved, guns saluted, townsfolk cheered, politicians made speeches, clergy intoned prayers, fathers beamed, younger brothers watched with envy, and mothers, sisters, wives, and girlfriends wept while more than one hundred Henry Flemings boarded the ship. The sons of Newport were real people, however, not characters in a novel. Henry and William James and Thomas Perry were there in the crowd not to write or sketch the scene but to see their friends Duncan "Archie" Pell and Wheaton King off to war. That the company of volunteer soldiers from Newport also included Henry Bull, Jr., son of one of the signers of the 1835 antiabolition resolutions in Newport only served to underscore the mixture of motivations involved in their enlistment, preservation of the Union being the one cause to which they could all rally. John P. Peckham, son of a Newport carpenter, and Thomas Harrington, Jr., who listed himself as a resident of Kerry County, Ireland, were also among the volunteers in Company F; presumably their friends and families were among the crowd cheering them as they embarked.

The raw recruits who answered the initial call for volunteers had little time for training, since, as requested by President Lincoln, they were only to serve for ninety days and were officially mustered into their units as of May 2. By July 4, they had already completed two-thirds of their service and were as yet untried in battle. The Fourth of July rhetoric in Newport, however, heated up the battle of words. Henry James, Sr., was invited to give the annual address, a speech which was later published as "The Social Significance of Our Institutions." He began his oration by attacking the very foundation of Newport's pride, the wealth of upper-class citizens and summer visitors: "It does not seem to me a particularly creditable thing, that a great number of people annually grow richer under our institutions than they do anywhere else. . . . Every one knows . . . how meagre and mean and creeping a race we permit our rich men to be, if their meanness is only flavored with profusion."[73] Although his father had rapidly accumulated a fortune of three million dollars, the inheritance was divided among numerous relatives, so that what Henry James, Sr., inherited was $100,000, about the same amount Richard Arnold and Zachariah Allen had inherited from their fathers' estates. The essential difference was that James chose to invest his inheritance so that he could live off the income and be free to pursue the intellectual and cultural life in America and Europe. Arnold and Allen chose to invest their money in businesses in the hope of accumulating more money and property. It would not matter to James that Allen used "free" labor in his mills, because James's belief in the philosophy of Fourierism saw wage labor as another form of slave labor.

James reserved his most scathing rhetoric for those men like Arnold whose wealth was obtained through racial slavery.

> The cultivated intelligence of the race abhors the claim of any human being to possess an *absolute* property in any other being, that is, a property unvivified by the other's unforced, spontaneous gift. Slavery affirms this diabolic pretension,—affirms the *unqualified* title of the master to outrage, if need be, the sacredest instincts of natural affection in the slave, and to stifle at need his feeblest intellectual expansion.[74]

Mary Rotch Hunter writing to her husband on July 7 did not comment on the elder James's speech, but the context was that all were holding their collective breath waiting for news from the war front, for "everybody has some relation or friend at the seat of war."[75] Exactly two weeks later, on July 21, the First and Second Regiments of the Rhode Island Volunteers, two Rhode Island batteries, and a regiment each from New York and New Hampshire, all under the command of Colonel Ambrose Burnside of Rhode Island, marched into the battle of Bull Run. In the first forty-five minutes, the brigade fought alone and suffered twenty-eight men killed, fifty-six wounded, and thirty missing, the heaviest casualties being incurred by the First Light Battery Rhode Island Volunteers. It was a rout, and some of the troops, scarcely trained and ill-prepared for battle, panicked and ran.

Exaggerated news of the battle and its casualties reached Newport the following evening by telegraph: "People were rushing thro the streets in the greatest state of excitement fathers left in the boat that night to hear, if possible, in Washington the fate of their sons, and mothers are almost distracted." The next day there was some relief from the tension, the news being that "the loss [of life] was not as great as had at first been reported," but that was small comfort to the families of Privates Peckham and Harrington, whose deaths had been confirmed by private telegram. Conflicting reports and lack of confirming news, however, created "an agony of suspense" for the King family. On the afternoon of July 23, "Doctor King was telegraphed that Wheaton had been wounded in the hip, and left upon the field—Edward [King, his brother] & himself went in the boat that night. We have since heard that Wheaton is in the Rebel hospital at Manassas, a prisoner—the Doctor cannot see him—Mrs King is almost wild with fear."[76]

The following day, after three days of anxious uncertainty, the Pells learned that their son Archie was safe. "Poor Mr Pell looked 10 years older during the uncertainty, & went with his brother immediately to Washington." But the ordeal for the King family continued: Doctor King wrote to his wife that "the last known of Wheaton, he was wounded & lying upon the field, when some one passing, heard him groan & call for water, this person gave him a drink, and placed him in a more comfortable position." It was not until August 13, three weeks after the first news of the battle, that the Kings learned "that Wheaton had been reported, by a Secession Physician known personally to Doctor King, as alive in Richmond—his wound was not dangerous—no bone broken, but the ball had not been extracted."[77] The family's relief at the news was mixed, since they had not yet heard from Wheaton directly; all the letters written to him were returned undelivered. In desperation "Mrs. King has written to Mr. George Jones to supply all his wants." but the Doctor is very depressed and "very sad when he speaks" of Wheaton.[78]

Wheaton died January 28, 1862, in Philadelphia, en route home in the care of his parents. He died of complications resulting from the operation to extract the bullet from his thigh, a procedure that left him so weak he was unable to recover. Indeed, a premature rumor of his death had reached Newport on December 18, causing Mary Hunter to blame the South: "One more victim of this wicked rebellion!"[79] She could just as well have blamed the Union army for his death, sending untrained volunteer troops into battle. Better to blame youth: an indifferent scholar at the Berkeley Institute, he could not compete with the well-read James boys and the studious Thomas Perry. His older brothers were making a career for themselves in China. The war and the patriotic call for volunteers was a godsend to whatever fantasies of romantic heroism he had dreamed as a youthful recruit marching down the streets of Newport to the cheers of his former classmates. His was a long-drawn-out agony, not the heroic death he might have envisioned as the *Empire State* passed Newport on its way down Narragansett Bay on April 20, 1861, and he saw his home town for the last time. He was dead long before Stephen Crane wrote his *Red Badge of Courage* or Henry James was to publish his first fiction dealing with the return of a wounded soldier who made it back home to die.

The return of the surviving Newport volunteers on July 28, 1861, was in sharp contrast to the cheers that had sent them on their way to war: "They requested there should be no demonstration, and marched quietly to the Armoury—the wounded were in carriages—All looked worn & wearried. They walked *fifty miles*, after the fight with only two hard crackers, to eat, each."[80]

The plight of the Rhode Island volunteers after the Battle of Bull Run brought home the reality of the war, and on August 9 the Association for the Relief of Volunteers was organized in Providence with Louisa (Mrs. Samuel

G.) Arnold as president and her husband as a member of the board of advisers. The purpose of the association was "to aid in fitting out the Rhode Island Volunteers, and in contributing to their comfort when absent."[81] Humanitarian aid was very much a part of the public image of the Arnold family and a safe topic of conversation within the family circle. But it did seem odd that the ladies of the Volunteer Relief Association "in the hope of replenishing their now almost exhausted treasury," sponsored a lecture on January 6, 1862, by Dr. Robert A. Fisher entitled "GUNPOWDER, CANNON & PROJECTILES: ILLUSTRATED BY BRILLIANT CHEMICAL EXPERIMENTS."[82]

This was wartime Rhode Island, where Richard and Louisa Arnold lived in exile from their two sons, Thomas and William Eliot, suffering the same kind of anxieties experienced by the parents of the young soldiers in the Union army. Henry Middleton, for example, Confederate soldier and son of Henry A. Middleton of Newport and Charleston, was also wounded on July 21, 1861, at the Battle of Bull Run. He died six days later, but unlike Wheaton King, his father was not with him when he died.[83]

Providence was no escape for the Arnolds. The volunteers from Providence had suffered even more casualties in the first Battle of Bull Run than had the Newport contingent. Arnold, therefore, decided not to attend the commencement exercises and related activities at Brown University, September 1, 1861, even though he received a special invitation from his old friend William S. Patten, who had served with him on the 1831 Race Riot Committee and who addressed him by the courtesy title of *Colonel* Richard J. Arnold, in deference to his Dorr War service:

> As to your not coming to Commencement & participating in social life from low spirits, I think you make a mistake. I think you would receive and give great pleasure, at any rate to yourself relief, by pursuing the accustomed tenor of your way, at least to a considerable extent. . . . There is probably no more devoted Union man than you are, in the Union. . . . You and your family are "middle men" between the North & South say "*border*" inhabitants—Your own native interests, education & association are North—Your wifes at the South.[84]

The image of themselves as mediators between North and South and good Samaritans who opened house and heart "to the sick, the needy, the afflicted, or the social" was consoling to the Arnolds, but it was no guide to living in Rhode Island during the war. Newport in wartime, as Henry James described it, "in fine, the hurrying troops, the transfigured scene, found a cover for every sort of intensity, made tension itself in fact contagious—so that almost any tension would do, would serve for one's share."[85] Even a walk from his house to the Newport Reading Room to pick up his mail would be a reminder for Arnold of the war, since the United States Naval Academy had been moved lock, stock, and students from Annapolis, Maryland, to the safety of Newport. The cadets were living in the Atlantic House across from Touro Park, and they paraded daily there, just a block from the Newport Reading Room. And even if he never left home, Arnold would be aware of the United States Navy, since he had a view of the training ships from his house high above the harbor. The navy with its blockade of southern ports, including Savannah, threatened most of Arnold's southern business interests.

What was the *right* thing to do? Should Arnold attend the Brown commencement and chance being insulted, the center of an unpleasant "incident," especially since Colonel Burnside was to receive an honorary degree and feelings were still running high against the South after the Battle of Bull Run? Should Louisa Arnold join the ladies of Newport, the same women who in the 1850s as members of the Queen of Clubs had set the social pace of Newport and who had now formed a "Women's Aid Society," vying to be the first to send supplies to the soldiers, said aid acknowledged in a letter from Frederick Law Olmsted, now Secretary of the United States Sanitary Commission? And if she did, should she say, by way of conversation, "We knew Olmsted; he was our house guest in Georgia, he wrote all about our slaves in *A Journey in the Seaboard Slave States?*" On the other hand, would it be the *wrong* thing to do, to stay away, especially during the winter of 1861–1862 when the women "cut out and issued to be made by the families of the Volunteers, 75,000 army-shirts, under a contract with the Quarter-Master Genl's Department"?[86]

Gone were the charades of more innocent years—gone were the southern social leaders like the Joneses who led them. The social events in wartime Newport were the fairs and concerts arranged to raise money for the sanitary commission in its humanitarian work. Everyone participated, and the ladies vied in setting up booths at the fairs to sell handmade articles as their contributions. Young Henry James ushered at one of the concerts in which Annie Porter sang. After the concert, they all went to a party at the home of Dr. David King. Yet the tension Henry James felt could not have been far below the surface at such events, for Annie Porter, a friend of the James boys and the Temple girls, was the daughter of a slave owner who remained in Newport.

On June 6, 1862, Mary Hunter wrote to her husband, "I called upon Mrs. Arnold today, & feel so sorry for her. She told me two of her sons were in

Georgia protecting their property and Mr Arnold at Chicago. She says she is wretched about this Rebellion, her husband no sympathy with it—Those are the people who feel it the most where their interests & sympathies are divided." Obviously, the Arnolds had walked a tightrope since last fall when two detectives arrived in Newport looking for property of southerners to confiscate and inquiring about Henry Middleton in particular.[87] Arnold, however, was a Rhode Island citizen and thus legally safe from having his property in the North confiscated as contraband of war. Indeed, the only time Arnold ran afoul of the law during the war was when a writ was served on him for not licensing his dog! Even though he insisted he was not liable to pay for the license or the writ because he kept his dog chained, his son Richard, Jr., paid $1.24 for the license and $0.90 for the writ. Richard, Sr., thought his son had made a mistake to pay it, but on October 7, 1862, he reimbursed him for the cost.[88]

It was, in fact, an indication of a return to a more normal life for Arnold that he felt free to travel to Chicago, attending to what he would usually be doing during the summer season, that is, looking after his northern business and property. He invested in commercial blocks and a dock company in Chicago and in mining companies in Michigan and Canada. He and Louisa went to Washington in March 1863 to attend Samuel Arnold's swearing-in as United States senator from Rhode Island. He returned to Chicago in June where, as a delegate to the National Ship-Canal Convention, he was elected to the executive committee.[89] And he and Louisa made frequent visits to New York City, where their daughter lived.

At Sunny Lawn, the Arnolds maintained a relatively large staff of servants, mainly Irish, during those early years of the war—Frances Hicks, cook; Margrate [sic] Jones, chambermaid; Katy Murr, laundress; Bridget Cain, waitress; Edward McNamara, gardener; James Dolan, coachman. Lincoln's Emancipation Proclamation freed the Arnolds from dependency on Irish servants, and on June 27, 1863, Arnold fired "Mary Jane Corcoran (waitress) to Mrs. A's joy," and began to hire black servants. Although the Arnolds' social life now centered in Newport, they still maintained contact with friends in Providence, and on October 23, 1862, they traveled to Providence with four servants. Arnold still maintained business interests and investments in Providence, and his son Richard, Jr., acted as his rental agent. He had enough varied accounts to keep his brother-in-law Zachariah Allen busy as trustee of the original family holdings and to hire William Bailey as a business agent as well as using Richard, Jr. In July 1864, he sold some of his inherited wharves on the Providence River to the Neptune Steamship Company of New York for $60,000. In all of this activity he continued to record dividends for his sons Thomas and William Eliot. He also continued buying real estate, purchasing, for example, in November 1864, a tract of land in Newport "in speculation" for $6,000.[90]

But the war was never far away. On September 17, 1862, at the Battle of Antietam, Lieutenant Robert H. Ives, Jr., the only son of Arnold's close friend, was mortally wounded in the thigh, dying on September 27, scarcely a month after receiving his commission as a volunteer aide to General Isaac P. Rodman of Rhode Island, who was also mortally wounded in the same battle. Almost the same age as Thomas and William Eliot Arnold, Robert Ives was born in Providence in 1837, graduating from Brown University in 1857, shortly after the Arnolds had moved to Newport. He had a bright, promising future as a partner in the family firm, Goddard Brothers of Providence. Zachariah Allen, recording the death of this "very excellent young man, in early life, with bright prospects of future wealth, and to the blight of the hopes of his father and mother centered in this only son," ended the eulogy with an angry observation: "How much have the wicked politicians among the Slaveholding aristocracy to answer for."[91]

Like Robert Ives, Tristam Burges, the Arnolds' nephew, was mortally wounded in the thigh, dying ten days later of congestion of the lungs, on May 23, 1863. But unlike Ives, he had had no bright future except in battle, where he "acted bravely and valiantly." His uncle Zachariah Allen, who had been so praiseworthy of Ives's character, wrote of Burges, "He lacked calm and reflective judgment, and was more governed by impulse than by discretion."[92] At about the same time, the Arnolds' nephew Crawford Allen was wounded at the second battle of Fredericksburg on May 3, 1862, but his wound was slight and he went back to active duty to command Battery H of the First Regiment Rhode Island Light Artillery. Lieutenant Frederick Ogden, only son of the Edward Ogdens of Newport, was killed in action at the battle of Trevillian Station, Virginia, on June 11, 1864, the same battle in which Colonel Joseph McAllister was also killed while commanding the Seventh Regiment Georgia Cavalry to which William Eliot Arnold belonged.

The war had come close to home for the Arnolds. They were all caught in the web of history. The interlocking connections of family, friends, and relatives, North and South, were like the filaments of a spider's web, every touch or breath of air vibrating the whole structure. It required Henry James's sense of Newport and its reverberations to sit in the garden of his father's house in Newport on the afternoon of July 1, 1863, observing his New York cousins restlessly strolling as they seemed to *hear* "the boom of faraway guns"

at Gettysburg, as united they "actually *listened* together, in their almost igno-
bly safe stillness: to a turning point in the war."[93] It would require so acute an
ear to hear in Newport the cry of joy on Chemonie plantation of George
Noble Jones's slave who upon learning that she was freed by Lincoln's proclamation "was so overjoyed with her new state that she completely forgot she
had been a cripple on crutches, much to the disgust of Jones, who had been
saving her from real work for seven years."[94]

Not *knowing*, not being able to communicate with Thomas and William
Eliot in Bryan County was agonizing for the Arnolds, despite the seeming
peacefulness of their lives in Newport. It would have been difficult to approach, even through intermediaries, the Reverend Edward B. Hall for possible news; the reverend's son, Lieutenant William Ware Hall, had resigned
his commission in the summer of 1862 because of ill health and was teaching
the "contrabands" at Port Royal, near Savannah. But William Hall died in
August 1864, never fully regaining his health.

It would have been almost impossible to approach the James family for
news of Thomas and William Eliot, even though Wilky James was also at
Port Royal. Wilky was adjutant to Colonel Robert Shaw, abolitionist commander of the Fifty-fourth Massachusetts Regiment, a black regiment. His
brother Bob had joined another Negro regiment, the Fifty-fifth Massachusetts. Wilky had been brought home to Newport on a stretcher in August
1863, wounded in the assault on Fort Wagner, the same battle in which Colonel Shaw had been killed. Even though Wilky and Bob had attended the
school in Concord, Massachusetts, organized by the radical abolitionist
Frank Sanborn, an appeal could have been made to Wilky through Andrew
Robeson III, who had been a classmate of the James boys at the Berkeley
Institute and had attended the Lawrence Scientific School in Cambridge
with William James. But after the burning of Darien, Georgia, only a few
miles from White Hall, in June 1863, no southerner would trust anyone
connected with Colonel Shaw and his regiment. Shaw himself had opposed
the pillage and burning of the deserted village, but his regiment participated.
To make matters worse from the point of view of the Arnolds, a section of
Light Battery C, Third Rhode Island Artillery, under Lieutenant William A.
Sabin, took part in the operation.[95]

On December 2, 1863, Arnold made an accounting decision which perhaps more than the Battle of Gettysburg or the Emancipation Proclamation
meant for him a turning point in the war and the end of an era: he wrote off a
debt of $94.10 owed to him by his former overseer, C. W. Ferguson, "he
having died and no prospect of my receiving anything from his effects." On

the same day he debited "Family Expense" the amount of $37.16 for "Articles for Prisoners." He did not indicate whether these were northern or southern prisoners.[96]

Closing the books on Ferguson was not a surrender but a recognition of the realities of war. His donation of articles for prisoners was a way of doing what he knew best, giving humanitarian aid. Thus, in the spring of 1864, having received the sum of fifty dollars from Mrs. William Coleman "for the relief of Southern Prisoners" he sent the full sum in greenbacks to George Troup Maxwell, prisoner at Johnson Island, Ohio.[97] Maxwell, a physician and son of a rich Bryan County planter, had been captured at the Battle of Missionary Ridge on November 23, 1863, and sent to Johnson Island to wait out the war as a prisoner.[98] In giving aid for the relief of southern prisoners, Arnold sometimes acted as a conduit for Mrs. Coleman and sometimes sent his own money. Mainly he concentrated on helping prisoners from Georgia and Bryan County, as the tide of battle turned against the South.[99]

The tensions within the Arnold family heightened with the beginning of the spring offensive in Virginia in May 1864 in which General Lee's army defended Richmond against Union forces under General Grant. During this campaign Colonel McAllister was killed and many of his regiment killed, wounded, or taken prisoner. One of those wounded and taken prisoner on June 11, 1864, was First Lieutenant F. A. Barnard, who was eventually transferred to Fort Delaware. Arnold wrote Barnard asking if he could help by sending money and boxes of clothing and provisions. In his reply Barnard provided firsthand news about Thomas and William Eliot:

> When I wrote you before I alluded to your son Elliot; he is a member of My Company, and consequently was on the field when I was taken prisoner. I saw him a short time before I was captured; and I am pretty certain he escaped unhurt. Joseph L. McAllister of Bryan County was Col. of the Regt., he was killed. Capt. J. P. Hines of Bryan was also killed. I left Bryan about the middle of April. I saw Your Son Tom nearly every day I staid in Bryan; he is enjoying excellent health.[100]

Richard Arnold sent Lieutenant Barnard money the same day he received the letter.

The Arnolds undoubtedly were relieved to learn that Thomas was well and that William Eliot had probably escaped unharmed, but Lieutenant Barnard's news about William Eliot was sketchy and the battle had continued after Barnard was wounded and captured. The fact that so many of Colonel McAllister's regiment had been casualties or had been captured in that battle was a source of continuing anxiety for the family. Therefore, on August 13, on the same day that he sent twenty dollars to H. R. Harrison, a prisoner from Savannah at Fort Delaware, he went to nearby Portsmouth Grove, the site of Lovell General Hospital, where hundreds of wounded soldiers, some of them southern prisoners, were treated or were convalescing prior to being transferred.[101] Two years earlier, in August 1862, young Henry James had walked Whitman-like among this "vast gathering of invalid and convalescent troops," establishing a "tragic fellowship" with their pain, a spontaneous affection in keeping with what his father had so often preached philosophically as the only true relationship of one human being to another.[102]

Arnold achieved no such catharsis. He paid out twelve dollars in small sums as presents to the sick at Portsmouth Grove that afternoon in the hope that he would receive in return some news of William Eliot, but apparently he learned nothing new. The family's anxiety was unrelieved, and on August 29 Eliza Harriet Greene (Mrs. William Brenton Greene) inserted the following advertisement in the *New York Daily News:*

> CAN ANY ONE give information of W. E. Arnold, a member of the Seventh Regiment Georgia Cavalry, and greatly relieve the anxiety of his sister.
>
> EANY
>
> Richmond, Charleston and Savannah papers please copy.[103]

Not until late November did the Arnolds learn William Eliot's fate, finally receiving a long letter from Thomas carried through "enemy" lines. The news about William Eliot was good:

> E [William Eliot] has been in Virginia for six months & lost three horses & has come home on sixty day furlough to get another [horse] which I have already got for $2000 which is not high   every one says E is one of the best soldiers in the regiment   he has been in most of the battles of the campaign & not recd a scratch   his comrades tell me he is perfectly cool in action   he saw poor Joe McAllister a few moments before he was killed perfectly exhausted & Eliot told him he would go and bring his horse but before he could get back Joe had been killed with enemy men between E and his body   he died a most gallant death   his body was recovered the next day & interned. . . . Eliot says that all the soldiers in Virg[inia] say they will fight until the last man is killed before they will go back in the union & I think this is the expression of the whole country.

Thomas Arnold's commitment to the Confederate cause was matched by his optimism concerning the military situation in Georgia: "Sherman is now advancing (as Hood has blocked his rear) upon Augusta with the intenson of comming to Savannah   I do not think he will ever succeed in doing this & I expect his whole army to be destroyed." Four weeks later Savannah surrendered. Thomas was more a realist than a military strategist: "If he [Sherman] should get to Savannah I shall move my people to Montgomery county where I have a Plantation & have made enough to support them this year."[104]

Lieutenant Barnard had apparently been repatriated, returning to Bryan County, for Thomas wrote that he "spoke most feelingly of your kindness to him   T. Maxwell also in his letters to his mother and Dr Wragg also on the part of his son." Thomas urged his father to help Captain William Brailsford, who had been captured and was a prisoner of war at Johnson Island, Ohio: "If you could send him a little money and some comforts I would be glad as he had been kind to me."[105] There is more than double irony in this plea, for William Brailsford, one of the wealthiest cotton planters in coastal Georgia before the war, was the opposite of Richard Arnold in his life-style, more akin to George Noble Jones: "He was probably the last of his class in Georgia. Money with him was made only to spend, not in his own enjoyment but in contributing to the enjoyment of others. Ready at all times to serve a friend, even at the risk of his life, he was often identified with affairs of honor in the days when men were called upon by public sentiment to recognize the code *duello*." During the war, Brailsford made it his special task to recapture runaway slaves from the Georgia rice islands; black troops made it their special task to destroy his plantation and mansion. If Brailsford's life before the war was scandalous, his life after the war was outrageous by Arnold's standards, for he lived openly with his natural daughter, Catherine Brailsford, a mulatto servant "to whom he bequeathed all his property" upon his death in 1887.[106] Whatever help and comfort he received from his northern friends, it did not extend to getting him released from the prisoner-of-war camp. He was not released until May 30, 1865.

Thomas Arnold assured his father that

> the People are all well except Charlot who has been sick for some time but she is improving   Sambo['s] Celia (not Nero's wife) Elviria & Lually I think are the only addults that have died since you left and very few children   my gang has increased some fifteen or more since you were here   the Children are all in Montgomery County with the exception of four or five.

Thomas had thus divided the families to be assured of their continued loyalty. To clothe the people was too much for him, however:

> Could you not send me [illegible] winter clothes and shooes for the people for they are quite destitute and it is not possible to get anything for them as every

thing is taken for the soldiers   you might devide what you sent in two parcels
so that if I lost one I might get the other   I have cut up most of the carpets in
the house for blankets but still they suffer   I never new them to behave better
than they do no[w] and expect to loose very few if I have to move them   I am
afraid that many of the children are now suffering for the want of a blanket.

Inflation was rampant, and

shoes are $100 and cannot be got for negros as the army must have them
first   I have taned some leather and will make some myself, but only a few,
wollen is out of the question   I now some planters in B C [Bryan County] who
have clothed and shod their people through the blockade by sending a few
bales of cotton but this requires a great deal of influence to get your cotton
taken out. [107]

Thomas, if nothing else, was his father's son, and he continued to buy land
in the midst of General Sherman's devastating campaign to the sea: "I have
paid for Hays place $20000 and also $46000 for the place in Montgomery
County with stock."[108] It was not, however, a measure of Thomas's gulli-
bility that he paid $46,000 for a plantation complete with "stock" already
proclaimed free, since he paid in Confederate money.

Thomas and William Eliot were prepared to fight for the land: "I am,"
Thomas wrote, "Capt & a dc [aide-de-camp] to Maj. Genl McLaws and assigned to duty in Bryan. If I have occassion to move my people I expect to go
into active service."[109] But the swiftness of events overcame Thomas and
William Eliot Arnold. Thomas had to move the people hurriedly to his plantation, Mount Vernon, in Montgomery County. William Eliot stayed behind
to defend Fort McAllister. He was captured and taken prisoner on December
13, 1864.

On December 11, two days before the capture of Fort McAllister, Colonel
George S. Acker, commanding officer of the Ninth Michigan Volunteer Cavalry regiment, reported: "Moved across the Ogeechee River marching toward
Fort McAllister. Captured one prisoner, and encamped at Whitehall for the
night."[110] General Hazen's division crossed the Ogeechee at King's Bridge
early on the morning of December 13, the engineers having quickly rebuilt
the bridge destroyed by the Confederates. General Sherman watched the
capture of the fort from the roof of the rice mill on the Cheves plantation,
which Thomas Arnold was to purchase after the war. That night, General
Sherman slept at Strathy Hall, McAllister's house.[111] Savannah surrendered
a week later, but for William Eliot Arnold the war ended on December 13.

Wilky James, writing to his brother Henry a few days later, could not keep
from sounding triumphant, although he and his regiment had not taken part

in the action: "The taking of Fort McAllister the other day was a splendid thing—we got 280 prisoners and made them go out and pick up the torpedoes round the fort."[112] William Eliot Arnold was not one of the 16 Confederate soldiers killed in the defense of Fort McAllister nor was he one of the 54 who were wounded, but undoubtedly he was one of the prisoners who were detailed to clean up the live ammunition around the fort. This detail was not without its dangers, for many of the Union casualties in the capture of Fort McAllister, 24 killed and 110 wounded, were caused by the mines planted by the Confederate defenders on the western approaches to the fort, next to White Hall plantation.[113]

In Newport the Arnold family's joy upon receiving Thomas's letter was short-lived. The news that Fort McAllister had been captured and that Savannah had surrendered increased the level of anxiety to its highest point since the Arnolds had left Georgia in 1861. Richard and Louisa Arnold were determined to go to Georgia and find out for themselves what had happened to their sons and to their property. Whatever their own individual attitudes toward the war and its causes, the Arnold family closed ranks in seeking permission for Richard and Louisa to travel to Savannah. Samuel Arnold's letter to the secretary of war, dated January 6, 1865, was a model of diplomatic language and political pressure:

> The undersigned ex US. Senator from R. I. hereby makes application for a permit for Rich^d J Arnold, a loyal citizen of the State of R. I. to go to the city of Savannah accompanied by his wife & one servant, in order that the said Arnold may look after his estates in Bryan C° on the Ogeechee River; or in case Mr. Arnold's health will not allow of his going in person then that he may be permitted to send an Agent in his behalf for the same purpose; and that he or his Agent may be allowed to take such articles as may be required for the maintenance of the colored people lately belonging to him.
>
> Mr Arnold was compelled to leave Georgia in the spring of 1861 on account of his efforts in the cause of the Union—& has not since been able to return, having rendered himself obnoxious to the sentiments of the people at that time prevailing in Georgia.[114]

Since Samuel Arnold was personally in Washington on that day, action on his application was immediate. Permission was granted by C. A. Dana, acting secretary of war, that same day.[115]

On January 12 in the midst of preparations for the trip to Savannah, Richard Arnold received startling news in a brief letter from William Eliot at Hilton Head, South Carolina: "I am a prisoner of war. I was taken by surprise and came here unprepared. I am well and hope you are all well. I long to see you all. The last time I saw Tom he was well."[116]

The whole purpose of the trip had shifted to visiting William Eliot at Hilton Head and attending to his welfare. Since Arnold's loyalty to the Union had been emphasized when permission had been requested earlier, to admit at this point that his son was a captured Confederate soldier would not be wise. Therefore, on January 15, Samuel Arnold, now back in Providence, wrote to Senator John Sherman in Washington:

> May I presume upon our brief but pleasant association in the Senate to ask of you a favor?
>
> Mrs. Arnold's father Richard J. Arnold Esqr has obtained a permit from the War Department to go to Savannah to look after his property in Bryan County on the Ogeechee River. Mr. Arnold is a Union man who has always preserved his citizenship in Rhode Island altho' residing in the winter for the last 40 years in Georgia; and in the outbreak of the rebellion was obliged to leave & of course has been unable & unwilling to return until now that your brother has made it possible.
>
> What I have to ask is that you will send me a letter of introduction for Mr Arnold to your brother Genˡ Sherman.

On the same letter Senator Sherman penned a note to his brother: "The statement of Senator Arnold as to the bearer of this—his near relative will show you that he is deserving of protection   I trust you will do all you can to promote the purpose of his visit to Savannah."[117]

Leaving nothing to chance, nor to the whims of the Sherman brothers, the Arnolds asked Francis J. Lippit to write a letter, dated January 31, 1865, to Brigadier General John W. Geary, commander of Savannah, introducing Arnold as "a gentleman of the highest standing among us, who long since made himself obnoxious to many people in the South by his attachment to the Union."[118] Two days earlier, on January 19, while still in New York, Arnold handed $30 to the Reverend S. W. Magill also on his way to Savannah "to give my People should he see any [of] them at the South."[119] But before the Reverend Mr. Magill saw them, the Arnolds had met Amos, George, Lewis, Cato, and Sylvia in Savannah on January 25 and had given them a total of $21. That was less than he gave to Mrs. Hines and Mr. Nichols but more than he handed to Mr. Demere, Mr. Baker and his daughter, Mr. Anderson, and Mrs. Schley; in all he gave $179.50 in greenbacks to now-destitute southern friends, black and white, to say nothing of clothing, tea, coffee, wines, and brandies.[120]

All this largess was meted out before he reached White Hall, where he discovered, according to his old Boston friend William Amory, "that his Plantation was stript, his house & store-houses with all their contents worth $80,000 in greenbacks were burnt, & that his son—ill, with a fever chills &

jaundice had been sent north on the same day he—Mr. A.—reached Savannah."[121] The Arnolds immediately returned north to seek permission to visit William Eliot, now at Point Lookout, Maryland, and if possible, obtain his release or parole to Samuel Arnold. Arnold probably understood but did not appreciate that in order to return north he had to receive an official travel voucher from the provost marshal general's office at Hilton Head, granting permission to "R J Arnold & Lady, 1 Man Servt. 1 Woman Servt. 1 Child (Col'd) to go to New York."[122] Sylvia, her husband, Derry, and their child, former Arnold slaves, were the accompanying servants. Before the war, slaves traveling anywhere alone, even within the state, had to carry tickets signed by their masters.

This time, the Arnolds did not correspond with mere generals. They, or their influential friends, wrote to President Lincoln and his secretary of war, Edwin McMasters Stanton, requesting that William Eliot be paroled. Lincoln wrote on the request, "Let this be done," and it was done.[123] Fifteen days after the Arnolds left Savannah, William Eliot was released to Samuel Greene Arnold on "solemn parole of honour" by which he agreed "that he will hold no correspondence with, or afford any aid or comfort to any enemies or opposers to the U. States."[124] The jargon of military law meant in real terms that William Eliot had given his word of honor not to communicate with or give aid and comfort to his brother Thomas, who was now "the enemy."

The war, however, did not end for Thomas Arnold as suddenly and completely as it had for his brother. True, some things had returned to normal, and on February 10, 1865, Thomas was able to send a short note to his father: "I have this day drawn on you at five days sight for two thousand dollars which please honor. I am well."[125] The dividing line for him between war and peace was invisible and ambiguous, for it depended on an attitude of mind rather than a specific date in history, April 9, 1865, when General Lee surrendered to General Grant. To Thomas, "home" was no-man's land, where anarchy reigned and the enemy was the black man who turned against his former master. On May 28, 1865, five months after the occupation of Savannah by Union troops, Thomas wrote to his father from Savannah:

> I arrived here last evening from Montgomery County   everything was well on
> the place and I have a good prospect of maching [sic] four thousand bushels of
> corn provided I can keep enough hands   none have as yet left me but it is only
> because the enemy has not been in that county   I have not one on the place
> that I trust except Cane [Cain], Old [Big] Peter was hung for attempting to

*Travel pass granting the Arnolds and "servants" permission to go from Georgia to
New York after the fall of Savannah, February 1865. (Courtesy of the Rhode Island
Historical Society.)*

raise my people against me   he said he would kill me himself   I found out the
plot and turned him over to the County   he was one of the worst negroes that
ever lived   Since then the people in the up country have behaved very well,
but I do not depend upon them. I was obliged to draw on you for money twice
since I left Bryan, for old Peter had sold most of the corn that I had on the
place and when I got up there I was obliged to buy corn and am still halling
corn a distance of sixty miles to feed free negros with, but if I can keep them a
month or six weeks longer until I lay my corn, I would then like to come north
and see you all. I have seen Amos   he is as true as steel. The money I drew
from was to pay for corn   I have still to pay for three hundred bushels of corn
in green backs that will carry me until the new crop comes in   I am glad to
hear that you have got Eliot out of prison   I hope he has got well. I am very
sorry to hear that Addy [Eliza Harriet Greene, his sister and wife of William
Brenton Greene] is sick   do give my love to her. If it is convenient do send me
some money for I have no clothes and no money. I understand the negroes are
behaving very badly in Bryan   they murdered six returned prisoners the other
day passing through Bryan on there way home   I intended to go to Cherry
Hill but I shall not do so until the Yankeys will give me protection   do give
my love to Mother and all the family   I long to see them all. I am well   If the
Yankeys will let me go north in about a month I will do so. I shall return to

Montgomery County next Wednesday   But if you write me care of mr Champion   he will be able to send it to me by some one   hoping to hear from you soon I remain

> Your truly attached
> Son   T. C. A.

P.S. I can not even borrow a few dollars   Money is so scarce in Savannah   Do let me hear from you what I shall do with the negros in the up country   Shall I let them go or try and keep them until fall. If I cannot avoid [and] can get some one to except [accept] a draft on you for $300 I will draw on you tomorrow.[126]

Whether on his father's advice or on his own initiative, Thomas let his people go: on June 30, 1865, it was reported that "Mr. Arnold from Bryan had turned off all of his people from Mount Vernon and told them to go to the Yanks: he would feed them no longer."[127]

That is as good as any date for the end of the war for Thomas Clay Arnold. He went north to stay with his family in Newport for the summer as in the old days before the war. The two lives of Richard J. Arnold were now reunited in his two sons.

CHAPTER NINE

Epilogue

On April 10, 1865, the first full day of peace, the Reverend S. W. Magill, returning from the North to organize schools for the American Missionary Association among the freed slaves in Georgia, wrote to his old friend and former parishioner that he had met Amos Morel and his wife Cretia in Savannah and that they were trying to "save money for the passage" to New York, their ultimate destination being their former master's estate in Newport.[1] If Thomas Arnold was having difficulty borrowing money until he could return to his father, the obstacles for Amos Morel were tremendous. All the credit accumulated on the plantation books was wiped out by the war and the confusion and chaos after the fall of Savannah, and Confederate paper money was worthless. Amos was now forty-five years old, a free man under the law, but he had known only slavery and dependency on his master. He had known the "best" that slavery had to offer—status, a position of authority and respect among his peers, even money and "possessions," although he himself had been a legal possession first of Louisa Gindrat, then of her husband, Richard Arnold, and finally of their son Thomas. Freed by proclamation, January 1, 1863, he was freed again by the surrender of Savannah in December 1864, and he was frightened. The benevolent paternalism of his former plantation life made him turn to the one person who had rewarded him in the past for his loyalty and services. On May 19, 1865, another friend wrote Arnold that Amos and his wife were even more determined to go north and be with him: "I advised him to remain but he says he had rather starve with you than to remain here."[2]

Whatever else Arnold, a shrewd businessman, was doing in Newport, he was not starving at Sunny Lawn. His investments in real estate, mining, and railroads in the North and West brought in money that more than compensated for any losses incurred during the war to his plantation property, including the monetary value of two hundred former slaves. Amos Morel need

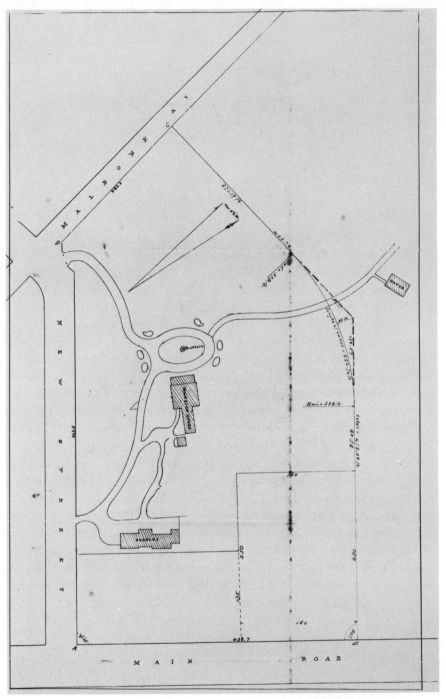

Map of Sunny Lawn, Arnold's Newport estate, from deed of the Arnold family estate, Newport. (Courtesy of the Rhode Island Historical Society.)

not have worried. Arnold made sure immediately after the fall of Savannah that "said plantation be considered exempt, for the present, from the designation 'abandoned rice fields,' as used in 'Special Field Order No. 15.'"[3] Issued on January 16, 1865, by Major General William T. Sherman, this order declared that the abandoned rice fields from Charleston south along the rivers for thirty miles back from the sea, to the country bordering the St. John's River, Florida, "are reserved and set apart for the settlement of the negroes now made free by the acts of war and the proclamation of the President of the United States."[4] Arnold's former plantation lands lay in the middle of the area.

Amos Morel reached Newport eventually, and he was rewarded as a free man by being paid the wages worthy of his hire. Arnold paid "Amos Morrell my former slave" $100 in wages for four months work and bought him clothes to make him presentable as a waiter in the Arnold household, the work Amos had spurned nearly thirty years earlier as a plantation slave in order to learn blacksmithing. But Amos was needed back on the plantation for the reconstruction of the rice mill destroyed during the war, not as a waiter in Newport. He returned to Georgia with Thomas and William Eliot in November 1865, working as a mechanic and blacksmith, just as he had while a slave, except that now he earned a daily wage. Before he left Newport, Amos Morel received a dozen photographs as a going-away gift from Richard Arnold—"taken of Amos at his request & presented him"—and it was the first gift Arnold had given him that he could not in honor take back.[5]

Thomas Arnold, having returned to White Hall in November 1865 for the first time since he had abandoned it nearly a year before to the approaching Yankees, reported back to his father on the condition of the house:

> We slept in the new Parlor as it was half filled with straw   this room is hardly injured at all   the picture that the Yankeys spared the negroes have since destroyed   they have also commited other depredations since Middleton was last here, such [as] breaking the Marble Mantlepeece in the little room out of the new parlor   the new dining room is not much injured but the wall as you go down the stares to the new dining room is torne away so that you can look through to Eliots room   they knocked out the back of Eliots chimney through to the new part of the house   the old Parlor has the hearth torne up, in my room the Mantelpeece & hearth are both gone, the liberry is not much injured . . . but every peece of furniture in the house is gone . . . the kitchen is gone & also the Gin house   not a vestige of them remain.[6]

Houses can be restored, and White Hall was brought back to life, but the attitude of the former slaves toward their former master had undergone a drastic change:

I have hired the stranger [not one of the former Arnold slaves] who is staying at Whitehall to hoe around the house and take the straw out of the house and clean it up, but there is no telling whether he will do so or not   no reliance can be placed in the negroes. Col. Sickles [chief of the Freedmen's Bureau] told him that he would be held responsible for every thing on the place . . . when we drove up [to Cherry Hill] no one came out   the Col. called William & Charles   when they came out they stood by the carriage but neither spoke to me. Col. Sickles then told them that the lands had been returned to its owners and if they would not contract [sign a labor contract to work for specified wages] or if I did not want them they must leave the place again & they must leave. We then went to the settlement [the former slave quarters at Cherry Hill] and Col. Sicles addressed thirty or forty of them telling them that I would be their best friend & advising them to contract, but Batteast spoke up in behalf of the whole plantation and said they had made up their minds never to work for me again, the Col. told them that they were very foolish and asked Batteast what he intended to do   that they must vacate   he did not know but that God would point out the way. The Col. left them in great disgust & he says if I can only get enough white labor to start my plantation, that before a month is passed the negroes will come to me and beg to be taken back. Not one of them old or young came up to speak to me.[7]

Thomas seemed genuinely puzzled that none of the former slaves spoke to him—neither Battist nor William nor Charles. Battist could not be trusted anyway, since he nearly lost Arnold twenty head of cattle in April 1847; and William, who never knew which way to jump, had lost his drivership in 1853 because he had been lazy and played favorites but had failed to win it back even though he tried to appease Amos by informing on Carpenter Peter. And Charles was the one who was always carting out the manure—when he was absent in April 1847, Cyrus had to do the work until Charles came back three days later and started carting manure again. Among all the former Cherry Hill field hands, only Cain was trusted by Thomas, and perhaps Cain was still grateful to the Arnolds for having bought his wife, Lissy, from Colonel Morris back in 1847, but if Cain was present that day not even he came up to speak to Thomas Arnold.

   In his reactions Thomas experienced the typical but nonetheless traumatic "moment of truth" that slave masters throughout the South were experiencing at the time. As Eugene Genovese in *Roll, Jordan, Roll* suggests, they expected faithfulness from their former slaves, for they were all part of the family; it was a self-deception based on paternalism, that devotion to the slave's needs in turn would command their loyalty during and after the war.[8] Arnold would not have reacted to the rebuff any differently from the way his son did; despite his experience and age, he was even more committed to paternalism and more in need of self-deception to justify nearly forty years of slave ownership. Thomas Arnold went through the gamut of rationalizations to maintain his image of the good master: Amos Morel was the faithful and loyal servant and therefore he was "true as steel"; Cain was a "good nigger" and therefore, could be trusted; old Peter was a "bad nigger," "one of the worst negroes that ever lived," and therefore deserved hanging. But the fact that none of the Cherry Hill hands, old or young, would speak to him could not be explained away. That some of the house servants remained loyal to the Arnolds was not enough. The Arnolds recognized that if they were ever to start over again producing rice they had to *depend* on their former slaves' agreeing as *freedmen* to work for them and that never again could they *force* them to do so by fear or favor.

Early in November 1865 Arnold purchased back the plantation lands from his son Thomas for twenty-five dollars and "other considerations." The transaction was a legal maneuver to prevent possible confiscation of the plantations owned by Thomas, lately of the Confederacy; two years later, when all danger of expropriation was gone, Richard Arnold sold back the land and stock to Thomas for $75,000. Since he valued "all Plantations and Hands and Stock" at $175,000, he recorded a loss of $100,000 to balance the books and set a price on the loss of "property," two hundred "hands," his former slaves.[9] Despite this legacy of the past carried in the books, the transfer was symbolic of a new beginning. This northerner, this transplanted New Englander who forty years before had committed himself to becoming a slave-owning planter in Georgia, would now in his seventieth year commit himself to becoming the largest rice planter in all of Georgia, second only to the Heywards of South Carolina in the coastal South. He would work his plantations with free labor, paying wages to his former slaves, whose labor would be negotiated through the Freedmen's Bureau.

Why he embarked on such an extensive business "adventure" in the South so late in life is not difficult to fathom. He had uprooted his family from Sabin Tavern in Providence, where he himself had been born, to live in Newport, which always carried the air of a summer resort. White Hall now was "home," where most of the children and their mother had been born. More important, it was where his sons Thomas and William Eliot had their roots and a commitment to the land that had been reinforced by the war itself. At the beginning of the war, Thomas, age twenty-five, had been untried as a rice planter, but after four years of managing the plantations on his own during the war he was ready to take over from his father. It

Dr. Expenses Planting, 1866 *Cr.*

Page from Arnold's ledger recording planting expenses on the plantations for 1866. Arnold and his sons, with a free black and Irish work force, undertook the reconstruction of White Hall and Cherry Hill plantation using northern capital exclusively. (Courtesy of the Rhode Island Historical Society.)

was for them, his sons, especially Thomas, that Richard Arnold committed his financial resources to the rebuilding of the rice plantations, hiring Irish laborers to dig the ditches and trenches, spending $3,000 in February 1866 for seed, and hiring sixteen Negroes on March 30 for the planting, paying them $85.50.[10] Managing a rice plantation was what he and his sons knew best. Besides, he now faced a dilemma similar to the one that had concerned him when he first started out forty years earlier—either he had to put more money into the land to build up the plantation into a viable business or else he would have to sell out cheaply, except that this time he did not have a choice between selling the land or "the people."

From a statistical perspective Arnold was only one of thousands of northerners who purchased or leased southern plantations during the Reconstruction era, fertilizing the land with greenbacks in the hope of a good profit from raising cotton.[11] But there was an essential difference between Arnold and the vast majority of these Yankee planters: he brought to the land more than forty years of experience as a planter and as a user of Negro labor, albeit as an "old" master of the slaves. The typical Yankee planter immediately after the war was a Union army veteran in his early thirties and well educated, "lawyers, doctors, teachers, and engineers" accounting for "60 percent of the total."[12] They were, in other words, young men of Thomas and William Eliot's generation, sons of the middle class, professionals rather than farmers or mechanics, having not even a small fraction of the experience in planting that the Arnold brothers possessed. Furthermore, Arnold separated himself from most of these postbellum Yankee planters by his decision to concentrate on rice culture rather than cotton production, producing as much as one million pounds of rice in 1869.[13]

If the typical postbellum northern planter knew little about farming and less about cotton planting, he knew nothing about rice culture and wisely stayed away from it. The system of dams, canals, floodgates, drains, and ditches essential to tide-flow rice culture had generally deteriorated or been destroyed during the war, as had the barns to store the rice and the mills to process it for market. The labor and effort that had been required to clear and repair Sedgefield plantation when Arnold purchased it from Edward Pynchon in 1848 was only an indication of the reconstruction required of Arnold after the war to restore his plantations to productivity and the rice mill and storage barns to useful capacity. Furthermore, work in the rice fields was the least desirable kind of labor to a freedman: "Indeed so resistant were the former rice slaves toward resuming their pre-emancipation labor patterns . . . that many observed rice to be the one staple of the Old South that could be produced successfully and profitably only with massive slave forces."[14] While Arnold's paternalism could be counted on to retain the loyalty of some of his former house servants, for large work gangs he had to depend on contracts arranged by the Freedmen's Bureau.

Richard Arnold believed that with a large infusion of northern capital he could reconstruct and expand his antebellum holdings beyond past productivity. He had the experience and expertise necessary to make the land productive and profitable again and the labor force efficient. His sons, especially Thomas, would provide the youthful energy and hard work needed for the day-to-day management of the estate, they being about the same age (William Eliot exactly so) as their father had been when he started out in 1823. This commitment to the land in Georgia far surpassed anything he had envisioned in his youth when he first decided to become a southern planter. It was as though he had set out to prove Olmsted's thesis that it would be more profitable to run the plantation with free labor than with slave labor. It was also as though, having been forced to exile himself from the South during the war, he returned with renewed vigor to the life of the planter.

Arnold's dream was far removed, however, from that of idealistic visionary southerners like Wilky and Bob James or Henry Lee Higginson of Boston and his two friends, Charles F. Morse and Channing Clapp, who hoped to aid the newly freed slaves on the cotton plantations they purchased for that purpose. Arnold was a businessman, not an idealist or reformer, and his vision was the establishment of a family enterprise that would rival in size and fortune anything in the old rice kingdom. He would accomplish this despite the loss of capital assets which resulted from freeing the slaves without compensation. In contrast, the James brothers were utopian in their vision. Having both served as white officers in black regiments from Massachusetts, they decided after their discharge from the army to establish nothing less than Swedenborg's New Jerusalem for the freedmen on the principles described by Charles Fourier. Since Henry James, Sr., had himself prophesied such a heaven on earth for the emancipated slaves, he blessed the enterprise financially as well as spiritually, so that Bob and Wilky James together with five others from Massachusetts formed the Gordon colony, a Yankee cotton planting community in northern Florida.[15]

Like many utopian communities before and after, the Gordon colony foundered spiritually and financially, ending abruptly in 1870, the victim of agricultural depression and local hostility. Similarly, the Higginson project collapsed. More humanitarian than utopian in outlook, Higginson and his partners purchased Cottenham, the Rogers plantation in the neighborhood of

White Hall. Morse, one of the partners, had participated in Sherman's march to the sea and "had fought over this very territory of Cottonham."[16] Their purpose was to make the plantation a reasonably profitable enterprise while at the same time providing work for the newly freed slaves at good wages as well as teaching them how to read and write at the school they established on the plantation. Unfortunately, like many of their fellow Yankee planters, they knew nothing about running a cotton plantation, and in two years they were bankrupt, having originally paid too much for the land but too little for a lawyer to clear the title so that they paid for twice as much land as the title granted. In the end, they lost their illusions even about being able to teach the blacks, to whom they paid high wages, yet who mistrusted them.[17]

Certainly, Arnold's dream had nothing in common with that of his new neighbors, William and Ellen Craft, who in 1870 purchased Woodville, a cotton plantation near White Hall. The Crafts had been fugitive slaves from Georgia who fled to England with the help of Samuel Gridley Howe and other Boston abolitionists when the Fugitive Slave Law was passed in 1850. The Crafts returned to their native state under the auspices of various old-time Boston abolitionists, for the Crafts had a dream also. They dreamed of establishing a community along the lines of the Ockham school in Surrey, England, where the Crafts had studied and taught. The Ockham school, financed by Lady Byron and Lord Lovelace, and run by Lady Lovelace, Lord Byron's daughter, combined practical, vocational training with a classical education. The Crafts' intention on Woodville plantation was to teach blacks various practical skills, such as carpentry (William Craft was a carpenter), mechanics, and domestic arts, as well as the fundamentals of reading and writing. The plantation and the school, financed in part with contributions obtained by Craft in the North, had some success until 1875, when George Appleton, who by then had married Arnold's granddaughter Luly, motivated others to print the charge in a Boston newspaper that Craft was a charlatan, that no such school existed, and that Craft was personally pocketing the money contributed for the school. Craft's unsuccessful libel suit the following year was the beginning of the end to his experiment, for the northern money dried up.[18] By then George and Luly Appleton were living at White Hall.

Richard Arnold's attempt to reconstruct and unite the two separate strands of his life was quite different from George Noble Jones's return to the land after the war. Although Jones, like Arnold, sought to bring back the plantations to profitable productivity, it was not and never could be the same, for unlike Arnold, he was a defeated southerner. His Georgia plantation had stood directly in the path of General Sherman's army and all had been destroyed, including 500 bales of cotton worth more than $100,000;[19] the liberated slaves presumably either followed the army or stayed, living off the land as best they could. The Florida plantations had remained productive throughout the war and were largely untouched by the destruction of the war. But neither El Destino, the home plantation, nor Savannah would ever again be the center of life for the Jones family, and Newport was but a distant memory. Jones himself spent some time in Florida straightening out plantation affairs so that his son Wallace Savage Jones could take over management of the estate, and he went to Savannah to survey the damage. Another son, George Fenwick Jones, settled in Savannah to practice law. The rest of the family lived in exile in France.[20]

Jones had never been committed to the life of a working planter, and his attempt to reconstruct the antebellum plantation world was doomed to failure. His son Wallace was even less suited to the detailed demands of managing a cotton plantation in the postbellum period. Wallace had been educated abroad (St. Cyr Academy and the Sorbonne) and was more studious than Arnold's sons, translating Alfriend's *Prison Life of Jefferson Davis* for publication in France in 1867. On June 5, 1868, for example, David F. Horger, the overseer of Chemonie, wrote to Wallace Jones that he had been unable to obtain the meat ration for the work force from the commissary run by the Freedmen's Bureau, and therefore Horger had to provide meat out of the plantation's supply. Wallace wrote to his father explaining the situation, perhaps including Horger's comment "that if all the Elections were over with for this year the poor devels [the Negroes] would not have smelled the meat from them [the Commissary]." Jones replied on July 7, blaming the Freedmen's Bureau: "I wonder when the negroes will find out those rascally Yankees." Jones, however, was feeling less than tolerant toward his former slaves three weeks later: "The news which you send of Fla. affairs is going from bad to worse. Such must be the case where niggers are left to themselves."[21]

In one important respect, nothing had changed for George Noble and Mary Nuttall Jones, and in this they remained different from the Arnolds: the plantations, whether worked by slaves or free labor, were a means to the end of sustaining their absentee way of life; the center of their social life had changed from Savannah and Newport to Paris and Montpellier, but the graciousness of southern hospitality remained. If "the sense of Newport" was now "the sense of the past," it was also a time for reconciliation, and it was fitting that it should be with the King family of Newport.

In February 1868 Mrs. David King and her daughters Mary and Georgiana, traveling in Europe, visited the Joneses in Montpellier. The reunion was like old times before the war—friends meeting, dining together, talking, amusing one another. It was such a treat to talk to old friends, Mary Jones said, because the French provincial families were socially dull and "so dreadfully stiff & particular." As if the war had never intervened, Mary Jones was "as nice as she can be" to the Kings, who dined with her every day of their stay in Montpellier. Although southern hospitality and the social graces were maintained as before, the years of exile had left their mark: "Mrs. Jones looks the same," Georgie King observed, "except that she is terribly lame." Symbolic of Mary Jones's expatriation, if not her ex-slave-owning status, was the fact that she refused to learn to speak French, so that her daughter Lillie "has to do every thing for the family."[22]

At about the same time that the Kings were traveling in Europe visiting the Joneses, Luly Arnold, the Arnolds' granddaughter, was visiting White Hall. On December 14, 1867, the first morning of her visit, she looked out the window of her bedroom. Whether it was the same window from which Frederick Law Olmsted looked out upon waking his first morning at White Hall fourteen years earlier, the view was the same:

> When I got up & looked out the window what an exquisite sight meets my
> view   the orange trees loaded with fruit   the japonica bushes with a quantity
> of flowers & beyond the garden the great tall live-oaks & pines as they used to
> be long ago. The Avenue stretching down in front of the house with the trees
> arching for some distance & draped in the beautiful long gray moss which I
> always admired so much![23]

It was paradise seen again (she had visited White Hall during the winter of 1858–1859, when she was nine), a paradise that never changed, for it was as beautiful as she remembered it from the past. That the past included the fact that her grandfather had owned slaves seemed irrelevant to an eighteen-year-old who had first read *Uncle Tom's Cabin* a year earlier:

> In the PM I practiced some & read some of Uncle Tom's Cabin which I
> finished in the evening. I think it very fine, Tom's character is *beautiful* & little
> Eva lovely & then George Harris has a fine character, & many others which I
> will not mention may well be admired for their good traits & then the *atro-
> ciousness* of Legree!! How thankful *Americans* ought to be that slavery no longer
> exists under the skies which cover our land.[24]

Her grandfather was a good, kind man, and *her* Uncle Tom was no Simon Legree.

White Hall seen again through the fresh eyes of an innocent observer made time stand still on that first day of Luly's visit. Her arrival was like old times, reduplicating her great-aunt Eliza Harriet Allen's experience visiting "the people" at Cherry Hill: "Old Mam Daphne jumped up & down & screamed at seeing me Miss Louisa's daughter as they all call Mother."[25] Thirty years earlier, Mrs. Allen had visited the people in the Cherry Hill slave quarters, including Daphne, "the sister of Phebe & saw her and her husband Ben."[26] Soon Luly was reading the Bible to the Negroes on Sundays. The observance of old traditions reinforced the sense of continuity with the past: Thomas Arnold killed a cow for "the people" at Cherry Hill on Christmas Day, 1867, and on the fifth day of Christmas the Arnold family sat on the piazza of White Hall to hear "the people sing."[27]

On the morning of the second day at White Hall, a Sunday, Luly wrote in her diary: "I sat in the parlor after breakfast—toasted my feet read & dozed & then sat looking out at the splendid old trees. Oh this place is beautiful   as beautiful as it was pictured in my memory." The idyllic setting of this paradise was reinforced for her in the afternoon when she went for a walk down to the river with her grandfather:

> Oh how beautiful the walk was   more so than when I was here [in 1858–1859] the trees have grown up so on the left side & form an arch a good part of the way   we came back & went out the "over yonder" avenue where the grand old trees meet above our head & make it more beautiful than the front avenue   we went out the gate & round the road from the front avenue. I cannot describe all the beauties for everything is so lovely   but the woods all around make the walk an exquisite one.[28]

But time does not stop, and in the midst of this loveliness "there is a grave in the avenue of one of our officers, a lt of Ill. Inf. Simmons is his name." Luly drew no moral lesson from this sobering sight, but as her concluding remarks for the day, she wrote in her diary that she "staid in the house the rest of the day & spent the evening in the parlor with a great wood fire."[29] That she identified Lieutenant Simmons as one of "our" officers indicates that her sympathies had been with the Union side. But Luly was soon caught up in the Savannah social season, courted by John McKay Elliott through a whirlwind of dances and parties and befriended by his cousin, Sada Elliott, the Maria McIntosh of her generation, an unreconstructed rebel and apologist for the southern way of life, which included slavery. The confusion of values and loyalties troubled Luly. On the one hand, her parents and friends had been active Unionists, though not abolitionists; even Grandpa Arnold had declared his loyalty to the Union. On the other hand, her uncles Tom and William Eliot had fought on the Confederate side, and her new friend Sada was still fighting the war.

Samuel Greene Arnold feared that his daughter was being unduly influenced, if not indoctrinated, by unregenerate southerners, for when, two years later, Luly was again staying at White Hall with her grandparents and renewing her friendship with Sada who had spent the summer with her in Newport, he (in London at the time) gave his daughter some fatherly advice about matters "too serious to be disregarded or to permit of ones views being concealed under the mark of courtesy":

> While you are at the South it is both proper & polite that you should not introduce the subject of the Rebellion—but remember this, if others introduce it you are not to shun it or evade it, for by so doing you leave room for them to misinterpret your motives or misrepresent your sentiments. Let your opinions in opposition to theirs be expressed, courteously but decidedly so firmly that there shall be no room for misunderstanding what they are, no excuse for the people to continue a discussion of the subject.[30]

The politics of manners and the manners of politics were united.

In the same letter, however, Samuel Arnold revealed a division within the family that seemed to mirror the continuing conflict between the North and South long after the war had ended:

> *Private*. Your mother's letter of 21 ult. rec[d] yesterday speaks of Saida [Sada Elliott] & the trouble she caused you in Prov. by her absurd secession talk with young Foster & others & mentions your excuses to him as to the delicate position she [your mother] held during the war on account of the ground taken by most of her immediate family. Your grandmother repeatedly said in her violent attacks upon the government that *all* her children agreed with her sentiments. This simply ignored your Mother & Aunt C [Mary Cornelia Talbot] who did not agree with her altho' all the rest did, but it placed me as a soldier first, then as Governor, then as Senator in a most dangerous as well as delicate position at a time of universal distrust, when even the private correspondence of men in high civil rank, as I was, was liable to be opened by super-zealous friends of the Union.[31]

Samuel Arnold's personal fear was that his daughter would marry young Elliott, for he was "not quite reconciled to the idea of having you marry a Southern man."[32] Luly in the end did not marry John McKay Elliott but a northerner, George Lyman Appleton, related to the Lymans of Waltham and the Appletons of Beacon Hill, Boston; Appleton was a convert as dedicated to the southern cause as any born southerner, serving in the Confederate army during the war and in the lost cause after the war.

The northern faction of the family feared for their inheritance. Richard

Arnold put so much capital into the reconstruction of his southern estate that the Talbots and the Samuel Arnolds were alarmed. Louisa (Mrs. Samuel G.) Arnold wrote to her daughter Luly, "Uncle Willie [William Talbot] told me not long ago that they were sinking thousands every year in rice planting & Grandpa was taking property from here & from the west & sinking it at the South—& it did not seem right to him but he did not know what could be done about it."[33] Reconstructed dreams are costly, but constructed fears are even more dear: at this time (the spring of 1870) Thomas Arnold was engaged to marry Elizabeth Screven of Savannah, and William Eliot was courting her cousin Helen Foreman, also of Savannah.[34] The fear of a southern hegemony was real, and plantation economics being what they were, the plantations were managed through complicated financial arrangements and loans between Thomas and William Eliot.

For all that Richard and Louisa Arnold sought to recapture the days before the war by restoring and redecorating White Hall and by surrounding themselves with loyal servants—Pompey and Tom and his wife Peggy; Nero and Celia; Abby and Netti and Cora, Lizze's daughter; Lizze and Cain; Daphne and Sylvia; and of course, Amos Morel and his wife, Cretia—the relationship between whites and blacks in the South had changed fundamentally. The blacks were no longer property, and if they were to be hired for their labor in the fields, terms had to be negotiated. The common method for hiring field hands on the larger southern rice and cotton plantations after the war, used by the Arnolds and the Joneses alike, was to draw up a contract, a written document insisted upon by the Freedmen's Bureau to protect the former slaves against de facto enslavement. The black workers were understandably suspicious of the contracts, for the written word was an all-powerful weapon and tool of the white man, which could enslave them for generations or free them.

The black workers at Cherry Hill, continuing their distrust of Thomas Arnold, refused in December 1865 to sign any contract with him "upon any terms," would not leave the plantation, and threatened to resist any attempt to force them to leave. "Moreover, they threatened those other freedmen Arnold had persuaded to contract and come to work for him."[35] The Freedmen's Bureau most often functioned as a mediator in Georgia, where the bureau saw its mission as maintaining the status quo rather than operating as a protector of the rights of the emancipated slaves. For example, on December 23, 1867, Captain Cook, from Rhode Island, arrived to speak "at the negro meeting" at Strathy Hall, the McAllister plantation. In the company of

Mr. Middleton, Captain Cook dined with the Arnolds at White Hall.[36] In the evening, accompanied by Middleton and Thomas, Cook went to Strathy Hall, where he spoke to the assembled Negroes. What Cook said at the meeting is not known, but he would not have said anything that in any way reflected upon the reputation of the Arnolds, for not only had he dined with them, but he stayed the night and "seemed in no hurry at all to go."[37] Apparently all had gone well for the Arnolds at the meetings in the area; on that Christmas Day Thomas had killed the cow "for the people" at Cherry Hill. Considering that in the two-month period of May and June 1867 the Arnold payroll was over $1,700 and that from January 1866 to January 1868 expenses for planting were over $60,000, it is no wonder that the settlement of contract negotiations in December 1867 was a cause for celebration.[38]

The following year, however, was a time of political and social unrest in Georgia, resulting in acts of violence by the Ku Klux Klan as well as in Negro riots. The most serious unrest among the Negroes was in the immediate area of the Arnold plantations at the end of December 1868 and the beginning of January 1869. Known as the Ogeechee Riots, they were, as described by C. Mildred Thompson in *Reconstruction in Georgia*, raids by armed bands of Negroes "who plundered and seized loads of rice, just ready for market. The rioters were pursued by a sheriff's posse and by army troops; fourteen Negroes were captured and arrested."[39] The Arnolds played down the seriousness of the riots in writing to their relatives in the North. On January 1, 1869, in the middle of the riots, Louisa Arnold assured her granddaughter Luly back in Newport, "We feel perfectly Easy about the Negroes, every thing is exaggerated."[40] On Janaury 13, however, less than two weeks later, Richard Arnold wrote to his friend Manton Marble, editor of the *New York World*, that accounts of the riots are "far from being exaggerated." "It was so threatening at one time before the U States arrived, that it was not considered safe for the women & children to remain on our side of the river, notwithstanding the Negroes with very few exception behaved very well, and I took them all from my immediate Neighborhood to Sav^h where we were exiled for six days." Arnold made no mention of Ku Klux Klan activities in the area at the time. His main concern was that the riots not be used as an excuse to suspend the Georgia Constitution and reinstitute military rule: if that happened, then "all Rice Planters on the Ogeechee will nearly all abandon planting, notwithstanding they have spent some thousands of dollars [in] preparation of our lands for this years Crops." As though to prove his objectivity, Arnold concluded, "You can say [this] comes from a

Northern man who had been a large planter on the Ogeechee for many years & who only gave it up upon the breaking out of the war."[41] Needless to say, rice planting was not abandoned.

The cause of this social disorder in Georgia was summed up by C. Mildred Thompson:

> The increase in social disorder in the years after 1867 was due to racial antag-
> onism between whites and blacks. The task of the dominant white population
> in the first years after the war was to keep the negro to his old labor; in 1867 to
> this task was superadded that of keeping the negro to a realization of his
> inferior social status though the law declared him equal to the white in political
> and civil rights and privileges. On the one side was law and on the other was
> the social custom of generations.[42]

The legacy of ambiguities within the Arnold family, North and South, in their attitudes toward blacks was made clear by Samuel Arnold's report to his daughter Luly of the reaction of her sister on her first visit to White Hall in April 1869: "Addeus [a former Arnold slave and Mrs. Samuel G. Arnold's nurse] went in to the room & fell on your Mother kissing her all over her face to Nina's great horror, which was turned to intense disgust when she fell upon Nina & repeated the dose. Nina at once betook herself to the wash basin & would not let her mother kiss her till she had also washed her face."[43] Since in this same letter Samuel Arnold revealed that he was not reconciled to the idea of Luly's marrying a southerner and that there had been divisions within the family during the war over the issue of secession and slavery, the ambiguities were indeed complex.

The one who remained loyal to Richard Arnold throughout all the post-bellum unrest was his former slave Amos Morel. As a reward for his loyalty, Amos and two other former Arnold slaves were deeded an acre near White Hall in 1869 for "25¢ in hand" so that the blacks could build their own church, Amos being identified as a preacher. But outright ownership of land in order to farm was Amos Morel's dream, a small plantation of manageable size for himself and his family, purchased with money earned working as a mechanic for the Arnolds after the war. On February 8, 1871, he purchased from the trustees of Joseph and Caroline Stiles that tract of land "known as 'Brisbanes Plantation,' bounded on the North by the land of George Waters, on the East by lands of Mrs. Morris Miller, on the South by lands of Joseph Stiles, and on the West by lands of Lewis Hines," all white plantation owners, friends and neighbors of the Arnolds.[44] The land lay across the road from Cherry Hill, south of the Ogeechee River, separated from William

Craft's plantation, Woodville, by the plantations of Stiles and Hines to the south and west. In all, Amos purchased more than four hundred acres of land. It was not the vast estate owned by the Arnolds both before and after the war, but neither was it the humble "forty acres of tillable land" promised in General Sherman's Special Field Order number 15 of January 15, 1865.

Amos Morel sold one-fourth of the plantation in 1875 to a fellow preacher and former Arnold slave, London Harris, for nearly $1,300, or $12 per acre, a good price. In 1879 he purchased 122 acres of White Oak plantation for his daughter, Sharlot Mattox, for only $250. He was apparently feeling his age by then, since in the 1880 census he listed himself as sixty-six years old instead of the sixty years he would have been by Arnold's calculation! He continued to sell small parcels of Brisbane plantation from the original tract, leaving some of it to bequeath to his wife, Lucretia, and his son-in-law and daughter, Andrew and Shartlot Mattox.

Louisa Gindrat Arnold died in Newport on October 15, 1871, in exile from her beloved White Hall.[45] Richard Arnold made the trip back to White Hall without her, the last time he made the pilgrimage south to the plantation. Depressed, he wrote to his daughter Mary Cornelia, "[I] have no difficulty in believing fully in Jesus Christ & that is the only way I can be saved and I try to do every thing I think my dear wife would have me do yet I feel as if I had no interest in the Holy Spirit, and that some thing must be radically wrong with me." His depression and religious doubts were not caused by his wife's death: "I have become perfectly reconciled to part with your mother & would not recall her if I could. tho' I spend a long time each day in looking at her picture every day and forming good resolutions from it."[46] The depression, if not the religious doubt, was caused by ill health. On New Year's Day, 1873, Zachariah Allen recorded in his diary, "I passed some time with Mr. Richard J Arnold yesterday. He is very infirm and feeble, and confined to his bed most of the time at the home of his son Richard" in Providence.[47] It was the end of an era; its legacy continues to this day.

Richard James Arnold died in Providence on March 12, 1873, leaving to each of his seven children the equivalent of $100,000, more or less the same amount he himself had inherited from his father fifty years earlier and which he had invested in the plantations. As for the plantation land, William Eliot received Cherry Hill in the division of the estate. He built a new house for himself and his wife in 1874, but he was not the manager his father or his brother Thomas had been. In the end Cherry Hill was sold at a sheriff's auction to pay off his debts.[48] Thomas received White Hall with its mansion house, and he lived there with his wife, Elizabeth Screven, daughter of a prominent Savannah businessman and politician. Since he had in effect taken over the management of the plantations after the war from his father, his life did not change drastically with his father's death. He and his father had carried out their extensive plans for expansion by 1873, having purchased the Cheves rice plantation the previous year. Thomas was only thirty-seven at the time of his father's death. The future was ahead of him.

Thomas Clay Arnold died December 23, 1875, signaling the end of the Arnolds' dream. Reconstruction was finished in Georgia by the end of 1872. The last of the occupying federal troops were withdrawn from the South in 1877. The last of the Arnold plantations was sold at auction that same year, some of the land having been sold in 1873 and 1874 to satisfy the division of property under Richard Arnold's will. The breaking up of the estate that Arnold had put together over a span of fifty years was completed in 1877 when Paul T. Haskell purchased Cherry Hill at a sheriff's sale, and George Appleton purchased White Hall at public auction.[49] Thus, the Arnolds did not entirely lose their connection with the land, for Luly Arnold Appleton had returned to her beloved White Hall. But White Hall had been the paradise of her youth. It was no longer a viable rice plantation, and George Appleton turned the Arnold plantation lands, as he had Cottenham, the Rogerses plantation, into a hunting and fishing preserve for himself and his friends (among whom was William Brailsford). The Negroes no longer labored in the rice fields. Where Captain Bailey's schooner, *Cotton Plant*, unloaded the bricks to build Arnold's sugarhouse, and Captain Thompson's sloop, *Science*, loaded 2,200 bushels rough rice to be delivered to Habersham and Company in Savannah thirty years earlier, the steam yacht *Gem* could be docked by its owner, George Appleton, for the Arnolds had rebuilt the wharf after the war. The windows at White Hall had been changed, but they still looked out on "the great tall live-oaks & pines as they used to be long ago."[50]

On March 28, 1914, the japonica trees at White Hall were in bloom and a large Japanese quince at the corner of the house was in full flower even though the house itself was deteriorating; the piazza had collapsed, and parts of the house were unsafe to enter. The moss hung heavily from the live oaks: "it was all most quiet and peaceful," that last full day in the life of the neglected and decaying old manse. By the next evening White Hall was in flames. "Many of the trees caught and the moss laden boughs blazed in festoons of flame. Wisps of the moss sailed around in the current made by the gigantic bonfire and one outstretched limb of live-oak thickly covered with Poly Pody burned in a long line of fire." The house and two outbuildings burned to the ground beyond repair. Two white adults, strangers to the Arnold family but friends of the Clays, and two black children were the only witnesses to the fire.[51]

The white woman wrote, "I feel as if I had been close to something which was dear to you [Mary Arnold, daughter of Thomas], had ministered to it in its last hours and now bring its farewell message." The message, the correspondent thought, was that it was better to go in a "burst of glory rather than slowly and pitifully decay." But what the two black children felt or said or what message the old manse had for them is unrecorded.[52]

Notes

Chapter One

1. In the original "Yeoman" letters published in the *New York Daily Times* during
   1853 and 1854, upon which Olmsted's book *A Journey in the Seaboard Slave States*
   (New York, 1856) was based, Mr. X was called Mr. A. Positive identification of
   Richard J. Arnold as Olmsted's host was first made by the editors of the
   Olmsted Papers on the basis of an annotated copy of *A Journey in the Seaboard
   Slave States* in which Mary Cornelia Arnold Talbot, Arnold's daughter, identified her father. See Frederick Law Olmsted, *The Papers of Frederick Law Olmsted*,
   ed. Charles E. Beveridge and Charles C. McLaughlin (Baltimore, Md., 1981),
   2:163–164, n 6. It is important to note, however, that Olmsted's description of
   Mr. A. as a man "trained in the rugged fields of New-Hampshire, among the
   looms of Lowell and in the counting rooms of Boston" has no basis in fact in
   Arnold's life (Yeoman letter no. 24, dated June 14, 1853). One can assume that
   these were attempts by Olmsted to disguise the identity of Richard Arnold for
   purposes of publication. In contrast to Mr. A, Mr. X is described in general
   terms: "Mr. X himself is a New England farmer's son, and has been a successful
   merchant and manufacturer." Corroboration of Beveridge and McLaughlin's
   identification of Arnold as Mr. X is to be found in a letter dated February 1,
   1853, written by Mrs. R. J. Arnold to her daughter Louisa: "Last Saturday
   [January 29, 1853] just after dinner Tom came down and said there was a
   gentleman in the parlor   father went up and found a Mr Olmsted the author of
   Walks & Talks [*Walks and Talks of an American Farmer in England*]   he brought a
   letter from Mr Mc'Curdy [of McCurdy, Aldrich & Spencer, commission merchants of New York]   he remained until this morning   we found him quite
   pleasant tho' I was quite ready for him to go" (Arnold-Rogers Papers, private
   collection).
2. Olmsted, *Journey*, 411.
3. Olmsted, *Papers*, 2:155.
4. Louise Brownell Clarke, *The Greenes of Rhode Island* (New York, 1903), 1:289–
   293.
5. Richard J. Arnold to Samuel G. Arnold, December 12, 1823, Welcome Arnold
   Papers, John Carter Brown Library, Providence. Arnold's initial reluctance to

invest money in land in Georgia was undoubtedly caused in part by the fact
that his cousin Welcome Arnold Greene had recently returned from a journey
to the Georgia backcountry in search of information about their long-lost uncle,
Jonathan Arnold. In 1796 Jonathan Arnold had invested a large sum of money
in shares and land claims in the Tennessee Company, one of the speculative
land companies formed to promote the Yazoo land grants based on Georgia's
claim that her boundaries extended all the way westward to the Mississippi
River. Jonathan sold a claim to a large tract of land near what is now Muscle
Shoals, Alabama, to his older brother Welcome, Richard's father, for 6,000
silver dollars. In 1806 Jonathan packed all the land deeds and traveled to western Georgia to see the land for himself. As far as Welcome Arnold Greene could
determine, Uncle Jonathan had been murdered by Cherokee Indians in
November 1806, near Muscle Shoals. Compensation for Yazoo land claims was
finally passed by Congress in 1814 and payment was made on presentation of
legal documents. Welcome Arnold's heirs were able to substantiate his share but
unable to obtain compensation for Jonathan's shares, since the documents had
disappeared with him. See *The Journals of Welcome Arnold Greene*, ed. Howard
Greene and Alice E. Smith (Madison, Wisc., 1957), 2:3–7, and C. Peter Mac-
grath, *Yazoo: Law and Politics in the New Republic, The Case of Fletcher vs. Peck*
(New York, 1967), 85–100.
6. Richard J. Arnold to Samuel G. Arnold, January 30, 1824, Welcome Arnold
Papers.
7. Eliza Harriet Allen to Richard J. Arnold, December 11, 1824, Richard J. Arnold Papers, Rhode Island Historical Society Library, Providence (hereafter
cited as Arnold Papers).
8. Clarke, *The Greenes of Rhode Island*, 293.
9. Olmsted, *Journey*, 420.
10. Richard J. Arnold to Samuel G. Arnold, December 12, 1823, Welcome Arnold
Papers.
11. Robert Manson Myers, ed., *Children of Pride* (New Haven, 1972), 1491.
12. Eliza Harriet Allen to Richard J. Arnold, December 11, 1824, Arnold Papers.
13. Mary Arnold Burges (Mrs. Tristam Burges) to Richard J. Arnold, March 26,
1820, Arnold Papers.
14. Eliza Harriet Allen to Richard J. Arnold, March 14, 1820, Arnold Papers.
15. General Greene had first proposed to his cousin Patience Greene, who instead
married Welcome Arnold, one of his close friends.
16. Jay Coughtry, *The Notorious Triangle: Rhode Island and the African Slave Trade,
1700–1807* (Philadelphia, 1981), 28, 83.
17. Ibid., 266, 268.
18. Zachariah Allen's tree experiments, particularly in Lincoln, Rhode Island, on
Arnold farmlands inherited by his wife, are well known. See Charles and Tess
Hoffmann, "Zachariah Allen's Vacant Lot: A Pioneering Experiment in Silviculture," *Horticulture* 60, no. 11 (November 1982), 42–47.

19. Recent excavations at Cherry Hill and Richmond-in-Ogeechee have uncovered Indian camping sites and villages.
20. Allen's estimate of "loss" per yard of wool cloth in the 1820s included a "profit" of 6 percent return on his capital investment. See Allen's diaries and business records, passim, in Zachariah Allen Papers, Rhode Island Historical Society Library, Providence.
21. Sabin Tavern, where Arnold was born, had been built about 1758 by Captain Woodbury Morris, a slave trader who had lost his life on the coast of Africa in 1763 while transporting 120 slaves to Barbados. Welcome Arnold, Richard's father, had leased the house from Morris's heirs in 1773, purchasing it in 1785. The house was known as Sabin's Tavern because a section leased as a tavern to James Sabin was where the plot to burn the British frigate *Gaspee* was hatched in 1772. Richard Arnold's heirs eventually sold the house, saving the Gaspee Room, which was incorporated into Mary Cornelia Arnold Talbot's home on Williams Street (known as the Gaspee House). The site of the Sabin Tavern, on the corner of South Main and Planet Streets in Providence, is now a parking lot.
22. Richard J. Arnold to Samuel G. Arnold, December 29, 1823, Welcome Arnold Papers.

Chapter Two

1. Olmsted, *Papers*, 2:161.
2. Olmsted, *Journey*, 422.
3. Ibid.
4. James O. Breeden, ed., *Advice among Masters: The Ideal in Slave Management in the Old South* (Westport, Conn., 1980), 114.
5. Ibid.
6. Olmsted, *Journey*, 439.
7. Ibid. The account books indicated that in the 1830s Arnold tended to use the Negro store to buy sundries for the family (eggs, fowl, etc.), but that by the late 1840s he was buying from individual slaves.
8. Eliza Harriet Allen, "Journal of a Visit to Georgia in 1837," April 12, 1837, Allen Papers.
9. Olmsted, *Journey*, 442–443.
10. Richard J. Arnold, Account Book, vol. 8, December 6, 1854, Arnold Papers.
11. Olmsted, *Journey*, 428–429. Philip D. Morgan, while disclaiming "that slavery was a beneficent school," emphasizes that the task system "was characterized by, and indeed encouraged, a number of traits—an ability to lengthen or shorten the working day, a sense of personal responsibility, a commitment to and economic underpinning for the slave family, and attitudes of collective solidarity and communal worth. All these features manifested themselves, and

in one sense reached their fullest expression, in the ability of low-country slaves to accumulate property" ("The Ownership of Property by Slaves in the Mid-Nineteenth-Century Low Country," *Journal of Southern History* 49, no. 3 [August 1983], 405). It is essential to remember that, whatever the advantages of the task system and the ownership of property by individual slaves such as Tom and Amos Morel, they were all slaves and not protopeasants learning how to be free, responsible citizens. Arnold and the other rice planters in the area accepted the task system because it worked economically despite its obvious inefficiencies and it enhanced their self-image. As Eugene Genovese points out in *Roll, Jordan, Roll: The World the Slaves Made* (New York, 1974), "Southern paternalism, like every other paternalism, had little to do with Ole Massa's ostensible benevolence, kindness, and good cheer. It grew out of the necessity to discipline and morally justify a system of exploitation" (p. 4). The price Amos Morel paid for his possessions was a lifetime of servility to his master.

12. Memorandum summarizing rice and cotton production and sales for 1836, Arnold-Screven Papers, Southern Historical Collection, University of North Carolina Library, Chapel Hill.

13. James M. Clifton, "Twilight Comes to the Rice Kingdom: Postbellum Rice Culture on the South Atlantic Coast," *Georgia Historical Quarterly* 62, no. 2 (1978), 146.

14. James M. Clifton, *Life and Labor on Argyle Island* (Savannah, 1978), xii–xiii.

15. Olmsted, *Journey*, 480.

16. Ibid., 418–419.

17. Ibid., 485.

18. Richard J. Arnold, Account Book, vol. 7, November 19, 1833, and May 17, 1836, Arnold Papers.

19. Ibid., April 3, 1832.

20. Ibid., January 23, 1834.

21. Richard J. Arnold, memorandum dated February 16, 1837, Arnold Papers.

22. Richard J. Arnold, Account Book, vol. 7, April 15, 1837.

23. Ibid.

24. Richard J. Arnold to Mrs. Mary Nuttall, February 7, 1839; Mrs. Mary Nuttall to Richard J. Arnold, December 20, 1838; Richard J. Arnold to Mrs. Mary Nuttall, February 8, 1839; all in Arnold Papers. Mary Savage Nuttall was the widow of William B. Nuttall, the niece of William Savage and the future wife of George Noble Jones. Arnold addresses her as niece and she calls Arnold uncle.

25. Richard J. Arnold, memorandum dated November 1846, "Observing the longevity of Negros they having been given to Mrs Arnolds Mother 1785 & 86. In all that time—12 of these same Negros from 45 are now living on the Plantations," Arnold-Screven Papers. See also slave list dated December 9, 1846, with additions of births and deaths through 1847, Arnold-Screven Pa-

pers. The Gindrat genealogy (Harry Alexander Davis, *The Gindrat Family* [Washington, 1933]) describes Barbara Clark Gindrat as Captain James McKay's granddaughter, but his will does not include her among his grand-children, although she inherited a share of his estate in her own right. Apparently, Barbara's grandmother had married McKay as his second wife (Mabel F. La Far and Caroline P. Wilson, comp., *Abstracts of Wills, Chatham County, Georgia, 1773–1817*, Lachlan McIntosh Chapter DAR [Savannah, 1933]).

26. Colonel Lewis Morris to Richard J. Arnold, January 14, 1847, Arnold-Screven Papers.

27. Copy of letter from Richard J. Arnold to Colonel Lewis Morris, January 20, 1847, Arnold-Screven Papers.

28. Olmsted, *Journey*, 485.

29. Richard J. Arnold to Louisa Arnold, April 29, 1824, Arnold Papers; Richard J. Arnold to Samuel G. Arnold, May 15, 1824, Arnold-Screven Papers.

30. Ibid., November 10, 1824.

31. Richard J. Arnold, Agreement with J. J. Snead, 1827, Arnold-Screven Papers.

32. Richard J. Arnold, Agreement with A. M. Sanford, 1829, Arnold-Screven Papers.

33. Philip D. Morgan, "Work and Culture: The Task System and the World of Lowcountry Blacks, 1700 to 1880," *William and Mary Quarterly* 39, no. 4 (October 1982), 566.

34. Ibid., 565–566, 578.

35. Olmsted, *Journey*, 435, 439.

36. Eliza Harriet Allen, "Journal," April 1, 1837, Allen Papers.

37. Olmsted, *Journey*, 439.

38. Olmsted, Yeoman Letter no. 30 to *New York Daily Times*, July 21, 1853.

39. Charles Ferguson to Richard J. Arnold, July 16, 1852, Arnold Papers.

40. Olmsted, Yeoman letter no. 30 to *New York Daily Times*, July 21, 1853.

41. Thomas S. Clay, *Detail of a Plan for the Moral Improvement of Negroes on Plantations*, presented before the Georgia Presbytery, 1833 (N.p., n.d.), 19.

42. Olmsted, *Papers*, 2:187.

43. Bill from Isaac D'Lyon, August 23, 1824, Arnold Papers. The odd three-quarter cents in Sheriff D'Lyon's bill is accounted for by the fact that he charged Arnold $1.87½ for apprehending Sampson and $2.56¼ for jailing him for sixteen days.

44. Richard J. Arnold, Account Book, vol. 6, May 22, 1827, and January 14, 1828, Arnold Papers.

45. Richard J. Arnold, Agreement with Overseer, 1841, Arnold-Screven Papers, passim.

46. Thomas S. Clay to Richard J. Arnold, September 29, 1837, Arnold Papers.

47. Gilbert Osofsky, *Puttin' on Ole Massa* (New York, 1969), 18–19.

48. Ibid., 19.

49. Richard J. Arnold to Thomas Butler King, July 15, 1841, Thomas Butler King

Papers, Southern Historical Collection, University of North Carolina Library, Chapel Hill.

50. Richard J. Arnold, Overseer Agreement for the years 1846, 1847, and 1848, dated December 9, 1845, Arnold-Screven Papers.

51. Richard J. Arnold, Plantation Journal, January 9, 1847, Arnold-Screven Papers.

52. Zachariah Allen to Richard J. Arnold, January 24 and April 19, 1831, Arnold Papers.

53. Richard J. Arnold, Account Book, vol. 8, April 15, 1848, Arnold Papers.

54. Ibid., April 21 and 28, 1848.

55. Ibid.

56. Ibid.

57. Eliza Harriet Allen to Richard J. Arnold, February 22, 1848, Arnold Papers.

58. Myers, *Children of Pride*, 1662–1663.

59. Richard J. Arnold, Account Book, vol. 8, January 15 and January 22, 1849, Arnold Papers.

60. Ulrich B. Phillips and James A. Glunt, eds., *Florida Plantation Records from the Papers of George Noble Jones* (St. Louis, Mo., 1927), 20–21. Because of the debts incurred by William Nuttall, Mary Jones's first husband, El Destino plantation was sold at a foreclosure auction in 1844, at which time George Noble Jones purchased it.

61. Ibid., 22.

62. Ibid., 235, 210–214.

63. Ibid., 21–22.

64. The most complete account of Welcome Arnold's life and times is to be found in a Brown University dissertation by Franklin Stuart Coyle, "Welcome Arnold (1745–1798), Providence Merchant: The Founding of an Enterprise" (1972). Welcome's son-in-law, Tristam Burges, also published a eulogistic overview, *A Memoir of Welcome Arnold* (Providence, 1850).

65. Richard J. Arnold, memorandum dated Spring 1842, "Directions for Planting Rice," Arnold-Screven Papers.

66. Ibid.

67. Genovese, *Roll, Jordan, Roll*, 353; see also pp. 353–365 for further discussion of the mammy's role.

68. Amos's birth date is computed from Arnold's slave list, but there is a discrepancy, since in the 1880 Census Amos lists himself as being sixty-six years old.

69. Richard J. Arnold, Account Book, vol. 7, May 25 and December 19, 1837, Arnold Papers.

70. Ibid., June 8, 1837. Phebe is listed as a "member" of the Arnold family, "consisting of self, wife, four children, Miss Cushing & servant Phebe."

71. Eliza Harriet Allen to Richard J. Arnold, December 31, 1841, Arnold Papers.

72. Richard J. Arnold, Instructions to Overseer, May 22, 1837, Arnold-Screven Papers.

73. Richard J. Arnold, Account Book, vol. 7, October 14, 1837, Arnold Papers.
74. Richard J. Arnold, Agreement with Overseer for years 1846, 1847, and 1848, Arnold-Screven Papers.
75. Richard J. Arnold, Instructions to Overseer, 1837, Arnold-Screven Papers.
76. Eliza Harriet Allen, "Journal," April 22, 1837, Allen Papers.
77. Ibid.
78. Ibid., April 23, 1837.
79. Ibid., April 9, 1837.
80. Quotation from Olmsted, *Journey*, 450; for a detailed history and analysis of the southern Afro-Baptist religion, see Mechal Sobel, *Trabelin' On: The Slave Journey to an Afro-Baptist Faith* (Westport, Conn., 1979), 139–217.
81. Samuel G. Arnold, *Address Delivered Before the Charitable Baptist Society on the One Hundredth Anniversary of the Opening of the First Baptist Church, Providence, R.I. for Public Worship, May 28th 1875* (Providence, 1875), 38.
82. Henry Melville King, comp., *Historical Catalogue of the Members of the First Baptist Church in Providence, Rhode Island* (Providence, 1908), 87. See also Arnold, *Address*, 19: "In 1838 the growth of the city having encroached on the shore between Fox and India Points, where the ordinance of baptism had formerly been administered, a baptistry was constructed at the cost of $605."
83. Arnold, *Address*, 19.
84. Irving H. Bartlett, *From Slave to Citizen: The Story of the Negro in Rhode Island* (Providence, 1954), 36.
85. For a discussion of the relationship of spirituals to the desire for freedom, see John W. Blassingame, *The Slave Community: Plantation Life in the Antebellum South*, rev. ed. (New York, 1979), 137–148.
86. Information about Magill is from Joseph Anderson, ed., *The Town and City of Waterbury, Connecticut from the Aboriginal Period to the Year Eighteen Hundred and Ninety-Five* (New Haven, 1896), 636–637; about Winn, Myers, *Children of Pride*, 1735.
87. Myers, *Children of Pride*, 1567.
88. Erskine Clarke, *Wrestlin' Jacob* (Atlanta, 1979), 12–15. For a more sympathetic account of Jones's dilemma, see Donald Mathews, "Charles Colcock Jones and the Southern Evangelical Crusade to Form a Biracial Community," *Journal of Southern History* 41, no. 3 (August 1975), 299–320. Even Mathews suggests, however, that Jones lacked the moral courage to renounce slaveholding and slavery.
89. Mathews, "Charles Colcock Jones," 318.
90. Clarke, *Wrestlin' Jacob*, 65.
91. Clay, *Detail of a Plan*, 7, 10.
92. Charles Colcock Jones, *A Catechism . . . for the Oral Instruction of Colored Persons*, as quoted in Andrew E. Murray, *Presbyterians and the Negro—A History* (Philadelphia, 1966), 58.
93. Eliza Harriet Allen, "Journal," April 11, 1837, Allen Papers.

94. Ibid.
95. Ibid., April 16, 1837.
96. Ibid., April 17, 1837.
97. Richard J. Arnold, Account Book, vol. 7, March 26, 1838, Arnold Papers.
98. Clay, *Detail of a Plan*, 16.
99. Clarke, *Wrestlin' Jacob*, 74, 168.
100. Jinny to Richard J. Arnold, October 21, 1838, Arnold Papers. Whether Jinny could read and write is not known, but the letter is signed with her name in the same handwriting as the rest. The question of whose penmanship appears in letters from slaves can never be adequately documented or proved. Even Amos Morel's letters reveal differences in handwriting, and we know that he could read and write.
101. Eliza Harriet Allen, "Journal," April 16, 1837, Allen Papers.
102. Jinny to Richard J. Arnold, October 21, 1838, Arnold Papers.
103. Julia Comstock Tolman to Frank Hagadorn, February 3, 1853, Hagadorn-Wells Papers, Rhode Island Historical Society Library, Providence. Emphasis in the original. "Christy's Minstrels" were first organized in 1842 by Edwin P. Christy (1815–1862). By the early 1850s they were at the height of their popularity and success, touring in America and England. They were instrumental in popularizing Stephen Foster's songs "Oh! Susannah" and "Old Folks at Home," the latter being first published under Christy's name in 1851. Julia Tolman was not given to ironic statements, but her underlining of the minstrel group's name emphasized the unintended irony that the slaves' singing was "equal" to a group of professional white singers dressed up with blackened faces to look like plantation slaves.
104. Louisa G. Arnold to her daughter Louisa (Mrs. Samuel G. Arnold), February 11, 1853, Arnold-Rogers Papers.
105. Ibid., February 18, 1853.

Chapter Three

Arnold's plantation journal is in the Arnold-Screven Papers, written in a fragile unruled volume with pages torn from both front and back. It is in Arnold's handwriting and covers the tasks set and accomplished at both Cherry Hill and White Hall as well as miscellaneous information about guests, weather, etc. At best, Arnold's punctuation and spelling is erratic and idiosyncratic with heavy use of hyphens, dashes, periods, and contractions. It would appear that Arnold is often working from notes, so that there are blank spaces where information about rice and cotton production was not readily available to him at the time of writing. Occasionally also he makes errors in dating entries. In transcribing the journal, we have tried to be as faithful as possible to the original.

1. The Maxwells and Hardens were friends, owners of plantations in the vicinity of

White Hall. J. P. Maxwell later moved to Florida, returning just before the outbreak of the war.

2. Amos Morel had been trained as a blacksmith and engineer in Savannah, returning to the plantation to oversee the steam engine. Eventually, he became not only a trusted servant but the watchman who greatly impressed Olmsted during his visit in 1853.

3. Distances between plantations were often great, and the Arnolds, like so many of their neighbors, kept open house. Thus, the Demeres, the Starrs, the Rogers family, the Pattersons, arrived to spend the day. Many others, however, made extended visits. The list includes family (their oldest daughter, Harriet, and son-in-law, William Brenton Greene, of New York City); clergymen, such as the Reverend Mr. Rogers, the Reverend Mr. Winn, and Dr. Carroll; business acquaintances, such as the Habershams and the Champions; close family friends like Mrs. George Noble Jones and her children.

4. Since his purchase of Cherry Hill in 1824, Arnold had been buying additional land so that eventually he owned 11,000 acres, including wood lots on the Canoochee River, pine lands, and old plantations. His goal was to achieve self-sufficiency.

5. Arnold often hired help off the plantation, particularly builders like Manvill and engineers like Lacklison as well as black men (free or slave) who had specialized skills.

6. The outbuildings at both plantations were numerous, if one is to judge from the journal and from Arnold's insurance policy on Cherry Hill (September 1860, Arnold Papers). His $5,500 policy covers the rice mill and thrashing machine, an elevator building with shafting and gearing, a sugarhouse, a brick engine house, a steam engine and boilers, a grist mill in the elevator building, a corn house, and a stable.

Chapter Four

1. Robert J. Cottrol, *The Afro-Yankees: Providence's Black Community in the Antebellum Era* (Westport, Conn., 1982), 55; see pp. 52–57 for a more detailed discussion of the riot. See also Howard P. Chudacoff and Theodore C. Hirt, "Social Turmoil and Governmental Reform in Providence, 1820–1832," *Rhode Island History* 31, no. 1 (February 1972), 21–31.

2. William G. McLoughlin, *Rhode Island: A Bicentennial History* (New York, 1978), 107–108.

3. Cottrol, *The Afro-Yankees*, 55.

4. Richard J. Arnold to Louisa G. Arnold, April 29, 1824, Arnold Papers.

5. Ibid. Louisa, who was pregnant with her first child, had stayed behind in Providence and needed Phebe during her approaching confinement.

6. Eliza Harriet Allen to Louisa G. Arnold, January 17, 1825, Arnold-Rogers Papers.

7. George M. Fredrickson, *The Black Image in the White Mind: The Debate on Afro-American Character and Destiny, 1817–1914* (New York, 1971), 11, 28.

8. Chudacoff and Hirt, "Social Turmoil," 25–26.

9. Ibid., 26.

10. Blodget, Dexter, and Carrington represented solid middle-class virtues with which the Allens and Arnolds identified, and it is not surprising that members of these families intermarried and continued to prosper as part of the Providence elite.

11. Newspaper copy of the 1831 Riot Committee Report, dated September 20, 1831, and found in the Zachariah Allen Papers, headed in Allen's handwriting "Account of the Riots in Providence."

12. Zachariah Allen to Richard J. Arnold, November 22, 1832, Arnold Papers. Two days later, South Carolina passed an ordinance of nullification, but any threat of civil war was averted when Calhoun and Clay worked out a tariff compromise the following year.

13. Eliza Harriet Allen to Richard J. Arnold, April 26, 1832, Arnold Papers.

14. Leonard L. Richards, *"Gentlemen of Property and Standing": Anti-Abolition Mobs in Jacksonian America* (New York, 1970), 3. Richards asserts that the northern anti-abolition mobs which broke up antislavery meetings, arrested abolitionists, and destroyed property were largely planned and organized by antiabolitionist "gentlemen of property and standing"—doctors, lawyers, merchants, bankers, etc. (p. 5).

15. Account of Providence Anti-Abolition Society meeting in *Providence Journal*, November 4, 1835.

16. U.S. Census, 1830, Providence, R.I., p. 35.

17. Eliza Harriet Allen to Richard J. Arnold, November 4, 1833, Arnold Papers.

18. *The Report and Proceedings of the First Annual Meeting of the Providence Anti-Slavery Society* (Providence, c. 1834), 6.

19. *Providence Journal*, November 4, 1835.

20. Ibid.

21. The Providence Anti-Abolition Society included such establishment figures as Walter Danforth, editor and joint owner of the *Providence Gazette;* Amos Denison Smith, cotton textile manufacturer and president of the Providence, Warren & Bristol Railroad; and William Blodget, Samuel Dexter, and Edward Carrington, all members of the 1831 riot fact-finding committee. Carrington, the most prominent of these business associates of Richard Arnold was one of Rhode Island's leading shipping merchants and cotton manufacturers, owning at one time twenty-six merchantmen and a couple of cotton mills, as well as being on the board of directors of several banks and insurance companies.

22. Richard J. Arnold, Account Book, vol. 7, September 7 and August 17, 1835, Arnold Papers.

23. *Newport Mercury*, September 19, 1835.

24. Benjamin Hazard was a partner of the Arnold family in the development of the Lyman Mill in North Providence (William R. Bagnall, *The Textile Industries of the United States* [Cambridge, Mass., 1893; reprint, New York, 1971], 1:550–551).

25. *Newport Mercury*, September 19, 1835. Italics in the original.

26. "Declaration of the National Anti-Slavery Convention of 1833," passim, as published by the Providence Anti-Slavery Society as part of its statement of "Abolition Principles," c. 1835. Boldface type and capitals in the original.

27. "Abolition Principles," Providence Anti-Slavery Society, 4–5.

28. *Proceedings of the Rhode Island Anti-Slavery Convention* (Providence, 1836), 2.

29. Ibid., 17–59, passim.

30. Ibid., 38.

31. Eliza Harriet Allen to Richard J. Arnold, February 18, 1836, Arnold Papers.

32. Ibid., 28.

33. Arnold was often asked by neighbors to oblige them in the purchase of Negro cloth in the North. One such request came to Arnold through a third party: "Mr Stiles is about commencing his settlement at Brisbane   When I saw him a few weeks since he desired me to request you to procure for him One Hundred Yards of Negro cloth such as you purchase for you own negroes" (D. M. Winston to Richard J. Arnold, August 21, 1833, Arnold Papers).

34. Bartlett, *From Slave to Citizen*, 39–40.

35. Marvin E. Gettleman, *The Dorr Rebellion: A Study in American Radicalism, 1833–1849* (New York, 1973), 60.

36. Ibid., 63–64.

37. Ibid., 90.

38. Zachariah Allen, "An Account of the Rebellion, 1842," contains insert of newspaper account of his talk to the Rhode Island Historical Society, Allen Papers, 115 and 115½.

39. Ibid., 134.

40. Arnold had been appointed acting adjutant general of the state militia as early as 1822 (Governor William C. Gibbs to Richard J. Arnold, November 23, 1822, Arnold Papers).

41. Richard J. Arnold, memorandums and bills dealing with provisioning Rhode Island forces during Dorr War, 1842, Arnold Papers.

42. Hon. Tristam Burges, Sr., to Richard J. Arnold, June 27, 1842, Arnold Papers.

43. Zachariah Allen, "An Account of the Rebellion, 1842," 151–152, Allen Papers.

44. In October 1843, Thomas Dorr voluntarily returned to Providence and was immediately arrested and jailed. Tried for treason the following spring in Newport County, where conservatives dominated the court and the jury, he was

shown no mercy and was found guilty. The sentence handed down ordered that "the said Thomas W. Dorr be imprisoned in the State prison at Providence in the county of Providence, for the term of his natural life, and there be kept at hard labor in separate confinement." The severity of the sentence, including a strict adhrence to the provision for solitary confinement, led to a counter-reaction of sympathy for him and a movement for clemency to obtain his release from prison. It took another year and the election of Governor Charles Jackson, who had campaigned on a "liberation" platform, for Dorr to be released from prison in 1845. His liberation was the work of many individuals, including some of his opponents and his family. But perhaps the most curious effort to obtain Dorr's release from prison was the private initiative of his uncle Zachariah Allen, who, on June 26, 1844, one year after Dorr's second attempt to gain control of the state government by military action, wrote to Governor James Fenner suggesting that his nephew be granted amnesty. It was not the expected plea of a relative for mercy but rather a devastating indictment of the man and his politics: after first agreeing with Governor Fenner's opinion of Dorr's "nefarious conduct" and "deeming his sentence perfectly just," Allen suggested that Dorr's "obstinate turn" of mind, his "strangeness" of conduct toward his relatives and parents, his "unsettled state of mind" which has made him unfit "for any regular business, like other men who have had the advantages of education, which he has enjoyed," were evidence of insanity and therefore he was not responsible for his actions. To Zachariah Allen, only a madman would betray his class (Zachariah Allen to Governor James Fenner, June 26, 1844, Allen Papers).

45. Arnold returned $6,000 to the treasury on September 13, 1842. He was able to return $3,125.03 to Governor King on October 7, 1843, when he finally closed the books on the Dorr War. It is obvious that the charter government had planned on a much longer and more expensive campaign against the Dorrites (Arnold Papers).

46. Arnold's fellow members on the salary committee epitomized, as was often true of handpicked members, the establishment. Burgess (1779–1856) was a Phi Beta Kappa graduate of the class of 1800 at Brown and had made his reputation as a lawyer and judge in Providence. Brown (1797–1874), who descended from the Browns who made their fortune in the slave and China trades and gave their name to the university, was a Phi Beta Kappa graduate with the class of 1816, receiving also an A.M. and an LL.D. (1852). His crowning achievement was the founding of the John Carter Brown Library to house his collection of incunabula and manuscripts. He was also a merchant and cotton manufacturer.

47. The Reverend Francis Wayland, an ordained Baptist minister, was president of Brown from 1827 to 1855, assuming from 1834 to 1855 the additional role of professor of moral and intellectual philosophy.

48. Undated document (1842), Arnold Papers. Upon reconsideration of the salary

issue, referred back to committee by the Corporation, the committee made minor adjustments in salaries subject to enrollments, but since this was a period of declining enrollments at a time when professors' salaries were largely paid out of student fees, the reconsideration was meaningless.

49. Walter C. Bronson, *The History of Brown University, 1764–1914* (Providence, 1914; reprint, New York, 1971), 259.

50. Richard Fuller and Francis Wayland, *Domestic Slavery Considered as a Scriptural Institution* (Boston, 1847), 35.

51. Ibid., 43–44.

52. Ibid., 222, 223.

53. As quoted in William Goodell, *Slavery and Anti-Slavery* (New York, 1852; reprint, New York, 1968), 503.

54. Fuller and Wayland, *Domestic Slavery*, 251.

55. Ibid., 253–254.

56. Richard J. Arnold, Account Book, vol. 8, April 21 and May 1, 1848, Arnold Papers.

57. Ibid., May 25, 1848.

58. Ibid., October 31, 1848. Arnold was compensated $7,054.81 for principal only, "nothing else having been allowed" (ibid.).

59. Ibid., June 1, 1848. Providence eventually annexed large tracts of land in the town of Cranston as it expanded to the south.

60. Ibid., June 5, 1848.

61. Ibid., May 10 through May 24, 1848, passim.

62. Louisa G. Arnold to Richard J. Arnold, August 13, 1848, Arnold Papers.

63. Ibid., August 15, 1848, Arnold Papers.

64. Richard J. Arnold, Account Book, vol. 8, October 2, 1848, Arnold Papers.

65. Samuel G. Arnold to his mother (Mrs. Samuel G. Arnold, Sr.), May 12, 1847, Arnold-Rogers Papers.

66. Eliza Harriet Allen to Louisa G. Arnold, March 31, 1842, Arnold Papers.

67. Zachariah and Eliza Harriet Allen to Richard J. Arnold, January 21, 1843, Arnold Papers. Mrs. Allen informed her brother that she had given Andrew Robeson, Jr., the message inviting them to stay at White Hall.

68. Eliza Harriet Allen to Richard J. Arnold, January 30, 1838, Arnold Papers.

69. "John H. Clarke," *Biographical Cyclopedia of Representative Men of Rhode Island* (Providence, 1881), 1:199.

70. "Reverend Edward B. Hall," *Biographical Cyclopedia*, 1:154–155.

71. "Amos Chafee Barstow," *Biographical Cyclopedia*, 2:345.

72. Clipping from *Providence Journal*, August 27, 1847, pasted in Louisa (Mrs. Samuel G. Arnold) Arnold's scrapbook, 1:5, Arnold-Rogers Papers.

73. Eliza Harriet Allen to Richard J. Arnold, February 22, 1848, Arnold Papers.

74. Richard J. Arnold, Account Book, vol. 8, May 3 and October 17, 1848, Arnold Papers.

75. Ibid., September 22 and 30 and October 23, 1848.
76. Ibid., October 27, 1848.
77. Arnold's inventory of his library, October 26, 1847, Arnold Papers.
78. Zachariah Allen to Richard J. Arnold, February 15, 1841, Arnold Papers.
79. Zachariah Allen, *The Science of Mechanics* (Providence, 1829), ii.
80. Zachariah Allen, *The Practical Tourist* (Providence, 1832), 1:332.
81. *Proceedings of the Rhode Island Anti-Slavery Society*, 86.
82. Fuller and Wayland, *Domestic Slavery*, 170, 48. Emphasis in original.
83. Records of the Rhode Island Chapter of the Daughters of the American Revolution, Rhode Island Historical Society. The Arnold Bible was purchased in 1965 from a used-book dealer as a rare book by Russell E. Bidlock of Ann Arbor, Michigan, who sent a transcript of the Arnold genealogy to the DAR. Mary Cornelia Arnold Talbot was a founding member of the Rhode Island Chapter.

Chapter Five

1. Arnold allowed trusted slaves to keep guns and to hunt on the land.
2. Arnold bought produce and meat not only from his own slaves to supplement the diet but also from slaves on neighboring plantations.
3. As in the first section of the journal, the Arnolds are seen in constant motion, visiting neighbors and Savannah, and being visited by the Pynchons, Rogerses, Demeres, Footmans, Pennys, Winns.
4. Arnold's hospitality was also well known among his northern friends, who often stopped at White Hall (as did Olmsted) while traveling south to escape the northern winter. Thus, New Yorkers like Sam Howland, Peleg Hall, Mott Francis, and Marion McAllister and Bostonians like William Dexter and George Timmins stayed with the Arnolds. All these men also had connections in Newport, particularly Francis and McAllister, who were cousins of Julia Ward Howe.
5. Arnold is opening negotiations to buy Sedgefield plantation from Edward Pynchon.
6. Among the Arnold visitors are friends who suffer from consumption and have come south to be cured of the disease. The nursemaid Catharine and young Carroll are examples of this common medical fallacy.

Chapter Six

1. Samuel G. Arnold to Richard J. Arnold, March 29, 1845, Arnold Papers.
2. C. W. Greene to Richard J. Arnold, March 12, 1846, Arnold Papers.
3. McLoughlin, *Rhode Island*, 139.
4. Bartlett, *From Slave to Citizen*, 54.
5. Ibid.
6. Dorothy Orr, *A History of Education in Georgia* (Chapel Hill, 1950), 412.

7. Ibid., 171.
8. Elizabeth Brown Pryor, "An Anomalous Person: The Northern Tutor in Plantation Society, 1773–1860," *Journal of Southern History* 47, no. 3 (August 1981), 389–392.
9. Richard J. Arnold, Account Book, vol. 8, March 28, 1848, Arnold Papers.
10. Richard J. Arnold to John P. Hines, May 2, 1843, Arnold Papers.
11. Maria J. McIntosh, *Woman in America* (New York, 1850), 116, 118.
12. Brown University Archives. Since Olmsted talked to two of Arnold's sons, according to *A Journey to the Seaboard Slave States*, he must have met Thomas and William Eliot.
13. Thomas Arnold to Richard J. Arnold, April 24, 1856, Arnold Papers. Sears himself went to Germany in 1833 for postgraduate study, having graduated Phi Beta Kappa from Brown University in 1825.
14. Thomas Arnold to Richard J. Arnold, July 18, 1856, Arnold Papers.
15. Thomas Arnold to Richard J. Arnold, July 3, 1856, Arnold Papers.
16. Richard J. Arnold, Account Book, vol. 8, November 28, 1856, Arnold Papers.
17. Richard J. Arnold to Richard J. Arnold, Jr. (copy of letter in Richard J. Arnold's handwriting), December 26, 1856, Arnold Papers.
18. Ibid.
19. Richard J. Arnold, Jr., to Richard J. Arnold, July 21, 1857, Arnold Papers.
20. Richard J. Arnold, Account Book, vol. 8, February 17 and July 3, 1857, Arnold Papers.
21. Louisa G. Arnold to her daughter Louisa (Mrs. Samuel G. Arnold), December 16, 1852, Arnold-Rogers Papers.
22. Richard J. Arnold, Account Book, vol. 8, April 29, 1853, Arnold Papers.
23. William E. Tolman, "Can the Institution of Domestic Slavery be defended on the principles of Political Economy?" September 5, 1849, Brown University Archives.
24. Julia C. Tolman to Frank Hagadorn, February 3, 1853, Hagadorn-Wells Papers.
25. Ibid.
26. Clay, *Detail of a Plan*, 4–5. Although there is no indication that Arnold ever formally adopted the plan propounded by his friend and neighbor, he did practice most of the suggestions incorporated in it.
27. Ibid., 9.
28. Richard J. Arnold, Account Book, vol. 8, March 28, 1855, Arnold Papers.
29. Phillips and Glunt, *Florida Plantation Records*, 28–29.
30. Olmsted, *Journey*, 427.
31. Ibid.
32. Richard J. Arnold, Journal C (1831–1838), vol. 7, May 5, 1837, Arnold Papers.
33. Amos Morel to Richard J. Arnold, August 22, 1841, Arnold Papers.
34. Richard J. Arnold, Cash Book C (1829–1842), vol. 10, October 16, 1841, Arnold Papers.

35. Olmsted, *Journey*, 427.
36. Ibid.
37. Zachariah Allen to Richard J. Arnold, December 29, 1843, Arnold-Screven Papers.
38. Amos Morel to Richard J. Arnold, July 18, 1843, Arnold Papers.
39. Richard J. Arnold, Ledger B (1825–1873), vol. 11, August 11, 1844, Arnold Papers.
40. Amos Morel to Richard J. Arnold, August 29, 1845, Arnold Papers.
41. Ibid.
42. Olmsted, *Journey*, 426.
43. Amos Morel to Richard J. Arnold, June 20, 1852, Arnold Papers.
44. Olmsted, *Journey*, 438.
45. Richard J. Arnold, Account Book, vol. 8, December 6, 1852, Arnold Papers.
46. Louisa G. Arnold to her daughter Louisa (Mrs. Samuel G. Arnold), February 18, 1853, Arnold-Rogers Papers. Between 1844 and 1860 Amos Morel married four times. What happened to his first wife, Mary, and the names and fate of his second and third wives are not known.
47. Amos Morel to Richard J. Arnold, June 22, 1852, Arnold Papers.
48. Charles W. Ferguson to Richard J. Arnold, July 16, 1852, Arnold-Screven Papers.
49. Amos Morel to Richard J. Arnold, June 2, 1853, Arnold Papers.
50. Ibid.
51. Amos Morel to Richard J. Arnold, August 28, 1856, and July 29, 1858, Arnold Papers. See the first entry in Arnold's plantation journal, where Carpenter Peter is reported as being on good behavior.
52. Amos Morel to Richard J. Arnold, July 29, 1858, Arnold Papers.
53. Charles W. Ferguson to Richard J. Arnold, March 24, 1859, Arnold Papers.
54. Amos Morel to Richard J. Arnold, July 16, 1860, Arnold Papers.
55. Charles W. Ferguson to Richard J. Arnold, July 16, 1852, Arnold Papers.
56. Agreement with Overseer for the years 1846, 1847, and 1848, December 9, 1845, Arnold-Screven Papers. It was recognized generally by the planters of the area that it was good medical practice to remove the slaves from the swampy rice fields to the drier pine land of the plantation during an epidemic.
57. Richard J. Arnold, Instructions to Overseer (J. Swanston), May 22, 1837, Arnold-Screven Papers.
58. Richard J. Arnold, Mr. Sanford's Instructions for the year 1839, Arnold-Screven Papers.
59. Charles W. Ferguson to Richard J. Arnold, July 7, 1849, Arnold Papers.
60. Phillips and Glunt, *Florida Plantation Records*, 577–578.
61. Richard J. Arnold, Account Book, vol. 8, November 20, 1852, Arnold Papers.
62. Olmsted, *Journey*, 423–424.
63. Clay, *Detail of a Plan*, 14–15.

64. Letter of John Evans to George Noble Jones, July 30, 1852, in Phillips and Glunt, *Florida Plantation Records*, 73.
65. Ibid., 90–91. D. N. Moxley to George Noble Jones, August 6, 1854.
66. Ibid., 96. John Evans to George Noble Jones, dated autumn of 1854 by Phillips; original letter undated.
67. Ibid., 110–111. John Evans to George Noble Jones, October 18, 1854.
68. Kenneth M. Stampp, *The Peculiar Institution* (New York, 1956), 296. According to Peter H. Wood in *Black Majority: Negroes in Colonial South Carolina from 1670 Through the Stono Rebellion* (New York, 1974), Africans were less likely to suffer from malaria than whites: "The immunity among slaves was partial, but it was also heritable, passing from one generation of Negroes to the next." He attributes this partial immunity to the presence of sickle-cell hemoglobin which can produce sickle-cell anemia but which also increases resistance to malaria (p. 88). Todd L. Savitt in *Medicine and Slavery* (Urbana, 1978) substantiates Wood's finding (see pp. 8–35). Stampp, however, flatly states, "The belief that Negroes were practically immune to malaria was altogether incorrect, as ante-bellum doctors and slaveholders knew all too well. . . . Malaria may have been somewhat less severe and less often fatal among Negroes than among whites, but even this is uncertain" (p. 300). Inherited partial immunity or not, Henry Ford, who bought White Hall in 1927, took no chances with the descendants of the Ogeechee River plantation residents, white or black. He impartially sprayed the swamps of Richmond-on-Ogeechee and Cherry Hill plantations to kill the mosquitoes, knowing that infected female mosquitoes tended to be color-blind.
69. Matilda Harden to Richard J. Arnold, July 19, 1834, Arnold Papers.
70. Richard J. Arnold, Account Book, vol. 7, April 10, 1835, Arnold Papers.
71. Ibid., August 17, 1835.
72. Dr. T. P. Charlton to Richard J. Arnold, September 10, 1835, Arnold Papers; italics his.
73. Richard J. Arnold, Account Book, vol. 7, November 3, 1835, Arnold Papers.
74. Olmsted, *Journey*, 418.
75. Charles W. Ferguson to Richard J. Arnold, July 7, 1849, Arnold Papers.
76. Stampp, *Peculiar Institution*, 308.
77. Ibid., 311.
78. C. W. Greene to Richard J. Arnold, April 9, 1845, Arnold Papers.
79. Zachariah Allen, *Solar Light and Heat* (New York, 1879), 231.
80. Louisa G. Arnold to her daughter Louisa (Mrs. Samuel G. Arnold), November 26, 1852, Arnold-Rogers Papers.
81. A contemporary of Richard Arnold's brother, Samuel, Samuel Bridgham was a fellow member of the board of trustees of Brown University and since 1828 had served as its chancellor. Joseph Bridgham was nearly twenty years younger than Arnold, but his sister Julia had recently married Arnold's old friend George Curtis, a fellow member of the committee investigating the 1831 riot in Provi-

dence and currently a director of the Manufacturers Mutual Fire Insurance Company that Zachariah Allen had recently founded.

82. Joseph Bridgham to Richard J. Arnold, February 26, 1836, Arnold Papers; italics his.

83. Eliza Harriet Allen, *Journal*, March 26–May 15, 1837, passim, Allen Papers.

84. Olmsted, Yeoman letter no. 23, *New York Daily Times*, June 11, 1853.

85. Eliza Harriet Allen to Richard J. Arnold, February 11, 1840, Arnold Papers. Timothy Green was born March 16, 1806, in Malden, Massachusetts, and although he was a lawyer in New York City, he had close connections with Providence. He married Cornelia Elizabeth Arnold, Richard Arnold's niece, on October 20, 1835, and in the same year became a trustee of Brown University. At the time of his death, he was on the board of directors of the American Bible Society.

86. Cornelia Arnold Greene to Richard J. Arnold, March 10, 1842, Arnold Papers. The remains of the Greenes (as well as the Samuel G. Arnolds) eventually came to rest at Swan Point Cemetery in the Arnold plot.

87. Richard J. Arnold, Instructions to Overseer, A. M. Sanford, 1839 and 1840, Arnold-Screven Papers.

88. It is possible that she ran away or was sold, but the most likely explanation is that she died. Business records for this period have not survived.

89. Louisa G. Arnold to her daughter Louisa (Mrs. Samuel G. Arnold), December 16, 1852, Arnold-Rogers Papers.

90. Eliza Harriet Allen to Richard J. Arnold, January 24, 1852, Arnold Papers.

91. Louisa G. Arnold to her daughter Louisa (Mrs. Samuel G. Arnold), December 16, 1852, Arnold-Rogers Papers.

92. See Blassingame, *Slave Community*, 303–304, for a discussion of the Sambo stereotype.

93. Louisa G. Arnold to her daughter Louisa (Mrs. Samuel G. Arnold), December 16, 1852, Arnold-Rogers Papers. Sambo, age twenty-two, was presumably Daddy John's grandson, not a stereotype.

94. Louisa G. Arnold to her daughter Louisa (Mrs. Samuel G. Arnold), December 28, 1852, Arnold-Rogers Papers.

95. Ibid.

Chapter Seven

1. The route back and forth to Providence varied for the Arnolds. They could travel by boat, taking the Fall River Line from Providence to New York, visiting relatives and friends in the city, and then embarking for Wilmington and either going by stage and railroad or by boat to Charleston, where again they might remain for a few days, leaving for Savannah by boat.

2. Eventually, Arnold agreed to Ferguson's terms.

3. During the period covered by this section of the journal there were three slave marriages and a number of births.

4. The position of the watchman was an important one on plantations like Arnold's, since Arnold liked to keep control over his slaves and over his overseer. When Amos Morel was made watchman (still during Ferguson's tenure), Arnold was able to have the best of the bargain because Amos's loyalty was never in question and he could be counted on to keep Arnold in touch with what the overseer was or was not doing.

5. The Ogeechee, a tidal river, not only provided easy transportation to the Savannah market but also was a rich source of food. In keeping with Arnold's practice of using every possible asset, it is not surprising that he leased out the fishing rights to his stretch of the river.

6. Rice culture is a particularly labor-intensive activity. Arnold, in seeking to renew canals, ditches, and squares that had fallen into disrepair, set his slaves and his overseer an incredibly difficult job.

7. Among the buildings at White Hall was obviously a large barn to store the cotton and rice produced on the plantation.

8. As with most of his planting, Arnold kept records and tried to compare methods of cane and rice culture to guarantee the best results.

9. Robert Hale Ives, a manufacturer and entrepreneur allied to the Brown family, was a Providence as well as Newport neighbor.

Chapter Eight

1. Richard J. Arnold, Account Book, vol. 8, August 1, 1857, Arnold Papers.

2. Richard J. Arnold, Account Book, vol. 8, April 17 and August 1, 1857, Arnold Papers.

3. Clipping pasted in Louisa Arnold's (Mrs. Samuel G. Arnold) scrapbook, 1:48, Arnold-Rogers Papers.

4. Ibid.

5. Conservative Republicans in Rhode Island were formerly members of the old Whig party who did not want to join the Democratic party but who were opposed to the more radical Republicans led by Seth Padelford.

6. Richard J. Arnold, Account Book, vol. 8, August 10, 1857, Arnold Papers.

7. Richard J. Arnold, slave list, January 1, 1856, Arnold Papers.

8. B. W. Pearce, *Matters and Men in Newport As I Have Known Them, 1858–1891* (Newport, R.I., 1891), pt. 2, p. 5.

9. Olmsted and his firm were landscape architects for many of the Newport mansions, including Chateau-sur-Mer (built for William S. Wetmore in 1852 and enlarged by Richard Morris Hunt in 1870–1874), and the Breakers, built for Cornelius Vanderbilt in 1895.

10. Carl Bridenbaugh provides a detailed study of the southern enclave in colonial

Newport in his two articles "Colonial Newport as a Summer Resort," *Rhode Island Historical Society Collections* 26, no. 1 (January 1933), 1–33, and "Charlestonians at Newport, 1767–1775," *South Carolina Historical and Genealogical Magazine* 41, no. 2 (April 1940), 43–47.

11. Eliza Clay to Richard J. Arnold, July 5, 1830, Arnold Papers; italics hers.

12. Eliza Harriet Allen to Richard J. Arnold, July 17 and July 23, 1832, Arnold Papers.

13. Trinity Church Records, Newport Historical Society, Newport, R.I. Mary Nuttall, Mary Jones's daughter by her marriage to William B. Nuttall, married George Wymberley Jones, who was George Noble Jones's uncle. George Wymberley Jones later changed his name to Wymberley de Renne.

14. George Noble Jones to George J. Kollock, August 15, 1842, in Edith Duncan Johnston, ed., "The Kollock Letters, 1799–1850," *Georgia Historical Quarterly* 21, no. 4 (December 1947), pt. 6, pp. 311–312.

15. Ibid., July 12, 1844, in Johnston, "Kollock Letters," *Georgia Historical Quarterly* 32, no. 1 (March 1948), pt. 7, p. 39. The hotel built opposite Jones's cottage was the Ocean House.

16. Ibid., October 6, 1849, in Johnston, "Kollock Letters," *Georgia Historical Quarterly* 32, no. 2 (June 1948), pt. 8, p. 131.

17. Samuel G. Arnold to Richard J. Arnold, September 25, 1843, Arnold Papers. Sam Arnold handled the delicate negotiations with Miss Mumford.

18. C. W. Greene to Richard J. Arnold, August 12, 1845, Arnold Papers.

19. The Robesons, Izards, Mrs. Harper, and R. H. Ives also built cottages in Newport.

20. Henry James, Jr., "The Sense of Newport," in *The American Scene* (New York, 1967), 211.

21. Mary Edith Powel (MEP), "Newport Worthies," in volume of memoirs, Newport Historical Society.

22. James, *American Scene*, 218.

23. J. Walton Ferguson, *Kingscote* (Newport, R.I., 1977), 14–15.

24. Zachariah Allen, Diary, September 13, 1855, Allen Papers.

25. Frederic Bancroft, *Slave Trading in the Old South* (Baltimore, 1931; reprint, New York, 1959), 224–233.

26. Katharine Prescott Wormeley, "Reminiscences of Newport in the Fifties," *Newport History* 41, no 129 (Winter 1968), 7.

27. Ibid., 11. The ladies must have been under pressure when Mrs. William Wetmore, a member, ran away with the Irish coachman. For details of Mrs. Wetmore's escapade, see Walter Barrett, *The Old Merchants of New York City* (New York, 1864), 299.

28. Wormeley, "Reminiscences," 7.

29. "By Laws and Standing Rules," *Annual Report of the Newport Reading Room*

(Newport, R.I., 1858), 10. Among the newspapers to which they subscribed was the *Savannah Republican*.

30. Arthur Tuckerman, *History of the Newport Reading Room* (Newport, R.I., 1954), 3, 4.

31. Ibid., 21–22.

32. Two books have recently been published describing the activities of the Secret Six: Jeffrey Rossbach, *Ambivalent Conspirators: John Brown, the Secret Six, and a Theory of Slave Violence* (Philadelphia, 1982), and Otto J. Scott, *The Secret Six: John Brown and the Abolitionist Movement* (New York, 1979).

33. Clarence L. Mohr, *On the Threshold of Freedom: Masters and Slaves in Civil War Georgia* (Athens, Ga., 1986), 7.

34. Ibid., 6.

35. Mary Cornelia Arnold to Thomas Arnold, August 24, 1859, Arnold Papers. Samuel Arnold's speech, as did Dr. David King's, celebrated the Revolutionary War and the capture of the British ship *Gaspee* on June 9, 1772, when "the first blood shed in the great struggle crimsoned the waters of Narragansett bay" (George C. Mason, *Reunion of the Sons and Daughters of Newport, Rhode Island* [Newport, R.I., 1859], 108). The plot for capturing the *Gaspee* was planned in a room of Sabin Tavern, which was later purchased by Welcome Arnold as the Arnold family home in Providence.

36. Charles A. Battle, *Negroes on the Island of Rhode Island* (Newport, R.I., 1932), 30.

37. Lawrence Grossman, "George T. Downing and Desegregation of Rhode Island Public Schools, 1855–1866," *Rhode Island History* 36, no. 4 (November 1977), 100.

38. Ibid.

39. Battle, *Negroes*, 21. The Sea Girt Hotel was gutted by a fire on December 16, 1860, which was deliberately set. Downing rebuilt his establishment the following spring.

40. Grossman, "George T. Downing," 101.

41. Clipping from *The Evening Press*, February 21, 1860, pasted in Louisa Arnold's (Mrs. Samuel G. Arnold) scrapbook, 1:81, Arnold-Rogers Papers.

42. Grossman, "George T. Downing," 104. Downing effectively argued against the "separate but equal" concept by protesting as a *taxpayer* that the *cost* of a truly equal school system for blacks would be prohibitive and wasteful. See James M. McPherson, *The Negro's Civil War* (New York, 1965), 266–268.

43. *Newport Daily News*, September 7, 1859.

44. Ibid.

45. Edith Wharton, *A Backward Glance* (London, 1972), 82–85.

46. Mary Cornelia Arnold to Samuel Arnold, March 1, 1860, Arnold Papers; italics hers.

47. Ibid.

48. Zachariah Allen, Diary, July 6, 1860, Allen Papers. The Parrish house was later owned by the Astors and was renamed Beechwood.

49. Ibid., October 13 and 17, 1860.

50. Ibid., October 20, 1860.

51. Mary Rotch Hunter to Lieutenant Charles Hunter, July 2, 1861, Hunter Family Papers, Newport Historical Society, Newport, R.I. (hereafter cited as the Hunter Papers).

52. Richard J. Arnold, memorandum, February 25, 1861, Arnold Papers.

53. Richard J. Arnold to Luly Arnold, March 29, 1861, Arnold-Appleton Papers, Southern Historical Collection, University of North Carolina Library, Chapel Hill.

54. William Brenton Greene to William Talbot, May 7, 1861, Arnold Papers.

55. Handwritten copy of deed, Richard J. Arnold to Thomas C. Arnold, May 7, 1861, Arnold Papers. As of April 25, 1860, Arnold held 201 slaves.

56. Zachariah Allen, Diary, April 14, 1861, and September 15, 1862, Allen Papers.

57. Mary Rotch Hunter to Lieutenant Charles Hunter, June 11, 1861, Hunter Papers.

58. Willie Lee Rose, *Rehearsal for Reconstruction: The Port Royal Experiment* (New York, 1967), 14.

59. Kathryn T. Abbey, "Documents Relating to El Destino and Chemonie Plantations, Middle Florida, 1828–1868," *Florida Historical Quarterly* 7, no. 1 (January 1929), pt. 1, p. 193.

60. Ferguson, *Kingscote*, 16. Sarah Fenwick Gardiner owned slaves in Jefferson County jointly with her brother and sister.

61. James, *American Scene*, 223.

62. Mary Rotch Hunter to Lieutenant Charles Hunter, July 29 and June 16, 1861, Hunter Papers.

63. John T. Morse, *Thomas Sargent Perry* (Boston, 1929), 8. Mrs. Porter returned to Louisiana in 1864 in order to sell Oak Lawn, her plantation.

64. Mary Rotch Hunter to Lieutenant Charles Hunter, June 16, 1861, Hunter Papers.

65. Harriott Middleton to her cousin Susan Middleton, January 24, 1862, "The Middleton Correspondence, 1861–1865," ed. Isabella Middleton Leland, *South Carolina Historical Magazine* 63, no. 1 (January 1962), 37.

66. Mary Rotch Hunter to Lieutenant Charles Hunter, June 16, 1861, Hunter Papers.

67. Harriott Middleton to her cousin Susan Middleton, January 24, 1862, "The Middleton Correspondence."

68. Samuel G. Arnold to Luly Arnold, December 5, 1869, Arnold-Appleton Papers.

69. Harriott Middleton to her cousin Susan Middleton, January 24, 1862, "The Middleton Correspondence."

70. *Rhode Island Adjutant General's Report, 1865*, 2:707.

71. Ibid.

72. Ibid., 708.

73. Henry James, Sr., "The Social Significance of Our Institutions," in *Henry James, Senior: A Selection of His Writings*, ed. Giles Gunn (Chicago, 1974), 106.

74. Ibid., 118.

75. Mary Rotch Hunter to Lieutenant Charles Hunter, July 7, 1861, Hunter Papers.

76. Ibid., July 27, 1861.

77. Ibid.

78. Ibid., September 22, 1861.

79. Ibid., December 17 and 18, 1861.

80. Ibid., July 29, 1861.

81. Clippings from *Providence Journal*, August 9 and 21, 1861, pasted in Louisa Arnold's (Mrs. Samuel G. Arnold) scrapbook, 1:114, 115, Arnold-Rogers Papers.

82. Ibid., 119. Flyer inserted in front of page. Boldface type, italics, and capital letters in the original.

83. Harriott Middleton to Mrs. David King, n.d., King Family Papers, Newport Historical Society, Newport, R.I. (hereafter cited as King Papers).

84. William S. Patten to Richard J. Arnold, August 30, 1861, Arnold Papers.

85. Henry James, Jr., "Notes of a Son and Brother," in *Autobiography*, ed. Frederick W. Dupee (London, 1956), 415–416.

86. Wormeley, "Reminiscences," 9.

87. Mary Rotch Hunter to Lieutenant Charles Hunter, June 6, 1862, and September 22, 1861, Hunter Papers.

88. Richard J. Arnold, Account Book, vol. 9, October 7, 1862, Arnold Papers.

89. Memo dated June 16, 1863, Arnold Papers.

90. Richard J. Arnold, Account Book, vol. 9, June 27, 1863; October 23, 1862; July 1864; and November 5, 1864, Arnold Papers.

91. Zachariah Allen, Diary, September 27, 1862, Allen Papers.

92. Ibid., May 23, 1863.

93. James, "Notes of a Son and Brother," 423.

94. Abbey, "Documents Relating to El Destino and Chemonie Plantations," pt. 4 (October 1929), 80.

95. Luis F. Emilio, *A Brave Black Regiment: History of the Fifty-Fourth Regiment of Massachusetts Volunteer Infantry, 1863–1865* (Boston, 1894; reprint, New York, 1968), 41–44.

96. Richard J. Arnold, Account Book, vol. 9, December 2, 1863, Arnold Papers.

97. Ibid., May 9, 1864.

98. Myers, *Children of Pride*, 1619–1620.

99. Richard J. Arnold, Account Book, vol. 9, Spring, 1864, passim.
100. Lieutenant F. A. Barnard to Richard J. Arnold, July 23, 1864, Arnold Papers.
101. Richard J. Arnold, Account Book, vol. 9, August 13, 1864, Arnold Papers.
102. James, "Notes of a Son and Brother," 421–422.
103. Clipping pasted in Louisa Arnold's (Mrs. Samuel G. Arnold) scrapbook,
     1:156. EANY is an acronym for Eliza Arnold of New York.
104. Thomas C. Arnold to Richard J. Arnold, November 23, 1864, Arnold Papers.
105. Ibid.
106. Myers, *Children of Pride*, 1471. For Brailsford's wartime activities, see Mohr,
     On the Threshold of Freedom, 79.
107. Thomas C. Arnold to Richard J. Arnold, November 23, 1864, Arnold Papers.
108. Ibid.
109. Ibid.
110. Colonel George S. Acker, Ninth Michigan Volunteer Cavalry Regiment, De-
     cember 11, 1864, in *The War of the Rebellion: A Compilation of the Official Records*
     (Washington, 1893), vol. 44, ser. 1, p. 97.
111. William T. Sherman, *The Memoirs of General William T. Sherman* (Bloomington,
     Ind. 1957), 2:202.
112. James, "Notes of a Son and Brother," 468.
113. "Fort McAllister," brochure, Georgia Department of Natural Resources, n.d.
114. Samuel G. Arnold to Secretary of War, January 6, 1865, Arnold Papers.
     Earlier, Sam had urged Richard Arnold to go by himself to what was, after all,
     a war zone: "I do not think Aunt L. ought to go with you. Mr. Magill, who
     dined with us on Tuesday is the very best man I know of; and he is going out
     to Bryan in Feb. anyhow. As to Aunt, she is too nervous and unstrung. She
     would be likely to get herself into trouble and you too." But Louisa Arnold
     was not to be denied the chance to see her sons after an absence of almost four
     years; and by January 6, there was no question of leaving her behind. (Copy of
     a letter from Samuel G. Arnold to Richard J. Arnold, December 23, 1864,
     Arnold-Rogers Papers.)
115. Hon. C. A. Dana to Samuel G. Arnold, January 6, 1865, Arnold Papers.
116. William Eliot Arnold to Richard J. Arnold, January 12, 1865, Arnold Papers.
117. Samuel G. Arnold to Senator John Sherman, January 15, 1865, Arnold
     Papers. Senator Sherman's appended note is dated January 17, 1865.
118. Hon. Francis J. Lippit to General John W. Geary, January 21, 1865, Arnold
     Papers.
119. Richard J. Arnold, Account Book, vol. 9, January 19, 1865, Arnold Papers.
120. Ibid., January 19, 1865.
121. William Amory to Hon. Daniel Clark, February 18, 1865, Arnold Papers.
122. Travel Pass issued at Hilton Head, S.C., February 10, 1865, by order of
     Lieutenant Colonel S. L. Woodford, Arnold Papers.
123. Henry Bowen Anthony and the Hon. William Sprague to President of the

United States, February 24, 1865. Endorsed by Lincoln, "Let this be done, A. Lincoln, February 24, 1865." Lincoln Collection, John Hay Library, Brown University. Anthony was the influential editor of the *Providence Journal;* Sprague, the wartime governor of Rhode Island.

124. Copy of order signed by A. G. Brady, Major and Provost Marshall at Point Lookout, Maryland, February 28, 1865, by command of Brigadier General James Barnes.

125. Thomas C. Arnold to Richard J. Arnold, February 10, 1865, Arnold Papers.

126. Ibid., May 28, 1865. Old Peter is not to be confused with Carpenter Peter, a younger man by nearly twenty years. Peter, who was sixty-four at the time of his death, was called "Old" to distinguish him from his son, "Little" Peter, age twenty-six at the time of his father's death. Old Peter's attempt to lead a rebellion against Thomas Arnold and his threat to kill him, for which he was hanged, should be seen in the context of slave revolts and unrest throughout the South during the war and in the coastal rice plantation area of Georgia in particular, because the Union forces had captured and occupied the Georgia sea islands early in the war, freeing the slaves there as "contraband." Many of these same freed slaves joined the Union army. Numerous uprisings took place during the war, for which the leaders were oftentimes hanged. By the time Tom Arnold wrote to his father in May 1865, even he admitted that "my people" were free and that he was only holding onto them until he got the corn planted. Nonetheless, he had moved them to Montgomery County, out of the path of Sherman's army, only a few months before to keep them from escaping to Union lines. For a detailed study of slave rebellions, see Herbert Aptheker's pioneer study *American Negro Slave Revolts* (New York, 1943; reprint, New York, 1963, especially pp. 359–367, "The Civil War Years." For a more detailed study of the tensions between masters and slaves in Georgia during the war, see Mohr, *On the Threshold of Freedom*, especially pp. 68–119.

127. Myers, *Children of Pride*, 1278.

Chapter Nine

1. Reverend S. W. Magill to Richard J. Arnold, April 10, 1865, Arnold Papers.

2. Aaron Champion to Richard J. Arnold, May 19, 1865, Arnold Papers.

3. Document exempting Richard J. Arnold, "a loyal citizen of the United States," from Special Field Order No. 15, Arnold Papers.

4. Sherman, *Memoirs*, 250. Blacks were given only "possessory title" to the land, however, not final ownership.

5. Richard J. Arnold, Account Book, vol. 9, October 25, 1865, Arnold Papers.

6. Thomas C. Arnold to Richard J. Arnold, November 7, 1865, Arnold Papers.

7. Ibid.

8. Genovese, *Roll, Jordan, Roll*, 97–112.

9. Richard J. Arnold, Ledger, vol. 11, p. 449, Arnold Papers.

10. Richard J. Arnold, Ledger, vol. 11, "Expenses Planting 1866," 528.

11. Laurence N. Powell, *New Masters* (New Haven, Conn., 1980), xii.

12. Ibid., 10.

13. Clifton, "Twilight Comes to the Rice Kingdom," 146.

14. Ibid., 148.

15. Powell, *New Masters*, 29.

16. Bliss Perry, *Henry Lee Higginson* (Boston, 1921), 250.

17. Ibid., 248–266.

18. R. J. M. Blackett, "Fugitive Slaves in Britain: The Odyssey of William and Ellen Craft," *Journal of American Studies* 12 (1978), 41–62.

19. Abbey, "Documents Relating to El Destino and Chemonie Plantations," pt. 1, 200.

20. Phillips and Glunt, *Florida Plantation Records*, 22–23.

21. Ibid., 23, 175, 177, 179.

22. Georgiana King to her family in Newport, February 6, 1868, King Papers.

23. Louisa (Luly) Arnold Appleton, Diary, vol. 39, December 14, 1867, Arnold-Appleton Papers.

24. Ibid., vol. 36, June 8, 1866.

25. Ibid., vol. 39, December 14, 1867.

26. Eliza Harriet Allen, Journal, April 16, 1837, Allen Papers.

27. Louisa (Luly) Arnold Appleton, Diary, vol. 39, Christmas, 1867, Arnold-Appleton Papers.

28. Ibid., December 15, 1867.

29. Ibid.

30. Samuel G. Arnold to Luly Arnold, December 5, 1869, Arnold-Appleton Papers.

31. Ibid.

32. Ibid., April 12, 1869.

33. Mrs. Samuel G. Arnold (Louisa) to her daughter Luly, March 14, 1870, Arnold-Appleton Papers.

34. Thomas Arnold and Elizabeth Screven were married on December 1, 1870; William Eliot Arnold and Helen Foreman, on August 18, 1871.

35. Edward Magdol, *A Right to the Land: Essays on the Freedmen's Community* (Westport, Conn., 1977), 168.

36. John Middleton, a friend of Thomas Arnold, was a cousin of the Middletons who were summer residents at Newport.

37. Louisa (Luly) Arnold Appleton, Diary, vol. 40, December 24, 1867, Arnold-Screven Papers.

38. Memorandum listing amounts paid by Arnold to weekly and monthly contract hands for May and June 1867 transcribed by Arnold from his overseer's account books, Arnold-Screven Papers. See also Ledger, vol. 11, "Expenses Planting 1866," Arnold Papers.

39. C. Mildred Thompson, *Reconstruction in Georgia, 1865–1872* (New York, 1915, reprint, Gloucester, Mass., 1964), 359.
40. Louisa G. Arnold to her granddaughter Luly, January 1, 1869, Arnold Papers.
41. Richard J. Arnold to Manton Marble, January 13, 1869, Arnold Papers.
42. Thompson, *Reconstruction in Georgia*, 369.
43. Samuel G. Arnold to his daughter Luly, April 12, 1869, Arnold-Appleton Papers.
44. Land Evidence Records, J 151, 154–156, April 20, 1869, Bryan County Courthouse, Pembroke, Ga.
45. It was fitting that Maria J. McIntosh, who had extolled the virtues of southern womanhood, should write Louisa G. Arnold's obituary.
46. Richard J. Arnold to Mary Cornelia Talbot, February 11, 1872, Arnold Papers.
47. Zachariah Allen, Diary, January 1, 1873, Allen Papers.
48. Land Evidence Records, K 316, Bryan County Courthouse, Pembroke, Ga.
49. Ibid., K 339.
50. George Lyman Appleton directed in his will that Elizabeth Screven Arnold (Mrs. Thomas C. Arnold) be deeded White Hall, a commission which his daughter Mary carried out. Mrs. Arnold sold to Henry Ford in 1927.
51. Edith Case Skeele to Mary Arnold (daughter of Thomas Arnold), March 29, 1914, Arnold-Rogers Papers.
52. Ibid. The letter, though lengthy, provides a fitting coda to the passing of the Arnold dynasty. We quote it in full.

"Myrtle Grove"
Ways Station, Georgia
29th March, 1914

My dear Miss Arnold:

It is a singular chance that brings to you from the hand of a stranger this word of the passing of your old home. I beg you to believe that it is not at least an unsympathetic hand; for as I watched the burning of "Whitehall" I thought of its owners and told my husband that I should write.

Through the kindness of the Gordons we are staying for a few weeks at "Myrtle Grove" and yesterday walked over to the Whitehall plantation.

Since the remarkable ice storm a month ago the woods which were much broken at that time are unusually full of debris, making the accustomed burning over of the ground peculiarly menacing.

There were fires in the woods yesterday and as we left Whitehall we saw in old Avenue that they were approaching rather closely. Mr. Skeele called my attention to them and thought them so threatening to the house, which was piled high in front with boards, the evident wreckage of a fallen porch, that we took pine boughs and he and I and our little daughter beat out the blaze. We went on toward the Clays and returning an hour later found that the light flames had started up again and gone some fifteen feet nearer the building.

It was a pretty fire burning in a circle of little leaping flames, suggesting Brunhilda and old legends of which we spoke. Again we put out the blaze and then lingered about for some time watching until we were sure that for the present the danger had passed.

We went around the building and Mr. Skeele and Elizabeth [her daughter] climbed up an old stairway, and went all over the house where it was still safe to go. There is something greatly appealing about such a place and we all talked of it, for though they were not our own, we felt it to be a place of memories.

The Japonica trees were blooming beautifully and a Japanese Quince of great size at the corner of the house was in full flower. The magnificient [sic] oaks were heavily draped in moss and some splendid cedars stood around like stately wardens of the spot and it was all most quiet and peaceful.

Elizabeth came out of the house about five o'clock and was I think the last human creature under its roof.

We went to church with the Clays this morning and spoke of the impression the place had made upon us in its beauty and desolation. We talked about the menace of the fires congratulating ourselves that we had saved it this time. Just as it was growing dark Mr. Skeele called to me that Whitehall was burning and we could see from Myrtle Grove the sheet of flame through the trees and hear the roaring. Together we hurried over and we with two negro children were the only witnesses of its last hours.

We found the fire in full headway and it must have been burning for an hour or more. The floors had fallen but none of the roofs and the whole building stood clothed in fire.

They tell me that you are an artist and so you can picture the splendor of it all. The light as it fell on the masses of foliage on the trunks of the trees and how they stood out from the depths of darkness in the forest beyond. It was lurid and splendid! Like Doré and the Inferno! [Gustave Doré, illustrator of Dante.] Many of the trees caught and the moss laden boughs blazed in festoons of flame. Wisps of the moss sailed around in the current made by the gigantic bonfire and one outstretched limb of live-oak thickly covered with Poly Pody burned in a long line of fire.

The house seemed in many portions past repair and l wondered as I watched if its owners wouldn't be glad to have it go in a burst of glory rather than slowly and pitifully decay. Two outbuildings caught fire, blazing up brilliantly and made one think of ancient days and customs when retainers and horses were killed upon the graves of warriors to bear them company in the land of shadows.

Do not try to answer this letter. I know it must be painful to you and yet I thought you would like to hear about it from the only woman who was there.

I feel as if I had been close to something which was dear to you, had ministered to it in its last hours and now bring its farewell message. Believe me,

Very sincerely yours,
Edith Case Skeele.

Sent to Miss Mary Arnold
c/o Reverend Frederick W. Jackson
107 Clark Street
Glen Ridge, New Jersey.

Selected Bibliography

Manuscripts

Zachariah Allen Papers, Rhode Island Historical Society Library, Providence. The papers contain Zachariah Allen's diaries, letters, autobiographical sketches, and newspaper clippings of letters to the editor and descriptions of his activities. Filed also with this collection is Eliza Harriet Arnold Allen's journal of her 1837 visit to White Hall plantation.

Arnold-Appleton Papers, Southern Historical Collection, University of North Carolina Library, Chapel Hill. The papers contain Louisa Arnold Appleton's diaries and letters from the Arnold and Appleton families.

Arnold-Rogers Papers, private family collection (Lazy Lawn Realty Trust). The collection contains miscellaneous papers, family letters, and scrapbooks dealing with Samuel G. Arnold, his wife, Louisa, and their descendants.

Arnold-Screven Papers, Southern Historical Collection, University of North Carolina Library, Chapel Hill. The papers contain Richard J. Arnold's letters, plantation journal, instructions to overseers and agreements, as well as letters and business records of his son, Thomas Clay Arnold.

Richard J. Arnold Papers, Rhode Island Historical Society Library, Providence. The papers contain business ledgers, account books, family letters, wills, deeds of Richard Arnold and his family.

Welcome Arnold Papers, John Carter Brown Library, Brown University, Providence, R.I. The papers contain early letters of Richard J. Arnold, mainly business letters to his brother, Samuel.

Bryan County Courthouse Records, Pembroke, Georgia. The records include vital statistics, deeds, land evidence records.

Clay Family Papers, Georgia Historical Society, Savannah.

Hunter Family Papers, Newport Historical Society, Newport, R.I.

Jones Family Papers, Georgia Historical Society, Savannah.

King Family Papers, Newport Historical Society, Newport, R.I.

Books and Articles

Abbey, Kathryn T., ed. "Documents Relating to El Destino and Chemonie Plantations, Middle Florida, 1828–1868." *Florida Historical Quarterly* 7 (January 1929), pt. 1, pp. 179–213; 8 (April 1929), pt. 2, pp. 291–329; 9 (July 1929), pt. 3, pp. 3–46; 10 (October, 1929), pt. 4, pp. 79–111.

Adams, Alice Dana. *The Neglected Period of Anti-Slavery in America, 1808–1831.* Radcliffe College Monograph no. 14. Boston and London, 1908. Reprint. Gloucester, Mass., 1964.

Allen, Zachariah. *The Philosophy of the Mechanics of Nature.* New York, 1852.

———. *The Practical Tourist.* 2 vols. Providence, 1832.

———. *The Science of Mechanics.* Providence, 1829.

———. *Solar Light and Heat.* New York, 1879.

Anderson, Joseph, ed. *The Town and City of Waterbury, Connecticut from the Aboriginal Period to the Year Eighteen Hundred and Ninety-Five.* New Haven, 1896.

Aptheker, Herbert. *American Negro Slave Revolts.* New York, 1943. Reprint. New York, 1963.

Armstrong, Thomas F. "From Task Labor to Free Labor: The Transition along Georgia's Rice Coast, 1820–1880," *Georgia Historical Quarterly* 64, no. 4 (Winter 1980), 432–447.

Arnold, Samuel G. *Address Delivered Before the Charitable Baptist Society on the One Hundredth Anniversary of the Opening of the First Baptist Church, Providence, R.I. for Public Worship, May 28th 1875.* Providence, 1875.

———. *History of the State of Rhode Island and Providence Plantations.* 2 vols. New York, 1860.

Bagnall, William R. *The Textile Industries of the United States.* Vol. 1. Cambridge, Mass., 1893. Reprint. New York, 1971.

Bancroft, Frederic. *Slave Trading in the Old South.* Baltimore, 1931. Reprint. New York, 1959.

Bartlett, Irving H. *From Slave to Citizen: The Story of the Negro in Rhode Island.* Providence, 1954.

Battle, Charles A. *Negroes on the Island of Rhode Island.* Newport, R.I. 1932.

Biographical Cyclopedia of Representative Men of Rhode Island. 3 vols. Providence, 1881.

Blackett, J. M. *Building an Antislavery Wall: Black Americans in the Atlantic Abolitionist Movement, 1830–1860.* Baton Rouge, 1983.

———. "Fugitive Slaves in Britain: The Odyssey of William and Ellen Craft," *Journal of American Studies* 12 (1978), 41–62.

Blassingame, John W. *The Slave Community: Plantation Life in the Antebellum South.* Rev. ed. New York, 1979.

Breeden, James O., ed. *Advice among Masters: The Ideal in Slave Management in the Old South.* Westport, Conn., 1980.

Bremer, Fredrika. *The Homes of the New World.* 2 vols. Reprint. New York, 1968.

Brennan, Brother Joseph, F.S.C. *Social Conditions in Industrial Rhode Island: 1820–1860.* Ph.D. Dissertation, Catholic University, Washington, D.C., 1940.

Bridenbaugh, Carl. "Charlestonians at Newport, 1767–1775," *The South Carolina Historical and Genealogical Magazine* 41, no. 2 (April 1940), 43–47.

———. "Colonial Newport as a Summer Resort," *Rhode Island Historical Society Collections* 26, no. 1 (January 1933), 1–23.

Bronson, Walter C. *The History of Brown University, 1764–1914.* Providence, 1914. Reprint. New York, 1971.

Buckingham, J. S. *The Slave States of America.* Vol. 1. London, 1842. Reprint. New York, 1968.

Chapin, William Waterman, comp. *Genealogy of the Family of Jonathan Arnold of Smithfield, Rhode Island.* Providence, 1910.

Chudacoff, Howard P., and Theodore C. Hirt. "Social Turmoil and Government Reform in Providence, 1820–1832," *Rhode Island History* 31, no. 1 (February 1972), 21–31.

Clarke, Erskine. *Wrestlin' Jacob.* Atlanta, 1979.

Clarke, Louise Brownell. *The Greenes of Rhode Island.* 2 vols. New York, 1903.

Clay, Thomas Savage. *Detail of a Plan for the Moral Improvement of Negroes on Plantations.* Presented before the Georgia Presbytery, 1833. N.p., n.d.

Clifton, James M., ed. *Life and Labor on Argyle Island.* Savannah, 1978.

———. "Twilight Comes to the Rice Kingdom: Postbellum Rice Culture on the South Atlantic Coast," *Georgia Historical Quarterly* 62, no. 2 (1978), 146–154.

Conley, Patrick T. *The Dorr Rebellion: Rhode Island's Crisis in Constitutional Government.* Providence, 1976.

Conway, Alan. *The Reconstruction of Georgia.* Minneapolis, 1966.

Coolidge, John. *Mill and Mansion.* New York, 1967.

Cottrol, Robert J. *The Afro-Yankees: Providence's Black Community in the Antebellum Era.* Westport, Conn., 1982.

Coughtry, Jay. *The Notorious Triangle: Rhode Island and the African Slave Trade, 1700–1807.* Philadelphia, 1981.

Dillon, Merton L. *The Abolitionists.* Dekalb, Ill., 1974.

Douglass, Frederick. *The Narrative and Selected Writings.* Ed. Michael Meyer. New York, 1984.

Drago, Edmund L. "How Sherman's March Through Georgia Affected the Slaves," *Georgia Historical Quarterly* 57, no. 3 (1973), 361–375.

Dumond, Dwight Lowell. *Antislavery: The Crusade for Freedom in America.* Ann Arbor, 1961.

Dunwell, Steve. *The Run of the Mill.* Boston, 1978.

Eaton, Clement. *The Growth of Southern Civilization, 1790–1860.* New York, 1961.

———. *A History of the Old South.* New York, 1949.

Elkins, Stanley M. *Slavery: A Problem in American Institutional and Intellectual Life.* 3d ed. Chicago, 1976.

Emilio, Luis F. *A Brave Black Regiment: History of the Fifty-Fourth Regiment of Massachusetts Volunteer Infantry, 1863–1865.* Boston, 1897, reprint. New York, 1968.

Franklin, John Hope. *From Slavery to Freedom.* New York, 1956.

Fredrickson, George M. *The Black Image in the White Mind: The Debate on Afro-American Character and Destiny, 1817–1914.* New York, 1971.

Fuller, Richard, and Francis Wayland. *Domestic Slavery Considered as a Scriptural Institution.* Boston, 1847.

Garrison, William Lloyd. *Thoughts on African Colonization.* Boston, 1832. Reprint. New York, 1968.

Genovese, Eugene D. *From Rebellion to Revolution: Afro-American Slave Revolts in the Making of the Modern World.* Baton Rouge, 1979.

———. *The Political Economy of Slavery: Studies in the Economy and Society of the Slave South.* London, 1966.

———. *Roll, Jordan, Roll: The World the Slaves Made.* New York, 1974.

Gettleman, Marvin E. *The Dorr Rebellion: A Study in American Radicalism, 1833–1849.* New York, 1973.

Gifford, James M. "The Cuthbert Conspiracy," *South Atlantic Quarterly* 79, no. 3 (Summer 1980), 312–320.

———. "Emily Tubman and the African Colonization Movement in Georgia," *Georgia Historical Quarterly* 59, no. 1 (Spring 1975), 10–24.

Goodell, William. *Slavery and Anti-Slavery.* New York, 1852. Reprint. New York, 1968.

Granger, Mary, ed. *Savannah River Plantations.* Savannah Writers' Project. Savannah, 1947.

Green, Constance McLaughlin. *Eli Whitney and the Birth of American Technology.* Boston, 1956.

Green, Fletcher M. *The Role of the Yankee in the Old South.* Athens, Ga., 1972.

Greene, Lorenzo Johnston. *The Negro in Colonial New England.* New York, 1942. Reprint. New York, 1971.

Grossman, Lawrence. "George T. Downing and Desegregation of Rhode Island Public Schools, 1855–1866," *Rhode Island History* 36, no. 4 (November 1977), 99–105.

Helper, Hinton Rowan. *The Impending Crisis of the South.* New York, 1857.

Heyward, Duncan Clinch. *Seed from Madagascar.* Chapel Hill, N.C., 1937.

Hoffmann, Charles, and Tess Hoffmann. "The Limits of Paternalism: Driver-Master Relations on a Bryan County Plantation." *Georgia Historical Quarterly* 67, no. 3 (Fall 1983), 321–335.

———. "North by South: The Two Lives of Richard James Arnold," *Rhode Island History* 43, no. 1 (February 1984), 19–33.

———. "Zachariah Allen's Vacant Lot: A Pioneering Experiment in Silviculture," *Horticulture* 60, no. 11 (November 1982), 42–47.

House, Albert Virgil. *Planter Management and Capitalism in Ante-Bellum Georgia.* New York, 1954.

Huxtable, Ada Louise. "Progressive Architecture in America, Allendale Mill—1822," *Progressive Architecture* 37, (December 1956), 123–124.

James, Henry, Jr. "Notes of a Son and Brother," in *Autobiography*. Ed. Frederick W. Dupee. London, 1956.

———. "The Sense of Newport," in *The American Scene*. New York, 1967.

James, Henry, Sr. *Henry James, Senior: A Selection of His Writings*. Ed. Giles Gunn. Chicago, 1974.

Johnston, Edith Duncan, ed. "The Kollock Letters, 1799–1850," *Georgia Historical Quarterly* 30, nos. 3–4 (September, December 1946), 218–258, 312–356; 31, nos. 1–4 (March, June, September, December 1947), 34–80, 121–143, 195–233, 289–322; nos. 1–2 (March, June 1948), 32–67, 119–143.

Jones, Charles C., Jr. *The Dead Towns of Georgia*. Collections of the Georgia Historical Society, no. 4. Savannah, 1878.

Jones, Charles Colcock. *The Religious Instruction of the Negroes in the Southern States*. Philadelphia, 1847. Reprint. New York, 1969.

Kemble, Frances A. *Journal of a Residence on a Georgian Plantation in 1838–39*. New York, 1863.

King, Henry Melville, comp. *Historical Catalogue of the Members of the First Baptist Church in Providence, Rhode Island*. Providence, 1908.

King, Spencer B., Jr. *Georgia Voices: A Documentary History to 1872*. Athens, Ga., 1966.

Kiven, Arline Ruth. *Then Why the Negroes: The Nature and Course of the Anti-Slavery Movement in Rhode Island, 1637–1861*. Providence, 1973.

Lawrence, Alexander A. *A Present for Mr. Lincoln*. Macon, Ga., 1961.

Leland, Isabella Middleton, ed. "The Middleton Correspondence, 1861–1865," *South Carolina Historical Magazine* 63, nos. 1–4 (January, April, July, October 1962), 33–41, 61–70, 164–174, 204–210; 64, nos. 1–4 (January, April, July, October 1963), 28–38, 95–104, 158–168, 212–219; 65, nos. 1–2 (January, April 1964), 33–44, 98–109.

Levin, Linda Lotridge, ed. *Federal Rhode Island: The Age of the China Trade, 1790–1820*. Providence, 1978.

Litwack, Leon F. *North of Slavery: The Negro in the Free States, 1790–1860*. Chicago, 1961.

McIntosh, Maria Jane. *The Lofty and the Lowly; or, Good in All and None All-Good*. 2 vols. New York, 1854.

———. *Woman in America*. New York, 1850.

McLoughlin, William G. *Rhode Island: A Bicentennial History*. New York, 1978.

McPherson, James M. *The Negro's Civil War*. New York, 1965.

Magdol, Edward. *A Right to the Land: Essays on the Freedmen's Community*. Westport, Conn., 1977.

Mallard, Robert Q. *Plantation Life Before Emancipation*. Richmond, Va., 1872.

Marx, Leo. *The Machine in the Garden*. New York, 1970.

Mason, George C. *Reunion of the Sons and Daughters of Newport, Rhode Island*. Newport, R.I., 1859.

Mathews, Donald G. "The Abolitionists on Slavery: The Critique Behind the Social Movement," *Journal of Southern History* 33, no. 2 (May 1967), 163–182.

———. "Charles Colcock Jones and the Southern Evangelical Crusade to Form a Biracial Community," *Journal of Southern History* 41, no. 3 (August 1975), 299–320.

Miller, Elinor, and Eugene D. Genovese. *Plantation, Town and Country: Essays on the Local History of American Slave Society.* Urbana, Ill., 1974.

Miller, Floyd J. *The Search for a Black Nationality: Black Emigration and Colonization, 1787–1863.* Urbana, Ill., 1975.

Mohr, Clarence L. "Before Sheman: Georgia Blacks and the Union War Effort, 1861–1864," *Journal of Southern History* 45, no. 3 (August 1979), 331–352.

———. *On the Threshold of Freedom: Masters and Slaves in Civil War Georgia.* Athens, Ga., 1986.

Morgan, Philip D. "The Ownership of Property by Slaves in the Mid-Nineteenth-Century Low Country," *Journal of Southern History* 49, no. 3 (August 1983), 399–420.

———. "Work and Culture: The Task System and the World of Lowcountry Blacks, 1700 to 1880," *William and Mary Quarterly* 39, no. 4 (October 1982), 563–599.

Morse, John T. *Thomas Sargent Perry.* Boston, 1929.

Mowry, Arthur May. *The Dorr War or the Constitutional Struggle in Rhode Island.* Providence, 1901. Reprint. New York, 1968.

Mullin, Gerald W. "Rethinking American Negro Slavery from the Vantage Point of the Colonial Era," *Louisiana Studies* (Summer 1973), 398–422.

Murray, Andrew E. *Presbyterians and the Negro—A History.* Philadelphia, 1966.

Myers, Robert Manson. *The Children of Pride.* New Haven, Conn., 1972.

Olmsted, Frederick Law. *A Journey to the Seaboard Slave States.* New York, 1856.

———. *The Papers of Frederick Law Olmsted.* Ed. Charles E. Beveridge and Charles Capen McLaughlin. Vol. 2: *1852–1857.* Baltimore, 1981.

Orr, Dorothy. *A History of Education in Georgia.* Chapel Hill, N.C., 1950.

Osofsky, Gilbert. *Puttin' On Ole Massa.* New York, 1969.

Ostrander, Gilman M. "The Making of the Triangular Trade Myth," *William and Mary Quarterly* 30, no. 4 (October 1973), 635–644.

Pearce, B. W. *Matters and Men in Newport As I Have Known Them, 1858–1891.* In four parts. Newport, R.I., 1891.

Perry, Amos. *Memorial of Zachariah Allen, 1795–1882.* Cambridge, Mass., 1883.

Perry, Bliss. Life and Letters of Henry Lee Higginson. Boston, 1921.

Phillips, Ulrich B. *Georgia and State Rights.* Yellow Springs, Ohio. 1968.

———. *Life and Labor in the Old South.* Boston, 1929.

———. *The Slave Economy of the Old South.* Ed. Eugene D. Genovese. Baton Rouge, 1968.

Phillips, Ulrich B., and James A. Glunt, eds. *Florida Plantation Records from the Papers of George Noble Jones.* St. Louis, Mo., 1927.

Pierce, Edward L., ed. *Memoir and Letters of Charles Sumner.* Vol. 1. Boston 1877. Reprint. New York, 1969.

Pierson, William H. *American Buildings and Their Architects.* Vol. 2: *Technology and the Picturesque.* New York, 1978.

Powell, Lawrence N. *New Masters: Northern Planters During the Civil War and Reconstruction.* New Haven, Conn., 1980.

Proceedings of the Providence Anti-Slavery Society. Providence, c. 1834.

Proceedings of the Rhode Island Anti-Slavery Convention. Providence, 1836.

Pryor, Elizabeth Brown. "An Anomalous Person: The Northern Tutor in Plantation Society, 1773–1860," *The Journal of Southern History* 47, no. 3 (August 1981), 363–392.

Rammelkamp, Julian. "The Providence Negro Community, 1820–1842," *Rhode Island History* 7, no. 1 (January 1848), 20–33.

Rawley, James A. *The Transatlantic Slave Trade.* New York, 1981.

Reid, Whitelaw. *After the War: A Tour of the Southern States, 1865–1866.* New York, 1866. Reprint. New York, 1965.

Rhode Island. *Annual Report of the Adjutant General for the Year 1865.* 2 vols. Providence, 1866.

Richards, Leonard L. *"Gentlemen of Property and Standing": Anti-Abolition Mobs in Jacksonian America.* New York, 1970.

Robinson, William H., ed. *The Proceedings of the Free African Union Society and the African Benevolent Society, Newport, Rhode Island, 1780–1824.* Providence, 1976.

Rose, Willie Lee. *Rehearsal for Reconstruction: The Port Royal Experiment.* New York, 1967.

Rossbach, Jeffrey. *Ambivalent Conspirators: John Brown, the Secret Six, and a Theory of Slave Violence.* Philadelphia, 1982.

Savitt, Todd L. *Medicine and Slavery.* Urbana, Ill., 1978.

Scarborough, Ruth. *The Opposition to Slavery in Georgia Prior to 1860.* New York, 1968.

Scarborough, William K. *The Overseer: Plantation Management in the Old South.* Baton Rouge, 1966.

Scott, Otto J. *The Secret Six: John Brown and the Abolitionist Movement.* New York, 1979.

Sherman, William T. *Memoirs of General William T. Sherman.* New York, 1875. Reprint. Bloomington, Ind., 1957.

Shyrock, Richard Harrison. *Georgia and the Union in 1850.* New York, 1968.

Small, Sandra E. "The Yankee Schoolmarm in Freedmen's Schools: An Analysis of Attitudes," *Journal of Southern History* 45, no. 3 (August 1979), 381–402.

Sobel, Mechal. *Trabelin' On: The Slave Journey to an Afro-Baptist Faith.* Westport, Conn., 1979.

Stampp, Kenneth M. *The Era of Reconstruction, 1865–1877.* New York, 1965.

———. *The Peculiar Institution.* New York, 1956.

Staudenraus, P. J. *The African Colonization Movement, 1816–1865*. New York, 1961.

Taylor, Clare. *British and American Abolitionists: An Episode in Transatlantic Understanding*. Edinburgh, 1974.

Thomas, Benjamin P. *Theodore Weld: Crusader for Freedom*. New Brunswick, N.J., 1950.

Thompson, C. Mildred. *Reconstruction in Georgia, 1865–1872*. New York, 1915. Reprint. Gloucester, Mass., 1964.

Tuckerman, Arthur. *History of the Newport Reading Room*. Newport, R.I., 1954.

Van Deburg, William. *The Slave Drivers: Black Agricultural Supervisors in the Antebellum South*. Westport, Conn., 1979.

Van Slyck, J. D. *Representatives of New England*. Vol. 1: *Manufacturers*. Boston, 1879.

Ware, Caroline E. *Early New England Cotton Manufacturers*. New York, 1966.

Weinstein, Allen, and Frank Otto Gattel, eds. *American Negro Slavery: A Modern Reader*. 2d ed. New York, 1973.

Weld, Theodore D. *Slavery and the Internal Slave Trade in the United States*. Reprint. New York, 1969.

Wiecek, William M. "Popular Sovereignty in the Dorr War—Conservative Counterblast," *Rhode Island History* 32, no. 2 (May 1973), 35–51.

Wood, Peter H. *Black Majority: Negroes in Colonial South Carolina from 1670 Through the Stono Rebellion*. New York, 1974.

Wormeley, Katharine Prescott. "Reminiscences of Newport in the Fifties," *Newport History* 41, no. 1 (Winter 1968), 1–17.

Zimiles, Martha, and Murray Zimiles. *Early American Mills*. New York, 1973.

Index